The OPL Sourcebook

The OPL Sourcebook

A GUIDE FOR SOLO AND SMALL LIBRARIES

Judith A. Siess

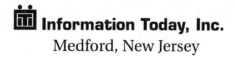 **Information Today, Inc.**
Medford, New Jersey

Library of Congress Cataloging-in-Publication Data

Siess, Judith A.
  The OPL sourcebook : a guide for solo and small libraries /
by Judith A. Siess.
    p. cm.
  Rev. ed. of: The SOLO librarian's sourcebook. 1997.
  Includes bibliographical references and index.
  ISBN 1-57387-111-7
    1. Small libraries--Administration. 2. Special libraries--Administration. I.
Siess, Judith A. SOLO librarian's sourcebook. II. Title.

Z675.S57 S54 2001
025.1'9--dc21

                                            2001024192

Printed and bound in the United States of America

Publisher: Thomas H. Hogan, Sr.
Editor-in-Chief: John B. Bryans
Managing Editor: Deborah R. Poulson
Copy Editor: Michelle A. Sutton-Kerchner
Production Manager: M. Heide Dengler
Cover Designer: Victoria Stover
Book Designer: Kara Mia Jalkowski
Indexer: Laurie Andriot

Dedication

This book is dedicated to my mother, Helen Siess,
who died just before my previous book was published.
I know she would be proud.

Table of Contents

Acknowledgments xv

Introduction xvii

Chapter 1 What Is an OPL? 1

A Brief History of the OPL Movement. 2
Where OPLs Work 5
  Law Libraries 5
  Prison or Jail Libraries 6
  Hospital Libraries. 7
  Museum or Zoo Libraries. 8
  Church or Synagogue Libraries 8
  Public Libraries 9
  Public or Private School Libraries. 9
  Others. 10
Characteristics of an OPL. 11
A Week in the Life of an OPL 19
  Monday 19
  Tuesday 20
  Wednesday 21
  Thursday. 22
  Friday. 22
Conclusion. 23

Chapter 2 An International View 25

The Universality of One-Person Librarianship 25
United Kingdom. 26
Germany 28
Australia. 36

South Africa. 38
Israel 45
Latin America. 46
Canada. 49
The Rest of the World 50
Profiles of OPLs Around the World 51

Chapter 3 General Concepts 55
Know Thy Organization: Organizational Behavior
    and Corporate Culture 56
The User Is Job One—Customer Service 61

Chapter 4 Time Management, Planning,
              and Prioritization 67
Ten Myths About Time. 68
Stop Wasting Time 69
    Avoid Procrastination 74
    Check Your Timing. 76
    Practice Saying "No" 76
    Value Your Time. 78
    Manage Your Routine Activities 78
    More Time-Management Hints 82
    Manage Your Absences. 84
    Get the Most from Conferences 85
Prioritization 86
    Question Things 87
Planning. 88
    Why Plan? 88
    What Is Planning? 89
    How Do You Plan?. 90
    Is Planning the Same as Creating Goals,
       Mission Statements, or Visions? 91

Chapter 5 Financial Matters 95
Budgeting. 95
Bookkeeping 98

How to Charge Back Without Pain 100
Financial Crisis 100
Evaluating Your Library 102
Money-Saving Tips 104
Conclusion 105

Chapter 6 Working with Others 107

Communication: An OPL's Guide to Connecting 107
   With Whom Do You Communicate? 107
   What Do You Need to Communicate to Others? 111
   How Can You Better Communicate? 111
The Annual Report 115
Oral Presentations 116
Working with Your Boss 117
The Care and Feeding of Nerds,
   or, How to Work with Your Computer People 120
Interpersonal Networking 123
Library Promotion: Self-Serving
   or Just Good Sense? 125
   Why Use Public Relations? 127
   When Do You Promote Your Library? 127
   How to Publicize Your Library 128
   Other Public Relations Techniques 131
   A Last Word on Public Relations 134
Professionalism 134

Chapter 7 Along the Information Superhighway:
The OPL and Technology 139

Past: Where Have We Been?
   How Far Have We Come? 139
Present: How Do Librarians Use Technology?
   Finding Our Role. 141
   What the Internet Is and Is Not 144
   Defining the Librarian's Role in the
   Information Society 147

Collection Development in an Electronic World:
Choosing Formats and Evaluating Resources. 151
Dealing with Electronic Journals 156
Purchasing Online 157
Future: Where Are We Going? 159
What About the Virtual Library?. 162

Chapter 8 Other Issues: Education, Downsizing and Outsourcing, and Knowledge Management

Chapter 8 Other Issues: Education,
Downsizing and Outsourcing,
and Knowledge Management. 165
Education for One-Person Librarianship. 165
Are Special Librarians and OPLs Different? 169
One More Pair of Hands—Or One Less:
Downsizing and Outsourcing 175
Downsizing 175
Outsourcing 189
Knowledge Management 196
What Is Knowledge?. 196
What Is Knowledge Management? 196
Which Skills Are Required for Effective
Knowledge Management? 198
What Are the Consequences of Not Having
a Knowledge Management System?. 199
How Does Knowledge Management Require
Changing of the Corporate Culture? 200
Who Is Doing Knowledge Management Now? 201
Can a One-Person Librarian
Do Knowledge Management?. 202
Is Knowledge Management for Everyone? 203

Chapter 9 The Future of One-Person Librarianship

Chapter 9 The Future of One-Person
Librarianship 205
Technology. 205
The Library of the Future 212
Future Roles of the Librarian 214

What Changes Might We See in Our Roles?........215
The Future for Specific Types of Librarians 218
The Future of One-Person Librarianship............221
My View of the Future 223

Chapter 10 Organizations 227

Especially for OPLs...........................228
General Library Organizations 228
Specialized Library Organizations 231
Law Library Organizations......................231
Medical Library Organizations..................232
Church and Synagogue Library Organizations 233
Other Organizations 233
Alternative Careers...........................235

Chapter 11 Books and Journals 237

One-Person or Solo Librarianship.................238
About the Profession 240
General Management 242
Space Planning.............................246
Business.................................247
Communication 248
Doing Business Worldwide.....................249
Marketing and Public Relations 251
Financial Matters 252
Strategic Planning...........................254
Time Management 255
Outsourcing and Downsizing 256
Knowledge Management 257
Technical Services 261
Medical and Hospital Libraries..................262
Law Libraries..............................268
Small Public Libraries 272
Church and Synagogue Libraries 274
Other Kinds of Libraries.......................275
Technology, Internet, and Online Searching 277

Education and Alternative Careers 280
Non-U.S. Essential References 282
Miscellaneous. 283
Publishers. 283

Chapter 12 Vendors and Suppliers 285

Guides to Products and Services. 287
Printed Resources. 287
   Booksellers and Bookstores 287
   Used Books 293
   Subscription Services 293
   Competitive Intelligence and Market Research 296
   Document Delivery. 297
   Patents 299
   Standards 300
Electronic Resources 301
   Library Automation 301
   Online, CD-ROM, and Other Electronic Media. 303
Other 307
   Suppliers 307
   Library Consultants 309
   Miscellaneous 310

Chapter 13 Discussion Lists and
World Wide Web Sites 313

Electronic Discussion Lists. 313
   Other OPL Lists 314
   General Library Lists 314
   Church and Synagogue Libraries 317
   Museum, Art, and Zoo Libraries 317
   Law and Government Libraries. 317
   Medical Libraries 318
   Science and Technology Libraries. 318
World Wide Web Sites 319
   Just for OPLs 320
   General Reference 320

News 324
Business Resources. 325
Strategic Planning Resources 328
Directories 328
Law Resources 329
Government Resources 332
Intellectual Property Resources. 334
Library and Information Science Resources 335
Knowledge Management Resources 338
Technical Services 339
Medical and Health Resources 340
Science and Technology Resources. 344
Internet, World Wide Web, and Computer
      Technology Resources 345

Annotated Bibliography 349

About the Author 359

Index 361

Acknowledgments

As is usual here, I want to thank those people without whom I could not have written this book. John Cruikshank of Mississippi State University verified most of the Web sites and Andrew Sprecher of Barton Business Services checked most of the book and journal citations for me while I traveled to the U.K. One-person librarians (OPLs) from various countries and electronic lists (especially SOLOLIB-L) gave me advice, pointers to resources—electronic and otherwise—and case histories. I could never do this without the Internet, so I thank all those invisible people who make it work. I also owe a debt to John Bryans of Information Today, Inc. for his flexibility and encouragement and to Tom Hogan, Sr. for getting me started in the book writing business.

Everyone always thanks his or her family, but the patience and forbearance of my husband, Steve Bremseth, enabled me to take the time to work on this book at the exclusion of all else—including him. Thank you, Sweetie.

Introduction

It has been four years since I wrote *The SOLO Librarian's Sourcebook*. A lot has happened since then—in the library profession, in the world of solos or one-person librarians (OPLs), and in my own life. Hence I've written this book, which is designed to update and expand its predecessor.

On the off chance that you have not heard of me, I will give you a little of my background. This may help you understand this book and my somewhat idiosyncratic way of looking at things. (Once, Guy St. Clair—the father of one-person librarianship—referred to me as a provocateur. I asked him if that meant "rabble-rouser." When he responded, "yes," I considered it a high compliment. You may not agree with everything I say, but if it makes you think, then I have done my job.)

I think I was destined to become a librarian. I started reading at 2-1/2 years of age and got my first library card at age four. Before I was 10, I had read all the children's books in the Urbana Free Library (Illinois, U.S.) and was sneaking upstairs to read the books for teenagers and adults (with the permission of the librarians, I hasten to add). After college and graduate school (resulting in interesting but relatively useless degrees in anthropology), I finally went to library school. I had worked in libraries in grade school and junior high and had done term papers in high school and college using the great collection of the University of Illinois. I had even run a couple of small corporate libraries (and didn't do a bad job at all, looking back on it). Now I had a chance to get a formal library education.

I thoroughly enjoyed library school at the University of Illinois. I did a thesis, which wasn't required (or even encouraged). I did an internship at the U.S. Army Corps of Engineers Construction Engineering Research Laboratory under the late Martha Blake. (The internship was not required either, but it was here that I learned much of what I know about customer service and relationship building from my mentor, the late Martha Blake.) While in school, I worked for the Department of Agricultural Economics, first as a secretary, then as a statistical assistant, and finally running the Agricultural Economics Reference Room. The last was like having my own private laboratory. As I learned to do things in class, I put them into practice. We had online searching, a primitive online catalog (remember, this was 1980–1982), and even e-mail.

My first professional position involved starting a library for a small biotechnology research and development (R&D) firm in Ashland, Ohio. I got this job through the placement service at the annual conference of the American Society for Information Science (ASIS). I didn't know anything about enzymes (the area in which the company was doing research), but I knew enough to ask questions. Before I left for my final interview, I asked the librarian at the chemistry and biology libraries at the University of Illinois for a list of books and journals that they considered essential. These suggestions were invaluable. When I started the job, there was nothing in my "library" except a desk, chair, and telephone. Because I couldn't do much with these, I got my boss to send me to the mid-year meeting of ASIS. There, I met a professor from the College of Wooster (20 miles from my new job) who was teaching chemistry undergraduates to search chemical abstracts online. I figured that if he could teach chemists who knew nothing about searching, he could teach a searcher who knew nothing about chemistry. I took lessons from him for 10 weeks and became proficient enough to be effective in my job. This is an example of the creative solutions that OPLs often must use.

As happens so often, the company did not last. I was neither the first employee hired nor the last let go. About that time, my husband's job led us to Cleveland, Ohio. I worked a while for a friend who had started his own biotechnology company, serving as librarian (organizing his extensive reprint collection), secretary, administrative assistant, bookkeeper, and payroll officer. I finally found a job subbing for a librarian on maternity leave at a contract chemical research facility. The work was interesting and I had a chance to familiarize myself with their large reference collection, but working in a library run by chemists was not what I had in mind either. Next was another maternity leave situation, this time at the National Aeronautics and Space Administration (NASA). I got to use their even larger reference collection and to learn from the large staff of librarians, but it, too, was not right.

Finally, I got a call from the chapter placement officer at my local Special Libraries Association (SLA) about a job at Bailey Controls Company (now a part of ABB Automation). I had seen the advertisement in the newspaper but thought I was overqualified because the position did not call for a library degree. The placement officer assured me that it was just what I was looking for—and she was right! I got the job and stayed nearly eight years. The job was interesting, challenging, frustrating, and rewarding. I was the only information provider for over 16,000 employees in what became a U.S.$2 billion global firm. The job was reclassified as professional (at my insistence), and the library changed from the Engineering Library to the Corporate Information and Research Center. However, I eventually tired of trying to make sense of an increasingly bureaucratic organization and of trying to implement current information practices (especially knowledge management) in a company that was historically unwilling to share information between departments.

As I approached my 50th birthday and its attendant mid-life crisis, I decided this was not what I wanted to be doing. My first book, *The SOLO Librarian's Sourcebook*, had just been published. I left Bailey to start my own business, Information Bridges International, Inc. (IBI), with the intention to facilitate visits and exchanges among librarians around the world. Shortly thereafter, Guy St. Clair called and asked if I was interested in purchasing his newsletter, *The One-Person Library: A Newsletter for Librarians and Management*. I said "Yes!" and we made it happen. The exchange part of IBI was set aside while I learned the newsletter editing and publishing business. I turned this part of the business over to Mel Westerman, retired business librarian from Pennsylvania State University, because I find writing *OPL* and teaching workshops consumes all of my time.

I have always been active in our professional associations, dating back to library school and the excellent example set by Linda C. Smith. My proudest accomplishment is helping to birth the Solo Librarians Division of SLA. Barbara Borrelli and I took it from caucus to division in six months—ignoring "everyone" who said it couldn't be done. (Hey, we OPLs do the impossible every day!) The division celebrates its 10th birthday in 2001 as the fourth or fifth largest division in SLA (out of 28 divisions) with about 1,000 members. I have served on local, division, and national committees and boards. I also make it a point to go back to my alma mater about once a year (and anywhere else that invites me) to tell library school students what life is like in the "real world." The library profession has been good to me, and I feel it is vital to give back to it.

Librarianship has changed since 1996. Knowledge management has not emerged as a trend, but as a new way of thinking about and organizing information. Neither the Internet nor the World Wide Web have gone away, nor the unfortunate management perception that "it's all on the Internet and it's free," but more and more companies are realizing that librarians have much to add. Library education has moved somewhat more to the information technology side of the profession. Yes, librarians are still being downsized out of existence as organizations merge, scale down, cut expenses, or even go out of existence, but new positions are being created in technology, research, and smaller enterprises.

This last trend has had great implications for OPLs. More OPLs are being created both by downsizing and the creation of new libraries. We are being recognized more and more as a unique type of librarian. Articles on one-person librarianship have appeared in *Spectrum* (published by the American Association of Law Libraries) and *American Libraries* (from the American Library Association). *Library Journal* featured an OPL, Olga Wise of Compaq Computers, on its cover. Dan Trefethen, an OPL at Boeing in Seattle, Washington (U.S.), has been named a Fellow of the Special Libraries Association—the second OPL honored. (Guy St. Clair was the first so honored.) The Library Association (U.K.) has created a new focus on special libraries, many of which are OPLs. This OPL renaissance has been repeated all over the world.

This book also benefits from my four years of publishing *The One-Person Library*. I have learned so much from my readers and contributors; from the various electronic lists (14 at last count) that I monitor to keep updated; from my travels to Australia, New Zealand, Germany, Canada, and the U.K. to give workshops; and from the extensive reading I have done on librarianship, management, time management, and technology. I have added a large number of Web sites to Chapter 13 to reflect the increasing amount of information on the Web and librarians' increasing reliance on gateways and lists of links. I have also become a member of library associations around the world (SLA, MLA, AALL, CSLA, ALIA, CLA, LIASA, CLA LA, and ASLIB at present—see Chapter 10 for more information on these and other associations). Reading their publications and attending their conferences has increased my awareness of not only the diversity of OPLs but also of how much we have in common. Therefore, I hope that all types of OPLs worldwide will benefit from this book. I enjoyed writing it. I hope you enjoy and benefit from it.

Judith Siess
April 2001

Author's Note:

If there is anything you think should be added to this book (Web sites, electronic lists, publications, organizations, vendors, experiences, or facts), please direct them to me by mail, fax, or email so they can be considered for inclusion in the next edition:

Judith Siess
477 Harris Road
Cleveland, OH 44143-2537, U.S.A.
voice: 1-216-486-7443, fax: 1-216-486-8810
e-mail: jsiess@ibi-opl.com, Web site: http://www.ibi-opl.com

What Is an OPL?

An OPL is a one-person librarian. Yes, I know that all librarians are just one person, but, in this case, it means someone who works in a one-person library. And what does that mean? Often called a solo librarian, an OPL is the only librarian (or only professional librarian) in a library or information center.

The OPL does everything: acquisitions; cataloging; circulation; reference; even dusting the shelves and vacuuming the library, if necessary. It is a situation where there are no professional peers with whom to share problems, share ideas, or commiserate when things get tough. It is a challenging position but also a rewarding one. The OPL often does not have to go through layers of administration to get approval for purchases or new programs. The OPL knows exactly what is going on in his or her library: what is being checked out, the questions being asked, who is using the library, and such. The OPL is often perceived as the "information guru" in the organization—the one to whom everyone comes for answers. Finally, any and all successes (and, of course, failures) of the library are also those of the OPL. He or she can make of it whatever is in his or her vision and power.

Other names for an OPL are "solo" in the U.S., the U.K., and Israel, and sometimes "Sole-Charge Librarian" in Australia and New Zealand. I will use OPL in this book. The Association of Libraries & Information Bureau (ASLIB) has a division called "One-Man Bands." In 1996, Guy St. Clair wrote, "Until about 25 years ago, one-person librarianship as a recognized branch of specialized librarianship and information services did not exist." (St. Clair 1996c). The movement and even the term OPL can be attributed to St. Clair, former librarian at the University Club in New York, founder of *The One-Person Library: A Newsletter for Librarians and Management*, and principal in SMR International.

A BRIEF HISTORY OF THE OPL MOVEMENT

- 1972: Guy St. Clair was invited to lead a discussion at the 1972 Special Libraries Association (SLA) Annual Conference in Boston, Massachusetts, on "The One-Man Library." He said he would do so only if the title was changed to "The One-Person Library." This is the first instance of the term OPL being used. Hundreds of OPLs attended the session, overflowing the room.

- 1976: St. Clair's first article on the OPL was published, followed by several workshops and seminars.

- 1984: St. Clair founded *The One-Person Library* newsletter with Andrew Berner, also of the University Club of New York.

- 1986: *Managing the One-Person Library* was published, the first book on OPLs, by St. Clair and Joan Williamson.

- 1987: The first two-day, continuing education course on one-person librarianship was taught at the SLA Annual Conference in Anaheim.

- 1988: At the SLA Annual Conference in Denver, Martha Rose (Marty) Rhine led two roundtables on OPLs. She distributed a list to get participants' names and addresses so they could keep in touch; 99 people signed the list.

- 1988: Using the list as a base, Marty formed the Solo Librarians Caucus of the SLA with an initial membership of about 100.

- Late 1980s: The One-Man Bands group of ASLIB (U.K.) was formed.

- 1991: The Solo Librarians Caucus became a full-fledged division of SLA, with Judith Siess as the first chairperson.

- 1991: Guy St. Clair was inaugurated as president of SLA. OPLs are recognized as leaders.

- 1991: *The Best of OPL* was published, consisting of selections from the first five years of the newsletter.

- 1995: One-Person Australian Librarians (OPAL) was formed as a special-interest group of the Australian Library and Information Association (ALIA) after the Health, Law and Specials Conference in Sydney. Georgina Dale, Toni Silson (now Kennedy), and Therese Bendeich were its first leaders.

- 1996: The first German OPL roundtable was held, organized by Evelin Morgenstern of the Deutsches Bibliotheksinstitut (German Library Institute), Berlin, Germany.

- 1997: AspB (Arbeitsgemeinschaft der Spezialbibliotheken, the German Special Libraries Working Group) devoted its biennial conference to small special (OPL) libraries.

- 1997: VdDB (Verein der Diplom-Bibliothekare, one of the professional librarian associations in Germany) established the OPL Kommission, with Regina Peeters as chair. This special working group offers continuing professional education programs for OPLs at least twice a year.

- 1997: *Das Robinsoon-Crusoe Syndrom und was man dagegen tun kann (The Robinson Crusoe Syndrome and What You Can Do About It)* was published with reports from 24 German OPLs describing their work.

- 1997: *The SOLO Librarian's Sourcebook*, by Judith Siess, was published.

- 1997: First meeting of SLIM, Special Librarians (many of them OPLs), in the Midlands, was held in Birmingham, England; Chris Crabtree and Margaret Brittin were the founders.

- 1998: *A Most Delicate Monster: The One-Professional Special Library*, by Jean Dartnall, was published in Australia.

- 1998: Information Bridges International, Inc., with Judith Siess as the new editor and publisher, purchased *The One-Person Library* newsletter.

- 1999: First meeting of Special Librarians in London (SLIL) was held; Bert Washington of Sports Marketing Surveys was the founder.

- 1999: Workplace Libraries discussion list was launched in April 1999 by the Library Association (LA) in the U.K.

- 1999: An electronic discussion list just for OPLs was established by the LA (U.K.).

- 1999: Workplace '99 Initiative was started by the LA (U.K.) to increase awareness of commerce, industry, government, and voluntary institutional libraries by Lyndsay Rees-Jones and Mark Field, professional advisors from the LA.

- 1999: A solo professional network was set up by Steve Witowski of the East Midlands Branch of the LA (U.K.).

- 2000: First meeting of Special Librarians in Cambridge (U.K.) was held; Lis Riley was the founder.

- 2000: OPAL published its first book, *Evaluating Websites*.

• 2001: Initiative Fortbildung für wissenschaftliche Spezialbibliotheken und verwandte Einrichtungen (Initiative for Special Libraries and Similar Institutions) formed in Germany as Deutsches Bibliotheksinstitut (DBI) was being dissolved.

WHERE OPLs WORK

Most OPLs work in special libraries. A special library is one serving a specialized or limited clientele, with specialized or limited materials and services. The emphasis is often on providing information, rather than books. The collection is often small. The OPL nearly always reports to a nonlibrarian, and the library is part of but not considered critical to the parent organization's main mission. Although many OPLs work for corporations, there are other opportunities. Some examples follow.

Law Libraries

Librarians serving private practice, small law practices, and bar associations are often OPLs, as are law librarians in government institutions such as courts or agencies and some public law libraries, but these make up only about 15 percent of law librarians. Most law librarians in academia and law schools, where a library is required for accreditation, are not OPLs. Only 29 percent of law librarians have law degrees, but almost all (80 percent) have library degrees. Most employers use their law librarians to save lawyers' billable hours, to save attorneys' time looking for information, and to add to revenues by librarians doing billable information searches for clients. Sometimes OPLs are used to perform other functions, such as archiving, managing records, managing dockets, conflicts checking, and supervising paralegals. The future probably will see an expansion of the law librarian into many other areas: skill-based resource management; client current awareness services; research for client and practice development; support for speaking opportunities, such as seminars; research, reference, and technology training for clients; support for internal and client newsletters, Web page design, Web content management, coordination of continuing legal education programs, management of paralegals, and formal legal research training for new staff. (Note: When asked to perform research for clients, the librarian should be sure it is included in the firm's profitability analysis.)

The issues facing legal OPLs are the need for rapid delivery of information, often with price insensitivity; the currency and accuracy of the information; the high degree of confidentiality expected; decisions regarding the fine line between legal research and interpretation; and employment of summer interns or law clerks. These temporary employees have high expectations of librarians and add to the workload of librarians. Also, academic law librarians are becoming increasingly responsible for teaching legal research techniques to students. Other issues not unique to law librarianship are timeliness, currency, accuracy, thoroughness, detail, rising costs and burnout, and emphasis on the practical uses of information. Academic law librarians get more involved in research, history, and comparative law. In a summary of several studies of how lawyers find information, researchers found that 50 percent to 60 percent of them do not go to librarians for help, even if they have trouble finding the information themselves. They do not use the librarian to learn how to search, only to provide the documents they identify from their own search. (I would wager that similar results would be found in surveying any constituency—engineers, doctors, and even the public.)

Prison or Jail Libraries

According to the 1996 Directory of State Prison Librarians, there are now more than 1,000 prison libraries. Most states require the provision of access to legal materials to inmates (although some states have decided to close all their prison libraries). Most prison libraries remain one-person positions, despite staffing level recommendations. Most prison librarians are professionals. Prison librarians have problems motivating their inmate assistants, due to turnover and lack of a strong work ethic. Prison libraries are also concerned with confidentiality and the dividing line between legal reference and legal advice. Another hot current issue is the computerization of prison libraries. Prisons are reluctant to replace books with computers, with their potential for online crime. Jail libraries are usually smaller and less likely to hire a professional. The emphasis is on access to legal materials and recreational reading as a form of behavior control or self-improvement. Lack of funds, censorship, and low status are major issues. Personality traits needed by prison or jail librarians include an understanding of the political climate of the institution, survival skills, patience, a sense of humor, ability to follow the rules, and a professional demeanor.

Hospital Libraries

In the past, hospitals were required to employ professional librarians for accreditation. Today, they are only required to provide access to appropriate materials. However, most hospitals still have libraries and librarians. Except in the large medical schools and hospitals, the librarian is often an OPL. The needs of physicians are similar to those of lawyers; that is, rapid delivery of current and accurate information having practical application, with cost usually being irrelevant. Many hospital librarians are also involved in patient services, archives, consumer health information, and administration of physician continuing education. Some librarians are even a part of the treatment team. This practice is increasing with the advent of higher training levels for librarians and the computerization of medical information. Hospital libraries frequently have a staff of volunteers, possessing varying degrees of training and commitment, with which to work. Having volunteers may or may not help the OPL's workload. The Medical Libraries Association offers a certification program in medical librarianship. Although certification is not required for all medical librarian positions, it is strongly encouraged.

Museum or Zoo Libraries

Museums, zoos, and libraries acquire, describe, and make accessible to us the records of human experience, covering life sciences, education, business, philosophy, and art. Not all museums and zoos have libraries. The American Zoo and Aquarium Association/Librarians Special Interest Group (AZA/LSIG) consists of zoo and aquarium librarians as well as other persons working in zoos and aquariums who are responsible for the institution's library and operations. Formed in 1978, AZA/LSIG now has over 90 members from zoos and aquariums on three continents. The Directory of Zoo and Aquarium Libraries, compiled and edited by Jill Gordon, librarian at the Saint Louis Zoo, lists 41 U.S. zoos along with four zoos from Australia, three from Canada, and one each from Brazil, Germany, the U.K., and the Netherlands. A number of zoos use volunteers to staff their libraries, while many other zoos combine the job of librarian with another position. These libraries have historically been underfunded, understaffed, and underused. Facilities range from just a collection of books and magazines for staff use to a full-fledged library. The library is very likely to have a relatively large number of volunteers. Nearly all the libraries provide reference service to staff, members, and the general public. Few of these libraries circulate items beyond the staff, provide online searching, perform document delivery, or have access to the Internet.

Church or Synagogue Libraries

Many churches and synagogues have libraries. Some are staffed by volunteers (often a retired librarian or schoolteacher), and some of the larger ones hire professional librarians. Nearly all of these are one-person positions. The church library functions as a centralized place for materials for church programs (a sort of learning and resource center), with the specific aim of promoting the spiritual development of its users. There are no specific educational requirements for the church librarian, but dedication, friendliness, an enjoyment for working with details, neatness, patience, and a sense of humor are suggested—the same criteria as for an OPL. Funding and pay are usually minimal, but it is a rewarding field for the dedicated.

Public Libraries

Surprisingly, a large number of OPLs work in public libraries. Nearly 80 percent of public libraries serve populations of under 25,000 and are staffed by only one professional (Vavrek 1987). Times are changing in small public libraries. The library director is the heart of the library, representing the library to the community, library board, and staff. Public librarians face similar issues, as do corporate and other types of librarians: a sense of intimacy with their patrons, overwork, "doing it all," and dealing with nonlibrarians as supervisors (the library board). They also face some unique issues such as building maintenance, raising money for new buildings, bond issues, and other related matters. Regarding library boards, the librarian and the board are often at odds as to the role each should play. Another issue unique to public libraries is their relationship to the school system. Some communities may not understand the need to support two separate library systems. Although the pay for small public library directors is often abysmal and there are long hours, as with all OPLs, you "run the show."

Public or Private School Libraries

School librarians and media specialists are very often OPLs. Many of them serve two or more school libraries, with volunteers (often students) staffing the library when the librarian is not there. All professional school librarians must also have a teaching certification. They are seen as an extension of the classroom and often assist teachers with special projects as well as run the library and teach library skills to the students. Some even have additional duties, such as holding story hours, teaching reading or English, providing computer instruction, advising student groups, running the bookstore, and supervising the lunchroom.

Others

Information Brokers or Consultants

The work of information brokers falls into two main categories: information retrieval and delivery and information organization, or "information consulting." An "infopreneur" is just a fancy word for an information entrepreneur. The infopreneur may design and produce databases, perform primary and secondary research, obtain documents, do abstracting and indexing, evaluate libraries, manage libraries, perform outreach and public relations, arrange for having materials translated, act as a records manager, train librarians, write or edit books and articles or newsletters—and almost anything else you can imagine. What does it take to be a successful infopreneur? It takes a combination of many different things: good speaking, writing, and telephone skills; good organizational skills; the ability to prioritize; the ability to solve problems; a broad base of knowledge; good computer skills; patience; a sense of humor; perseverance; dedication and hard work; enjoyment in working alone; enjoyment in decision-making; self-motivation; energy; creativity; confidence; optimism; intelligence; the ability to integrate disparate concepts; and the ability to sell yourself and your services. In other words, it takes the same skills as needed to be a good solo librarian. The newest buzzword is "intrapreneur," a library-based information entrepreneur.

Market Researchers

An increasing number of librarians work in the competitive intelligence (CI) field. Competitive intelligence is the gathering of information that will assist a company in maintaining its competitive edge. (It is not, as some think, only gathering information about one's competitors. It also includes information about a company's customers, keeping up with technology, and anything else that makes the company better able to compete.) Librarians are exceptionally well qualified to do CI. We are trained to search for, analyze, organize, and disseminate information. We are experienced in working in an interdisciplinary environment. We already have our own networks. Other traditional library competencies that transfer well to CI include online searching, the reference interview, current awareness, knowledge of bibliographic tools, computer skills, written presentation skills, and time management.

The non-traditional sector is probably the fastest-growing area of librarianship. A librarian's skills can be applied in many fields. You can be a representative for a library supplier, a writer or publisher, or a consultant. You can work for a market research firm, a nonprofit organization, a government agency, a document delivery service, an association library, in Web site development, or for a library consortium or network. The job opportunities are limited only by your imagination, creativity, interest, and persistence.

CHARACTERISTICS OF AN OPL

How does an OPL differ from a so-called regular librarian? First of all, the OPL is most likely in a small library, without extensive holdings or resources. Secondly, OPLs are expected to do it all— ordering, cataloging, referencing, bibliographic instruction, online searching, filing, budgeting, and so on. They may have a part-time assistant, volunteers, or—if they are lucky—some full-time clerical assistance. But the OPL is the only trained librarian on the staff. The OPL has no counterpart in the organization performing the same job to which he/she may refer for help, advice, or job-related sympathy. The OPL is probably working for a nonlibrarian—a boss who does not really understand what the OPL does or how it is accomplished. (It's hard to get approval to buy an automated acquisitions system if your boss doesn't even know what one is.)

You, as an OPL, have more in common with other OPLs than you do with librarians in larger libraries in the same subject field. At least that is what I've discovered in my travels and through talking with all kinds of librarians. Guy St. Clair (1997) observed four common traits of OPLs: OPLs love their work; OPLs communicate; OPLs are sophisticated; and OPLs are confident. I have found that about 80 percent are OPLs by chance, only 20 percent by choice. However, many who started by chance now like it so much they wouldn't go back to a large library.

According to St. Clair and Williamson (1992), a library with an OPL may be the organization's first library, newly established and unsure of how many staff persons it needs, destined to grow to include a larger staff. It can be a downsized library that formerly had several librarians but, because of less demand, less money, or less awareness of need, now is reduced to one professional. It can also be a library that is just the right size, one that needs only one well-trained, efficient professional to serve the organization's information needs. This is probably the most common situation.

How many OPLs are there? Because of the small size of the library and staff, there is no accurate count of OPLs, but the following figures are available. The SLA estimates that 50 to 60 percent of their over 14,000 members are OPLs, i.e., 7,000 to 8,400 OPLs in North American special libraries alone. (The SOLO Librarians Division of SLA is now 10 years old and in that time has grown from 350 to over 1,000 members—the fourth or fifth largest division in the organization.) U.S. Department of Education figures show that most U.S. public libraries have no more than one professional librarian. Most school libraries have only one professional (if that many), as do most hospital libraries. Small law firms are very unlikely to have more than one professional, and prison and church or synagogue libraries are lucky if they have a library staff person who holds a degree.

The question might be: Why would anyone want to be an OPL librarian? The three most common reasons are independence, variety, and an enhanced feeling of self-worth. OPLs enjoy the ability to "run their own show," i.e., set their own schedules and plan their own priorities, with a minimum of supervision and interference. "Doing what I want to do, when I want to do it" has great appeal. OPLs can make their own mistakes and successes. They know exactly what's going on and the level of quality going out to customers. They value the close relationship developed with their customers, and the wide variety of tasks that must be done (including those pesky clerical ones) keeps them busy and not bored. OPLs have the freedom to be creative in their solutions. They gain the respect of their colleagues by being the sole information authority in the organization. They are the recipients of all the appreciation for library services (and all the complaints, too). As Harry Truman said, "The buck stops here." But OPLs also have the opportunity to shine and show others what trained information professionals can do. As one OPL phrased it on a questionnaire, "Librarianship, especially solo librarianship, is a terrific career for liberal arts graduates with a passion for learning, a knack for problem-solving, a touch of creativity, and a sense of humor."

The life of an OPL has its drawbacks, as well. The most commonly mentioned problems include professional isolation, lack of clerical support, reporting to a non-librarian, and low pay. Other negatives about being an OPL include a lack of preparation for the job (in library school, on the job, and elsewhere); lack of management support; lack of job security (downsizing is always a possibility); poor physical working conditions; lack of time; frustration at not being able to "do it all"; lack of status; and lack of control concerning policy, personnel, or budget (or all three). There never seems to be enough time to get everything done. Filing, reading, public relations, and professional development fall victim to too little time. The lack of feedback and interaction with other professionals takes its toll; there is no one with whom to brainstorm; they may feel they are underappreciated within their organizations; they tire of being the only ones. "Mindless" clerical work seems to get in the way of doing "real" work. (Perhaps this requires an attitude transplant; clerical work isn't mindless. It can be a welcome respite from high-pressure decision-making and planning. It must be done, and who can do it better, faster, and more efficiently than an OPL?) Often OPLs tire under the strain of constantly having to explain themselves and their work to managers who do not understand them. The lack of feedback, status, and often credit for their efforts has its negative effects. If you are the type who needs constant reinforcement, this is not the job for you.

When I asked OPLs around the world "What do you wish you'd known before going solo?" I received some interesting replies:

- I should have been older with more experience under established librarians. (South Africa)

- I wish I knew how isolated I would be, how to network better, how useful a mentor would have been, how to learn about areas with which I wasn't familiar or had no experience. (Australia)

- I wish I developed better time-management and marketing skills. (Australia)

- I am glad that I did not know how much work it is. (U.K.)

- I wish I realized that I needed to know more than I learned at the library school. (U.K.)

- I wish I knew more about managing a library (administration). (U.K.)

- I wish I knew more about time management and information about the business world. (U.K.)

- I wish I had more information on time management and general management of the library (e.g., negotiations with companies, the staff of the institute, and such). (U.K.)

- I wish I learned accounting as it is practiced in a firm; library schools teach only about accounting practiced at government institutions. (U.K.)

- I wish I knew more about budgeting, administration, and human relations. (U.K.)

To the question "How could library schools have prepared solos better?" there were many suggestions:

- Grounding must be very thorough; pupils should have been encouraged to experiment, e.g., a "what if" situation. (South Africa)

- Schools should teach time management and how to search for information with limited reference works. (South Africa)

- There should be more concentration on practical work, and the fact should be highlighted that traditional systems of classification and style are not appropriate for many small special libraries. (Australia)

- Smart ways to do things, time management, and how to set priorities and limits should be the focus. (Australia)

- Much more hands-on practical work and better work experience programs should be offered. (Australia)

- The basics of software selection, such as which features to look for, should be taught. (Australia)

- One-person library internships should be available. Reading about problems of working in an OPL should be a requirement. (U.K.)

- You should be trained to build up contacts with all sorts of librarians. (U.K.)

- I don't think they can prepare you better. What you must have is experience in different jobs at different libraries. (U.K.)

- They should not only teach about public libraries but also about the structures in business, the role you play as an OPL, and time management. (U.K.)

OPLs outside the U.S. liked these things most about being on their own:

- Freedom, no sharing of personal space is necessary. (South Africa)

- Being responsible to myself, setting my own parameters, making my own rules, working alone are all benefits. (South Africa)

- There is freedom to prioritize based on known customer needs and work pressures. There is no hierarchy. There is personal satisfaction in meeting customer needs. (South Africa)

- The variety of tasks involved in running the library keeps me interested. (Australia)

- Being responsible for the quality of work is great. (Australia)

- I most enjoy the responsibility, the creativity in designing library management, and being able to see the results of my work by dealing directly with the users. (U.K.)

- I like working independently, the variety of tasks, having close contact with the users and knowing their interests. (U.K.)

- I enjoy the freedom of deciding what to do and when, and doing all that is necessary. (U.K.)

- I like the possibility of conceptual work, the self-responsibility, and the complexity of the work. (U.K.)

- I can decide how to organize my time and my work; I think I can work more creatively than in a bigger library. (U.K.)

The following are the parts of being an OPL they liked least:

- There is no one to rely on when you are absent or overworked. (South Africa)

• Not having a colleague to whom one can bounce off "library" ideas and problems. (South Africa)

• There are constant interruptions. (South Africa)

• There is isolation; the frustration of juggling too much work and not enough time or staff; the difficulty trying to keep up with new developments; and the difficulty of finding a good, approachable person who is a good communicator to assist with and train on new technology applications (loading software, using software, or software applications). (Australia)

• The heavy workload and the frustration of trying to convey to colleagues the nature of my work is a negative. (Australia)

• There is too much work. (U.K.)

• Lack of acknowledgment and a bad reputation are drawbacks. (U.K.)

• There is no information network; whether or not you get the right or most important information or, even more importantly, whether you find the right person to ask, depends on your own initiative. (U.K.)

• There is a lot of work, forcing meetings (e.g., with other librarians) to be possible only during free time; there is not enough exchange of experiences with colleagues. (U.K.)

• There is a feeling of being isolated. The library is underestimated within the association. (U.K.)

• The fact that decisions are made by non-librarian scientists and the director of the museum is frustrating. (U.K.)

• There is too little contact with other librarians. There is no communication about professional problems. (U.K.)

• You have to do your own lobbying. (U.K.)

Because many OPLs are OPLs by choice, obviously the pros must outweigh (or at least equal) the cons. Most OPLs are very happy, as shown by these quotes:

- "I love doing what I do. I cannot imagine not being involved with all aspects of running a library. It keeps me learning and constantly on the go."

- "It is a bonus being able to see interrelations of library functions. It makes you accountable."

- "I'm overworked and underpaid, but I love what I do partly because it has so many facets. The frustration is in not being able to juggle everything in the available time. I prefer being solo to being someone lost in a big library."

- "I like being a solo librarian so much that I can't imagine ever being interested in working in a big library."

- "This is an immensely satisfying business career."

Perhaps the key is in fitting the right person to the job. What kind of person should an OPL be? Most agree that the main requirements include being flexible and creative; having a bias toward service, sharing, coalition-building, and idealism; being resourceful; finding enjoyment in working alone; being able to manage time, think analytically, and see the big picture; being naturally curious; and having good recall. Also required are good communication skills, good organizational skills, self-confidence, a sense of humor, patience, and a high frustration tolerance. Can all these things be taught? They probably cannot, but specific tools and techniques can be learned, either in library school, on the job, or through continuing education. In general, OPLs wish they had known more about financial matters, management, corporate culture, networking, computer skills, assertiveness, time management, and public relations. In short, they wish they had learned more about the job on which they were about to embark.

What does it take to become an OPL? I followed the SOLOLIB-L e-mail support list for several months on the Internet, eavesdropping on discussions among list members regarding this subject. Their replies indicate that an OPL must have confidence in making good decisions, an entrepreneurial attitude, comfort with networking, proficiency in gathering supporters, a lot of flexibility, good time management skills, the ability to balance priorities, a love for the profession, the ability to cope with many bosses and patrons who think they are the only client, a readiness to take risks and learn something new every day, passion and enthusiasm, and a willingness to dive into any task.

A WEEK IN THE LIFE OF AN OPL

The best way to illustrate exactly what an OPL librarian does is to review a week in the life of one. What follows is a summary of my activities for one week, in one job, at one corporation. It may or may not be typical of the work of an OPL, but it will give the reader a taste of what it could be like.

Monday

Starting at 7:30 a.m., I read my e-mail, read my news groups, and listen to about five phone messages. E-mail can include "to do's" from my boss, requests for engineering document numbers to be assigned, and press releases. Phone messages are usually follow-ups on orders placed: "Can you get this?" or similar questions.

At about 8:30 a.m., I go to the mailroom for the first part of the mail. Monday is the heaviest mail day. I go back at about 11 a.m. for the rest (and to deliver what I've gotten done), and then return after 1 p.m. for the packages. On a busy day, I will go back once again at 3 p.m. for the rest of the afternoon mail. The mail consists of ads for new services (much of which I recycle without opening), bills to be approved, magazines to be checked in (and some read), and internal requests for information and books or magazines to be ordered.

As usual, I eat lunch at my desk. If I'm lucky, I'm only interrupted a couple of times. I don't mind, because lunch is the only time some people can get to the library so I deliberately leave my door open to be available to help. Remember, their questions do not interrupt my job; they are my job.

On Mondays, I usually check with my boss to see if he has any special projects for the upcoming week. Because he is an engineer and not a librarian, this can be anything from creating a new database, cleaning up an existing one (making abbreviations and words consistent), to locating an overhead projector for him to take on a trip.

The rest of the day consists of odds and ends. For example, I may write purchase orders for a couple of books and for new locks for the lab book files. I'll pick up the locks later in the week and have maintenance install them.

On this particular Monday, I prepare for my annual Open House, which is tomorrow. I spend about an hour getting my computer set up outside the library. It doesn't work immediately, which is normal. Nothing is ever as simple as it seems. I then leave for home about 5:30 p.m.

Tuesday

This Tuesday happens to be my Library Open House. At 8:30 a.m. the coffee is delivered, and at 9:00 the cakes arrive (one for morning, one for afternoon—if I put out both they will disappear quickly because food is a big drawing card around here). I also have lollipops, bookmarks (which read "When you absolutely, positively have to know ... ask a librarian."), stickers ("I visited my library today."), and notepads ("Have you tried the library?"). I placed announcements regarding this event in the company weekly update, in my monthly letter, and via large signs on bulletin boards on each floor. I also reminded everyone (vice presidents, in particular) via e-mail. By the end of the day, 110 people signed in (actually more were probably present since

200 pieces of cake disappeared). I answer many questions about the library. I even do some demos of library services. It's a very successful event.

Near the end of the Open House, the president's secretary appears. She needs me to find a press release on a new joint venture but, of course, I can't answer right away since my modem is in my office and my computer is out here. I call another special librarian whom I know has Dow Jones News Retrieval, but she is unable to locate the release. As soon as the open house is finished (3 p.m.), I reassemble the computer in my office, go on Dow Jones myself, and find the article. I send it to the secretary via e-mail—another satisfied customer. I go home at about 5:15 p.m.

Wednesday

Yesterday was the Open House, so I didn't get any "real" work done except for putting out *The Wall Street Journal*. (If I don't produce *The Wall Street Journal* first thing every day, the engineers get nervous.) Thus, I do two days work in one day. This is what occurs every time I am out, whether for a meeting, training session, SLA conference, sickness or vacation. However, it is worth my time to go to meetings or training sessions because I have to keep up with this ever-changing profession. Besides, if I never left they would take me for granted, "a piece of the woodwork, a permanent fixture." While I am gone (and no one is doing my work), they realize what I do for them and are somewhat more appreciative.

Three purchase orders are written today. One is for five articles that are needed as soon as possible for a manager's presentation to a potential customer. I send this order to an information broker; the articles arrive the next day, making the patron very happy. It is also a big interlibrary loan (ILL) day, and my boss wants 12 articles on measuring research and development (R&D) productivity. I locate them on the Online Computer Library Center (OCLC), the world's largest online catalog at area libraries. This takes about an hour, including looking up the ISSNs and checking the local union serials list. (Note: By one week later, five are in, one is not available, and the rest have been shipped.) I typically do about 30 ILLs a month, but have done as many as 60 in one day. Occasionally, I even have the opportunity to loan an item. Today, I actually go home on time (more or less) at 4:30 p.m.

Thursday

I continue working with a vendor's technical rep to fix a hardware problem. This has been going on for over six months, and the patrons and I are a bit aggravated. The system works, but not as it should. I am trying to get them to make some monetary concessions as well as fix the problem. A significant part of my job is dealing with vendors who may or may not give the desired service, and this vendor is not the only one with whom I have problems, just the only one of the day.

The vice-president of engineering appears with an information request; he needs information on software licensing. I do a quick search on a CD-ROM database and get about 30 full-text articles. I send them to him via e-mail and get a nice note thanking me for my promptness and professionalism.

Today is a light-load day, only one purchase order is written. It is a rush order for four copies of a computer book. I fax it to our book vendor, requesting next day delivery. The books arrive the next afternoon, and the patron is happy. The day ends at 4:45 p.m.

Friday

This Friday signifies the end of the month, time for my monthly report. I put together the statistics, which include the number of items circulated; the number of books, patents, standards, or ILLs ordered; and the questions that were answered. Then, I write a narrative of what I did this month. This includes direct patron service (e.g., tours of the library, special research projects, and such), new services added, and continuing efforts. I also include my activities with SLA and my local multi-type library consortium—to remind my boss that I am a professional. This month for SLA I have worked on the local chapter directory, attended one meeting, counted ballots for the Sci-Tech Division, and served on the nominating committee for the Engineering Division. I also attended one consortium meeting this month, titled Special Library Directors. We had a one-hour information sharing session, which is very helpful since we learn the resources of the other libraries. These meetings are invaluable for maintaining a network of local contacts from whom I can borrow items and ask questions. This report goes to my boss, who abridges it to his boss, who summarizes it for his boss, and so forth. I printed a list of overdue books, but I am not sure what to do with it. It is time-consuming to send out notices, which involves printing them, addressing them, and delivering them to mail slots. The return rate is under 50 percent, and it antagonizes the patrons. I put it in the "hold" file for now.

I perk up when Barbara Quint, editor of *Searcher* magazine, calls. I sent her an e-mail praising the timeliness and pertinence of the latest issue, and she asks if she can print my letter. We talk about library education, SLA headquarters, vendors, and the general difficulties of our profession today. She is a fascinating speaker and really knows what is happening in the information industry. Today I leave for home at about 4:45 p.m.

CONCLUSION

There are certain defining characteristics of OPLs. OPLs must be functioning as librarians or information professionals. They must be the only information professional in the immediate organization (although it is permissible, and encouraged, that they be part of a larger network). They may have a staff, but not consisting of other professionals. Regardless of where they are employed, they need to understand the corporate culture of the organization of which they are a part. They must be creative, patient, adaptable, committed, behave professionally, be able to work well with others, and have a sense of humor.

Some people resent the idea that OPLs even exist. Herb White, former dean of the library school at Indiana University, said that "perhaps we need to postulate that 'one-person library' is an oxymoron ... they are clerical centers for buying, lending, and recalling" (1988, 56). But the fact remains that there are OPLs, a lot of them, and library educators, researchers, management consultants, and even the rest of the library profession have ignored them. This needs to be brought to the attention of the profession, our user populations, and the public—as often and as forcefully as possible.

2

An International View

THE UNIVERSALITY OF ONE-PERSON LIBRARIANSHIP

There are OPLs all over the world. We go by various names—one-man bands, solo librarians, sole charge librarians—and work in different subject areas—hospitals, law firms, public libraries, corporate libraries, prisons, churches and synagogues, academia, and so on. We have a variety of titles—librarian, information specialist, researcher, technician, manager, supervisor, and many others. Some of us work entirely alone; others have an assistant or two or volunteers to help out.

Over the past few years I have traveled to South Africa, Germany, England, Canada, Australia, and New Zealand and have made it a point to talk with OPLs in each country. Through the miracle of e-mail I have been able to "talk" with OPLs in many other countries. Combined with 20 years of talking with librarians in the U.S., I have found that, fundamentally, we are all the same. We work in relatively small libraries, often for small firms or in small towns. We report to non-librarians, who likely do not completely understand what we do. We work in isolation, with no other information professional nearby to share our trials and triumphs. We do all the jobs in a library—acquisitions, cataloging, circulation, reference, research, and administration. We face the challenges of constant change, organizational politics, gaining the respect of our management and users, and using the Internet. We also, more than likely, love what we do.

There are some differences, however. In some countries, library resources and organizations are less plentiful. Problems with currency fluctuations and the resultant high cost of online services and journals can cause major problems for many OPLs. Outside the U.S., more libraries are likely to be OPLs and the OPL is more likely to be a non-professional. Educational systems outside the U.S. are structured quite differently. In many countries, there are two kinds of library education: the academic and the practical.

UNITED KINGDOM

"These are exciting times for solo librarians in the UK," wrote Sue Lacey Bryant, a library consultant and author, for *The One-Person Library* in November 1999. "New networks are emerging in the East Midlands and in London. The development of active, self-confident groupings of OPLs willing to learn from each other can only be of benefit to the profession as a whole." The Library Association (LA) has helped greatly by the appointment of two liaisons to the special library community, Lyndsay Rees-Jones and Mark Field, and by starting the solo e-mail list (see Chapter 13 for details on joining the list).

Bryant continues: "It has been clear for some time that an accurate assessment of the number of solo information professionals is vital. Without identifying the significance of OPLs within the profession and establishing a reliable picture of the sectors in which they are deployed, the various professional bodies cannot possibly serve the interests of solo librarians. For example, the need for access to affordable Continuing Professional Education, structured in such a way that solo librarians can participate, is crucial."

Based on 1999 LA subscription renewal figures, 1,506 of the 24,506 personal members identify themselves as OPLs. (The first year the LA gave members an opportunity to check a box marking them as a solo librarian or an OPL was 1999.) Deleting those not actively working in libraries, leaves 1,381 OPLs working in the U.K. who are members of the LA. Most OPLs work in school libraries, industry, or commerce.

In 1999, the Library and Information Statistics Unit of the Department of Information and Library Studies, Loughborough University, re-surveyed 897 organizations surveyed in 1997. Of the 435 responses, 128 had no library and 22 had a very small library and thus were not included in the analysis; all national, public, and academic libraries and those firms with overlapping sectors were included. The 285 responses used were comprised of government departments and organizations; voluntary (not-for-profit) organizations; professional, trade, and learned associations; legal organizations; commercial and financial companies; energy organizations; pharmaceutical companies; management and information consultants; and food and drink manufacturers (as an arbitrary example of manufacturers). Response rates varied from 36 percent to 59 percent.

OPLs made up from six percent (government departments) to 48 percent (government organizations) of the total (depending on the sector), with a mean of 35 percent. This compares favorably with the 50 to 60 percent estimated by the U.S. Special Libraries Association (SLA) for its members and a survey by Roberta Pitts (1994) estimating that 27 percent of U.K. librarians are OPLs.

SOLO librarians in the U.K. have quite a few networking resources. These include the Association of Libraries & Information Bureau (ASLIB), Institute of Information Scientists, LA, Royal Society of Information Science (RSIS), Women in Libraries, British Business School Librarians Group, Careers Information Officers in Local Authorities, European Business Schools Librarians, Management Librarians, Trade Union Librarians, Bank Librarians, British Library Information Officers, City Law Librarians, Construction Industry Information, Home Office Library & Information Science, Information Officers in Voluntary Organisations, Regional Health Authorities Librarians, UK Online User, Network of Community Resource Centers, and Information Officers in the Pharmaceutical Industry.

One of the first OPL organizations outside the U.S. was the One-Man Band Section of ASLIB in the U.K. This group was very active for several years, but now has been inactive for a number of years. In June 1997, Chris Crabtree and Margaret Brittin organized Special Libraries in the Midlands (SLIM) in Birmingham, England. SLIM members meet about three times a year. A similar group, SLIL (Special Librarians in London), meets monthly, thanks to the hard work of Bert Washington. Lis Riley is working on establishing Special Libraries in Cambridge (SLIC), and other groups are being formed in the west and south of England and in Scotland. The LA launched its Workplace Libraries (British for corporate or company libraries) discussion list in April 1999 and the East Midlands Branch of the LA established a solo Professional network, set up by Steve Witowski. The Industrial and Commercial Libraries Group of the LA is made up primarily of OPLs and is quite active.

GERMANY

The success of the OPL movement in Germany has been a direct result of the efforts of the Deutsches Bibliotheksinstitut (DBI) and Evelin Morgenstern. Her responsibility at DBI was to identify issues that affect the Special Libraries branch of the profession and to organize activities for addressing these issues. The mission of DBI was twofold. The organization was officially chartered to work with all types of libraries and information organizations by giving support through publications, continuing education, and professional development programs; project work; database creation; evaluations and information audits; and so on. Within the organization, Morgenstern's position is what might be called an "enabling" one because it is her responsibility to give advice and orientation to special librarians as they deal with day-to-day problems in their work. What follows is Morgenstern's latest report on the state of one-person librarianship in Germany (communication 2000).

The story of OPLs in Germany can be told in two parts—before and after May 1995. What happened in May 1995? The first German OPL Roundtable was held, organized by Evelin Morgenstern, the Special Libraries' advisor of the Deutsches Bibliotheksinstitut, and led by Guy St. Clair. Morgenstern had a strong desire to help her colleagues in eastern Germany who were making it clear to her that they were finding it difficult to cope with the changing conditions in their work situation. They had been accustomed to very generous staffing levels and were not prepared to accept their downsizing as "rightsizing"— something to which those in western Germany painfully had become accustomed.

What were OPLs like before May 1995? The leaders of the profession found the following:

- The role and relative importance of the OPL in the organization varies greatly, depending in part on the librarian's own perception of her or his role. A library with frequent and satisfied users provides the librarian with a chance to prove his or her merit and capabilities to the organization. In some organizations, however, the library is viewed as more of a service center than a library, providing copying, bookkeeping, telephone, and messenger services.

- If the library is not found in a central location, it is most likely to be located in the department where it is most needed, such as R&D. Most libraries seem to have fewer than 10,000 volumes, but 10 percent have over 40,000 volumes. Most OPLs do not have professional librarian status and many have no permanently-assigned staff. In a great many of the OPLs, there is no automation and what there is may have been selected by the organization and not the librarian.

- The topic of professional isolation among OPLs is a serious one. If the librarian feels, or truly is, isolated from other colleagues, he or she will not be able to judge the quality of work he or she performs. Networking is strongly urged.

- Both planning and financial responsibility in OPLs seemed to come under the well-known rubric: "Go ahead and do what you want, unless it costs money. Then prove to me it is really necessary to the organization." A supportive organization can give the librarian a great deal of autonomy. Selection of software, books, journals, and so on, should be made with the participation of the librarian in all cases. Note that they didn't go so far as to say "by the librarian."

- There is a great need for networking. Much of the current exchange of ideas and making of new contacts comes from attending meetings of librarians from OPLs. Groups such as the APBB (Arbeitsgemeinschaft der Parlaments-unde Behordenbibliotheke) offer support, but it is up to the individual librarian to seek them out. It is also extremely important, and this cannot be stressed enough, that the organization allow and encourage librarians to attend meetings such as the annual librarians' day (Bibliothekartage), congresses, and workshops—not only for their continuing education, but also to cultivate professional contacts. Continuing education must be supported financially by the organization. If librarians are not permitted and encouraged in this area, they will lose interest in improving themselves, to the detriment of the organization.

- In many OPLs, services are restricted to providing books and periodicals as requested. In others, excellent and comprehensive provision of services is available. Librarians could use more information on specific marketing ideas and more time and support for putting them into action. If a librarian finds out which customers' needs are unfulfilled and conquers these new areas, it would be an excellent way to justify his or her existence.

Interviews with OPLs themselves yielded similar, if more simply expressed, results. They stressed four main points: professional isolation, lack of status (prestige), lack of time, and lack of specialized training. It is clear that, when starting to work as an OPL, they found themselves feeling a little "unprofessional" and full of admiration for their colleagues in academic libraries who were able to concentrate their energies on a single problem. In contrast, OPLs had to be generalists, making a decision to ignore much of what they learned at library school, fighting against the mode of the academic library, and not allowing themselves or anyone else to regard the OPL as no more than a scaled-down version of the academic library.

The Roundtable could not limit itself to just time management, image, and lack of specialization, but had to work to raise awareness—on both sides. It had to force leaders of the profession and practitioners to look at the OPL differently, acknowledging its unique role and accepting that it could even become an example for the academic library. The OPL can offer better and more relevant information services because of its closeness to the customer, the organization, and the collection. This was a lesson everyone needed to learn.

After the Roundtable, DBI saw how the meeting helped the research and support organization meet its basic goals to be a seismograph and interpreter of trends, to implement them in German and then pass the torch to others. All the specialized working groups (in medicine, the arts and museums, government and parliament, and church libraries) immediately started to offer continuing professional education courses or workshops for OPLs. They still do. In 1996, the first OPL workshop was organized by the APBB at Erlangen on Librarians' Day. The same year APBB also sponsored the first "Diplomarbeit" written at Fachhochschule Hannover on OPLs in the Hannover area. In 1997, the biennial conference of the Arbeitsgemeinschaft der Spezialbibliotheken (AspB), the Special Libraries Working Group, devoted a large part of its program to OPLs with Sue Lacey Bryant of the U.K. and Guy St. Clair of the U.S. presenting papers. The same year saw the birth of the OPL Kommission in the Verein der Diplom-Bibliothekare (VdDV), the association for academic or special libraries. They have been very active. They have compiled a database of OPLs with over 1,000 listings, set up an electronic list (to which nearly 100 librarians subscribed in the first week), and created a Web site.

For those not able to attend conferences, an impressive list of literature is now available. Two of Guy St. Clair's works were translated into German by DBI (and one is being translated into Japanese now!). Regina Peeters of the OPL Kommission edited *The Robinson Crusoe Syndrome and What You Can Do About It* with 24 detailed descriptions of OPLs in Germany with a strong emphasis on pragmatic approaches to problem-solving. The library schools (Fachhochscholen) have begun to introduce OPL-related issues in their curricula, although distinct training for one-person librarianship has not yet been established.

The Roundtable also laid the groundwork for 12 regional working groups all over Germany. They meet regularly (usually bimonthly) with 10 to 14 participants (about one-third of the OPLs in the area). Most meetings involve a visit to a library or other event followed by an informal meeting. Both parts are equally important. The

Berlin-Bradenburg working group chose *The One-Person Library* newsletter as the basis for their professional discussions. The groups seldom invite outside speakers. The groups are organized very informally and without bureaucracy. There was an OPL interest group under the DBI with representatives from all 12 groups, but it was not successful and has been discontinued. However, the OPL Kommission intends to take over the role of coordination and identification of unfulfilled needs.

In 2000, those who attended the 1995 Roundtable were surveyed about the "after" existence of OPLs. It was their unanimous view that professional isolation no longer exists. If it does, it is the choice of the individual OPL; with all the networks, lists, OPL Kommission, databases, and so-on, there is no reason to feel alone. Most of the other goals have been met to some degree—mostly depending on the attitude and personality of the individual OPL. In fact, personal competencies have begun to play a crucial role in Germany due to influences from the U.S. More continuing education courses are being organized to cover this area. OPLs themselves agree that they feel less isolated and are more aware of their own value. This self-confidence has improved the quality of professional service they deliver because they can measure their own performance against that of others. Both the leaders and the OPLs mentioned the problems of decreasing finances, which are now universal. This has sometimes led to quite a quality dilemma. OPLs have to take over other tasks involving as much as half their working time (especially at museum libraries). They feel doing so imposes quite a burden on their provision of high-quality service, but the smart ones have turned their non-librarian duties into a publicity campaign for the library.

Looking back on what has been achieved, it feels like a fairy tale—but it is not. The changes have been brought about by cooperation and investment of time and effort in the target group. Nevertheless, there is still much to be done and many questions remain unanswered:

- We [I include all OPLs] still need to bring about a certain mental change in our colleagues to make them understand that continued professional education is essential, even if not provided by the employers. It is a question of taking responsibility for one's own career. We also need to be concerned about the quality of the providers of such education. Volunteers are nice, but are they qualified? Are the courses still thought of as being "too American," especially since the German librarian often finds it difficult to see himself or herself as an entrepreneur?

- It seems to be fashionable for the leaders of the profession [in Germany, at least] to write one-person librarianship on their banner, but there are no visible consequences. The salary structure has not been reformed. Are OPLs in danger of becoming complacent and not seeking contact with fellow professionals in other fields? Is there an unrealistic expectation that any CE [continuing education] course should be customized for OPLs? [Such as preservation of historical library materials for OPLs—what's different for OPLs than others?]

All these problems are familiar and will probably go on forever, but we can hope it [they] will be approached with a positive attitude. As one OPL put it: "We must improve the information services, take them in a proactive way to management, and find at least one powerful advocate. That is my recipe for success and, indeed survival."

Since the early days of Germany's reunification there has been a major change in German society at all levels. Government, educational institutions, and, of course, professional organizations have been required to organize and manage the shift from what were two separate and distinctly opposite points of view to a "unified" one. With the fall of the [Berlin] Wall and the subsequent demands for reunification, challenges of a different sort had to be dealt with, since two different cultures and two different ways of thinking about work and the workplace (to say nothing about quality service delivery and similarly sensitive issues) had to be combined into one. The situation in Germany has been complicated by the transition from the practice of "traditional librarianship" to the development of an information delivery infrastructure for the 21st Century, requiring major shifts in thinking for information workers. A new perception about their professional status has come into play. Until 1995, OPLs were not even aware that they were in a position to raise awareness and "educate" these several societal entities about the role (and the *value*) of one-person librarianship. Now they are starting to do it!

With this raised awareness has come new responsibilities, new methodologies, and, perhaps as important as anything else, recognition. OPLs are no longer thought of as being (and the OPLs no longer think of themselves as being) modest, humble, or shy. They have identified their place in the library and information services workplace in Germany and they enthusiastically accept their role as change agents in the information management community.

Unfortunately, the DBI is disbanding, taking with it the Consulting Services for Special Libraries. To help fill that void, Morgenstern and some of her colleagues founded a new group on June 30, 2000, "Initiative Fortbildung für wissenschaftliche Spezialbibliotheken und verwandte Einrichtungen" (Initiative for Continuing Education in Libraries, Museums, and Archives). The association wants to continue and expand this work that for 20 years has provided consulting; organizational evaluation of special libraries; special projects; publication of professional literature; and, especially, the offering, planning, and carrying through of high-quality customized continuing education programs. The Initiative: " ... will make use of the innovative potential that is inherent in every situation of change: we will attempt a much broader conception of continuing education and thus be able to embark upon new ways not yet familiar to us. At the same time we will enlarge our spectrum of our target groups. The amazing thing is that LIBRARIANS are taking the initiative for founding this sort of association. [The] Initiative will concentrate on specific topics and problems relevant to is [it's] members. Some of these may be strategic planning, management skills, the Internet, and technology in general" (Morgenstern communication 2000).

AUSTRALIA

Australia is another hotbed of one-person librarianship, thanks to pioneering work by Guy St. Clair and Meg Paul and the continuing work of a dedicated group of One-Person Australian Librarians (OPALs). Australia has one of the largest Internet user bases in the world, enabling Australian librarians to embrace it and other new technologies at a rapid pace. The country has good special librarians, ones who are well educated, professionally well-read, and able to network well. However, they have had problems with downsizing, too, partly due to the lack of information to back up the need for library services.

A survey conducted by the Australian Library and Information Association (ALIA) in 1997 showed that only 47 of 83 top 100 companies responding had a library or information service (Walsh 1998). ALIA didn't expect this to change because 92 percent of the companies without a library said there was "no chance" of allocating funds for one in the next 12 months. The information competency most valued by management was "the ability to interpret requests for information and respond quickly." Surprisingly, nearly one-quarter of the respondents felt that their library resources did not meet the needs of their users. The Australian library work force was characterized as

• Aging—because 72 percent were over 40 years of age;

• Poorly paid—because they receive pay increases of only 3.4 percent compared with a national average of 4.5 percent;

• Highly unionized—because 57 percent were unionized vs. a national rate of only 31 percent;

• Insecure—because 17 percent were in "permanent part-time" positions vs. the national average of seven percent, over 50 percent were concerned about job security in the future, and one-third felt threatened by new technologies; and

• Dissatisfied—because over 40 percent said they had less say in decisions affecting their jobs than they had a year before, and over 60 percent experienced more stress at work.

Australia is the home of the One-Person Australian Libraries (OPAL) special interest group of ALIA. At the ALIA Health, Law and Specials Conference in Sydney in 1995, five members of the Health Section's program committee (Georgina Dale, Frances Bluhdorn, Claire Pillar, Marion Steele, Toni Silson [now Kennedy]) decided there was a need to meet with other OPLs at the conference. This meeting drew a large number of OPLs; therefore, Dale and Silson presented the case for a special-interest group to ALIA, which approved the idea in 1996. The first convenor was Georgina Dale, and the executive committee was made up of the five persons listed above plus Therese Bendeich. OPAL started a newsletter (*Opalessence*) in October 1996, an electronic list in December 1997, a Web page in 1998, a membership directory in 1999, and their first publication (*Evaluating Websites*) in 2000. There are now coordinators in each state organizing local meetings, the first being held in New South Wales in September 1996. In addition, national meetings are held at major conferences. OPAL has been sponsored by the Globe Subscription Agency from the very beginning. As of mid-2000, OPAL membership was nearing 300, and OPAL had regional groups in six of Australia's states and territories (Queensland, New South Wales, Victoria, Tasmania, South Australia, and Western Australia).

Frances Bludorn described Australian OPLs in 1996 by way of some wonderful analogies:

- "OPAL is an amorphous form of hydrated silica in the gel state. The amorphous nature is illustrated by its cross-sectional membership drawn from special libraries, health libraries, law libraries, public libraries .... "

- "OPALs are precious stones which have been used as gems."

- "Being the only gem of our kind in our organizations ... "

- "OPALs have existed underground since the beginning of time, their solid particles remaining suspended indefinitely, unaffected by bureaucracy. The formation of OPALs affords these suspended particles a sense of organisation in a loose but definite arrangement and [a] network while giving some rigidity and elasticity to ALIA's mixture."

- "The finest OPALs are found chiefly in Australia."

In 1996, Meg Paul at FLIS Pty Ltd., Melbourne, started *The Australasian One-Person Library*, a wraparound for *The One-Person Library* with local content. This publication was bought by Information Bridges International, Inc., in 1998, just prior to Meg Paul's retirement.

SOUTH AFRICA

In 1996, I had the privilege of visiting the Republic of South Africa and finding out about the solo scene first hand. I was one of 10 librarians who made up the first People-to-People Citizen Ambassador Delegation in

Special Librarianship and Information Services Management to the Republic of South Africa. The trip was arranged and led by Guy St. Clair of Infomanage/SMR International.

Although none of the group's official visits was to an OPL, I had three opportunities to meet with OPLs in a less formal setting. The first was at a meeting of the South Africa Institute for Librarianship and Information Science (SALIS) Special Libraries Interest Section at the University of Witswatersrand in Johannesburg. SALIS is an organization similar to the American Library Association (ALA). I also met with OPLs at a cocktail reception sponsored by the Special Libraries Interest Group of SALIS, Western Cape Division, and at a meeting with special library leaders at Ernst & Young in Capetown.

Most librarians (70 percent) attend one of the universities. There are three programs available at the universities: a four-year bachelor's degree, a fifth-year honors program, and a master's degree by research. Most graduates go to work at academic or national libraries. Librarians in corporate libraries are a mix of qualified and nonqualified employees. Compared with the Teknikon (technical or vocational school), the university program is more prestigious and the schools have more money to spend. The education is almost totally theoretical, although the University of South Africa (UNISA) requires two management courses. The internship is only three to four weeks long. Gill Owens, chair of the Special Libraries & Information Services (SLIS) group and librarian at the Cement and Concrete Institute of South Africa, said she didn't even know how to stamp a book when she graduated. She had been at university and her internship had been just cataloging a collection, involving almost no interaction with the librarian.

I asked briefly about salaries for qualified librarians. They range from 3,000 rand per month for public librarians to 7,000 rand per month for special librarians. In 1996, this range was equivalent to $8,000 to $20,000 per year. The University of Witswatersrand advertised for an assistant law librarian at up to R59,000 per year (U.S. $13,000) and had trouble filling the position with an experienced person. (To put this into perspective, I looked at job ads in the newspaper and found that most other positions were advertised at about 25 percent under U.S. salaries. The cost of housing, transportation, and food also seemed to be about 25 percent under U.S. levels.) South Africa also has a serious foreign currency exchange problem, with the rand going from U.S. $1.25 to about U.S. $0.25 in recent years. The implications for purchasing books and database and journal subscriptions are enormous.

Overall, the OPL situation is much the same as that in the rest of the world. All the OPLs I spoke with agreed that networking is very important and very helpful and also agree that library school does not prepare one to be an OPL. There is a need for more personal, people-oriented training and more interlibrary, multi-type library groups. Several of the library groups in South Africa are currently working together to form one association, presenting South African librarians with a unique opportunity to merge existing groups and cooperate.

In 1972, Anna Louw, a professor at UNISA, gave a talk at the South African Library Association. At the time, she was librarian at a Johannesburg financial, mining, and industrial organization. She was the company's first professional librarian, hired to organize 60 years' worth of materials. She began with an initial staff of three, which grew to seven (two of whom were "qualified" or professional), then she was downsized to a OPL. She found that South African libraries were not too different from those in Europe and the U.K., but suffered from a less reliable postal system and a weaker communications infrastructure. (When I visited in 1996 I was told that there was only one T-1—high-speed—communications line out of the country. When I enquired about the situation in 2000, I was told that it had not changed at all.) The responses to my questionnaire showed the South African OPLs to be somewhat smaller, with smaller staffs, in smaller companies, and having a little less automation than their counterparts in Europe and the U.S.

Louw noted the professionalism and difference in attitude needed by a corporate librarian:

- "It is not unusual for a newcomer to the staff of a company library to have to learn to accept [that the library staff is employed to save the valuable time of more highly paid officials] and to adapt to this approach, particularly if such a person had been working in a public library. This can be both more and less demanding on the librarian who must meet deadlines at all hours with little supervision and micromanagement.

- "The task of the company librarian becomes that of a source of information about sources of information" (not necessarily to have the information in stock, but to know where to find it).

- "The attitude of willingness to go to tremendous trouble, with total disregard of own convenience, in order to obtain the required information, is the factor that can make or break a company librarian."

Based on the findings of a short questionnaire sent to members of SLIS and the Organisation of South African Law Libraries (OSALL) in June 2000 (a total of 29 OPLs responded), Louise Flynn (personal communication 2000) described South African OPLs as follows:

> Although there are several library associations and groups in South Africa that cater to both public and private sector libraries, there is no distinct support group or branch devoted solely to the area of one-person librarians. Many OPLs belong to more than one group—generally having a membership in one, or even two, of the main library organizations, as well as regular liaison with informal library groups aimed specifically at the sector in which they operate. This makes it difficult to establish the exact number of OPLs operating in South Africa, as the figures overlap. Another factor that adds to the inaccuracy of current solo status in this country is the fact that not all one-person libraries have any association with a library body. However, with the recent formation of the Library

and Information Association of South Africa (LIASA) as a merger of three of the major library organizations, there is hope of more and easier networking among OPLs.

The majority of OPLs who participated in the survey were qualified professionals, holding degrees and post-graduate diplomas in the fields of library and information science or information management. Some respondents had additional qualifications in subjects such as social sciences and teaching. (Eleven had earned the Higher Diploma in Librarianship or its equivalent—comparable with the Master of Library Science (MLS) or Master of Library Science and Information (MLSI) in the U.S., 10 had earned a Bachelor's of Librarianship or equivalent, seven held another library degree, and only two were not qualified or degreed at all.)

The OPLs in South Africa cover both the private and public sectors, ranging from subject-specific [libraries] such as engineering, mining, medical, law and financial services, to academic and non-governmental organisation libraries, (law libraries 7, finance and insurance 4, government 4, science and technology 3, arts and religion 3, health and medicine 2, academic 2, engineering 2, manufacturers 2, associations 1, and 2 unclear as to type).

The responses received from the survey reveal that, in spite of the diverse range of one-person libraries in South Africa, they [the OPLs] appear to share many of the same issues in their daily work and in the long term. The most common problems and concerns are as follows:

1. Time management. Most OPL respondents expressed difficulty in managing their time effectively—in search of a balance between the demands of providing research and information services to their users and keeping up with general administrative duties. This was especially

of concern to OPLs who work part-time and have even less time to juggle their workload and develop the library services. A backlog of work resulting from no support staff or replacement when on leave was also a common issue.

2. Budgetary constraints. A common complaint amongst OPLs, particularly the smaller libraries and nonprofit organizations, was the lack of adequate funding, which restricted the general growth of the library and purchase of up-to-date materials. Many OPLs have had to be resourceful or "make do" in the light of frequent budget cuts, of which they are usually a prime target. The cost of maintaining special collections is becoming more difficult with price hikes, particularly in overseas subscriptions, a problem that leads to cutbacks in good-quality materials.

3. Computer support. The lack of IT [information technology] support is another cause for concern amongst OPLs in South Africa. A large number of respondents felt that they were not receiving adequate training or assistance on basic computer-related queries such as Internet search techniques and networking software to other users in their organizations. Also, not all OPLs benefit from library management software and have to either use whatever database software is given to them for information retrieval, or stick to a manual system of record management.

4. Technology. Keeping track of the latest technology in the information services field is of great interest to South Africa's OPLs, particularly the option of online versus hardcopy. The proliferation of electronic documents and management of these is also an issue. A number of OPLs are facing the added pressure of set-

ting up an Internet or Intranet site to create a virtual library for their organizations.

The majority of South African OPLs find networking with other libraries and library organizations invaluable to their work. Most network informally through contacts they have built up over time. They also benefit a great deal from attending meetings, workshops and conferences organized by their associations—as well as from ongoing liaison with other libraries by telephone or e-mail. South Africa's OPLs are gradually coming to grips with using list servers and understanding the benefits of this mode of communication. The Organisation of South African Law Libraries (OSALL) members in particular make extensive use of their listserv to help one another with locating and obtaining legal material and discussing any problems.

The full potential of electronic lists has still to be realized. The main hindrance is the fact that some of the smaller libraries do not have a network, but need to dial up in order to use their email and only get the chance to do this once or twice a day. So often, the responses only come days later. Some libraries, OPLs included, belong to informal support groups such as libraries using the same library management software (e.g., Inmagic, ILIS, and so on) or working in a similar field (e.g., financial services, engineering, law, and museums). As an example of a user group, the museum libraries have an exchange publication system in place between museums and art galleries in South Africa and internationally. Requests for materials are sent via e-mail, and the libraries have a mutual agreement to send one another brochures and other interesting items without charges. In addition to making use of other libraries in the specific fields, OPLs make extensive use of the larger libraries in South Africa for support, including municipal libraries and major academic institutions.

ISRAEL

OPLs are found in virtually every type of workplace in Israel: industries, hospitals, high-tech firms, high schools, banks, law offices, government offices, the army, and so on. The Israeli Society of Libraries and Information Centers (ISLIC), which every librarian can join, does not have a special section for these professionals despite several attempts. As a result, OPLs in Israel suffer from a lack of activities and an absence of organized contact with each other. ISLIC has an electronic list. It is not geared to OPLs in particular, but they make extensive use of it.

In 1999, Anat Antonir, an OPL at the Tahal Group in Tel Aviv, and a colleague tried to establish a forum for OPLs in Israel. They were motivated by the need to create an arena for OPLs to share problems, advice, information and experiences to help them deal with their special status within their organization. Their motto was: "We are Solo but not alone." An appeal to all OPLs resulted in a list of about 70 members. Unfortunately, they only had one meeting, which was attended by only eight people. A short time later, ISLIC organized a one-day seminar for OPLs in which about 30 people participated, but since then there have been no other meetings.

How do OPLs manage without any official representation? According to Antonir, "The answer is 'personal connections' [networking]. As a member of ISLIC, one attends all their meetings, where one rubs shoulders with librarians from other workplaces, allowing one to develop informal relationships with them. Israel is a small country and the people are strongly 'friendship' oriented, a trait that smoothes the way for interaction on a professional level as well. It is thus common to obtain professional help from a friend in another library rather than through a formal agency. It is nonetheless imperative that efforts be devoted to establishing a formal body for Solos. Israel indeed has much to learn from Solos in other countries."

LATIN AMERICA

In early 2000, I put a message on the biblio-progresistas electronic list looking for OPLs. Within a week I received a dozen replies, and they kept rolling in as the message was reposted to other lists throughout Latin America. By press time, I had heard from over 30 OPLs in Argentina, Cuba, Guatemala, Mexico, Peru, Uruguay, and Venezuela.

The first thing I found was that many of the librarians had not heard of the terms "solo" and "OPL." Once the terminology became clear, I found they had the same concerns as do OPLs in other parts of the world:

- Managers and even library directors are not library professionals.

- Library work is not valued.

- Salaries are low.

- Job responsibilities are often limited to technical processing.

- OPLs are responsible for arranging their own continuing education.

- Dedication to customer service is not always a priority.

- Lack of preparation for the information revolution exists.

- Concern exists over whether to drop the name "librarian" in favor of "information analyst."

- Lack of funding exists, with institutional cost-cutting hitting the library first.

- Concerns exist over assignment of unqualified or problem personnel to the library.

- Lack of adequate equipment exists, especially computers.

- School librarians are asked to "baby-sit" classes when teachers are absent.

- Public librarians are also asked to organize cultural activities.

- For some librarians the only work available is as consultants, organizing personal collections, or working on temporary contracts.

In 1988, Hammerly (1999) surveyed 392 librarians who graduated from schools of library science in Argentina from 1980 to 1983. Of the 288 respondents, 231 were working in librarianship and 66 were working in one-librarian-libraries (29 percent). A 1998 follow-up survey showed that 114 were still working in librarianship, with 27 (24 percent) as OPLs. "Of course this information does not reflect the unknown situation for the whole population of librarians in Argentina but anyway may provide a hint about some characteristics of them." One librarian who has been an OPL most of her career but is currently working in a large library with many librarians wrote that most libraries in Argentina are OPLs, especially in schools, museums, and public libraries. OPLs work without help. In Buenos Aires, the school librarians and public libraries have degreed librarians.

Examples of where OPLs work in Latin America follow.

Argentina:

- In a primary school: an OPL whose most gratifying experience has been creating a librarian information section on the Web, acting as a virtual librarian and facilitating networking. She is completing her degree by e-mail.

- As head librarian at the National University of Villa Maria in Córdoba: the OPL is in charge of two people who help with circulation and occasionally other administrative tasks. They have no library training. She does everything: collection, development, cataloging, purchasing, and so on.

- In a public library: a library school graduate and current psychology student is now supervisor of eight OPLs in the system.

- As a freelancer: one librarian is organizing a collection of 400 books and 20 journals for an economist who works for a bank. She used a general classification—business, economics, literature, music, history, and miscellaneous—and Excel to make a simple database.

Cuba: In the surgery department of a hospital.

Guatemala: In corporations. Many OPLs work in small and poorly funded libraries, for managers who do not understand our profession.

Mexico: In the central library of the national technical university. One OPL is the only professional out of 21 people in the library, including the director.

Peru: I heard from many Peruvian solos because my initial message was reposted on a Peruvian list.

- For an association of educational publishers.

- For a Venezuelan electric company, working completely alone.

- In a governmental agency in Peru, working with three assistants who have no library training.

- In a school library.

- For the National Institute of Health.

- In an information center in a small company.

- In a private teachers' college in Lima.

- For a private bank in Lima, serving nearly all employees in the institution's 23 departments, seven days a week with no clerical help. She catalogs, classifies, does current awareness, twice-weekly newsletters, and online searching "constantly." She has a very small collection (123 volumes and 79 journals) and has developed her own classification system.

- Running the library of the Superior Court of Lima. With just one assistant, the library is open from 8 a.m. to 8 p.m., including the lunch hour. She has gotten a lot of praise in the two years she has been there, even from upper management. She started with nothing and has accomplished much.

- Implementing library automation. He says that most libraries there use MicroIsis/WinIsis/WWWIsis. Others use Visual Basic, Sirsi (Unicorn), and two were using a Spanish system, Sabini.

- On a project in an information center for the blind. She has some help from library students.

- Running two libraries for the city of Lima plus the Historical Archives. Most of the time she can cope, but occasionally would like some help.

Uruguay: One OPL has been working alone for three years.

Venezuela: For the national electric company. A Peruvian now living in Venezuela, he worked at a university as an OPL for five years.

CANADA

Canada has been a leader in one-person librarianship. In 1986, a group of OPLs in Toronto formed the first formal OPL organization. The One-Person Library Support Group was established in October and the new chairperson, Penny Lipman of Rio Algom Ltd., became a member of the Chapter's board. The group is still active, meeting for lunch several times a year. It has nearly 100 members. The issues facing Canadian librarians are similar to those of other OPLs, but seem focused on the following:

- Copyright protection in Canada is biased in favor of authors, to the detriment of users. Canada looks to the U.S. to take the lead on this issue.

- The consolidation of information sources, especially in the area of directories, has led to higher prices and a concern for the completeness of information.

- The twin issues of electronic storage of information and the replacement of print by electronic sources have major implications for permanence (archiving) of information.

- With the decrease in value of the Canadian dollar, currency exchange issues and costs of non-Canadian sources become more troublesome.

- Because Canadian employers must allow up to 12 months of maternity leave, with 17 weeks of that paid by the government, there is both the problem of providing a replacement for an OPL and the opportunity of temporary employment for those not wanting or unable to find a permanent position. (This is also an issue in Australia and some European countries. It is not a major issue in the U.S. because maternity or family leave is not as generous.)

THE REST OF THE WORLD

Eide-Jensen found in Sweden that "the counties with a large number of one-man libraries do appear to have a worse library service than others" (1977, 15). In 1977 there were 40 municipalities with only one librarian, serving 8,000 to 20,000 people. Professional librarians are a recent addition, and the OPL is often an administrator for "local cultural administration," helping to establish small libraries, adult education, and so on. Eide-Jensen concluded that the OPL cannot do it all, and neglects long-range planning and personal and professional development. There is a high turnover because "the post of one-man librarian [in Sweden] is not a particularly attractive one" (1977, 16). This is due to the low salary, long hours, and lack of training for one-person librarianship. His solution is government intervention (salary support), better training (more administration and more continuing education), and more help from larger libraries. In Norway, Kristensen (1985) found over 1,400 libraries for over four million people, but most are small. There have been few changes in the past 15 years, and there are libraries serving as few as 750 people.

In Brazil, according to Maria Cleofas F. Alencar, professor of library science at Pontificia Universidade Catolica de Campenas, Sao Paolo, there are few corporate libraries, but most of these are OPLs. Most of the community libraries in small towns are OPLs as well. The university has 30 undergraduate library programs and six masters' level programs. All graduates find jobs, but the pay is low. If they have a library degree, they most likely will become department heads.

The concept of one-person librarianship in the rest of the world is somewhere between unknown and invisible. While there undoubtedly are very many OPLs around the world, in fact they might predominate, at present there is no good way of reaching them. They are most likely working in nations that are less developed, in very small libraries in very small communities or charitable institutions, and are unlikely to be degreed librarians (or to have even had any library training at all). In addition, they probably do not have access to the Internet, the World Wide Web, or even e-mail. The challenge of locating these OPLs and helping them network and become more efficient and effective information providers is a great one, but one with the promise of great rewards. I hope that all who read this book take up this challenge.

PROFILES OF OPLs AROUND THE WORLD

In South Africa I met an OPL who is retired from an aircraft plant where she was downsized to an OPL situation. She did have a professional assistant and clerical help, but each successive manager cut more. However, the company was very generous with funding and she said she nearly always "got what I wanted." She was able to get out and network a lot. She feels it is even more important for solo librarians to network than is for others to do so.

An OPL in a public library in South Africa found that patrons need more than just information and the librarian also serves a social function. She likes being an OPL because she has control and can often start her own programs without going through the bureaucracy. She is able to get a relief person so she can be active professionally, go to meetings, and present papers. She is very active in the Library and Information Workers Organization, a left-wing, nearly radical, quasi-trade union organization.

A part-time (14 hours per week) OPL at the South African Center for Health Policy—a government agency—doesn't feel too alone because she has lots of contacts, made before she retired from the Medical Library at the University of Witswatersrand. The Center is a very democratic organization, with no bureaucracy, but there is not good communication so she doesn't always know what's expected of her. She would like more time to get more done.

A new graduate of the Teknikon in Capetown, South Africa, described her library program. It is more like a U.S. junior or community college, providing a very practical education. The program is three years long, with an eight-month internship. Unlike in university education, theory, professionalism, management, public relations and marketing, customer service, and subject specialization were not taught. Fortunately, she developed a professional and customer-oriented attitude on her own and further developed it during her internship at Ernst & Young, an accounting and consulting firm. She said most students choose librarianship because they like books.

One OPL has worked in various types of libraries, especially in the rural areas of Guatemala where she worked on a project to distribute books to the most remote areas. She did this for three years, establishing six libraries for the GTZ of Germany. This has been the most satisfying job of her professional career. Now she is working for a Spanish-English cultural organization.

A library student at the University of San Marcos, Peru, is an information analyst for a press agency in Lima and is working on its Web page. In his organization, there are no fixed working hours, very short deadlines, and a great deal of pressure. In addition, user needs are constantly changing. The Internet is used "constantly." He is involved in a local networking group that is trying to make changes for the future of the profession.

OPLs Around the World—We Are
More the Same Than We Are Different.

3

General Concepts

One of the greatest concerns of OPLs is management of the library or information center. It is important to realize that, in addition to being in the library profession, OPLs are in the business of managing information and all its associated services. OPLs are "not just librarians .... The tasks that one-person librarians perform are not limited to information delivery anymore. And it's those management tasks that really separate the serious one-person librarians from the others .... " (St. Clair 1996a, 4). In a one-person library, you do all the management. What you do (and don't do) is the difference between whether or not the library succeeds. The success of your library is almost entirely up to you. There are always factors beyond your control, such as your prime users being laid off or the company going under. Because you can't control these things, forget about them and concentrate on what you *can* control.

You must ensure that the library is seen as a critical part of the organization and that it is involved in mission-critical issues. You need to write a mission statement and tie it closely to the mission of your organization. If you don't do this, you run the risk of being seen as peripheral to the organization. When it comes time to make cuts in the budget, space, or personnel, the library that is not seen as critical to the fulfillment of the organization's mission will be one of the first to feel the ax. You must make sure that the library is relevant to the lives of your users. Management must know that you know more than anyone else in the organization about its business; the users and their needs; and the collection, organization, and dissemination of information. To cut you or the library would compromise the organization's competitive advantage.

Early in my musings on one-person librarianship I came to realize what I now call the "Four Hard Truths":

1. We must make ourselves the information experts. No one will give us our place in the information society. We can make ourselves the experts by virtue of our education and our customer orientation.

2. We cannot demand respect, we must earn it. We can do so by keeping up in our field, participating in continuing education, and developing professionally.

3. We probably never will be paid what we are worth.

4. We are all in the marketing business. We market our institutions, our services, and ourselves, and we do so all the time.

KNOW THY ORGANIZATION: ORGANIZATIONAL BEHAVIOR AND CORPORATE CULTURE

"Power is one of the last dirty words." But it makes organizations run (Kanter 1997). Perhaps the most important thing you can do to survive and thrive in an organization is to know the organization in which you are working. Every organization has a corporate culture, whether it be a business, community hospital, law firm, or other entity. Corporate culture is made up of a system of shared beliefs, values, and assumptions. Whether or not you agree with these values, you must accept them as part of the organization. You need to know how the organization is formally structured and how it actually works, who is in power and who is not. You need to understand what information the organization needs, who needs it, how it is communicated, how it flows within the organization, and how to market your information products. You also need to know how team dynamics work, how to provide leadership and vision, and how to be customer-driven.

What do you need to know?

- To whom do you report? Higher is usually better, but if you report to a too-busy top executive you may not get the attention you need.

- Are you classified as a professional and treated and paid accordingly? If you aren't, find out why not and what you can do about it, then start working to change this.

- How does your budget compare with similar departments, and does it include money for travel, professional development, and continuing education? Is your equipment as up to date as that of others in the organization? Librarians are notorious for being too complacent about under-funding. You can't be expected to do a competent, let alone outstanding, job if you don't have the appropriate resources. Make sure you know where you stand. If you aren't getting your fair share, then complain, make a plan, and get something done about it.

- What do people think of the library? Do all the members of the organization know where the library is (or even that there is a library)? Do they know the services the library offers and what it can do for them?

- What are the critical issues facing the organization and its industry, i.e., the "hot buttons?" Where is the organization going in the future—the next year, five years, 10 years? How does it plan to get there? Who are the movers and shakers in the industry and the organization's competitors and partners? What are the key trade organizations, journals, and analysts?

• Every organization has written and unwritten behavioral rules:
work hours, work ethic, dress code, writing style, and communication style. You must find these out. Although you don't have to
follow the party line exactly, you do need to fit in. Remember
that the corporate culture operates on both the organization and
department level and that it may not be the same at both (St.
Clair 1994). Who eats lunch with whom? It's probably not a
great idea to always eat lunch with the secretary of your department. Invite a library user, non-user, your boss, or even your
boss's boss to lunch once in a while. Where you lunch may even
be important. If all the managers go out to lunch all the time,
what message do you send by eating in the cafeteria or at your
desk?

How do you find out all this? Talk to people, ask questions, listen
to the answers and even to the talk around the water cooler. Read mission statements, annual reports, long-range plans, organizational
charts, catalogs, policies and procedures, budgets, and any other corporate documents you can get your hands on. Arrange for site visits to
remote locations. I have found that the site visits were extremely useful. People not at your facility tend to assume that you serve only the
main location. Going out to the people assures them that you really
are there to help them, gives you a chance to see what their work is
like, and puts faces to names. Don't forget to tour your own facility,
including any manufacturing or maintenance areas. Knowing what
goes on in every nook and cranny of the organization is vital information you need to do your job well.

Part of being a successful OPL is the ability to communicate with
management. You need to learn what information management needs
and in what form it is needed. Then provide it—preferably *before* it is
asked for. The format in which you provide information is very important for how it is received. If management wants only a summary, summarize. If management wants detail, include everything. Usually, the
higher up an executive is, the less information he or she wants. What
management really wants is an answer, not information. If that is

beyond your scope, try to give whatever information you have in as concise a manner as possible. Provide the most important information first. Another key in dealing with upper management is to talk in their language. Management neither understands nor cares about library jargon. (For example, it took a lot of convincing for my boss to accept the work "weeding" as a real library term.) Read about management, and learn to use their jargon. Sprinkling your conversation and reports with terms such as "return on investment" (ROI), "turnover," and "mission-critical" will enhance your professional status in the eyes of management. It may seem like a game, but it is one in which management makes all the rules. Don't just communicate with management when a request is made. Feed a steady stream of useful information. Prepare an "elevator speech," a short conversation you can conduct when an executive speaks to you in the elevator or hall. Mentioning something you have just read in a trade journal, news feed, or financial journal shows that you keep up with business, not just librarianship. (One writer suggested you have a good answer prepared in case the CEO asks you, "How're things going in the library?" An answer along the lines of "Fine, but I really could use [fill in the blank with a service or product you really need but haven't had the money or approval to buy]." Be sure to be prepared to explain the value it would provide to the organization. Whether you want to go over your supervisor's head by doing this is up to you, but it is an idea.)

Speaking of supervisors, a good relationship with your immediate boss is absolutely necessary. Your boss probably does not and will never really understand and appreciate the library as you do, but when cultivated properly, he or she can be a powerful advocate for you and your library. A good technique is to make your boss look good. You will then look good, and he or she will support you when you really need it. Getting published inside and outside the company or winning an award enhances your (and your boss's) image. Go to your boss with "solutions, not problems" (Merry 1994, 68). Try not to go over your boss' head—except when it is absolutely necessary. This is sometimes necessary when a problem arises that will affect the library and your boss isn't willing or able to help. You must be involved or have input into decisions that will affect the library. You should keep your supervisor informed about what you are doing and what you plan to do so that he or she can respond to any suggested changes from upper management in the way that you would like.

What about library committees? Many OPLs swear by them; some probably swear *at* them. Library committees can be quite effective, but they must be advisory and not decision-making committees. All must know that you, the trained librarian, are the one responsible for the library. A library committee should not include your boss but should be composed of library users who are knowledgeable about the needs of the organization and how to get things done. If there is to be a committee, three members are ideal, with a maximum of five.

To succeed or even stay alive, the OPL must constantly justify its existence. This continual justification is necessary in all types of libraries, even in those once thought immune to budget cuts, downsizing, and even closing. You must be visible and indispensable, add value, and take risks (St. Clair 1994). You need to make sure that everyone, especially those in a position to affect you, knows how critical the OPL and the information you provide are to the organization. You must know and be able to show the economic impact of the library. One method is with a newsletter, another by periodic reports. St. Clair wrote that the annual report is "the single most important document the one-person librarian will give to management all year long" (1976, 236). He suggested it include a summary of what you have done over the past year and a plan for what you intend to do in the next year. Testimonials to your excellent service are very appropriate here. Try to get your annual report to management and your users, too. Williamson (1984) suggested showing your cost and time effectiveness, having a high profile, and changing your title from librarian. I do not really like the idea of removing "librarian" from your title. Many librarians think it makes people think of you as one who shelves books, not as the information leader in the organization. I would prefer to change the image of the librarian, but until that happens—if it happens—it may be necessary for your and your library's success to lose the terms "library" and "librarian." You are the best judge of this, but tread cautiously.

How does an OPL survive, thrive, and get promoted? O'Donnell (1976) writes that management requires the information center to demonstrate administrative competence, have adequate tools, and keep them informed. An OPL should have a mentor (as high up in the company as possible), publicize the library (e.g., using open houses and brochures), get supervisory experience, and know the company's culture. You need to find friends in the organization and make them your advocates. Unfortunately, often "the person who wields the most influence over the library [vice president, dean] tends to have the lowest level of knowledge of its operations" (Drake 1990, 152). Above all, "don't ignore politics" (St. Clair 1995a). Not realizing that the organization is a political animal is dangerous at best and fatal at worst.

THE USER IS JOB ONE—CUSTOMER SERVICE

It cannot be stressed enough that customer service, putting the user first, is the most important factor in library success. You can have the best collection, largest staff, biggest budget, nicest furniture, and most up-to-date computers, but you will not last if your users don't feel that the library helps them. It would be great if all librarians graduated from library school knowing this, but it isn't always so. If you are an OPL, you probably already know this, but, please, don't skip this section. A reminder of these basic issues is important.

One thing to remember is that you can't be all things to all people. You will have to be selective about services offered, i.e., which services and to whom they are offered. Choose what you can do best and what will be of greatest benefit to your parent organization, and then promote your services to those who can benefit most from them. It is also necessary, sometimes, to say no. Some requests made of you may be out of the scope of your position, out of your range of talents, or just impossible to fit in. It often helps to have written policies to support you at such times.

You are likely to face some special challenges that will tax your customer service dedication and try your patience. Every organization has prima donnas, clients who think the library and the librarian exist only to serve them. They will monopolize your time and resources—if you let them. That last phrase is the key. You are in charge of your own time. You have the right (and perhaps obligation) to say no. All members of the organization have an equal right to your services. You may have to remind the prima donna (gently) of this fact. Trying to teach him or her how to find their own answers or do their own research also may work. A related challenge is reporting to more than one boss. The key here is communication—from you to each boss and between the bosses themselves. They may not realize that you are getting assignments from two (or more) people. Ask them to prioritize their requests. If you have serious conflicts you should ask them to meet and decide how to handle this situation. And if all else fails, go to the human resources department or your boss's boss for guidance.

Who are your customers? They are those in management, other professionals, secretaries and other clerical staff, manufacturing workers, the mailroom staff, and even the cleaning staff. All of these are potential customers of the library. Ideally, all should be treated equally, but it would be foolish not to recognize that you will be much faster to respond to an inquiry from the president or managing director of your organization than from a worker on the assembly line. Just be sure that you are responding to the importance of the answer to the continued existence of the organization, not just the position of the customer on the organizational chart.

What do your customers want? This one is easy—they want answers. They want their problems solved. To that end, you need to produce a summary report with the answer to the question, not just a stack of articles or Web sites. This is how the library can best add value. Your clients also expect the library to help lower their costs of doing business—by saving them time and, therefore, money. Another desire is for you to make getting information convenient for them. This can mean anything from taking requests over the Internet to putting databases and research services on their desktop computers.

You must become client-centered, not library-centered. By this I mean you need to understand your clients' work and vocabulary by reading their journals, talking to them, and listening to them. Remember to be accessible, approachable, and friendly. Make sure your clients get what they came for—do more than point to the resource and forget them. Many clients are reluctant to ask the librarian for help. They try to find the information on their own, and they give up when they can't find it. Your desk should be situated where you can see your clients as they leave the library. If they do not appear to have found anything, gently ask, "Did you find what you needed?" If they say no, then offer to help them find the information. Some librarians offer to help clients when they enter the library. Because I have found that doing so may be intimidating, I prefer to ask clients as they are leaving. You may also need to encourage them to come again. Of course you hope that your excellent service and resources will do this, but you can make a big difference by saying something as simple as "Come back anytime."

Focus on your customers, not on yourself and the library. Emphasize how your services will benefit clients, not just how big or cool it is. Make things as easy as possible for your clients, even if it makes things a bit more difficult for you. Speak their language, that is, no library jargon (e.g., say "updating the collection" rather than "weeding," "buying books" rather than "acquisitions" or "collection development.") When entering items into the online catalog, be sure the subject headings are meaningful to your users. How many engineers would search for a computer book under "data processing?" You need to add "computers" to this record. Some small libraries even go so far as to arrange books by subjects rather than using call numbers. (Caution: This may cause problems if your small collection grows large.) It is good to centralize information in the library, making for one-stop shopping; however, it is often necessary and even desirable to house parts of the collection elsewhere. For instance, you might want to have a satellite library for staff at an off-site facility or house the marketing reports (which you buy for the entire company to get quantity discounts and avoid duplication) in the marketing department. Doing so will raise additional problems regarding security and cataloging, but you can find ways to solve them. *All* materials, wherever they are housed, should appear in your library catalog.

What about the "library without walls," or the virtual library or cyberlibrary? More information on this appears in Chapters 7 and 8, but a bit is appropriate here. These libraries are really just extensions of the traditional library, bringing information to people at their desktop computers instead of having clients come into the library. You still need to choose resources, order them, keep them up to date, enter them in a catalog, and train customers how to use them. Instead of dealing only with the books and journals you have in-house, you will be "in charge" of a much larger universe of information. In fact, electronic resources require more of your time rather than less. End-users doing their own searching will do the easy searches and come to you to perform the more difficult, complicated, and time-consuming ones.

Presentation is very important. Everyone is different, so you shouldn't give everyone the same information in the same way, i.e., customize your product to the needs of your users. Go through the information and arrange it first, summarize if appropriate, and clean up online searches. I worked for one library, however, that cleaned up the searches too much; the search strategy was stripped out so the user never knew exactly how I found the information. Therefore, I prefer to leave the searches in. Be scrupulous about leaving copyright statements in as well and putting your name or the name of your library on every page! That way the user can't take the information to his boss and say, "Look what *I* found." Instead, the user must say, "Look what *the librarian* found for me." Finally, use business language, not library jargon.

An OPL must be proactive. You must anticipate what your patrons will need and be sure you can meet the demand. Doing so involves planning, thinking, anticipating, and taking the initiative. As Stephen

Covey (Paul and Crabtree 1995) pointed out, you must see every "threat" as an "opportunity" and be able to turn "complaints" into new service ideas. St. Clair remarks that this proactivity is important because "the traditional library model, even the corporate library model, doesn't work in business anymore" (1995c, 1). We still need libraries, but different, more responsive ones. The keys are communication with and to customers and taking responsibility for information (evaluating it for content and quality). How do you find out what your customers need? Observe, listen, read both the library and industry literature, use your intuition, or do an information audit. (There is a wealth of information out there on information audits. Start with the Information Resources Center of the Special Libraries Association.) Make sure that when you undertake to offer a new service that you can meet the demand it will generate. Nothing turns off users more than unfulfilled promises. (Remember the old sales motto: A satisfied customer will tell a friend; a disgruntled one will tell ten.) Because you are unlikely to get more staff for your library, plan to add services by using technology, not people.

Traditionally, people (and too many librarians) think that the library, especially a "captive" institutional library, has no competition. But there is always competition. Customers will go to inside sources for information or they will go to outside information providers; the ultimate competition is—get ready for this—doing without.

There are many facets of management that the OPL needs to know about. (I started to write "master," but no one can master management. You do need to understand the concepts and how to implement them.) Chapter 4 deals with time management, the number one problem expressed by OPLs. It also covers planning and setting priorities because you cannot manage your time if you don't plan and prioritize. Chapter 5 discusses basic budgeting and other financial issues. (I am not an accountant and cannot tell you how to do this, but I can tell you the questions you should ask and the things you should watch out for.) Chapter 6 deals with how to relate to your colleagues (including how to work with your information technology or computer people), including networking and public relations, professionalism, and continuing education. Finally, Chapter 7 covers all the other management-related issues: education and preparation for the profession, the information revolution and technology, how to avoid downsizing, outsourcing of selected services, and knowledge management.

4

Time Management, Planning, and Prioritization

If I had a nickel for every time an OPL said to me, "How do I find the time to do it all?" I could retire to Freemantle, Western Australia, or Puerto Vallarta, Mexico, or Victoria Island, British Columbia, Canada (my current favorites). Let's look at the question more closely.

1. How do I (the OPL, who has little or no help in the library)

2. find the time (which is finite and cannot be managed [see below])

3. to do it *all*? (You cannot and should not do it all; do only the most important tasks)

In my previous book, *The SOLO Librarian's Sourcebook*, Andrew Berner, library director and curator of collections at the University Club in New York and co-founder of *The One-Person Library: A Newsletter for Librarians and Management,* wrote that the "Three Ps" of effective time management are planning, prioritization, and procrastination:

If ever there was a group for whom time management is an important concept, it's solo librarians. With so much to do and, generally, no one to whom work can be delegated, it becomes essential that the solo librarian be aware of the basic principles of good time management. Too often, however, the librarian seeks time management "tricks," things that will enable a job to be done more quickly. In other words, they seek efficiency, when in fact they should be seeking effectiveness. Time management is not just looking for ways to cut down on the time it takes to do specific tasks (though that certainly can be a part of it). To be sure, there is much more to time management than simply being aware of the importance of planning, priorities and procrastination. Much can—and has—been written on each of them, as well as on the many other aspects of good time management. Still, these are three powerful tools (two to use and one to avoid) in any solo librarian's arsenal of time management weapons. A knowledge of them can be used to help the librarian function not only in a more efficient manner, but—even more importantly—in a more effective manner as well. And after all, that's what being a one-person librarian is all about. (Berner in Siess 1997)

TEN MYTHS ABOUT TIME

1. *Myth*: Time can be managed. *Truth*: Activities are managed, not time itself.

2. *Myth*: The longer and harder you work, the more you accomplish. *Truth*: It is better to work effectively.

3. *Myth*: If you want something done right, do it yourself. *Truth*: Delegating is good if done properly, and for an OPL delegating is necessary.

4. *Myth*: You are not supposed to enjoy work. *Truth*: If you do not enjoy what you are doing, you will just become frustrated and feel as if you are always behind.

5. *Myth*: We should take pride in working hard. *Truth*: Librarians should take pride in working smart.

6. *Myth*: You should try to do the most in the least amount of time. *Truth*: It is better to do it right.

7. *Myth*: Technology will help you do it better and faster. *Truth*: Technology can speed up routine stuff but not creative work.

8. *Myth*: Do one thing at a time. *Truth*: Use your multi-level, multi-tasking abilities (or lose them).

9. *Myth*: Handle paper only once. *Truth*: This is an impossible and unnecessary rule. (What planet do they live on?)

10. *Myth*: Get more done, and you will be happier. *Truth*: No, you will just get more done.

STOP WASTING TIME

We all waste time. This is inevitable. What is important is that we learn how we waste it and work toward eliminating as many of the time-wasting behaviors as possible from our work lives. Here are some of the most common ones.

- Attempting too much. This happens if you haven't established priorities and plans, are prone to making unrealistic time estimates, haven't let go of perfectionism, or are a victim of under-staffing.

- Being confused about responsibility or authority. Perhaps you lack a job description, have been given responsibility without authority, or work with other employees who are unwilling to accept responsibility for certain projects.

- Having the inability to say no. This is the most common time-wasting behavior for librarians. (More on this later.)

• Having incomplete information. This is often the case for OPLs. You must go to someone else for the information and a decision, or you don't know what information is needed, or the information you need is not provided, or you lack the authority to make a decision.

• Managing by crisis. Many organizations function this way normally. Don't let the lack of contingency plans, overreaction to non-urgent issues, constant putting out of fires, procrastination of action until the last minute, and unrealistic time estimates invade your management style.

• Being personally disorganized. You have control over your own space and time. Do not allow fear to immobilize you. Let go of your fears of indispensability, loss of control, and forgetting. Don't allow a disorganized workspace, interruptions (including the telephone), and indecision undermine your plans.

Library managers may lack time-management skills because they often have been promoted from within and not trained as managers. Also, time management is seldom talked about in library school and is taught even less often. As a group, we tend to estimate time somewhat unrealistically and try to do too many things at once. Many of us feel overwhelmed by the new technology. Finally, we often feel that the work never seems to be done.

One step toward effective time management is to analyze your workday to determine how much time you spend on various activities. There are several ways to do this. The easiest way is to do a time study. First, write down how you *think* you use your time. Make a list of the tasks that comprise your workday. Include everything, even time at the water cooler or coffee or tea bar, chatting with a colleague, talking on the phone, and opening the mail. Then make up a sheet or grid with all these tasks listed (Figures 1 and 2). (Don't forget to leave some space for "other," which are those tasks you forgot to include.) You'll need one grid for each day of the study. For at least a week (and even better, two to four weeks), mark the time you spend on each task. Do this as you do the task; don't wait until the end of the day and try to recall how you spent your day. Write the time down, even if it is only one or two minutes. When the study is over, tally the totals for each task. (Don't do this every day because the results likely will influence how you use your time the next day.) Now you can see how you *really* use your time. Compare it to your pre-study estimate. I can almost guarantee that there will be some surprises. The next steps are to determine the priority of each task and to make a plan for your time. They will be discussed later in this chapter.

DAILY TIME LOG Day _____	quick reference	phone	circ'n	online & WWW	house- keeping	in-house meeting	outside meeting	prof'l activities	personal	other
time										
8:00										
9:00										
10:00										
11:00										
12:00										
1:00										
2:00										
3:00										
4:00										
5:00										
day's total percentages										

SUMMARY TIME LOG WEEK OF _____	quick reference	phone	circ'n	online & WWW	house- keeping	in-house meeting	outside meeting	prof'l activities	personal	other
day										
MONDAY TUESDAY WEDNESDAY THURSDAY FRIDAY										
week's total percentages										

Figure 1

Figure 2. Sample Time Recording Forms--Completed

DAILY TIME LOG
Day Tuesday, 15 September

time	quick reference	phone	circ'n	online & WWW	house-keeping	in-house meeting	outside meeting	prof'l activities	personal	other	total
8:00		answering machine (15)			filing (30)				eat muffin (15)		
9:00			enter circulation (10)	search for Jack Smith (35)	open mail (15)						
10:00						Intranet task force (60)					
11:00	Jones (10), Francis (15)	call for ILL (15)						reading (20)			
12:00					finish mail (25)				lunch with Nancy (35)		
1:00	Leslie (25)	various (25)								talk with Jill (10)	
2:00		various (10)		search for Jim (15), surf Web (20)	write supplies PO (15)						
3:00	Bill Harper (15)				work on monthly report (45)						
4:00				deliver searches (30)	meet with boss (30)						
5:00		various (15)									
day's total	65	80	10	100	130	90	0	20	50	10	555
percentages	11.7%	14.4%	1.8%	18.0%	23.4%	16.2%	0.0%	3.6%	9.0%	1.8%	100.0%

SUMMARY TIME LOG
WEEK OF 14-18 September

day	quick reference	phone	circ'n	online & WWW	house-keeping	in-house meeting	outside meeting	prof'l activities	personal	other	total
MONDAY	125	115	45	120	60				60	15	540
TUESDAY	65	80	10	100	130	90	0	20	50	10	555
WEDNESDAY	45	90	45	180	65	30			30	60	545
THURSDAY	35	105	10	180	35	120		25	30		540
FRIDAY	120	100	60	60	95		120		45		600
week's total	390	490	170	640	385	240	120	45	215	85	2780
percentages	14.0%	17.6%	6.1%	23.0%	13.8%	8.6%	4.3%	1.6%	7.7%	3.1%	100.0%

Figure 2

We now return to time management itself. There are a number of ways to manage your time more effectively. First, decide that you don't have to please everyone. You don't need everyone to like you. If you try to please everyone all the time, you will either wind up pleasing no one, including yourself, or lose your job, your mind, or both. Second, work efficiently. The Pareto 80/20 rule applies to time as well, i.e., 80 percent of your time is taken up by 20 percent of your tasks. Prioritizing and planning ensure that you are doing the right 20 percent. Here are five rules for decision-making using the 80/20 principle:

1. Twenty percent of decisions are important, the other 80 percent are not. The trick is to figure out the most important 20 percent. Don't agonize over the unimportant decisions, and don't overanalyze your decisions.

2. The most important decisions often are those made only by default. The critical decision point may come and go before you recognize it. Make sure you are asking the right questions. The right answer to the wrong question is meaningless.

3. Always make a decision. Act as if you are 100 percent confident that the decision is right. Once you have made the decision (to do or not to do), don't let yourself be pushed into changing your mind.

4. If it isn't working, cut your losses early and abandon the project or task.

5. If it is working, stay with it—and even redouble your efforts.

Third, don't complain; just fix the problem. Your boss does not want problems, only solutions, so don't waste time worrying about problems. Don't pursue lost causes. Yes, it may be an important issue, but if it's going nowhere because of managerial resistance, lack of money, or lack of interest, you can't afford to waste your time on it.

Fourth, let go; don't be a perfectionist. Sometimes "done okay" is better than "partly done but perfectly." In the same vein, resist the temptation to do small, insignificant tasks too well (e.g., making the monthly report a literary masterpiece). Emphasize self-service by being proactive with bibliographic instruction and handouts. Make a handout or a sign for questions that come up frequently or create a frequently asked questions (FAQ) list for the library on the organization's Intranet. Outsource what you can. Follow the rule, "Don't do what you can buy." (Examples are cataloging and interlibrary loans.) When you outsource or delegate, however, don't be overly critical and don't micromanage. Choose the best providers, and let them do the work. If you look over the provider's shoulder constantly, you won't be saving your time. Other outsourcing and delegating tips include making sure the provider has the information needed to accomplish the task. Delegate in advance or at least don't wait until the last minute. Delegate the whole task, giving the provider both responsibility and authority, then hold the person responsible for the outcome. Delegate for specific results, not individual steps. Accept someone doing something a way other than the way you do it, assuming of course that the task is accomplished. Keep track of the project's progress so you know immediately when things aren't going well.

Avoid Procrastination

The last of Berner's "Three "Ps" is:

> ... not something that you should work towards, but something that you should avoid, and that is procrastination. Accept the fact that everyone procrastinates sometimes, and understand that guilt will not help to solve the problem. It is very important, however, to keep in mind that you should not assume that because everyone procrastinates it cannot be a serious problem. It can, in fact, rob you of your effectiveness on the job. No matter what you may think and no matter what you may have convinced yourself over the years, no one works best under pressure. Procrastination only insures that you will have to rush to complete a project, and that you will have insufficient time to check your work and to create a superior product. Procrastination leaves no time for that great despoiler of work: Murphy's Law. If you leave yourself ample time for a project and something goes wrong, you'll be able to correct it and still meet your deadline. Without that sufficient time, however, your work will suffer, and no doubt your reputation will suffer along with it. (Berner in Siess 1997)

Why do we procrastinate? There are many reasons: the task may seem daunting, you may be afraid of failure, you may not have enough information, or you may be hoping someone else will do the task. The task may be so daunting or large that you don't know where to start. Divide the task into smaller parts and start somewhere; anywhere will do as long as you start. You can't avoid an unpleasant task forever, so you might as well get it over with. Some experts advise doing unpleasant tasks the first thing in the day so you don't have time to dread them. Fear of failure also is a factor in procrastination. Fear of failure often is paralyzing. Failure is not a bad thing, assuming you learn from your mistakes. I have never heard of an organization going under because of a librarian's mistake, nor are many librarians fired because of one error. Perhaps you don't have the information you need to do a task. OPLs are the information experts; we know how to find information. So, get the information and get on with it. Perhaps you think that if you put it off, someone else will do the task (negative delegation). This seldom works. One prioritization technique involves ignoring a task to see if anyone misses it, but that is a different matter.

Other common excuses for procrastination (note that I used the term "excuses" instead of "reasons," because procrastination is never acceptable) are an over-commitment to other projects (you haven't said "no" enough) or lack of motivation because you believe the task won't make a difference anyway. (If you think that, you have other problems that are dealt with elsewhere.)

Finally, interruptions can be a form of passive procrastination. If you let people interrupt you, you can avoid working on what you don't want to do. Speaking of interruptions, they are a part of the job. If no one asked questions, we wouldn't have jobs. You can try to anticipate the most common questions and have answers prepared in the form of guides and procedures that you can quickly hand to the client, minimizing the disruption to your work. You can also try closing your door or arranging your office to discourage people who drop by to chat, but I think this makes for an unwelcoming environment. I try never to close my door. A closed door sends a message that I don't want to send. If all else fails, hide. Go somewhere no one expects you to be and work there.

What else can you do to overcome procrastination? List the things you have been avoiding. Prioritize them. Try to do at least one of them each day until you catch up. SWAP, i.e., start with a part, break it down into smaller parts, and tackle just one part. Remember that it is not procrastination if you put aside a low-priority project to work on a high-priority one. Also remember that you *do not* work best under pressure. Almost no one does. This is just a rationalization for procrastination.

Check Your Timing

Timing is important in knowing when to work and when not to. Look at your workday routine. Is it efficient? Does it fit your personal clock? If not, change it. Write down how you want your day to go. Refer to your written routine frequently. Really try to follow the new routine. If it doesn't seem to be working, change it again, but give it at least a month. A routine makes your day more predictable, less stressful, and more efficient. It helps you get started in the morning because you know what you should be doing. Some experts suggest saving the easiest tasks for the end of the day so that you accomplish something and go home satisfied, not frustrated. (I really like this idea.) It is important to stay focused on high-priority activities and limit the time you spend on low-priority tasks, no matter how easy or how much fun they are. Get the most out of the first two hours of the day. Try not to be interrupted. Don't eat breakfast at work. Start with the most important work of the day when you are fresh and enthusiastic, and before you get involved in something else. Don't schedule meetings for this time.

Practice Saying "No"

One very important time management tool is the word no. As good librarians, obsessed with quality customer service, our first inclination is to say yes to every request that comes along—whether it's from a patron or the boss. But OPLs just can't do everything for everyone.

Sometimes the answer must be no. It is appropriate—even advisable—to say no:

- When the request is clearly out of your scope. (You do have a written mission statement, don't you?) I've never been afraid to tell a patron, "You should try the public library" when, e.g., I don't have the resources to answer the question or I am being asked a child's homework question.

- When someone else can answer the question better or cheaper. This could be another library, another department in the organization, an information broker, and so on.

- When you have been asked to do something illegal or unethical. This could be copying an entire book, ordering something on the company account for personal use, or industrial espionage. You simply tell the patron (or boss) that the request is illegal or unethical and your personal and professional code of ethics will not permit you to fill it.

- When you really don't want to do the job. This is a close call, especially when it comes to your boss, but you should never do something you really don't want to do. Sometimes you might have to decide between doing something you don't want to and finding another job. This is another issue, but it does come up and you should be prepared to address it.

Why are we afraid to say no? We are often driven by a desire to win the approval of others or by a false sense of obligation. We simply do not know how to say no or haven't the time to think of a better answer. If your objectives and priorities aren't clear to you and your clients, the thoughtless assumption by others is that you will say yes. Perhaps you feel you just can't say no to your boss. We all want to be liked, to win the approval of others. We also may feel that it is our obligation to do whatever others ask of us. We may be rushed into a response, and it's usually easier to say yes than no.

How should you say no? Not knowing how to refuse a request is a frequent problem for OPLs. First, remember that people take advantage of you only with your permission. Never say yes without thinking about it first. Say no to negative people who drain your energy and don't appreciate you. Don't just say no; offer a counter proposal, an alternative. Never make a promise you can't keep. Keep your goals and priorities in mind; if this project does not advance them, say no. When faced with a decision, focus on the business implications of your answer. It is your library and your responsibility. You have the right to set policy. Be firm.

Saunders (2000) suggests the following: "Don't say 'I'm sorry'—it weakens your 'no.' Make a simple explanation—a long-winded one weakens your 'no.' If you sense a request coming [that you don't want to do], be proactive and say 'no' first. Once you've said 'no,' stick with it. Rehearse and practice how to say 'no.' Don't let your body language defeat you (looking away, speaking softly or too slowly)."

Value Your Time

What is the value of your time? If you don't value it, no one else will. If it costs more to do it yourself than to hire someone to do it, hire someone. For instance, use a document delivery or fax rather than physically going and getting it. I found that it was "cheaper" to outsource document delivery vendors rather than to spend the time locating them and ordering on the Online Computer Library Center (OCLC). (An added bonus was the money we saved by dropping our OCLC membership, but the real reason was the time it took away from more important tasks.)

Manage Your Routine Activities

Meetings

Meetings can be another activity that wastes time. I try to avoid them because very little is ever accomplished in them. I have said that meetings are convened either to postpone making a decision or to share the blame if something goes wrong. I am only half joking. Some meetings, especially those involving planning or with your professional (library) colleagues, can be very worthwhile. However, many are not useful and you should minimize the number of these you attend.

If you have to hold a meeting, learn how to run it effectively. To cut down on wasting time, prepare and distribute an agenda with time limits set for each item. Have a goal or purpose for the meeting, and keep everyone on track. Guide the group decision process (i.e., stay on track, limit discussions, and try for consensus rather than a vote). Postpone long debates for another meeting and do not plan too much for one meeting. End the meeting at the time stated on the agenda. Keep the number of participants small and limited to only those who need to be there. Meeting productivity varies inversely with the number of people at the meeting. Could the problem be solved or a decision reached without a meeting? If so, don't meet! One suggestion I heard to get people to be on time to meetings was to make a rule that the last one to arrive must take the minutes. Because no one wants to take minutes, they will try harder to be on time. Finally, providing food only drags out the meeting.

Filing

Almost everyone dislikes filing. Filing is a great time-wasting activity if not done right. Here are some suggestions to save time. Never file envelopes unless the postmark is significant; put the address in your card file instead. Write a keyword on the item when you read it, before you put it in your filing tray, especially if someone else does your filing. File according to how you'll use it, not where it came from. Judy's first law of filing: If you have trouble finding something in the files, put it back where you first looked for it (or at least put a pointer sheet there).

You can do only three things with any piece of information: Toss it, file it, or act on it. The following "logic-based disposal" rules make deciding what to do with a piece of paper easy:

- Does it require action on my part? If not, toss it or file it.

- Does it exist elsewhere? If so (and it is easy to get to), toss it.

- Is it outdated? If so, toss it.

- Will I really use it again? If not, toss it. Don't use "just in case" logic.

- Are there tax or legal implications? If so, file it.

- What's the worst thing that could happen if I don't have this info? If you can live with the answer, toss it.

- Does anyone else need this info? If so, file it or give it to them.

Reading

What about that ever-increasing to-read pile, all those things you want to read—someday? Accept the fact that you probably will never be able to read everything you would like to (or think you ought to). Read with a pen in your hand. A quick scan is better than a complete reading that is never done. Delegate your reading (to a colleague—split your reading list, use a service, watch the lists). Peruse the table of contents. Rip out articles you want to read and put them in a folder you can take with you. If you don't want to tear out articles, at least mark them with a Post-It Note.

E-Mail

We all know that OPLs need to keep in touch with their colleagues and customers. Electronic discussion lists and e-mail are two excellent ways to do this. However, you can spend a lot of time on e-mail. Here are some tips for managing your e-mail (courtesy of the MEDLIB-L list). Check e-mail only once a day. Triage by source and subject fields, without opening messages. Use a filtering program (I use Eudora Pro), and store like messages in separate folders. Read lists at home. If you find something you want to save, send it by e-mail to yourself at work.

Don't print out messages and clutter your desk with them. (I disagree. Print them out and file them, like anything else.) Purge folders and delete files regularly. If it's been a couple of months since you've looked at the e-mail, you probably don't need it. One major exception is addresses. If you even think you might use an address again, file it somewhere. They're too hard to track down again. I have a separate folder labeled "addresses to save" and purge it regularly for ones that are no longer of use.

Telephone Calls

Although it may be faster to use the telephone rather than go somewhere, phone calls can be a large factor in wasting time when not handled properly. You don't have to answer every call. You should use the answering machine or voice mail when you are working on a rush project, when a project requires all your attention, or when a customer is in front of you. Don't pick up someone else's phone. You'll inherit their problem. Here are hints for cutting off a long-winded person. At an opening ask, "Now, what can I do for you?" You also can tell the caller you are on your way to a meeting and just have a minute, or say you have someone in the office so you must be quick.

There is nothing worse than not reaching the person you want, unless it is reaching a poor message on an answering machine. And, there is nothing better than reaching a good message. What's the difference? A good answering machine message will give the caller a brief but clear message and then encourage him or her to leave a detailed message. Ideally, it will give you the time and date of the call automatically (rather than relying on the caller to do so). The message you record should clearly identify your library, you, or both. The message also should be business-like (save the cute messages for your home machine). If you are out of the office for a day or more, the message should say when you will return and what to do or whom to call in the meantime. If you are just busy or on the phone, the message should say something such as: "I'm sorry that I can't help you right now, but I am currently serving another patron. Please leave a detailed message with your information need, and I will get back to you as soon as I can." (This says that you care about the client's question, are working with someone else, and will return the call). The message should be relatively short. Finally, you must return phone calls as soon as possible. Get in the habit of checking your messages as soon as you return to your desk. If your machine takes messages while you are on the phone, check it each time you hang up. You want to become known for answering messages promptly so that customers will not be reluctant to leave messages for you. (This is also true of your e-mail.)

More Time-Management Hints

Here are more time-management hints that can make your job easier.

- Use multi-tasking to get more done. Always have something to read or do while you wait; while on hold on the telephone, check e-mail or open mail.

- Substitute: Use electronic copy instead of hard copy; let vendors manage and store periodicals for you.

- Simplify: KISS, i.e., keep it short and simple; examine every repetitive task you perform to see if you can streamline it.

- Save time before money. Ask yourself, "Can someone else do this task?" Use the cataloging of others rather than doing your own. Outsource whenever possible (internally and externally).

- Find a place to hide when you need to work without interruptions or just to get away. It needs to be somewhere no one would look for you. (I used the mailroom.) One OPL hides in her car in the parking lot. (This is more feasible if you have a cell phone and a laptop computer.)

- Don't worry. It accomplishes nothing. Either do something about it or forget it!

- Carry a pen or pencil and paper or sticky notes with you at all times. Write down thoughts as they occur to you.

- Keep a set of boilerplate files on the computer. Include common answers to common questions, headers, references, order forms, interlibrary loan requests, and so on. Store all documents you might use again on your computer.

- Eliminate bad habits that waste time. Make a list of your time-wasting behaviors and post it as a reminder not to do them.

- Arrange your office and desk to increase efficiency. Put what you use most often close at hand. Keep it neat. Have a place for everything and put everything in its place. (Yeah, sure.)

- Remember, you don't have to be perfect, just good.

- Block out vacation time for yourself. Put it on your calendar and make it sacred.

- Allow time for unexpected problems. This will allow you to meet your deadlines without undue stress.

- Group appointments so all the interruptions are together and you have more blocks of time to work.

- Don't be afraid to leave a meeting if all that you needed, or were needed for, is over. Say you have another appointment rather than staying just to be polite.

- At the end of the day, check e-mail, check voice mail, go through the mail and to-do files, and review what you want to do the next day. You will feel better when you leave and can leave the office at the office.

Manage Your Absences

Speaking of leaving the office, it is inevitable that sometimes you will not be in your library. You have to plan for each type of absence: temporary, short-term, and long-term. Temporary absences are those that take a few minutes, such as delivering a document, getting the mail, buying a cup of coffee, and going to the bathroom. Put a sign on your door or desk that says: "The librarian will be right back. Please wait, or leave a message." (Make sure you leave notepaper and pencils nearby.)

You might also be away for a day or two during a short-term absence because of such things as illness, vacation, off-site training, or jury duty. If you know about the absence in advance, let people know with a sign or by e-mail. (It doesn't necessarily mean they will plan ahead, but at least they know you will be out.) Arrange to have your mail taken care of and be sure to leave an appropriate message on your answering machine or voice mail (or have the phone calls sent to someone else to answer). It's a good idea to have a place for people to leave books and journals, requests for materials, and other things for you outside your door. Make sure it is a secured box so people can't take items out of it as well.

As an OPL, it is mandatory that you get out of the office occasionally. You need to visit other libraries, make contacts, take continuing education courses, and attend professional conferences. You need to do so even more than librarians who work with large staffs, yet you may think you can't leave. You can. You are not indispensable. The organization can do without you; your career or family cannot. Take your vacation. Attend at least one professional conference per year.

What will your clients do without you? If you plan well for long-term absences, your clients will manage (not so well that they don't still need you, but enough to keep the organization running). Make sure you have a written manual of policies and procedures. Don't worry about journals for routing piling up, because they would pile up in someone else's office anyway. Leave a list of sources to consult for reference, document delivery, help, and so on. You could arrange a reciprocal agreement with a nearby library or librarian in your same field to handle emergencies, but it is better to give the name of a reputable information broker or consultant with whom you have set up an account. Thus, you can be sure your clients will get good service and there is an additional benefit—your clients will find out the real cost of obtaining information and then will better appreciate the services you provide. Prominently post "how-to" instructions. List Web sites that they may need to consult. If you will be gone a long time, notify vendors to expect delays in processing invoices if they send them during your absence. You may want to suggest they send invoices early unless they prefer to put the bills—and payments—on hold (guess which they'll choose). Secure sensitive files and other paper and electronic data, such as circulation records, computer passwords or access codes, and original copies of software or videos. Don't forget to set your e-mail to "nomail" for the duration, unless you can read it from home. Finally, let your customers know that you will be gone as far in advance as possible.

Get the Most from Conferences

While you are at a conference, be sure to continue your time-saving ways. Go there with a plan. Know what you need to find out and from whom, and have questions ready. Make a prioritized list of objectives (often in your request to your boss for funding). If you find you can't get to all the sessions and meetings you want to go to, try splitting your list with a colleague. Contact people you need to meet before the conference and make a date to get together. Be sure to take a notebook, pens, tape, markers, file folders, a highlighter for the program, and so on. Have plenty of business cards; if your organization doesn't provide them, go to an office supply store and have some made with your home address. During the conference, use files to keep papers straight (e.g., labeled "action required," "to file," "people," and "vendors"). Toss what you don't need to take home. Tear pages out of catalogs, vendor literature, or journals you pick up at the conference, taking home only what you need. Ship stuff home rather than carry it, although this might encourage you to save too much. Use the two-pocket business card system (one incoming, one outgoing); write a note on the back of each card before filing it; and toss cards you know you won't need. Keep receipts in one place (use a hotel envelope). Stay focused. Remember your objectives. When you arrive home, write a conference report for your boss; if one is not required, write it for yourself. File what you brought home, going over it once again to make sure you really need it.

The exhibit hall requires its own strategy. On your first visit to the exhibit hall, just look it over and locate vendors you especially want to see. Then, start on one side or the other (from left to right is counter to how most people work, so I do it that way) and systematically make your way through the hall. Don't waste time (yours and theirs) talking to vendors you aren't interested in. Say hello, and walk on. If you think you might be interested later or the vendor is new to you, pick up literature only. You can always go back. Make sure you go up and down every aisle and exhibit area. On the last day of the exhibits, return to vendors from whom you need more information. (This is a good time to stock up on pens and pencils. The vendor doesn't really want to pay for return shipping.)

PRIORITIZATION

Berner reminds us of the second of his "Three Ps": priorities.

> Not everything you do is of equal importance and you should be able to differentiate among your various tasks and duties to set your priorities. You should also be aware of the fact that priorities are not constant. While it is helpful to list tasks and goals in writing and to assign them a priority, you cannot make the mistake of thinking that they are carved in stone. Priorities are constantly shifting as new tasks and new developments come into play. Whatever you may be working on, for example, it is likely that if your boss calls

or comes in with a request, that request is going to become your number-one priority (unless, of course, your boss's boss calls with a request, and then you may have to reevaluate). The important thing is to recognize that whatever criteria you may use for determining priority—and there are many—you should always be working on your highest priority items at any given time. (Berner in Siess 1997)

Question Things

Just because you can do something doesn't mean you should. You must question things:

- What is the objective? Will doing the task help me achieve my business or personal goals?

- What's in it for me? What's the payoff going to be? How will I know if I'm successful? How will I be rewarded?

- Is this task something I want to do? Will doing it make me bored, unhappy, or even miserable?

- Is it something I have to do? Or, is it something someone else can do? Can I add value to the task? Or, is it something anybody could do?

- Do I have the time to do it? Am I willing to pay the price (in giving up my precious time) to accomplish the task?

- Is this trip necessary? Is there a better way to do it? Should it even be done at all?

- What if I don't do this? Will the world come to an end? Am I willing to accept the consequences that not doing the task may incur?

• What have I got to lose?

• Will it go away if I ignore it? If no one misses it, maybe it didn't need doing in the first place?

Deciding what to do and what not to do is critical and requires continually checking your mission statement (Wilson and Mount 1997, 21): "It is important to have a clear goal. However, this goal should be a stretch goal (one that seems at first glance to be impossible) and must relate directly to what your company is doing or is planning. It will be a moving target in that as you close in on it, it will change or you will be ready to upgrade it to something even more challenging, depending on the situation."

You don't have to do everything everybody tells you to do. Learn the difference between what you should do and what you need to do. What you should do is not always in your best interest. You also don't have to do everything the way other people tell you to do it. Nor do you have to do everything according to someone else's time frame. Finally, you don't always have to do everything yourself. Yes, you have to please other people, but you also have to please yourself.

You must be both efficient and effective. Efficiency is completing a task with the least possible amount of wasted labor, cost, or time. Effectiveness refers to the quality of the work. Above all, make sure you are doing the right things. Too many businesses spend lots of time making sure they are doing things right and not enough determining if they are doing the right things. Doing the right things well is the epitome of efficiency and effectiveness. This is where the strategic plan comes in.

PLANNING

Why Plan?

What will the future bring for your library? What do you want it to bring? If there is going to be any chance for the future to turn out the way you want, you must plan. If you don't plan the future of your library, someone else will. And it's not likely to be the future you envision. Berner says of planning:

> Without a sense of where you want to go, how can you ever know if you are going in the right direction? Without planning you merely struggle through the day-to-day operations of the library—relieved no doubt, to get through each day—but you never bring your library any closer to realizing its ultimate goals. How can you if you have no idea what those goals are? Yet isn't that movement toward specified goals—for our libraries, for our parent organizations, and for ourselves—one of the things that marks us as professionals? Without it we are really nothing more than clerks. The most often-heard cry is, "but I don't have time for planning!" I can only respond by saying you'd better find the time. Doing long-range planning will give you the direction you need for intermediate planning and for short-term planning. Before you know it, you'll have a sense of direction which may have been lacking in your work before, and suddenly you'll find that you can be making decisions about the work you do (e.g., do I really need to do this?) rather than simply filling your day with tasks that seem to have no purpose. Unfortunately, libraries rarely plan. Instead they react to what others have already decided in such areas as budgets and staffing and then "plan" to make the best of the situation. Proper planning, by contrast, is a proactive process.... (Berner in Siess 1997)

What Is Planning?

Have you ever heard "If you don't know where you're going, any road will get you there?" or "If you don't know where you're going, how will you know when you get there?" Strategic planning solves these problems. "Strategies are policies (written or unwritten) that guide organizational decisions, and they are tied inextricably to the nature, direction, and basic purpose of an organization" (Penniman 1999, 52). "Strategic planning is essentially a process of relating an organisation and its people to their changing environment and the opportunities and threats in the marketplace; it is a process in which purposes, objectives and action programmes are developed, implemented, monitored, evaluated and reviewed …. [It is] particularly concerned with anticipating and responding to environmental factors, taking responsibility for change, and providing unity and direction to a firm's activities. It is a tool for ordering one's perceptions about future environments in which one's decisions might be played out (Corrall 1995).

Planning also allows you to focus your thinking on the future. People (and especially OPLs) often get so caught up in the moment, fighting fires and keeping their heads above water, that they forget about the future—where they are heading. Planning also saves time, fights uncertainty, helps you focus on your objectives, and is critical for efficiency. In other words, planning equals control. "The greatest value of the plan is the process, the thinking that went into it" (Beckwith 1997, 61).

How Do You Plan?

First, take a look at the strategic plan you did last year. Which items did you accomplish? Which did not get done? Why? (Were they not possible? Were they deferred? Did you decide they weren't worth doing?) Then, talk to your boss. What does he or she expect for next year? What are his or her priorities? Next, talk to users. Get an idea of both their concrete needs and their dreams. Consider a user survey. Follow up on complaints or requests that you weren't able to fill. Finally, talk to non-users. Why don't they use the library? What could you do to draw them in? This is a good time for blue-sky thinking. Think not only of the possible but the impossible and see if you can make it happen. Encourage this type of thinking by your boss, your users, and your non-users. Now, take a look at your current services. Do all of them need to be continued? Can you justify continuing them? Which new services do you want to add? Why? How will the organization benefit from them? Go ahead and include some items from your wish list. Not only does doing so show that you are a forward thinker, but it also gives the powers-that-be something to cut (so they feel they've fulfilled their fiscal responsibilities).

You should now be able to make a list of goals for next year. Goals must be demanding, achievable, specific, measurable, flexible, and agreed to by those who must achieve them. Goals also must have deadlines and be put in writing. Remember that you should have a reasonable expectation of meeting these goals, given the budget you are seeking. It also is important that you and your boss have a way of measuring or knowing when you have met them.

Is Planning the Same as Creating Goals, Mission Statements, or Visions?

Sort of. Penniman writes that "[A] mission [is] a statement of 1) what the institution does, 2) for whom it does it, 3) how it does it, and 4) why." "A vision ... is a clearly articulated statement of what you wish your institution to become, i.e., a future-oriented statement" (Penniman 1999, 51). Goals must be measurable so you know you've achieved them. (Be sure to congratulate yourself when you reach them, and even reward yourself.) Put goals in writing so you can review them. Goals must be concrete, not abstract, to be successful. Goals must be achievable. List the key tasks required to achieve the goal, the order in which the tasks need to be done, and the resources needed to carry out each task. Set deadlines for your goals. Doing so keeps you moving forward and halts procrastination. Keep your eye on your goals. It is easier to determine what is important in the short run when you know what you want in the long run. If it doesn't help to get you where you want to go, is it really necessary?

Then set priorities. Priorities are ranked goals. Then relate daily activities to goals and priorities. Finally, list the resources you need to meet these goals. Resources are not just money; resources include staff, equipment, technology, space, coordination, and authority. Yes, I know these all boil down to money, but think in broader terms.

Your strategic plan should cover one year in detail and three to five years in a brief form. The long-range plan undoubtedly will change dramatically as time passes. Beckwith (1997) builds a plan on the "Three Cornerstones of Planning." The first cornerstone is predicting the future. This is hard. Eric Morgan (1999, 33) says: "Few, if any, people successfully predict the future with 100 percent accuracy, but there are experts who have wider perspectives than the rest of us and, consequently, are more apt to see what lies ahead. Librarians of the future will always be keeping one ear tuned to the experts and one ear tuned to their individual experiences. Use what you hear to plan your future. Your vision may not be the one everybody else sees, but at least it will provide a framework for future decision making, and will enable you and your library to evolve within our dynamic professional environment." Examine the environment: the corporate culture, competitors, the information needs of users, mandates from the community (e.g., regarding management and accrediting), and unmet market niches. What did last year's strategic plan say? What did you accomplish? What did you not get done? What does your boss or organization want? What are their priorities? What do your users want? What are their needs—and dreams?

The second cornerstone is to decide what you want your future to look like. You need a vision statement that will express your aspirations, core values, and philosophies. Your vision should be very general and probably not achievable. You must share your vision with the participants (staff, customers, and management) in order to achieve it. Let those affected read the plan or maybe even help write it. Make use of your library committee, focus groups, and surveys. You also need a mission statement. This should be a doable statement of institutional purpose. It should contain measurable objectives and targets. Develop alternative plots for the future.

Next, figure out ways to make sure your future comes out the way you want. Now it is time to write your strategic plan. This plan describes how you will respond to and flesh out the mission statement. (Write an executive summary if the plan exceeds five pages.) One format for a strategic plan is the following:

- Your vision and mission statement.

- A summary of environmental forces and market trends.

- The key objectives and priorities of your plan, with annual, measurable library-wide goals and objectives. Describe where you are now and where you want to go.

- The human resource strategy and financial projections. Include resources needed, such as staff, money, and technology, along with where they will come from. Don't plan for a specific technology; rather, plan for a specific mission and a specific vision, and then use the available technology to fulfill your mission and vision.

- A timeline for the implementation of the plan.

- Ways in which you will allow for feedback, evaluation, and adjustments to the plan.

The final cornerstone is to implement the plan.

To find samples of other libraries' plans, try the Internet. Use Hotbot at www.hotbot.com to search on "library strategic plan." These plans mostly come from larger libraries, but you can get ideas from them. You can also ask around your town or city. Be sure to get a look at your organization's plan. It might be a good idea to follow its organization.

You say, "I don't have time for this"? Well, you'd better make the time. How else can you decide what to do and, more importantly, what not to do? How to find the time? How about on the way to work or at the beginning of your workday? You might need to come in early, because planning at the end of day does not usually work as well. Once you have done your strategic or yearly plan, don't just forget about planning. Set time aside every week for planning. You may need to go somewhere quiet, away from the library.

Strategic planning is a valuable management tool. It is also about management of change. Strategic planning strengthens the role of the library in the organization. It can demonstrate the librarian's competence and improves the image and visibility of the library. Planning provides a framework for policy formulation and decision-making. Planning can help support your case for funding. Planning identifies critical issues and constraints. Planning can keep you on course. "[I]f a library does not know where it is going it is likely to go downwards, because the staff cannot commit themselves fully to a drifting ship ..." (Line 1995, 136).

What if all this doesn't work? You must give yourself permission to fail. Failure is okay if you learn from it, if you failed because a higher priority task came up, or if you did not get the resources you needed (such as cooperation from someone else). In fact, if you have not failed, it means you have not taken a risk and have not challenged yourself.

5

Financial Matters

Budgeting, bill processing, and other financial matters are the tasks most dreaded by librarians, that is, after hiring and firing. Because as one-person librarians (OPLs) we have no one to whom we can delegate, we must learn to dispel our fears and master some financial skills.

BUDGETING

The budget is a very important management tool that too often is ignored. The librarian must have input into the budget. Here are things to keep in mind: justify each item in terms of time and money saved; allow for inflation; be realistic, remembering the financial situation of your parent organization; and keep it simple.

There are three types of budgets, but there is no "best" budget for all libraries. What is best is what management requires. The line-item budget is a list of items along with their proposed costs. The functional budget groups related activities and most often includes expenses only, not revenues. The capital budget accounts for long-term resources.

Begin by forecasting the present, that is, where you will be at the end of the current budget year. Factor in known internal or external cost changes and inflation. Look at where you can cut current costs to add new services. Maybe you can consolidate operations, eliminate little-used services, or reduce expensive resources. If you charge for your services, consider increasing your prices. Also consider moving your costs to someone else's budget.

Get to know the budget or planning cycle of your organization. Budgeting is often a two-year, or longer, process and may go on all year long. If possible, find out what amount of funding other similarly placed departments have. Try to locate all pockets of library-related money, whether or not they are under your control (and try to get all that money under your control). Also get to know the finance people assigned to the library. Make sure you understand your budget, how the numbers are derived, whether they are actual or estimated, and who has responsibility for what. Talk to the finance people throughout the year, not just at budget time or when there is a problem. Make the accounts payable person and the person who puts out the monthly reports your dear friends.

You say your boss did not ask for your input on budget or that you do not even have a budget? Prepare one and give it to your boss anyway—for the record—even if your boss does not use it. Preparing a budget is a good exercise and identifies you as a forward-thinking, responsible professional. If you do not have a budget, don't worry too much about it unless the organization is expecting you to run a department without any money. Many OPLs do not have a library budget or have a so-called as-needed budget. This situation isn't all bad. At one organization, I never got to see what was approved for the library. I had no actual budget, the library was just part of the cost center's overall budget. This arrangement had advantages and disadvantages. The main advantage was that I didn't have to make spending decisions because I had no idea what I could spend. The main disadvantage was that I never knew when I was going to be told that the money had run out. This didn't happen often. My boss knew that I wouldn't ask for something unless I really thought it would help my customers (and I *always* couched requests in those terms). My boss also knew that I researched my purchases and always made the most economical choices. However, it is better to have a budget—like all the other managers in your organization—and most OPLs do have budgets.

Your boss probably doesn't really want to deal with all the library orders and would prefer that you handle them. I used this logic to get purchasing to let me handle my own ordering. I pointed out to those in purchasing that they probably would not want the work of dealing with my high volume of book, journal, and document orders.

Here are three things you can emphasize to management concerning your budget. First, point out that if the organization wants a library, it should be willing to fund the library appropriately. Although funds are available in an established library, they might not be in the library budget, but in the budgets of other departments. You need to gather those funds into your budget so you control and manage them. Because many companies base the next year's budget on the previous year's budget, it is important to have all information about expenses in one place, rather than having it spread over several departments. An organization having one librarian who is interested in and able to manage all information expenditures can affect tremendous economies of scale and cost savings. Second, make it clear to management that a budget is something you, as a professional, expect. Third, point out that if you are trusted to run the library and select materials, then you should be trusted with a budget for doing so.

Question everything when budgeting. Use the technique of zero-based budgeting (i.e., justify every expense, every year). Be realistic. You may include some pie-in-the-sky items, but realize that they are likely to be cut. Don't be limited by available money. If a service is important enough (and you present it in the right way), the money will be found.

Remember KISS in Chapter 4? It means keep it short and simple, but not so short that you do not provide adequate information. Be sure to prioritize your requests. The simplest way to do so is to put the most important first; however, the best way is to develop multiple scenarios. Know the difference between purchases that can be capitalized and those that cannot. Separate recurring and fixed expenses. Photocopy everything (e.g., invoices and copies of purchase orders). Remember to keep track of preparation time, bookkeeping, cataloging, and so on.

Offer alternatives or substitutes (e.g., cheaper, faster, and better). Justify every item in terms of its value to the organization. Budgets are often based on office politics, so be sure to show how a service will make the organization and upper management look good, produce more, and save time. Be ready to negotiate, because a negative response is not always a final one.

Some categories that you should include in your budget are the following:

- Periodical subscriptions

- Book purchasing

- Online database services

- Delivery services (Can these be charged back to the departments?)

- Office supplies (Central supply won't carry everything you need.)

- Your training and continuing professional education

- Computer hardware and software

Once the budget is finalized, forget it and go on with everyday operations. If a real problem arises, document it and put it into next year's file. Be sure to get the budget and its authorization in writing. An oral agreement isn't worth the paper on which it's printed.

BOOKKEEPING

In order to create a budget you need data, that is, figures. Data involves bookkeeping but needn't be complicated. You can use whatever works for you. Some OPLs use Excel or Quattro Pro spreadsheets to keep track of expenditures. You can make each cost center or category a separate spreadsheet and link the spreadsheets to a summary sheet for monthly or annual reports. You can keep a running total of expenditures and subtract them from available funds. Other OPLs use an accounting program, such as Quicken, or a database, such as Access. Some OPLs don't even use the computer for bookkeeping. You can make folders for each category and put all the information relating to that category into the appropriate folder. You need to track everything that goes through the library, including items ordered for others. Be sure to include costs for office supplies, services, dues and subscriptions, printing and copying, personnel, software and licensing, equipment and repair, books (you can even break them down by type), document delivery—including ILLs, training, travel, wages, furniture, and telephone. You can include cost codes and names of departments, vendors, and requestors. When using a computer program, be sure that you can print reports in a variety of ways, for example, by category and time period. Try to get monthly reports from your accounting department and check them against your records.

I used a database program to keep track of all library expenses. I was able to search for and rearrange the data in infinite ways, for example, by cost center, requestor, vendor, category, and date. Then I took the totals and put them into an Excel spreadsheet to present them to others. I would input all the information when the order was placed and, therefore, could use this system to watch for open orders or orders received but not paid for. (The latter happened more often than you would expect. Some vendors were very slow in billing.)

I did the same for subscriptions and ILL. I tracked ILL by cost, supplier, and the time taken to receive the item. I could then decide where to submit a request (either to an inexpensive supplier or a fast one), depending on customer needs. I also used this tracking method to eliminate some vendors from my preferred Online Computer Library Center (OCLC) list.

I highly recommend charging back, at least for out-of-pocket items. Yes, it takes some time and can be a hassle (although less so if you do it right [see below]). But your customers will value your services more because they will see how much information you provide for so little money. My clients were almost always surprised at how little online searches cost. If everything is provided for free, two things will result: the customers will tend to over-use your services and undervalue them. Things are perceived as worth what they cost. A high-cost service must be better than a free one. In addition, you should aim to have the departments and functions that use your services include in their budgets—not yours—the costs for your services as part of their cost of doing business.

I prefer not to charge for my time. It really is a pain. What OPLs do is so fragmented and fraught with so many interruptions that it is hard to keep an accurate record of how much time we spend on a particular project—not to mention the time it takes to keep track of your time and get it all to add up at the end of the time period. For example, on one job I spent at least one hour a week and an extra hour each pay period just making my time sheet add up. Just think of what I could have gotten done in those hours!

How to Charge Back Without Pain

Here is a way to charge back without pain. Create a request form that includes the cost center to be charged and a place for the signature of someone authorized to charge on the account. (In my case, the form had to be signed by the supervisor of the requestor.) Include the copyright and ILL statements on this form, so the requestor is—supposedly—aware of the rules. When the bill for the service or item comes in, you already have the approval. Just add the cost center, sign the bill, and send it to accounts payable. Using this method, you avoid sending the invoice to the requestor for approval, waiting for it to be returned, following up on it, requesting a second invoice when the requestor loses the original, and so on.

FINANCIAL CRISIS

It is highly likely that sometime during your career you will be asked to cut your budget or spending. There are some ways you can minimize the impact on your library. The most important thing to remember is to anticipate the worst. Have a plan so you don't panic and make a wrong move. Go back to basics. Ask yourself what the library is supposed to be doing? Are you fulfilling its mission or have you gotten off the track with new projects that are peripheral to taking care of your customers?

A cutback will not come as a surprise to you if you are plugged into what is going on. Because you are the information guru in the organization—you *are*, aren't you?—you should be in a position to hear all the gossip (e.g., promotions, lay offs, new projects, and newly won contracts). Your connections to upper management will pay off big in times of crisis.

R. Lee Hadden (U.S. Geological Survey, Reston, Virginia) wrote of this quite eloquently:

> Cut library services and hours. Then let patrons complain directly to the administration. The administration will turn instead to a less assertive office to cut budgets. The absolute worst thing you can do is absorb the cuts with no change in patron services. If you accept the cuts meekly, you will train the administration that you are a free service that can be cut at will and without cost. You must show that any cut in library staff and services will cut the services to the library patrons first. If they say you should cut back on buying books, smile and ask sweetly which departments should be cut first and by how much, and would they please put that in writing.

Library legend Herb White once said that if they tell you your budget has been cut by 50 percent, just ask, "What 50 percent of my services do you want me to cut?"

In her *OPL Column*, Anne Tomlin (2000) wrote:

> Even in the worst of times, someone turns a profit. [In financially hard times] look for ways to (a) cut costs reasonably—

in dollars or staff time, and (b) bring in departmental revenue by charging back costs to other departments, establishing fee-based services, or mining for grant monies. Even if the actual amounts [saved by the above measures] are small, it demonstrates your commitment to being a part of the cost-containment game.

If upper management wants to cut your continuing education budget, remind them that it is important for good customer service for the librarian to keep up to date.

You also need to position your library as a low-cost, high-value service. As far back as 1979, White (1995) observed, "The library cannot spend enough, no matter how extravagant we get, to affect earnings by even one cent per share ...." This is still true. In fact, it is far better, and most likely cheaper, to have information and research services in-house rather than relying on outside sources, although any number of outsourcing services will tell your management the opposite. But that is another matter (see Chapter 7).

A budget crisis is also the time to call in any favors you have done for your customers. As Tomlin (2000) says: "Gratitude can bring on generosity. Going the extra mile creates a strong customer base of people who will be the library's more ardent advocates in good time[s] and, more importantly, hard times." You should have built up a network of advocates within the organization (especially at high levels) that will fight for you. However, if all of your efforts fail to get the message across, polish up your resume! A company that does not value your contribution is not where you want to work.

EVALUATING YOUR LIBRARY

Evaluating your library is critical, because, as St. Clair (1976, 236) points out, "No one is going to value the librarian if no one knows what he is doing." First you must know what you are doing, what your products are, what your strengths are, and what value you add.

Then you have to share this information with your supervisor, your users, and upper management. Svoboda (1991, 240) wrote, "Quality information products are the measurable evidence of the library's value to a corporation." This means this information should be current, value-added, selected, sorted, classified, and analyzed. If you are typical, your most valuable services are online searching and quick response to questions, so try to get feedback from your users on the time (translated into dollars) saved by using the library. All information transactions add some value in that the question gets answered. The real measure is when you go beyond the basics and provide more than is asked for. This is *transformational librarianship*, that is, making a difference in the patron's life.

There is no easy formula for measuring the effectiveness of your services. Surveys usually produce skewed results: The unhappy user does not respond; the busy user does not respond, no matter how satisfied. In measuring your services, you cannot count or evaluate everything, because the enormity of the task will cause you to abandon it. Don't be tempted to take the easy way out and count activities (e.g., ILL, books cataloged, and circulation). Count results instead. If a process is very complex, break it down into its component parts and analyze each of them, all the while keeping in mind your long-term goals and those of the corporation.

Remember that information does not need to be free, only reasonable. Alsop (1995, 126) says, "It's not information but information *gathering* that costs money." I frequently had users come to me wanting information but only if it could be found for free, especially on the Internet. Sometimes I searched the Internet for them, usually finding nothing of value. Sometimes I just said that nothing is free and they would have to pay if they wanted information. For one user, I spent about 15 minutes on the Internet looking for a Microsoft book on some obscure subject. I finally asked the user, "Do you want it free or do you want the information?" We logged off the Internet and onto the Books in Print file in DIALOG. In two minutes, for $2.00, I had the title and price of the book he wanted. I then asked, "Did you learn anything from this?" We agreed that perhaps the free Internet was not always the best solution. Another example is that after an online search, patrons would sometimes complain about the cost (usually when it was only $35 to 50). I would then ask how long it would take them to get in the car, drive to the library, locate the information (if they could), and drive back. Then I would ask their departmental charge rate (usually about $65 per hour). Almost always that was the last I heard about information costing too much.

MONEY-SAVING TIPS

There are many easy ways to save money. Instead of purchasing expensive journals, you can retrieve articles from the Internet, from document delivery services, by reciprocal lending arrangements set up formally through library networks and consortia, and through informal networks of colleagues. You also can save on book orders by buying on the Internet or from a local discount bookseller, becoming a reviewer for library journals, or purchasing overstocked books directly from the government or the publisher. Take advantage of group purchases through consortia, vendor discounts, prepayment deals that save shipping charges, and multi-year renewals that cost less than annual renewals. You can usually negotiate costs, fees, and even payment terms with your vendors. One library allows coffee in the library only if people use lids sold by the library. I held annual book sales, offering the books removed from the collection to employees at a nominal cost. I made more than $500 over a period of five years. I used the money for direct patron services such as maps, atlases, and, of course, for goodies for the next open house. Fundraisers also can serve as a chance to promote the library and remind users of its place in their lives.

Revenue can be generated by doing research or purchasing documents for outside customers (if your organization's policy allows). Joan Gervino (1995), director, Center for Banking Information, American Bankers Association, wrote about the concept of establishing fees for service. First identify your customers, then decide what you will charge for and what will be free. Research, database searching, document delivery, prepackaged information, database design, and translations are usually charged for, whereas circulation (although you may charge an access fee for the collection) and quick reference (under 15 minutes) usually are free. You must focus on quality, 100 percent accuracy, timeliness, comprehensiveness; and you must have standards or metrics to keep track of and measure quality. Gervino (1995, 6) wrote, "A highly pro-active marketing effort is essential to the success of a fee-based library." Be sure to evaluate the program after a while, not only on its financial success, but on its reception by your patrons.

CONCLUSION

Budgeting and finances need not be complicated or time-consuming. Just use your common sense and streamline the process. Keep in communication with those who control your money. Make sure you understand what is going on in the organization, and make sure the organization understands what is going on in the library. Be sure your customers appreciate the value of information and of your services. Be prepared for the worst and aim for the best.

6

Working with Others

One-person librarians (OPLs) may be alone in the library, but they certainly are not alone in their organizations or profession. Knowing how to work well with others, therefore, is especially vital for OPLs. In this chapter you will find out about better communication, library promotion and publicity, networking, and professionalism.

COMMUNICATION: AN OPL'S GUIDE TO CONNECTING

Almost nothing is more important to an OPL than communication. No one will know what we can do if we don't tell them. We cannot serve our users unless we know what they need or want.

Doing so involves communication—not just public relations, talking, or the reference interview, but *communicating*.

Real communication is an interactive process. One person sends a message and another receives it. When you are the sender, the trick is to make sure that the message received is the same as the one you meant to send. When you are the recipient, the trick is to make sure you are receiving the right message.

With Whom Do You Communicate?

You communicate with your boss and your boss's boss (upper management). Former dean of the Indiana University library school, Herb

White (1995, 213), said that "The purpose of management communication ... is to get something accomplished." Therefore, it is important to communicate with your boss and upper management in the way they do. Make sure management is kept informed of your activities. Remember that management does not like surprises or problems. When a problem arises that you can't solve yourself, be sure you approach management properly. Managers don't want problems; they want solutions. Therefore, make it easy for them to solve the problem by offering several scenarios for a solution. You also need to have what is called an "elevator speech." Prepare a short (one minute or less) statement to use if you should encounter the chief executive officer (or another top management person) in the elevator or hall. Your speech can be about your mission, capabilities, current money needs, hot news about a customer or competitor, or a recent accomplishment.

You communicate with your users. In this type of communication, your marketing gene needs to kick in. Your users need to know which resources you have available in your library and which resources you have access to outside your library, such as electronic databases, the Internet and World Wide Web, interlibrary loan, and connections to other libraries. Your users also need to know that you and your library are a one-stop, full-service, low-cost supplier of high-quality information for your organization. Last, but definitely not least, your users need to know that *you* are the most important resource in your library. O'Leary (2000) wrote:

> Even the most information-literate end-user/customer is behind [the information tools learning] curve. Bob Schwarzwalder of the Ford Motor Company defines marketing as customer enlightenment, and describes his role as "Huckster-in-Chief," whose job is to sell and to really educate people on the power of information and the potential of what information technologies can do for them. Our customers understand their information needs, but they don't understand the tools that can satisfy them.

You communicate with your colleagues, who are other OPLs and other librarians. It is especially vital for the OPL to stay in contact with other librarians. Our collections usually are small and narrowly focused. Even so, we often receive questions for which we do not have answers. Therefore, it is good to know other librarians and the contents of their collections. I often called another library when I knew it had what I needed. I always got what I wanted because I had made the effort to visit other libraries and, thus, became more than a disembodied voice on the other end of the phone. I also had made it clear that I would reciprocate by providing information from my own collection whenever I could. You can find out whom you should visit by going to local, regional, and national conferences and meetings and talking with people and by looking in your association directory of members. In other words, practice *networking*.

You should also communicate with the public. When was the last time you read about an OPL in the newspaper or the non-library press? You say you can't remember. Then why not do something about the public image of OPLs by writing for the popular, business, medical, or legal press? You may think you have nothing worth saying or that you won't be able to get your article published. That's not necessarily true. Most publications, including the scholarly press, are hungry for articles, especially something they haven't seen before. For a medical journal, go to a doctor or nurse who uses and values your library and offer to co-write an article. It may turn out that you do most of the writing, but their names will get the article published. If the rest of the world doesn't know what we do, maybe it's because we haven't told them.

You also receive communication from others. You need to know what information your users need. A lot has been written about user information needs. Before I go further, I will get up on my soapbox and say a bit about them. Most of these studies are *not* about user needs. They are usually about user demands and sometimes about user wants, but seldom about needs. *Demands* are what the user asks for. *Wants* are what the user says he or she wants. *Needs* are what the user really wants but probably can't articulate without probing by the librarian. Here is an example from my own experience. A man came into the library and asked for an atlas (demand). I asked him what he wanted it for (to determine which one to give him). He said he was going to look up the mileage from Cleveland to Columbus (want). After further questioning, I found out he wanted this number for his expense account (need). So I gave him the official mileage our organization authorized for Cleveland to Columbus, an entirely different number. If I had just filled his information demand, I would have done him a disservice by not meeting his information need. (Off my soapbox.)

You find out what your users want and need from you by asking them. Ask your selected users questions such as:

- What tools do you use in your everyday information seeking?

- Where do you go for information other than the library? Why? Why not the library?

- How many times have you not looked for information because you didn't think you could find it, it would take too long, or cost too much?

- If money were no object, what would you like the library to do? (Caution: be sure to tell them that you cannot guarantee that you will be able to provide these things, but you will try.)

You also must be sure that you know what your management expects from you and your library. Does management want you to maintain the status quo or be on the leading edge of technology and librarianship? Are you supposed to serve the entire organization or just one area? You find these things out by asking. If you do not get an answer the first time, ask again. Keep asking (in different ways, if necessary) until you are satisfied that you understand exactly what is expected. After all, how can you be expected to meet the expectations of management if you don't know what they are?

What Do You Need to Communicate to Others?

Your users and your management need to know, and be reminded, that you are a professional. If you have an advanced degree (library or otherwise), hang your diploma on the wall of your office (or library) and consider putting it on your business card. Do not be intimidated by the degrees of your users. Remember that you, too, are an expert in your own field.

You need to communicate your value to others. Be sure your manager knows about it whenever a user says, "I couldn't have done this without you," or "Gee, now I have the information to cinch the contract," or "The information you gave me saved the company $xxx." Have the user document how you helped and send the documentation to your boss. Put testimonials in your newsletter or frame them and hang them on the wall. Schwarzwalder (O'Leary 2000) said: "We try to find leading consumers, those who are more aggressive in manifesting their information needs. These liaisons, as we call them, are the way that we popularize our services to others."

How Can You Better Communicate?

Words are not the only way we communicate. According to Leslie Dickson, President of Voice-Pro (a Cleveland, Ohio, firm specializing in helping others present a professional image), words (or content) make up only 7% of the message we send. The sound of our voice makes up another 38% of the message. But the major part of our message, the remaining 55%, is transmitted by how we look: our appearance, demeanor, and style. Beckwith (1999, 171) said, "If you deliver two messages, most people will process just one of them." Therefore, we must make sure that:

1. We look the part of a professional. Act and dress professionally. Clothing details depend on the dress code in your organization. (All organizations have a dress code, whether written or informal.) If managers wear suits, then wear a suit. If the only

women who dress up are secretaries, then dress like your users. Stand tall and proud.

2. We say what we mean, and we mean what we say. In oral communications, your tone and inflection are very important. To see what I mean, say the following sentence seven times, each time emphasizing a different word: "I didn't say you took the money." People like to hear their names, so use them frequently. Make eye contact. Use hand gestures only when appropriate. When writing, make sure you read over what you write, especially in e-mail because it is very tempting to send a hasty and perhaps imprudent reply. Determine whether the occasion calls for a formal or informal style. Avoid the use of slang and profanity in both speech and writing.

People have widely varying styles of communication. You must find out how the person you are communicating with wants to receive information. Some people want all the details; others want only an executive summary. If you send a long and detailed report to the executive summary–type person, he or she probably will ignore it. Is it better to report in writing or will an oral report in person be better (such as when there may be questions you will need to answer)? Because today most workplaces are multicultural, be aware of the ways different cultures interpret words, gestures, and personal space. If your intended audience is not fluent in English, provide a translation or at least communicate in writing. There are many books on cultural differences (see Chapter 11).

Sometimes you must deal with difficult people. We have all encountered someone who just isn't responding to us, who may even be obstructive or downright hostile. Sometimes you can just ignore the person, but what if this difficult person is your boss or an important customer? Brinkman and Kirschner (1994) identify "The 10 Most Unwanted List" of difficult people. Here are a few I have met personally and my ideas for dealing with them.

1. The know-it-all who doesn't like to be corrected or contra-
   dicted and blames you when something goes wrong. A common type, so keep him or her well informed of your activities
   and the consequences of any action.

2. The think-they-know-it-all who knows some stuff but likes
   being the center of attention. Sometimes you may just have to
   ignore his or her boasting.

3. The "yes" person who, to avoid confrontation, says yes to
   everything and winds up being overcommitted. You aren't one
   of these, are you? There is a simple cure. Learn to say no.

4. The "maybe" person who will do anything to avoid making a
   decision. Make it easy for him or her to make a decision,
   preferably in your favor, by giving several clear options and
   adding a box for him or her to check off an answer.

5. The "no" person who always knows why something will not
   work. Use the same technique as for number 4, while reminding him or her that your other ideas have worked out well.

6. The whiner who is overwhelmed and brings his or her problems to you, but really does not want a solution. This person is
   just looking for a sounding board. Listen, but not long enough
   to interfere with your own work.

How do you respond to difficult persons? First, you can stay and do
nothing but suffer, complain, and become frustrated. Second, you can
leave. Third, you can change your attitude and learn why they act that
way. Fourth, you can change the way you deal with them. I suggest a
combination of the last two. (Only if that does not work do I suggest
leaving. Suffering, complaining, and becoming frustrated should *never*
be an option.) Get a book—or two or three—about the subject, and
identify the types of difficult persons with whom you are dealing. Then
implement the appropriate remedies.

We all have to negotiate something from time to time, whether it be a salary, a contract with a vendor, a deadline, or job responsibilities. Be realistic, be flexible (leave room for negotiation), and present your side in terms of the benefits to the other side. As Guy St. Clair (1995d) put it, "Always stress the money angle." Show how you have progressed, and be patient.

Today we do a lot of communicating by telephone. Do not allow the telephone to run your life. You do not have to answer it every time it rings. In fact, you shouldn't, especially when you have someone in your office or when you need to concentrate on something such as an online search or major report. Answer the phone with your name and the name of the organization or library. Be prepared to repeat yourself, because most people really won't listen to your greeting. Get a good answering machine or voicemail. Think carefully about your message. It should be relatively short and very professional. (This is not the time to be cute.) Give callers an option other than leaving a message, such as another person to call if the situation is urgent. Listen occasionally to your greeting and make sure it is still appropriate. Check your machine frequently, and return calls religiously. When leaving a phone message, speak clearly and distinctly. Be brief and to the point. Do not ramble. Give your full name and phone number early in the message, in case you run out of recording time. Repeat your phone number for clarity.

Another frequent way of communication is in writing. On memos, Guy St. Clair (1993) writes: "If you don't need a permanent record of the interaction, use the phone. If there is room for misunderstanding, write a memo. If you need a written response, write. If you need to 'talk' to more than one person, write rather than call." When writing a report, first make sure that it will serve a purpose. Do not write reports that won't be read.

THE ANNUAL REPORT

You should definitely write an annual report, being sure to send it to your boss and your boss's boss and, if feasible, to your users. St. Clair and Williamson (1992, 138) say that the annual report may be "the single most important document the one-person librarians will produce during the year." You can use the report to inform management of the problems and strengths of the library. You can also use it as a tool in lobbying for changes.

Although writing an annual report may seem like a daunting task or one more bureaucratic requirement, it can be made easier with advance planning and some organization. Writing will be much easier if you keep statistics and notes during the year. Doing so will take care of the hardest part, that is, gathering the information. If you use a diary or calendar, note what you accomplish each day or special things you want to include in your report. I usually had to write a monthly report and used this as the basis for the annual report. (Remember: do not include everything—just the highlights.) Consider the reader. Be brief, avoid library jargon (business jargon is fine), and assume the reader is interested and educated. Do not be afraid to toot your own horn because that's what the report is for. Keep the report simple. Do not elaborate on problems or failures. Report problems as decisions made elsewhere in the organization, providing just the facts. Save your prose for your accomplishments and plans for the future. Finally, make it look good. Get help from your organization's graphics department if you can.

What should be included in the report? You want to begin with a short history of the library, just enough to put the report in context. Then state the role of the library in the organization. If you have a formal mission statement include it. Be sure to make clear the time period covered by the report (calendar year or fiscal year). If you have held significant events or had special visitors, be sure to mention them. Also include significant purchases or gifts that have added to the collection. For each of the above, show how it supported the parent organization. Reports should concentrate on results and benefits to the organization, not statistics. List the current services offered to your clientele and describe new and enhanced products and services introduced during the year. Were they successful? Will they be continued? Did any fail? A very important part of the annual report is a recounting of your professional activities (conferences or continuing education courses attended, offices held, papers written, and so on). Doing so reinforces your professional status and attitude. You will want to show the benefits that your organization realized from these activities. If you received an award or a thank-you letter for something you did, include it.

There should be a section of the report that contains hard numbers. These would include a financial statement (including fund surpluses and deficits), usage statistics (making sure they reflect actual library usage), figures on acquisitions and technical services (items purchased, cataloged, and removed from the collection), total size of the collection, and measures of customer satisfaction (if available).

You want to end the annual report with your plans and vision for the future. Which new services do you plan to implement or continue? Which might you be eliminating? How will your plans and vision affect the users and the budget? Write a conclusion. If written and used properly, the library annual report can be a record of what you have accomplished, what you hope to accomplish, an effective marketing tool, and a report to management. Be sure to make enough copies to last until the report is outdated next year.

ORAL PRESENTATIONS

At some point in your career you most likely will have to make an oral presentation. It may be to your colleagues or upper management, or you may give a workshop. You will be nervous—every time. (You need to worry if you are not nervous, because it means you aren't taking the presentation seriously enough.) Know your audience. Make sure you are giving them what they want to know. Do not worry about what they think of you. These "ego thoughts" are the number-one cause of stage fright. The best way to calm your nerves is to be prepared. Know your material inside and out. Do not be so concerned with the material you are trying to present that you cannot be flexible and prepared to skip sections in which the audience does not seem to be interested. Arrive early to check out the room and equipment. It is a good idea to have a backup (old-fashioned paper or transparencies) for audiovisual presentations. Having a backup is especially important when you are using a computer or a projector.

Your oral presentation should state your purpose, support it with strong arguments and stories, give the audience a specific action to take, explain the benefits of that action, and then sum it all up. People remember best what they hear last. Speak simply. Avoid jargon, acronyms, and idioms. When speaking to a multinational audience, avoid U.S.-centric examples. Pause when you change subjects or for emphasis. Make sure your gestures are appropriate (common gestures used by Americans may be obscene ones in other cultures). Make visual presentations clear and simple. Present numbers graphically. If you are using handouts, try providing only an outline during the presentation, followed by a more complete set or copies of visual presentations after the session. (Doing so will allow your audience to concentrate on you and not your handouts.) Breathe from your diaphragm. Do not allow your voice drop off at the end of sentences, which is a common problem. Stand with your feet parallel, about 8" apart, with hands at your sides. Take a deep breath, then relax. You know your material and the audience is ready to learn what you have to say. They are yours.

WORKING WITH YOUR BOSS

Perhaps the most important relationship an OPL has is the one with his or her boss. Yes, this is even more important that the librarian-user relationship. You can be the best librarian ever, but if your boss is not convinced of your worth you will not last long. You can take action to maintain and improve the boss-librarian relationship.

First, we need to examine the nature of the boss-librarian relationship. The OPL most likely reports to a non-librarian. (The exceptions are those OPLs that are part of a larger network or organization, such as all the OPLs in the far-flung IBM libraries.) The OPL's boss is probably not the top official in the company. The boss also can be someone entirely outside of the organization (such as a mayor or a board of trustees). The boss has many other people to supervise. The boss may not even set his or her own priorities. Priorities may be set by your boss's boss, with or without his or her input. The boss is not interested in the library's day-to-day operations or problems, but only cares that the library functions well. The library's budget is usually a small part of the organization's overall financial plan. In fact, the library may not even have a budget. Finally, the boss may or may not be a library user.

Given the information above, which issues need to be addressed by the OPL? You must educate your boss, especially if you are establishing a new library for the organization. Even if there has been a library at your institution forever, you will have to let the boss know who you are, your work style, and what you plan to do. Of course, you will have to learn the same about your boss. What are his or her priorities for the library? Is the budget expandable? To whom does your boss report? And what are the priorities of your boss's boss? Communicating with your boss is a high priority. How does he or she want to communicate? How often? Is reporting to be done in person, by written report, or by e-mail? Does your boss want all the details (probably not) or just a summary of your activities? Perhaps he or she wants only a report of major accomplishments or problems. (If you report a problem, be sure to include how you plan to address it. Remember that most bosses don't want problems, just solutions.) Maybe you should just list highlights and provide details only when asked.

Does your boss really have power, or is he or she just a supervisor with the real decision-making authority resting at a higher level? If your boss is just a supervisor, resist the temptation to go over his or her head and right to the decision-maker. Organizations want you to follow the rules and lines of communication. Of course, you can always copy your boss's boss on memos that you think your boss will be tempted to ignore or not act on. That way you can have your cake and eat it too. If you have a boss that is really blocking your ability to run the library, consider finding a new boss. I once reported to a manager who kept asking, "What *is* it you do again?" After about six weeks of this, I left a voicemail message for the president (an avid library supporter) saying, "Find me a new manager, quick, or I'll quit!" He responded (by voicemail, of course) almost immediately by telling me to be patient, he would work something out. After some searching on my part for a sympathetic boss in the right place in the organization, I had a new manager in a few weeks. Going over your boss's head may not work for you, and you must be prepared to accept the consequences. Sometimes, however, it is the only option.

Kevin Kearns (1997) advised that you do not have to use psychological tricks to deal with your boss, nor do you have to become friends with him or her. You don't have to change your style completely to get along with your boss, although you may have to make some modifications. Most importantly, you do not have to give in to your boss. Learn to disagree respectfully and constructively. According to Kearns (1997), to manage upward effectively:

- Be sure you understand the structure of the organization.

- Develop a realistic set of expectations regarding what you want from your boss. Look at your boss's style, strengths, and weaknesses, and see how they compare with your own.

- "Understand that managing upward is not about managing the boss; it is about managing yourself within a complex set of peer and hierarchical relationships."

Of course, nothing will help the situation of a cruel or incompetent boss. If you have tried all these strategies and still cannot get along with your boss, you have only two choices: put up with it or start polishing that resume to look for a new job. This should happen in very few instances. Let's hope it doesn't happen to you.

THE CARE AND FEEDING OF NERDS, OR, HOW TO WORK WITH YOUR COMPUTER PEOPLE

I have heard many OPLs complain about a lack of cooperation from the organization's computer people. Do you get quick and friendly service for your library hardware and software when you need it, or are the computer people unresponsive? Do you work together to bring new information services to your common users, or are you always in conflict over who is responsible for what? Your answers may make the difference between seamless service and chaos and frustration.

Martin writes (2000, 8): "Far from viewing nerds as superheroes who will save us from technology, many librarians often end up feeling frustrated, confused, or stupid after an encounter with a nerd. I think this is partly because we don't understand the language they speak and partly because we look at the world a bit differently than they do." I doubt if *they* feel the same way after talking to us, so why should we feel this way?

You need to know the inherent differences between the roles of librarians and information technology (IT) people:

- IT provides the pipeline, technology, expertise, project planning, and management, and IT usually has the money.

- IT gets the glory but must also deal with organization-wide, conflicting demands. All administrative departments are dependent on IT, creating conflicts and competition for resources.

- The goals of IT are a robust infrastructure and system availability and reliability.

- "Computer nerds don't necessarily want to share their knowledge with others .... [They] enjoy the mystique that surrounds them and they like knowing they're the only ones who can fix computer problems. Nerds also worry that if they give users too much information it might end up as more of a mess for the nerd to clean up later" (Martin 2000, 8).

- "Nerds have difficulty admitting they don't know everything about technology." [An OPL might say], "I don't know but I'll find out, but nerds may feel ashamed or uncomfortable about what they see as their lack of knowledge" (Martin 2000, 8, 10). Nerds may say that something can't be done when they really mean they don't know how to do it. You must state your requirements and expectations explicitly.

- The Library has a strong orientation toward service, and the librarian has expertise in researching. The Library provides a systematic, centralized, and coordinated method of retrieving, filtering, and storing information.

- The Library has niche software products that are out of the IT mainstream, with relatively few primary users. Library vendors may be small companies. It is not feasible for IT to train many help-line staff in library applications. Programs may not be as well debugged and require lots of IT staff time for a small number of users. It also may be better for some vendors to work with IT, not through the librarian. The library handles print, CD-ROM, and Internet services; IT provides a stable platform.

- Common goals include providing excellent service to the firm and clients, intuitive access at the desktop, and systems to increase communication and collaboration.

- Computer scientists and librarians "both believe in providing information for free, but they do so using very different methods. [The computer people might think], 'I'll do what I want and tough luck if you don't like it.' The people deciding whose needs get served by software that's given away for free are, for the most part, programmers who are fortunate enough to have the time and the freedom to putter around ... driven by their desire for the coolest toys rather than by the needs of most people. Libraries, in contrast, are built around the idea that they need to serve everyone. Instead of focusing on the latest toys, they focus on resources that everyone will be able to use." (Martin 2000)

The people in IT would like librarians to master the operating system, understand the network infrastructure used by the organization, subscribe to and read technology publications, help with system design, provide ideas for new services and content, and add value. Librarians would like IT to provide a list of current projects so the librarian can provide current awareness on hot topics, provide timetables on significant hardware and software upgrades, add value to new applications, track trends in technology to locate technologies that work with current systems, and develop a common user interface to minimize the learning curve.

Technology and librarians are two sides of the information coin. Too often, however, those that work in IT—not the librarians—get all the glory, money, and impressive titles. Librarians are relegated to acquiring and storing information in books. We librarians are increasingly dependent on IT because we are involved in organization-wide systems, not just a few terminals in the library. We have good idea of what customers are asking for, however, and should provide that information to IT. The library also can provide coordination of strategies and identification of knowledge or information leaders.

It is possible, and necessary, for IT and the library to work together. The first step is to make sure both groups understand each other's goals, jargon, and issues. It is critical to communicate frequently and electronically. Librarians should ask the advice of IT before purchasing new applications.

Librarians usually need IT more than IT needs them, so librarians need to make the major effort to improve the relationship. Martin

(2000, 10) has written, "If your nerd has a tendency to hoard knowledge, he can probably be trained to spill some of that knowledge, given proper rewards." Appreciation is the best reward, but food, especially chocolate chip cookies, works wonders. Martin (2000, 10) continues: "If you are searching for a computer nerd to work in your library, first test the nerd's ability to translate technospeak into English. Social skills are another important factor to consider." However, you may want to find your computer expertise closer to home. Tennant (1999, 8) says, "It's much easier to teach a warm librarian what he/she needs to know about technology than to make a cold-hearted geek care [about excellent customer service]."

Because the library often is one of the first groups to adopt and benefit from new technologies, librarians must move from dependency to collaboration. We help IT by providing instructions and cheat sheets for after-hours IT support for library services and by acting as liaison between users and IT for troubleshooting. We should provide IT with library plans for budget, staff, and products that will involve IT. Then we can begin to develop joint training and orientation programs. Developing these programs may involve collaboration with other departments on automation projects that may have organization-wide applications.

How does an OPL start making these changes? As the Nike firm and former SLA president Judy Field (it was the theme she chose for her presidential year) say, "Just do it!" Identify one critical area, and compile a few possible applications. Remember to think strategically. When users have a problem with a program or application, IT and the library should go to users as a team for technology and content, respectively.

INTERPERSONAL NETWORKING

It is safe to say that OPLs network in some manner. Networking can be informal or formal. Formal networking involves the use of established organizations and much of it, especially in special libraries and one-person libraries, arises out of necessity. One-person libraries are small, have limited resources, and have very specialized collections. Networking is a major factor not only in reducing the OPL's feeling of professional isolation, but also in reference, document delivery, interlibrary loan, acquisitions, and continuing education. All libraries and librarians depend on the support of others. We use interlibrary loan; the Online Computer Library Center (OCLC); consortia; vendors; temporary help; outsourcing; consultants; and other departments within our institution, such as management information systems, purchasing, accounting, and legal.

Informal networking involves contacts among personal friends, within the organization, with former colleagues, and with former co-students. Although often ignored in this age of electronic communication, informal or interpersonal networking is arguably more important than its formal counterpart. We rely on contacts with other professionals (e.g., through meetings, the Internet, professional reading, and phone calls) to make decisions on which books to buy, which vendors to use, and which meetings to attend. We call other librarians when we have a reference question that is out of our scope or need an answer in a reference book we do not own. We find these other professionals either by formal or informal means, but finding them is still networking. Be sure not to abuse nonlibrarian sources, thank your sources, and share information. I have found that informal networking, that is, calling a colleague, is often faster and less expensive than an online search. In large libraries, this is called *resource sharing*. The resources we are sharing are ourselves and our knowledge. Remember, as Quint (1996a, 4) has said, "Libraries do not cooperate, librarians do."

Our professional organizations (the American Library Association [ALA], Special Libraries Association [SLA], American Association of Law Libraries [AALL], Medical Library Association [MLA], Australian Library and Information Association [ALIA], Library Association [LA], Canadian Library Association [CLA], and so on) are the best sources of networking contacts. In addition to national meetings, there are local meetings which usually occur more frequently. Even if the topic is not of immediate interest to you, go to the meeting. First of all, you never know when you will need to know about outsourcing, acquisitions, or whatever the topic is this month. Secondly, you need to renew your contacts with your fellow librarians, both to maintain your own sanity and to make sure they remember you when you call with a question or request. One of my colleagues referred to a consortium meeting as a "support group." By this she meant that the members could share their complaints, fears, and concerns, feeling confident that the others understand and probably have the same feelings as she had. Talking with someone who has "been there" is frequently the only way to deal with some new frustration or challenge on the job. Being active in professional associations improves communication skills, makes us feel more connected, enhances professional awareness and personal growth, makes contacts, adds information to our resumes, helps us gain management skills and experience, and enhances self-esteem and self-worth. St. Clair (1989, 107) wrote, "Informal networking takes its value from relationships between people."

LIBRARY PROMOTION: SELF-SERVING OR JUST GOOD SENSE?

I often have heard librarians express reservations about public relations or promotion of their library and its services. Some are even more reluctant to promote themselves. This is not good. It is necessary to promote, or market, the library and yourself all the time. Every contact with someone outside the library is a marketing opportunity. Another name for this is public relations (PR) or promotion. Here are some of the common excuses for *not* doing marketing—and my counter-arguments.

- *PR takes too much time.* Actually, many of the best PR techniques take little or no time. Once you redo your stationery, routing slips, and so on, making sure the library's name (or yours) is on everything that goes out to users takes no time at all.

• *PR takes too much money.* It costs almost nothing to create an interesting bulletin board, write an article for your organization's in-house publication, or create a poster.

• *It is unprofessional to advertise.* On the contrary, it is unprofessional to hide your light under a bushel, let others take the credit for what you do, let your library be downsized or closed because no one knew what you could do.

• *I already have too much to do. Promotion would just bring me more work for which I do not have the time or resources.* When was the last time you looked at your priorities? Are you spending too much time on low-priority tasks and not enough on the high-profile, high-impact, very professional tasks only you can do?

• *Other departments in the organization don't do it, so why should the library have to?* If everyone else buries his or her head in the sand, should you do the same? Maybe those other departments have already done their marketing, and so everyone already knows how valuable they are? (Of course, they should continue marketing to ensure that people don't forget about them, as should you.)

• *Advertising sounds so self-serving. No one will believe it if it comes from the librarian.* There's a big difference between tooting one's own horn and reminding others of services that can help them. Ideally, you will be able to quote satisfied users (the higher-up in the organization the better) in your publicity. But if you don't tell people how good, useful, helpful, and knowledgeable you are, who will? Better you than no one.

• *I don't know what to do. PR wasn't covered in library school.* Lots of things we need to know weren't covered in library school. So, learn how to market. Take a class, read a book, subscribe to a journal, or ask a colleague.

Why Use Public Relations?

Kurtz (1993) said:

> Although information has intrinsic value, no special library or information is guaranteed its existence. Just because it has been around for years does not guarantee it will be around next year. With the possible exception of academic libraries (since most accrediting programs require an adequate library), no organization has to have a library in order to conduct its business. It may not be able to compete adequately in the long run without a library, but that in itself doesn't guarantee that a library will not be closed or down-sized.

When Do You Promote Your Library?

When do you promote your library? If your answer is anything other than "all the time," you aren't doing enough. Every time you meet someone and every time you put something in the mail (postal, e-mail, or inter-office), you have an opportunity—nay, obligation—to explain how you and your library can help your clients do their jobs "better, faster, cheaper" (the librarian's mantra). You should have a "30-second commercial" to be used whenever you meet people. It should go somewhat like this: "Hello, I am Jane Doe of the Brown Company Library. I provide pre-screened, quality information to keep you competitive in the widget industry." Your goal should be to make everyone in your organization aware of you and your library. Every single piece of paper (or electronic message) that goes out of your library should have your name or your library's name on it. A logo, mascot, or slogan can help get this message noticed. Avoid using a book as your symbol. Use a computer or abstract words (information) instead. Include this information in the running head of your search printouts so that it appears on every page. Another benefit of having your name on everything is that it keeps your users from going to their bosses and saying, "Look what I found." It is obvious that you found it.

Keep PR relaxed and friendly, but businesslike. Be sure it is not filled with library jargon. (Use "We can get information from almost any library in the state" rather than "We participate in the State ILL system.") Use bulleted text rather than straight text. A sense of humor never hurts. Have a library brochure, but keep it short, simple, and good-looking. Tie its style to the organization's design. In fact, get your organization's graphics people to design it for you. Give the brochure to everyone you can, and get it into all new-employee orientation packets. Finally, make sure you have business cards and hand them out liberally within the organization.

Of course, public librarians need to promote their libraries to their users and potential users. But they also need to make sure their elected officials know about them, their services, and the economic value of the library to their communities. They need to become masters of local politics. Making the city council involved and happy will pay off. Staying positive and upbeat will make your potential supporters more confident in your abilities.

Another area that library schools don't emphasize enough is publicity. Drake (1990, 153) has pointed out, "If you don't promote, you're doomed to defend." If no one knows what you can do and how well you can do it, you probably will not be doing it for long. The OPL is no place to hide your light under a bushel. You must constantly tell management and your users exactly how you can help them. No matter how satisfied they say they are, they will forget about you very quickly if you don't remind them.

How to Publicize Your Library

First, you need a library newsletter. The newsletter can be distributed by e-mail, posted on the bulletin board, offered as a handout in the library, or whatever method works in your organization. A newsletter is very easy to create. You can use your word-processing software for simplicity or get really fancy with a desktop publishing program. You can also find a plethora of good graphics on the World Wide Web. You might try to get someone in the graphics department to work with you on a total graphic package. At least get someone in the graphics department to design an attractive library logo and letterhead for you. Your brochures and other handouts should look professional and carry a common theme, as should your Web and intranet pages.

What should you include in a newsletter? You can include many things: new services; additional information about underutilized services; recent acquisitions of books, journal, and even standards and pictures; professional activities of the librarian; excerpts from articles by you in professional journals; testimonials from satisfied customers; sample reference questions to stimulate users' thinking about what you can do; jokes; and quizzes. You also can get promotional materials from your professional associations (ALA, ALIA, SLA, MLA, AALL, CLA, LA, and so on). In short, anything that will help promote to users and potential users the idea that the library can help *them.*

How often should a newsletter come out? Your newsletter should be published often enough to remind users that you are there, but not so often that it gets repetitive or stale or intrudes on your other work. Once a month is usually about right, but, for your organization, a weekly or quarterly newsletter might work better. You are the best one to decide.

The best advertising is by word of mouth from satisfied customers. Therefore, outstanding customer service is more important than ever. Whenever a user thanks you for special service, ask him or her to put it in writing. Not only make sure a copy of this "atta-boy" or "atta-girl" is placed in the personal file your boss keeps, but also use it (with the user's permission, of course) in your library newsletter, brochure, Web site, or wherever it fits best.

As with all promotion, you have to define your product and determine which services you will promote. You should probably concentrate on high-value services (such as online searching and competitive intelligence). However, these services are likely to be more time-consuming.

Be sure you can provide excellent service before advertising. You may want to increase volume by promoting lower-value but easy tasks, such as journal routing or document delivery. Next, you need to define your target markets. Is your market everyone in the organization or one department? Is your market the movers and shakers only? Do you want to serve outside clients as well? Do you need to turn a profit? These factors may influence where you do your marketing and to whom. Then define the competition. Even if you are the only library or librarian in the organization (or town, or branch), you have competition. Find out where non-users currently get their information and how you can compete with them. Find out what makes you and your library better than the competition. What are your advantages? What can you do better than anyone else? Finally, follow-up. Follow-up is critically important. One shot won't do it. You should plan to market a new service *at least* three times to have it really noticed. Check with your users after introducing a new service to see if they like it. One way of following up is to RBWA, i.e., reference by walking around. Get out of the library and visit your customers, stopping to talk to people if they are not too busy. Ask what they are working on and offer to help. Just the act of walking around—being seen—reminds people that you exist and that you might be able to help them. I can't count the number of times I have talked to someone at their desk, in the cafeteria, or in the hall and had them say, "Oh, yes, that reminds me. Can you get ...?"

More Promotion Ideas

Make sure information about the library is included in the new-employee orientation program or packet. The information you provide need not be fancy or complete, just enough to make sure new employees know that you and the library exist. Of course, it is even better if you can obtain the names of new employees and follow-up with a personal call or visit.

One OPL sends out a daily news alert, making sure that the library's name is on it. This is great if you have the time. Getting mentioned in company publications is very good PR, and public libraries should use the local newspaper as a PR vehicle. Even the free neighborhood newspaper is good for an article now and then. But don't stop there.

Michel Bauwens (1993), the first *cybrarian*, a librarian who operates exclusively in cyberspace (i.e., with no physical facility), has some suggestions for marketing your library in cyberspace. By proactively building virtual reference areas, the cybrarian anticipates user needs and creates a one-stop shopping mall for information. He suggests a three-part system, with access to Intranet (in-house) sources, general productivity tools (e.g., dictionaries, encyclopedias, and phone books), and organization-specific resources on the Internet. Among Bauwens' suggestions are:

- Offer something useful to attract new users and get current ones to return.

- Provide newsgroups, listservs, and other interest groups, creating a virtual community.

- Use newsletters, memos, e-mail, and other means to promote your virtual library.

- Make it easy for your clients to find information.

- Provide a means for user feedback.

Other Public Relations Techniques

Create a bulletin board. Bulletin boards serve many purposes. They catch the eye of users and invite them into the library. You can highlight new or important services on a bulletin board. Try posting tables of contents or copies of newly arrived newsletters. Highlight hot news in your organization or industry and new Web sites. Put the covers of new books on the bulletin board. Use an upcoming event as a theme or have a theme week (or month, or day). Post library procedures or frequently asked questions on a bulletin board near your office to reduce interruptions. Make your postings complex to make people stop to read them. (Simple boards can be read in a glance as they walk on by.) Be creative. Use pictures, jokes, puns, puzzles, and cartoons. Change them at least every two weeks.

Have an open house. Remember to provide food and giveaways: "Feed them and they will come." If you are providing free coffee or tea, put up a poster at every coffee and tea station in the building advertising your open house. Make sure you put publicity for the event in all in-house publications. Provide giveaways—something with the library's name on it for users to take back with them (e.g., pencils, sticky notes, or buttons). Have a raffle. You will want to get your customers to sign a register so you have a record of how many attended and for follow-up. Have a vendor fair by inviting representatives from databases and other services you provide. (Make sure the vendors provide the food and the giveaways. Often, vendors also can provide the publicity.)

Have a book sale. Charge 50 cents (or a similar sum) the first day, 25 cents the second, and give away the books on the third day. If someone wants to buy a book before the sale begins, charge double. Earmark the monies raised for something that the users want but that the organization would not usually provide, such as maps and travel guides.

Publish a special issue of your library newsletter. In it, highlight a new service of your library or interview a satisfied customer.

Write an article for the organization's newsletter or, better yet, write one for a local newspaper. Be sure to make sure your manager gets a copy of the article for your personnel file.

Don't forget vendors. Many of them produce very nice materials that you can use, for free, to publicize your library. Some will even focus on you and your library and not on their own products.

Use a special day to get publicity. The best days to highlight are those that relate to your users, such as engineers' week, doctors' day, law day, nurses' week, and so on. Celebrating during National Library Week is not as good an idea because it focuses on the library instead of the users. However, if you want to do something focused on libraries, here are some ideas. First, celebrate International Special Libraries Day (ISLD), not National Library Week, which focuses on public libraries (unless, of course, you work in a public library). Use the ISLD artwork available from SLA or make your own. Honor a library user of the year. Choose someone who has supported you, has checked out the most books, or requested the most searches. Post the client's picture, interview the client, and give the client an inexpensive gift to encourage others to use the library.

Celebrate one of the two patron saints of libraries. St. Lawrence the Librarian was one of the seven famous deacons of the early church and was noted for his patience and grace under pressure. Lawrence was a librarian and archivist, supposedly holding a list of the locations of the Vatican wealth. When captured by the Emperor Valerian, he refused to produce this wealth, instead bringing a large number of sick, orphaned, and crippled Christians to the Emperor and declaring, "These are the treasures of the church!" For doing so, it is said he was roasted on a spit in Rome. (Actually, he was beheaded, but this roasting story is more popular.) August 10 is the feast day of St. Lawrence, often celebrated with cold cuts in honor of the way he supposedly met his death. His head is held in the Vatican Library.

St. Jerome, another patron saint of libraries and librarians, was also known as Hieronymus, Eusbius, or Sophronius. Because he translated the Bible into Latin, he is also the patron saint of translators, scholars, and editors. Born in what is now Croatia/Yugoslavia in A.D. 347 and educated in Rome, he argued with church scholars early in his life. He withdrew to Bethlehem to found a monastery and convent based on his principles. While secretary to Pope Damasus I (A.D. 382–384), he helped establish the papal library and began his biblical translation activities. He died in A.D. 420 and is buried in the Church of the Nativity in Bethlehem. His feast day is September 30 (Hadden 1991).

A Last Word on Public Relations

I would like to end with some wisdom from a relatively unlikely source. Harry Beckwith is a super-salesperson and motivational speaker. I recommend his entire book to you, *Selling the Invisible*, which has many gems for those of us who specialize in *service* (referring to the term *invisible* in the title) (Beckwith 1997):

- "The core of service marketing is the service itself" (3). Make sure it is the best it can be.

- "You cannot be all things to all people; you must focus on one thing" (103). Find out the hardest thing your customers need to do, and "position yourself as the expert at that task" (107).

- "Your first competitor is indifference" (171). I have always preached that a library's biggest competitor is doing without. We learned in library school that if it is too difficult (or too expensive) the users will not use the library.

- "Attack your first weakness; the stereotype the prospect has about you" (176). Be approachable and technologically savvy. Never, ever, say "Shhh."

- "Talk about him [your customer], not about you" (209). Be customer- and answer-centric, not library-centric.

- "Services are human. Their successes depend on the relationships of people. The more you can see the patterns and the better you understand people, the more you will succeed" (245).

PROFESSIONALISM

Several issues are involved in librarians as professionals. We must be concerned about our image and guard our professional demeanor and ethics. We also have an obligation to continue to grow as professionals.

It is absolutely necessary that the library and the librarian have a professional image. In 1990, Drake (1990, 152) wrote, "Our profession suffers from an identity crisis, caused in part by supervisors (and users) who do not share our professional identity." Most people assume that anyone who works in a library is a "librarian." Thus, when a member of the clerical staff cannot answer their question, is rude, or gives misinformation, they assume that the "librarian" was not helpful. This situation is especially bad in public libraries but also holds true for other types of libraries. As OPLs we are especially vulnerable to this misconception even if we have clerical assistance. The other problem is that many libraries are not staffed by professionals. If they are not well trained and do not have the customer-service ethic, their performance hurts us all.

White (1984, 95) wrote, "Librarians are often taken for granted, and they are often patronized; it is assumed that many of their requests are well-meaning and idealistic, but not practical." One problem is there is no accounting of a librarian's accomplishments, "with no methods to evaluate library contributions to productivity and profits" (Prusak and Matarazzo 1990, 45–46). These statements are not unique to librarians, but that does not make them any less damaging to us.

What is even more damaging to the profession is our acceptance of this image. When I was in library school, I found the prevalent attitude was that our low salaries and low prestige was almost entirely due to the profession being predominantly women, which was taken as an immutable fact. I was not very popular when I suggested that the reason our salaries and prestige are low is that we accept them. Many library activists feel that we need to demand more respect and higher pay, but I strongly disagree. We cannot *demand* respect; we must *earn* it. Respect can be earned by a professional attitude and by producing results for our institutions and our users. We do not do our profession any good by failing to set up explicit standards for librarians. At present, there is no consistency in the degree of preparation offered by the ALA-accredited library schools, no competency requirements, and no requirements for continuing professional development.

In addition to updating standards, there are other ways to improve our image. We should be on the forefront in adopting technology, pay attention to the needs of our users, be active in the parent organization, represent our business in the community, get published outside the company, avoid the librarian stereotype, and provide information leadership in the organization. Librarians need to be more proactive and decisive. We have to promote and defend the library and get managers to see the library and the librarian as strategic resources. We must defend our turf against those who would deny our information collection, analysis, and dissemination expertise. Our title and place in the organizational structure need to be appropriate. Even if we do not manage a staff, we manage information. Therefore, the title of manager should be ours. Several experts suggest dropping the title "librarian" from our title. As much as I hate to admit it, they are right—at least for now. Until we can update management's preconceived notion of a librarian, we are better off with some other title.

What does it mean to be a professional? Herb White (1994, 53) writes, "The smaller the professional staff, the more important it becomes to select truly excellent professionals." Because an OPL is as small a professional staff as one can find, professionalism is especially important for us. As St. Clair (1996a, 3) puts it, "If you stop to worry whether you *should* be doing this or that part of the task, whether it is *appropriate* or not, you'll never get around to doing what you're supposed to be doing." Clerical tasks are just as much a part of the job as are the professional tasks, and St. Clair (1976, 234) says it is very important to "Always think of yourself as a professional, even when performing nonprofessional tasks." Often this may mean working longer hours, whatever it takes to get the job done. However, you can overdo a good thing. Herb White (1995, 210) reminds us that there is life outside of work, saying, "Burnout for librarians seems to me both foolish and unnecessary. Work hard, work well, work effectively. Work until quitting time. Then go home and enjoy the rest of your life. Let the people with the proportionately higher salaries do the higher proportion of the worrying."

Professionalism also requires a continuing commitment to maintain your skills, which includes spending time and money on continuing education. This important subject is covered in more detail in Chapter 7. All I will say here is that you must assume responsibility for your own continuing education to reinforce your standing as a professional dedicated to keeping current and to continue to provide users with the best possible service.

7

Along the Information Superhighway: The OPL and Technology

echnology. Just the word conjures up mixed feelings: excitement, anxiety, and stress. How are we going to keep up with something that, by the time we get a handle on it, has already changed into something else? Technology is one of the biggest aids to the one-person librarian, but many OPLs see it as a threat. The trick is to become the master (or mistress) of technology, not let it become *our* master. This chapter looks at technology in the framework of past, present, and future.

PAST: WHERE HAVE WE BEEN?
HOW FAR HAVE WE COME?

Technology has been part of libraries for decades. In the 1960s, large mainframe computers first appeared in major institutions. In the 1970s, personal computers were developed. Large, mostly academic, libraries began automating their card catalogs and circulation. The Online Computer Library Center (OCLC) began production of cataloging and catalog cards. In the 1980s, networking (local area networks or LANs) began to link computers within libraries. Later in the decade, networking and modems allowed libraries to start reaching out of their buildings, and e-mail became more common. The 1990s was the decade of personalized information at the desktops or in the homes of users and, most importantly, saw the Internet become a part of everyday life for many people.

The Internet began in the 1950s as a network for information exchange among defense researchers. It is now found in nearly every corporation and school and in most libraries. Let's see how the situation has changed since I wrote the first edition of this book, way back in 1996 (Siess, 1997). At that time I said, "Everyone agrees that there is a lot of information available on the Internet. Sometimes it is useful and someday it may become one of a librarian's most important resource[s]. BUT that's not today's reality." Well, that "someday" is today. The Internet is, or should be, an integral part of every library, no matter how large or small. I also quoted someone as saying, "There are 'no more gates to keep.'" We were wrong. Although our users think they don't need anyone to mediate between them and the Internet, they really *do* need us. Users need us to locate, evaluate, index, and make available the information they need from the electronic universe.

In 1995, Barbara Quint (1995) warned that the interfaces of the standard search services must catch up with the flash and ease of the Internet if they expect to continue to attract end users. To some degree the standard search services have caught up, but they still have some work to do to be as attractive to the end user as is the point-and-click World Wide Web (WWW). Quint was also concerned that librarians would abandon the major services (e.g., DIALOG, LEXIS-NEXIS, and Dow Jones) for the inexpensive full-text services on the Internet. The search services are trying their best to get us to do just that. However, we aren't yet willing to give up the greater flexibility of the proprietary interfaces for the user-oriented and "dumbed-down" WWW search engines.

The WWW, however, is not perfect yet. In 1996, Fletcher pointed out such disadvantages as wasted user time; unreliable searching and navigating; user overload, that is, too much information; and system overload, with its attendant delays and frustrations. Added value and completeness also may suffer. Fletcher (1996, 44) wrote, "Most people are not willing to pay for the added value of thoroughness unless there's a mission critical situation. Ease of search is more important ...." The simplicity of the search engines on the Internet passes some costs from the provider to the user. The longer it takes to find information, the more the user "pays" in extra time spent searching. All this is still true. We still have no way to convince the end-user of the cost of incomplete or incorrect information.

In *The SOLO Librarian's Sourcebook* (1997), I wondered what the effect of the Internet would be on published forms of information, such as directories? Would these be forced out of print by the economics of direct publishing on the Internet? If they were, how would those who cannot afford the Internet access this information? Now we know that many of these print resources *have* disappeared into the electronic world, albeit with improved search capabilities and faster updating. While the issue of access to all for all is still being debated, it is being thrust on librarians (primarily in public libraries), ready or not.

PRESENT: HOW DO LIBRARIANS USE TECHNOLOGY? FINDING OUR ROLE

In 1996, only a minority of librarians used e-mail for collection management activities, such as questions about vendors and library management issues (e.g., salaries), but many more wanted to be connected. Now most everyone at least has e-mail. Electronic lists are available for almost any group, issue, or purpose. (See Chapter 12 for ones of interest to OPLs.) We use electronic lists to stay informed, to stay connected, to follow library issues, to replace or in addition to professional meetings, for reference, and for interlibrary loan (ILL) and duplicates exchange. Early on librarians began to use the Internet to search library catalogs (OPACs) worldwide and to access commercial databases such as LEXIS-NEXIS and DIALOG to do the following: find and download documents, answer consumer health questions, find government statistics or publications, locate information about companies, obtain country-specific information and Centers for Disease Control and Prevention health advisories for travelers, locate working papers and conference announcements, and download maps and other geographic information. We still do search OPACs over the WWW, but most librarians prefer to access commercial databases using the proprietary software of the vendor, which is more powerful than the user-oriented WWW interface. In 1996, Mike Scully at the Swedish Medical Center in Seattle, Washington, wrote this testimonial on the usefulness of one electronic list: "Inside of an hour seven of the nine messages in our in-box were regarding my query. I have several good sources to check. The speed of the Internet and the helpfulness of the MEDLIB-L people never ceases to amaze me!" This is still true, and lists are used even more today.

Also in 1996, Bob Berkman, editor of *The Information Advisor*, did a survey on BUSLIB-L of how people use the WWW for business research. The top 15 responses were:

1. To locate obscure information not found anywhere else by using search engines such as AltaVista or Savvy Search.

2. To find government information, especially from the Census Bureau and the Securities and Exchange Commission.

3. To find information posted on the home page of a company.

4. To get alternative views found in non-mainstream journals published on the WWW.

5. To peruse primary sources, such as court options, press releases, and white papers.

6. To find information about communities or other entities.

7. To find news and information from professional societies and universities not previously available online.

8. For inexpensive, albeit incomplete, access to newspapers and magazines.

9. To find experts on an unfamiliar topic (via newsgroups).

10. For economical access to reference materials not accessible in print.

11. For access to graphical materials not available online.

12. To access sources formerly available in print but now only available on the WWW.

13. For one final check on a research project.

14. To find out who else might be interested in the same project in which you are interested.

15. To search a WWW version of a traditional database when doing so is less expensive.

All these uses are still common in libraries today as well as many we never dreamed of in 1996. Librarians now serve as Webmasters; act as Intranet coordinators; write Web-based training courses; use our expertise in choosing, using, and fixing hardware and software; order books and journals on the WWW; manage electronic journal subscriptions; and occasionally even serve as organizational chief information officers (CIOs) or chief knowledge officers (CKOs).

Technology also can put small law firms "more on a par" with large firms. Law firms still need someone to manage and support the automated research tools—a librarian. But technology may allow law firms to reallocate space from the library (historically the largest office, centrally located, and most expensive to build) (Stathis 1995). Baker (1995, B13) has pointed out that another concern is whether the Internet is "helping or harming law librarians. Right now it is doing both." The Internet distracts from other activities, not all information there is valuable, and not all valuable information is there. Some librarians become too accessible (to users) due to e-mail. Baker (1975, B14) also says, "Librarians ... must take steps to ensure that they are masters of the Internet, not its slaves."

How does the Internet compare with traditional reference sources? The Internet can be more current. However, you must check the date of the Web page, that is, the date the information was created, not the date it was posted or accessed. The Internet is wonderful for finding ephemera, such as company press releases, works in progress (such as committee reports, working papers, and draft standards), local resources not available elsewhere, and government documents and statistics. For instance, many of the series from the U.S. Bureau of Labor Statistics are no longer available in print form but are on the WWW. As with traditional online searching, you must construct the question properly. Start with the answer you want and work backward, taking advantage of advanced search capabilities on many of the WWW search engines. Analyze the results. Do they make sense? Are they corroborated elsewhere?

What the Internet Is and Is Not

I wrote this in 1996 (Siess, 1997), but it is still true today.

What It Is

- A great communications tool

- A great leveler (if made available to all, in public libraries or other locations)

- A giant "mail order" catalog

- A great information dissemination tool for business (technical manuals, product literature, catalogs, technical support, software)

- A great information dissemination tool for government (bills, position papers, feedback from people to government)—but not a substitute for print

- An ephemeral storage medium

- Cheap

What It Is Not

- A good reference tool (except for posting questions on lists among professionals)

- Secure

- The answer to all information needs (you still need verified sources)

- A substitute for libraries (books are more user-friendly and better for most reference)

- A substitute for librarians (we need them as information guides, consultants, evaluators, and indexers)

- An archival medium

- Fast

One of the biggest issues in electronic information and the Internet is how to evaluate the information on it. Hope Tillman (1995) has developed some criteria for evaluating Internet resources: Who are the authors? How does it compare to other sources? How stable is the information? How appropriate is the format? What is the cost? How easy is it to use? How convenient? How fast?

In the Information Strategies course at Purdue University in Indiana, students compare finding and evaluating information in print sources with the same process online to teach new strategies (Brandt 1996). There is a difference in how the information is "published." Print sources are usually peer reviewed internally and then externally and are indexed for public access. Internet sources are put up directly on the Net via newsgroups, electronic lists, and the Web. Indexing is done by computers, not human indexers; additional or controlled vocabularies are not used and sources are not evaluated. Search engines are not all inclusive, so sources may be missed. Some guidelines for evaluating the sources are to check the author's credentials and affiliation, to check to see if there is reason to assume a bias in the information or its source, and to make sure the information is appropriate for your purpose by checking its scope, coverage, and level.

Nancy Garman (1996), editor of the now defunct magazine *Online User*, cautioned that the librarian needs to be careful in how and what is looked for on the Internet—and online, for that matter. Be sure to look in the right place. Sometimes, however, online (or print) is a better choice. Think about and question the source of Internet information. Who is behind it and is it reliable?

Of course, there is a downside to the Internet as well. Information overload, excessive time spent surfing the Internet, too many e-mail messages, hardware crashes, software glitches, viruses, user-hostile interfaces, disappearance of well-loved print resources, lack of time to keep up with all the new sites and services, and poorly thought-out ventures by new dot.com companies are just a few of the everyday annoyances. There is also a perceived threat to our profession. The increase in end-user computing leads bosses to wonder why librarians are needed and leads librarians to wonder if they will be unemployed. There is hardly a librarian who hasn't heard "It's all on the Internet, and it's all free." This comment is just one aspect of the lack of respect for and understanding of our profession. We have a big job to do in educating our bosses and our customers. We need to emphasize that end users cannot do as thorough a search as librarians can. End-users may not find the best sources, just the easiest ones to find. Because we all have limited time and resources, we can let customers do the easy searches, leaving the more complex ones for us. End-user searching simply is not cost-effective. For example, does management really want a highly trained and highly paid doctor, lawyer, or engineer to search for information, when a highly trained and lower paid (unfortunately) librarian can search faster, better, and less expensively? The doctor, lawyer, or engineer does not really know how to search, does not know where to look, and cannot determine if the information found is reliable. In contrast, being proficient at all these things is part of the librarian's professional duties. Librarians need to convince customers of the truth behind the old adage, "Shoemaker stick to your last"—that is, everyone should do what they do best. Or, we can promise that we won't practice medicine, law, engineering (or whatever), if those in other professions don't practice librarianship. Fletcher (1996, 44) sees great opportunities for information intermediaries: "Knowing how to get information economically, how to synthesize material, how to distill facts to answer questions, and how to extract the right question from the client" are our core competencies and, at present, no online search engines exist that can do what we do. Fortunately for us, this is still true. Unfortunately, we haven't been able to convince all of our customers.

Defining the Librarian's Role in the Information Society

One of the most important issues librarians must address is which part we are going to play in the newly defined information society. We are increasingly called on to provide instant access, 24/7/365 (24 hours a day, seven days a week, 365 days a year), to all the information anyone could want, and all at the user's desktop with an interface that any child could learn in 20 seconds. The volume of information also has increased greatly. Information overload is a concern, but there also is concern about *mis*information. Where do we fit in? We must go back to basics, our core functions: our ability to manage knowledge resources, in all forms; our ability to focus on the users, which differentiates us from Internet service professionals; and our facility for using tools and technologies. I have divided our potential roles into four categories: searcher and navigator, teacher, evaluator, and policymaker.

Searcher and Navigator

Most people do not know how to find information efficiently. Too sweeping a statement, you say? Most people have trouble locating sites and need help they are not getting from automatic search engines. Leibovich (2000) found that students would rather do research on the WWW than in the library, even if they can't find the answers. They don't understand the importance of choosing the right key words, synonyms, and getting information from multiple sources. Students also are more likely to choose the first hits they find, rather than the best ones. They assume what they find is true, without checking for accuracy or bias. Although students may know how to use computers, they don't know how to formulate searches to get the results they want. Librarians must intervene. Libraries provide access and librarians provide assistance.

Although more and more people will find the easy answers for themselves using the Internet (and, occasionally print sources), we will still be needed to do the difficult searches. We also will be needed by those people who do not want to do their own searching for whatever reason. In fact, there have been several anecdotal studies showing that the Internet and other electronic resources actually add to librarians' workload. The reason is that users do the easy searches themselves, leaving the more difficult and more time-consuming ones for us, the experts.

Teacher

Again, people do not know how to search for information. We must teach our customers how to formulate searches, modify them, search multiple sites, and evaluate sources. The most significant way we can help our customers use the WWW effectively is the same way we help them with print sources, that is, by teaching them how to ask the right question.

We also need to teach users when to search for themselves and when they need to come to us by pointing our customers to the *right* source on the WWW, just as we do with reference books. Our role will continue to be one of information navigator. This teaching role is never-ending. Just when we get comfortable with one set of tools, technologies, or users, a new set will come along.

Here are some examples to illustrate the magnitude of our task. A customer asked me to use the WWW to see if Microsoft had a book. He didn't know the title and wasn't even certain of the subject. After about 10 minutes of working the Microsoft site (this was before search dialog boxes were common on Web sites), we hadn't found anything. I asked if he wanted the answer. I then logged on to Books in Print on DIALOG and had the answer in two minutes for $2.00. The moral of this story is that the librarian determined the best resource to use to answer the question. Another wanted me to look on the WWW for the definition of a word. I told him that we had a faster way to get the answer, a print resource called a dictionary. Still another employee called me to complain that he had been searching the WWW for an hour and still hadn't found his information. When I asked what he'd been searching for, he said, "It's the price list of one of our competitors." I asked if our company put our price list on the WWW. "Of course not," he replied. I then asked him what made him think our competitor would do so? If he had come to me before he began, I could have saved him an hour by telling him that the information wasn't on the WWW at all. I've also had customers who wanted me to look up the spelling of a word or a telephone number on the WWW. I introduced them to sources that could find these even faster and more accurately, a dictionary and telephone information.

Librarians also know how to obtain the materials found by searching. Tenopir (2000) writes, "Libraries must employ a variety of strategies for document access, including full-text databases, electronic-only journals, commercial document delivery services, automated interlibrary loan, and cooperative collection development." How much money and time would be wasted if our customers had to get their own

ILLs (and books, and subscriptions)? How many invoices and how much chaos would be created? Instead, the librarian can centralize purchases, plan acquisitions, negotiate terms, track their progress, and even make sure copyright regulations are followed.

Evaluator

Picasso said: "Computers are useless. They can only give you answers." A major role for the librarian will be to choose the appropriate resources, tools, systems, and interfaces. The tools we use may change, but the mediator role will not. We must use both the new and old tools. Although it will become less important to build physical collections, the selection, evaluation, and reevaluation of books, journals, and electronic sources will always be critical in an organization's ability to compete and thrive. If we don't do this, who will? Will it be end users, computer people, administrators, finance people? Imagine the chaos that would ensue if any of the above were to be put in charge of recommending information resources.

R.A. Schneiderman, a computer consultant and not a librarian, wrote:

> Librarians have been managing complex information for over two hundred years. If we were smart, we'd let librarians rule the Net. Computers aren't very good at cataloging information even when the information ... is already quite specialized. If we're going to catalog the web, people will have to do the bulk of the work. [Other professions have done some of this work,] "but if librarians [were] in charge, they would have insisted that every web author have access to simple programs that helped them briefly catalog any document or collection of documents they put up on the web. If someone moves their web, there is no easy way to find it .... As a result, extremely valuable information sometimes disappears off the web without a trace. Librarians have spent years handling these ... problems ... and their

experience would have been invaluable if computer scientists had been smart enough to use it.

Policymaker

Griffiths (1996) warns, "Technology can be a black hole for money." We can serve as the central point for the ordering of resources to ensure minimal duplication and maximal use of scarce monies. Many OPLs already serve this function for books and journals, but we should also be responsible for the electronic resources. Of course, it is inevitable that the computer people will be making the buying decisions for the hardware and even the software. However, we need to communicate with the computer people to ensure the technology will run the resources our mutual customers need. We must work together to keep the focus on the problems technology can solve and not on the technology itself. Crawford (2000, 49) recently wrote, "Your job is to recognize that technology offers tools, that those tools interact in complex ways, and that tools aren't ends in themselves .... Most tools should be nearly invisible. They should do their work without intruding on the task at hand. [Finally,] the only thing we really have to look forward to is more change." We must get comfortable with the constant change in technology; learn to take risks, identify opportunities, take action; and realize and accept that anything new will be obsolete within a couple of years.

Collection Development in an Electronic World: Choosing Formats and Evaluating Resources

I sometimes find myself thinking, "Gee, wasn't life easy when we just bought a book or subscribed to a print journal?" I must be getting old, longing for the good old days. But think of how little information we were able to provide then and how long it took. We now have the possibility of providing far more information, faster, in a more usable form, and to more users. Instead of looking back, we should be looking forward to the "good new days." Fasten your seat belts, it's going to be a wild ride!

First, look at your institution and your users. Where are the users located? Are they mostly in the same building or all over the world? Does the institution perceive itself as being on the cutting edge of technology and expect you to be the same? How technologically savvy are the users? Do the users want a virtual library? Do the users need 24/7 desktop access to information? If so, do the users need this access for all the information or just certain sources? Are the users willing to pay for this information, either directly or by giving the library (you) more resources? How often do the users need historical information, the kind that is neither in electronic form nor likely to be so for the near future?

Then look at your library. Is there information there that is "never" or seldom used? Have you been acquiring "just-in-case," and are you ready to move to "just-in-time" acquisitions? Do you have backfiles of journals that are covered by one of the major electronic services? How is your relationship with the information technology (computer) people? It had better be a good one if you are going to go electronic (or you'd better be a techie yourself). What is your collection development policy? (You don't have one? It's in your head? Don't feel guilty. Most OPLs do not have a written collection development policy, but maybe this is a good time to write down those intuitive guidelines under which you've been operating.)

Now, look at the available resources. What is available in electronic form? At what cost? Here are some items to look at when evaluating resources in print versus electronic formats:

• Reliability and continuity (Will it be here tomorrow?)

• Content (coverage and arrangement)

• Appearance

• Search and retrieval (options and ease of use)

- Access (A book can be used by one person at a time, CD-ROMs can be networked but have practical limits, WWW access is available to all at the same time.)

- Technology requirements (What is the cost? Who will update it?)

- Ownership (Often you only lease electronic information.)

- Archival properties (How long will the medium last?)

- Training requirements for staff and users (How much? By whom?)

- Cost (Unfortunately, often this is the determining factor.)

- Space requirements (Electronic is a clear winner here.)

As Smock (1995) points out, there are some other issues of consequence as well. What is the life expectancy of electronic documents? How well do electronic media preserve information? We assume that preservation of our cultural and intellectual history is one of the responsibilities of libraries. Therefore, we must be concerned whether the hardware and software to access the information will be there tomorrow and in 5, 10, 50, and 100 years. We also must ascertain what people *really* need online.

Will the new medium replace the old? Of course not. Crawford (2000, 49) recently wrote, "'Media' is a plural noun, implying that there will continue to be more than one medium of communications and entertainment. Librarians must decide which media work for their libraries and their users. The more media, the more complex that decision." There always have been and always will be multiple formats. When CD-ROM first came along it was predicted that it would revolutionize home entertainment (it has), eliminate low-density media (it has supplanted but not replaced floppies and now has been somewhat replaced by other, faster media), and revolutionize publishing (there has been some change, but definitely not a revolution). Why wasn't

CD-ROM more successful? Networking CD-ROM wasn't as easy as we thought it would be. Storage capacity, while better than for floppies, is being exceeded by the demands of new software and data. Although transfer and access speeds are increasing, CD-ROM is still slower than the Internet. The WWW is now supposedly the be-all and end-all, and CD-ROM is out of favor. In the future something new will come along and then the WWW will be passé; however, print, disc, CD-ROM, and the WWW will all continue to coexist. After all, we all still have some microfilm or microfiche, don't we?

We've always had to choose formats. Now we just have more choices and user and librarian training is a bigger concern. We have many more products available; some are just repackaging of old services in new formats, but some are really novel and exciting. Even for old products, there are multiple delivery options (dial-up, CD-ROM, print, the WWW). Yes, life was easier when print was our only option. Selection tools were easy to find. User training was almost unnecessary. There were many providers of information, most had been in business for a long time, and could be expected to stay in business in the future. Pricing was simple and straightforward. Ownership of the item was clear and permanent. Sharing (ILL) methods were already established and open to all. Our users knew what to expect and how information would be delivered (in print, on paper). Virtual libraries and 24/7 access to information outside our own libraries were unheard of.

Now we must choose whether to offer information in print, on CD-ROM, or on the WWW—in the library or at the user's desk. The criteria for evaluation of services are very complex and involve knowing about interfaces, random access memory (RAM) requirements, licensing agreements, contract negotiation, and other skills we didn't learn in library school. Using this information isn't "intuitively obvious" (a favorite phrase of a former boss of mine) and requires instruction on each different service. Publishers are merging and diverging at lightning speed; many old, established companies are disappearing entirely, being replaced by dot.com companies and electronic publishers that may be here today and gone tomorrow. Pricing is complicated, and information seems to be more costly than ever. License agreements may make borrowing articles from academic institutions more difficult and maybe even impossible. If we have to purchase information directly from the publisher, you know it will cost more and be more complicated to obtain than an ILL request. Users in the 21st Century expect to be able to get information from the library at their institutions in an instant (or at least within a few hours), at their desks, and at any time of the day or night. Users also expect us to be able to do the same for information not in our libraries or institutions and maybe even from halfway around the world.

If all this isn't enough to boggle your mind, there are some additional issues you should think about. This move to electronic information is going to change the thinking of the whole library world about collections. The number of volumes and journal titles a library has will become meaningless. Libraries will be judged by the breadth of sources they make available to their users. If large academic and public libraries no longer keep large backfiles of journals (or even current issues), what will small libraries do for document delivery, especially if electronic publishers restrict licenses to institutional users? We increasingly must rely on purchasing journals directly from the publisher. This adds time, complications, and most assuredly cost. Membership in multi-type library consortia may become more attractive than ever. What happens when a publisher goes out of business or discontinues a title? We had better hope that some library somewhere has decided to keep that journal in its collection in the old-fashioned but reliable print form. Another issue is that the licensing agreements for these electronic offerings usually are quite complex. Your legal department will get involved, adding another layer to the bureaucracy and another delay in providing access to that information.

There are two other issues to consider when looking at online full-text or Web-based journals as opposed to print: authorship and unauthorized duplication. Authorship concerns the rights of the author to keep from having his work "stolen" and presented under someone else's name. Authorship also can deal with downloading a work, editing it, changing its meaning, and uploading it back to the WWW. Zamparelli (1999) says: "Unauthorized duplication is when the work, or a substantial part of it, is copied and shared without payment to the author or copyright holder. These issues can be dealt with in two ways. We can forbid them by law and then use the technology to enforce the law or we can make it uneconomical or inconvenient so that obtaining a legal copy is safer, cheaper, and has added values." Most copying, or infringement, is not done by computer "pirates," looking for economic gain, but by ordinary people who are merely using the technology for what seems an obvious and "harmless" purpose. Computer hackers also infringe on copyrights just to test and show off their skills but constitute a minority of offenders.

Dealing with Electronic Journals

Electronic journals may be full-text electronic versions of print journals, published simultaneously, or journals available only online, never in print. More and more journals are going online, and there is no reason to expect this trend will stop or even slow down. Acquisition of serials is changing. More and more we are not acquiring but "pointing to" materials. When you cancel a print subscription, you keep the issues you have already received. When you cancel an electronic subscription, however, you usually lose access to both future and past issues because you only leased them. Electronic serials are more complex to buy, receive, access, service, regulate, and renew. The acquisition process is not standardized. Subscription services are only now beginning to deal with electronic journals, and many titles require dealing directly with the publisher. All these factors make more work for the already beleaguered OPL. Steps must be added to the process of acquisition, such as trials and demonstrations, legal review of leases, and installation of required hardware or software. We lease journals instead of buying them. Check-in becomes meaningless and claiming no longer applies. Instead of writing a purchase order, we negotiate a lease. (Our skills in negotiation during the reference interview will serve us well in this new environment.) In print, most subscriptions are "til forbid," that is, they are automatically renewed unless the publisher (or subscription vendor) is specifically instructed to cancel. Electronic journals may have such a clause, but contracts usually run for a set term only. In any case, annual reviews are even more important because lease terms, prices, and formats may and do change. Duranceau (1997) says, "It is no longer sufficient to assume a product purchased the prior year is still the best way to deliver a certain set of information."

As more libraries depend on electronic journals with licensing agreements for authorized users, they may be unable to lend outside that authorized population. Because the major research libraries (ones many OPLs depend on for document delivery) are more likely to have expensive electronic subscriptions, what will be the effect of electronic licensing on the cooperative ILL system libraries have worked so hard to create? Electronic publishing may have a major impact on collections only from about 1980 or so on, but these are the materials borrowed most often. Who is going to digitize the older materials? Publishers are not jumping on the bandwagon, but some major libraries might. Is there a role for private enterprise? Services, such as CARL Uncover, have been doing a good job at providing images over the Internet, but the cost may exceed what small libraries can pay. How will the new electronic copyright legislation being proposed in the U.S., Australia, and other countries affect ILL? Maybe *all* libraries will eventually have to pay copyright fees. Issues such as these ensure there will always be a place for paper copies, but their availability and cost will become problems. Information brokers that are a mere photocopying service are going to get hit badly, unless they specialize in "old" information.

Purchasing Online

It is becoming increasing advantageous to purchase even print materials via the WWW. Amazon.com and the multitude of other online booksellers offer many advantages to the librarian. These booksellers often are less expensive because they have no physical warehouse and often provide fast delivery. But you must make sure that you are ordering online for the right reasons. Because "everyone" is doing it, your purchasing department says you have to, or it is "fun" are not good reasons. Compare the *total* price with that of your old, reliable, low-tech book supplier. Remember to include tax and shipping. Don't forget about the cost to process multiple invoices. This last problem can be solved if you can use a company credit card. (Do not, I repeat, do not, get coerced into using your own personal credit card. If your organization wants you to pay by credit card, management should authorize one for you. Most organizations are slow to repay. A slow response can impact your ability to pay the credit card bill on time and, in turn, your personal credit rating.) If you can't use a credit card, you may have problems using Internet booksellers. Perhaps the vendor can provide a pro forma invoice so that you can use their service. Internet booksellers also may add delivery charges or surcharges. It is only worthwhile to purchase books on the Internet if you buy enough to offset the delivery charge and if the books are less expensive.

Will Internet sellers put traditional vendors out of business? Not likely. In a survey of 80 books, Allen and Miller (2000, 20) found, "The sum total for these 80 books is $273.68 less from the traditional library book vendor than the price offered by the Internet bookseller." Some Internet vendors advertise that they will send you e-mail to let you know when a forthcoming book is available, but the publisher or your book supplier can do the same. One use I make of the big Internet sellers is as a free "Books in Print." It is easy to find a book on amazon.com or barnesandnoble.com; then find the correct title and author, publisher, price, and ISBN number (and even reviews); and then send the information to my regular source for fulfillment. There's even a version of *Ulrich's International Periodicals Directory* (PubList at www.ppublist.com) on the WWW. Although it is neither free nor as complete as the printed version, it is enough for most users and is more current.

FUTURE: WHERE ARE WE GOING?

Smock (1995, B1) has said, "We have been spoiled by the computer on *Star Trek* which instantly answers Captain Kirk's requests." Our customers expected this level of service from the Internet and from us, and they still do. Unfortunately, this *still* is not possible. In 1995, *InfoWorld* writer Bob Metcalfe (1995) predicted the imminent collapse of the Internet due to lack of money and support. The Internet would not prove to be the cash cow some expected. He expected phone monopolies to raise prices, making access economically infeasible. Users would get bored with the Internet and its hype and lose interest. The security, privacy, and censorship issues and capacity problems would overwhelm the system. The impending collapse would be good, dispelling the myth of the Internet that Metcalfe (1995, 61) describes as a "wonderfully chaotic and brilliantly biological and homeopathically self-healing" system and lead to the realization that "it needs to managed, engineered and financed as a network of computers ... " George Gilder (1996) rebutted: "Will the Internet collapse? No Way!" He said that as the internet expands, each new user adds resources as well as using them. This process of growth pushes the Internet service providers (ISPs) to add more capacity and the backbone providers to follow suit, keeping the Internet from collapsing. Gilder expected communications power to grow at least 10 times faster than computing power over the next decade. One remaining obstacle to the fulfillment of the promise of the Internet would be government regulation. Gilder saw this obstacle being removed by the increasing need of business for the Internet and the resulting lobbying of regulators by business.

Well, Metcalfe certainly was wrong. The Internet and its main component, the WWW, has thrived and prospered. E-commerce, although still not a cash cow, is expanding rapidly. Phone charges have decreased and transmission speeds have increased, making access even easier and less expensive. Users certainly have not become bored, thanks to exponential increases in the quantity and variety of offerings available on the WWW. Still, there are serious problems.

Security, privacy, and censorship are major unresolved issues. Capacity problems sometimes cause system crashes. The WWW is chaotic and needs to be managed. However, there has not been, and does not appear that there will be, a collapse. Overall, the system works. Gilder was right about new users adding resources. In fact, this is one of the problems of the modern WWW, that is, the proliferation of uncensored, unfiltered, and uncontrolled sites. ISPs have added capacity far beyond what we could envision in 1996. Government regulation has been sporadic and inconsistent and has done little to hinder the use and growth of the Internet.

In 1996, Sharyn Ladner made this "fearless prediction":

> The Internet is not an end-all and be-all, but a catalyst, because it affects the rate of change. It will either make or break the small special library. If you don't grasp the technology, you will die. If you do run with it, especially if you implement the Internet, you will be viewed as more than a librarian, you will be viewed as a valued member of the company team.

All this is still *very* true. At that same time, I made the following predictions for the future of the Internet (Siess, 1997):

- "Copyright issues will be addressed, but not necessarily settled"—still true.

- "Security issues will be addressed, but hackers can crack security faster than it can be developed so security will always be an issue"—still true.

- "Censorship issues (both pornography and personal use in the workplace) will be addressed but, again, not necessarily settled"—still true.

- "Bandwidth problems may improve, but technology will
  find ways to exceed the improvements and the problems
  will reappear"—still true.

In late 1995, I predicted that if too many non-research/personal
users take over the Net, a parallel, fee-based, research/serious user network may develop, similar to where the Net was a few years ago. In
August 1996, the National Science Foundation announced grants to 13
universities to develop a very-high-speed Backbone Network Service
to connect 100 universities, national laboratories, and other research
organizations (InfoWorld 1996)—the alternative Internet I predicted.
(It's so nice to be right!)

Here are three related issues to consider: electronic myopia, archiving of electronic data, and longevity of electronic information.
Electronic myopia is the name I give to the increasing tendency of people, primarily the young, to discount any information that does not
appear in electronic form. For some, if it isn't in electronic form, it
doesn't exist. Some teachers even require students to use the WWW to
answer questions that could be answered faster and easier using so-
called old-fashioned print resources. If this trend continues, what are
the implications for all data that are not in the form of bits and bytes?
Will this data continue to be produced and find a market? What will or
will not be digitized? Gillies (2000) expected that materials not in
English, in non-Western alphabets, humanities and social science
information, historical documents, and non-word items and artifacts
(such as art, non-contemporary music) will not be digitized, or at least
will be far down in priority. Will an e-book be developed that is easy
to read, inexpensive, and can be taken to the beach or into the bathtub?
Will we throw away all learning before the early 1980s just because it
isn't available or even indexed online?

Next, who is going to make sure that the data we see today on the
Internet are available tomorrow, next week, next month, next year, or
even in the next century? Who is archiving electronic information? At
present, no one is archiving much of the WWW. Lists of uniform

resource locators (URLs) are out of date long before they can be distributed. Even if we create a system for archiving the Internet, who is going to decide what to archive and what to leave out? And most importantly, who is going to pay for this?

Finally, despite manufacturers' claims, we do not know the life expectancy of electronic media. It just hasn't been around long enough. Even if the media and the data survive for eons and eons, will the software and hardware to access the media and data survive? Vendors of these systems go out of business frequently, leaving "orphan" programs. What good is a "permanent" record if it cannot be accessed? Is it economically feasible to periodically convert data to a new system? If it is, who is going to take responsibility for converting data? And again the question, who is going to pay for all this?

WHAT ABOUT THE VIRTUAL LIBRARY?

As managers of technology, we are responsible for implementing new ways of thinking: One of the most common propositions is the virtual library (also called a library-without-walls, cybrary, or library of the future). One of the first such efforts was by Michel Bauwens (1993), who coined the term *cybrarian* to describe his role in the virtual library (see Chapter 6). At BP Nutrition in Belgium he recognized declining financial and personnel support. Bauwens first identified the information needs of senior management. They needed current, accurate, selective information on competitors, markets, and regulations in an attractive, readable, and usable form, and they needed it fast (Matarazzo and Drake 1994). To provide these things, he abolished his paper library, freeing up the time and money it had taken to manage it. He didn't try to compete with analysts within the company (he lacked the time and expertise) but worked with them. Information was seen as the property of the whole corporation, not just the person using or paying for it. Many other firms have done the same thing in the succeeding years, from Lotus Inc. to Ernst & Young, and even perhaps a small library near you. These virtual libraries provide desktop access to newswires, databases, market research, library catalogs, electronic newspapers, internal business documents, and many other services. Document requests are handled electronically and often there is an electronic mailbox for questions. Librarians may not even be located on-site, instead working at home. In-house collections are small or even nonexistent. Collection development consists of evaluating information services, negotiating license agreements and contracts, training, and user support. Reference interviews are conducted by telephone or e-mail, not face-to-face. In fact, librarians often never meet their users.

Many companies and law firms have eliminated paper-based records entirely, relying on computers to store all their files and documents, e-mail for most of their communication needs, and Internet-based databases for all their research. The law may have been the first area to have most of its primary materials available in full-text, machine-readable form, and the law is still a leader in this area. However, many lawyers, law professors, and librarians lament that this has resulted in poorer searching and retrieving of the complicated precedents of the law. Searching for rules or concepts is not what computers are best at doing. The two large online legal database providers, LEXIS and WESTLAW, are beginning to use concept-based systems and natural-language-search interfaces, but these tools do not replace human input (nor can computers replace human input in other fields where causation is important). When we search for information only manually in indexes and print sources, however, we frequently feel we may have missed something. The fact that most people think a computer search is somehow more complete inevitably leads to a false sense of security. (This seems to be especially true among lawyers, doctors, and young scholars of every stripe.)

I leave you with some words of wisdom:

"The information highway is paved with rhetoric, metaphors, and the scar tissue of misinformed executives." (Cisco Systems advertisement, 1996)

"Take a book, remove the cover, remove the title page, remove the table of contents, remove the index, cut the binding from the spine, fling the loose pages that remain so they scatter about the room. Now find the information you needed from that book. This is the Internet." (Michael Gorman, 1995)

"The roads are built by the communications companies. The vehicles are built by the computer manufacturers. The services are built by the content providers. What is the role of the information professional? We provide the signage, the travel guides, the maps and most importantly —the drivers' ed." (Jose-Marie Griffiths, Dean, School of Information, University of Michigan, U.S., 1996)

"In the long run, the only way the Net will rise to its true potential is if librarians become an integral part of the discussion of the Net's future." (R.A. Schneiderman, computer consultant—not a librarian), 1996)

8

Other Issues: Education, Downsizing and Outsourcing, and Knowledge Management

EDUCATION FOR ONE-PERSON LIBRARIANSHIP

I am, for the most part, disappointed in education for librarianship. Yes, I know it is changing. Yes, I know that some schools are doing a great job in preparing students for the real world. However, most could do a much better job. Too many librarians are graduating unprepared for the cold cruel world of work. They have not had enough exposure to the different types of libraries in which they might work. Special libraries and OPL positions are not even mentioned at some schools. How many students know about the opportunities in zoo or prison libraries? How aware are students of the realities of budgets, corporate culture, conflicting demands on time and resources, library boards and committees, the realities of planning and prioritization, the importance of networking and continuing professional education, and rest of the things they don't teach you in library school? How many have worked in a library, other than as a graduate assistant? How many have done an internship or, better yet, several internships in different kinds of libraries? Have students taken courses in business communications and presentation skills? Do they even know how to write an effective memo? Have students had extensive experience in conducting reference interviews, a critical skill most schools only teach about?

Another thing that disturbs me, and many others, is the removal of the word "library" from schools. (I also am very concerned about institutions renaming their libraries "information centers.") The computer people have co-opted the term "information" for what should really be called "data processing." What is stopping us from taking it back? We are the ones dealing with information, and we need to remind our clients and bosses of that fact. Instead of spending time looking for substitutes for the term library, why aren't we using that time to improve the world's perception of librarians? The terms "library" and "librarian" should come to mean state of the art, customer friendly, easy to use, complete, evaluated, reliable, time- and cost-effective, good for business, and indispensable.

When I began my first professional library position, as a one-person librarian, I found myself unprepared for many of the tasks confronting me. This was despite the fact that I had attended the library school ranked number one in the country and had taken courses specific to my work as a science-technology librarian. Unfortunately, I had no experience in interlibrary loan (ILL) or the Online Computer Library Center (OCLC), both indispensable in a small library with very limited resources. I also knew very little about acquisition processes, subscription services, and book jobbers. Although I had not been taught about the need to network with my fellow librarians, my naturally outgoing personality and curiosity led me to do so out of sheer necessity. Techniques for budgeting, managing a library, marketing my library and myself, managing time, and being effective in a large organization were unknown to me. At first, I had difficulty balancing all the demands of being an OPL, which created my continuing interest in how librarians are educated to be OPLs.

As I became active in the Special Libraries Association (SLA) and the SOLO Librarians Division, I began asking other OPLs if they had learned these skills in library school. Most agreed that their education had not adequately prepared them for life in the real world of special and one-person librarianship. Complaints about library education can be traced as far back as 1906 (Rothstein 1985). The nature of the complaints have been amazingly consistent: too little practical training, no education for leadership, educators being out of touch with the needs of the profession, instructors needing to be practitioners and not just teachers, the work not really being at graduate level, and courses being too geared toward public libraries. The debate between theory and practice in library education also has been ongoing for a long time. Some writers insist that the schools emphasize or concentrate on the theoretical background for the profession. However, most realize that a mix of the theoretical and the practical is necessary. Paris and White (1986) discuss the paradox of education versus training; they believe that schools cannot do both. Employers want training; the academics want education.

Despite this history of complaints, very little progress has been made. Increasing numbers of employers deem the Master of Library Science (MLS) degree irrelevant or even a negative factor, especially in the world of business or industry (Cronin and Williamson 1988). St. Clair (1995b, 8) wrote, "Traditional LIS [library and information science] education, as embodied in the MLS degree, is perceived by many practitioners to be out of sync with the demands of the emergent market." Library schools are adding courses to the core curriculum and changing the names of others, but I question whether content and orientation have changed. Cronin and Williamson (1988, 262) write, "LIS schools will need to revise not only their curricula but also their culture if they are to become successful players in this [emerging information] market." Note that he advises them to *become,* not to *stay,* players.

Obviously, the ideal library education program would be a mix of the broad, theoretical basics of information science and the specific, practical tools that will be needed on the job. Most students will not have another opportunity to learn the basics, but they will have opportunities to learn more techniques and technologies. But a purely theoretical education will not produce graduate librarians who are ready to face the real world. Perhaps the solution is to teach the basics, some of the technologies and tools, and then enough learning and reasoning skills so that students know how to find the answers in situations that develop once they are on the job. Students cannot be sure which kinds of libraries they will be working in later, so the school needs to educate very broadly, emphasizing the relevance of concepts to the preferred type of library. Graduates, especially OPLs, need to have knowledge not only of theory and skills but also must be prepared for what they do not yet know. They need to know the questions to ask and how to find the answers to situations that develop once they are on the job.

Another problem is how students select a library school. Most students select a library school based on geography, by a margin of two to one, according to a survey of students and alumni from 12 library schools (White and Mort 1995). Geographic location is *not* the best criterion to use in selecting something as important as education for your future career. However, library students are older (averaging about 35 of age) and are established, with many having jobs and family holding them to a specific area. The problem is a difficult one because library schools are not evenly distributed geographically. In the U.S., there are some Eastern cities that have more than one school, while many Western states have none. Outside the U.S., there are fewer library schools concentrated in a few countries. Students must travel long distances or relocate to attend library school. Many schools have some type of long-distance educational opportunities, usually within their own state; however, educational opportunities usually are offered in limited areas and at limited times.

Library education faces another difficulty because the type of library that students think or plan that they will work in often changes from enrollment to graduation and throughout their careers. In addition, there is very little additional information (such as listings or comparisons of specialties, and courses) available on which to base a decision. On their first job, less than half of the respondents were working in the type of library they expected to be working in when they enrolled in library school. After nine years on the job, nearly 30 percent were working in yet a different type of library (White and Mort 1995). The implication is that library schools need to concentrate more on basic, transferable skills and on introducing students to all types of libraries to give students a general idea of what they need to know for each type.

Are Special Librarians and OPLs Different?

Are special librarians different? Do they have special educational needs? Are OPLs even more different? Special libraries do have several distinct characteristics. They often are *the* library in an organization and, as such, serve all the organization's information needs. The risk exists of the library being closed when the costs of the organization are too high or when the parent organization cannot find enough benefit in the existence of the library.

There are over 14,000 members of the SLA. Not all work in special libraries (some are educators or former special librarians or students), and not all those who work in special libraries are members of the SLA. According to SLA figures, 52 percent of the membership works in corporate libraries. About 60 percent are employed in small libraries (six or fewer employees), with the most common library size being one employee (30 percent to 50 percent of members). The SOLO Librarians Division of the SLA has over 1,000 members, making it the fourth or fifth largest division in SLA, after only five years of existence.

In the report of the Special Libraries Association Presidential Study Commission on Professional Recruitment, Ethics and Professional Standards, chaired by Guy St. Clair, it was pointed out that, "Special librarianship is different from the other branches of the profession and as such requires knowledge, skills, and attitudes that are different from those needed in the other branches of the profession ... The standards for [ALA] accreditation ... are too general to insure adequate preparation for the special library environment." Also, although they may be aware of special librarianship as a career option, many students don't really know what a special library is.

A small library or OPL may have very different needs from a large one. Tees (1986, 191) points out that most studies of special library needs have been made of large libraries and are not necessarily relevant for the more common small libraries. In addition, many management courses assume management of a large library and not OPL situations. Because special librarianship is not emphasized in most library schools, it is more probable that the special librarian did not anticipate being in this situation and may not have chosen to take courses emphasizing skills needed in a special library. As an OPL, the librarian may now be responsible for all areas of librarianship and may not be adequately prepared. As Bierbaum (1986, 2) comments, "In graduate school you may have taken courses in reference, cataloging, serials, conservation, administration and the like, but it probably never occurred to you that you'd be responsible for *all* of those aspects of library work." OPLs assume a managerial role early in or even at the beginning of their careers. OPLs are much more likely to need entrepreneurial and business skills, because they are running their own little businesses.

When I speak with OPLs around the world, I always ask, "What do you wish you had learned in library school?" The most common responses are time management and more on management, corporate culture and office politics, finances and budgeting, and negotiation.

Library schools are doing a much better job of preparing graduates for positions in special and one-person libraries today than they have in the past. However, some issues still exist. Are the right people being recruited for and admitted to library schools? Are we looking for bright, creative, flexible, computer-literate, user-friendly persons who will become the information leaders of tomorrow? If we admit anyone less, we run the risk of dragging down everyone in the profession, including those already in the trenches. It may be unfair to fault library schools for not teaching one-person librarianship, but much of what they do teach is simply not relevant or does not work in a small library.

Recently, Tenopir (2000, 44, 45) wrote:

> More than one-fourth of the [accredited U.S. library] schools, however, do not require courses in the three areas of Information Systems and Technology, Research, and Information Policy .... The overall trend is to reduce the number of required (core) courses in the master's degree programs to allow more individual flexibility and chance for specialization .... Many [schools in the U.S.] are offering interdisciplinary degrees, joint degree or courses with other campus departments. New faculty are bringing new courses and more flexibility.

U.S. library schools, however, are aware of the importance of technology. Following the lead of library programs outside the U.S., such as in Australia and New Zealand, "Forty-five of the fifty-six accredited [U.S.] LIS programs offer some sort of distance-learning program. Options include a degree completely over the Internet, courses offered via interactive television, or faculty travel to off-campus site" (Tenopir 2000, 46). In addition to the MLS, 10 schools in the U. S. are offering an undergraduate major in LIS and 13 schools offer a minor. While this may make entry into the field available to more potential librarians, "students armed with a Bachelor's degree in information science and technology ... may get jobs as Webmasters, technology coordinators, or Intranet managers," possibly competing with MLS graduates (Tenopir 2000, 46).

Library school graduates really need practical experience in a library. Ferguson and Mobley (1984, 177) ask, "Do library school graduates possess the actual skills needed to function in the real world?" Although a large number of students today are already working in a library, the only library experience for some is an assistantship or other work in the campus library while they are in school. Thus, these students have experience in only one type of library, that is, the academic institution. Internships need to be available in a variety of library types: public, corporate, not-for-profit, large, small, and one-person libraries. Students should be encouraged to intern in a library type in which they have no experience or a type different from the one they plan to work in after graduation, when possible, because the first professional position for many is not in the type of library that they wanted or for which they prepared.

Two more issues need to be addressed. It is *very* important that special library courses be taught by practitioners rather than by academicians. Even professors who previously worked in a special library may not be aware of the current issues in the field. At minimum, there should be many guest lecturers in a special library course. Most local chapters of library associations can provide speakers, and few special librarians would turn down the chance to speak to students. Lectures can be done from home or work, using Internet chat rooms or interactive television. I also would like to see more integration of library course work. Cataloging is an extension of reference; customer service is part of library building; abstracting and indexing are related to acquisitions. We need well-rounded librarians who are entrepreneurs and professionals capable of handling all parts of librarianship. As a rule, students take a series of discrete courses and then graduate. We need a thesis, a senior project, a final course, or something that requires students to look at the totality and interrelation of what they have learned. Most other disciplines require such a summing up for a master's degree—how can we ask to be considered equals if we do not? For example, for my master's degree in anthropology, I was required to write a thesis and defend it to a committee of professors, pass comprehensive examinations in all four sub-fields of anthropology—physical, archaeology, cultural, and linguistics—and pass a language proficiency examination. Library schools should ask the same of their students.

We all must take the problem of library education seriously. In life, when we want things to improve, we take the responsibility of envisioning that future and then doing something about it. The same is true for library education. What have *you* done recently to improve things at your alma mater or local library school? Have you gone back to your library school and sat in on some classes to see what is being taught? (If your school is too far away or closed, go to the one nearest to where you work.) Have you volunteered to be a guest lecturer or even an adjunct faculty member? Have you spoken to the student chapter of your professional association? You say that it is too far, you are too busy, or whatever? Nonsense. Using the Internet, you can lecture from a distance. You could go out there on a Saturday or holiday—make it a vacation. Have you been a mentor or hosted an intern? This is a great way to let students find out about one-person librarianship and doesn't take as much time as you may think. Someone already in the profession probably helped you when you were getting started. Repay them by helping someone else. Repaying the debt is personally rewarding and it is a professional responsibility. The future of librarianship lies in the hands of this generation, not the next. *You* can make a better future for all of us. I urge you to get started now.

Finally, the MLS is only the beginning of a librarian's education. Recently, Mickey (2000) wrote, "New hires straight out of library school frequently still need extensive training before they're truly up to speed. Keeping up in this field is a classic case of adult continuing education. Schwarzwalder (in O'Leary 2000) says, "Library school graduates have very little of the skill set that I need. There is also a lack of good training opportunities and I'm really troubled by that." Who pays for this education? In some cases the employer will pay. However, many OPLs do not work for such enlightened organizations and must pay for their own training. If this is your situation, consider continuing education an investment in your future. If there is one comment OPLs make that really makes me angry, it is "If my boss won't pay to send me to the conference, then I won't go." If you are a professional, then you do what is necessary to keep your skills up-to-date. If this means paying your way to a conference or course, then pay. Just because your company isn't smart enough to realize the importance of continuing education doesn't mean you have to ignore it as well. Scholarships are available to many conferences. You can make the trip part of a family vacation. Remember that the information you receive will make you a better librarian; if being a better librarian does not help you on your current job, it will on the next. Cynthia Hill of Sun Microsystems (in O'Leary 2000) says, "People need to recognize that they have a professional portfolio. They take their competencies with them. They don't belong to the organization." Every conference and course I have attended has given me something. I always come away more confident of my abilities or with new information that would come in handy down the road. Continuing education is an opportunity a professional librarian cannot afford to neglect.

Where is this continuing education to come from? Library schools offer continuing education courses, but often they are only or primarily for their own graduates. They are usually only on campus or in a few locations, not exactly ideal for a working professional. Every library association provides continuing education opportunities: at conventions and conferences; through computer-based, self-study courses and teleconferences; and by way of the Internet. However, it is up to the individual to take advantage of these opportunities. A survey done by the SLA showed that 62 percent of SOLOs did not attend the most recent Annual Conference and 70 percent did not attend SLA education courses. However, 63 percent said they had gone to non-SLA courses in the past year (Bender 1994). Another source of continuing education, often forgotten, is training courses offered by library and computer software and hardware vendors. These are often in locations near you, cost little or nothing, are usually only one day, and are nearly always very relevant. OPLs must keep up-to-date by reading professional journals and newsletters and by networking. Often available are in-house training courses; online user groups; courses offered by regional library organizations; non-library sources, such as Toastmasters; and courses in the department of computer science, business, or communications at your local university or community college. If all else fails, you can visit other libraries (both like yours and different) to get ideas.

The U.K. Library Association has a Code of Professional Ethics requiring continuing education, which specifies that "Members must be competent in their professional activities ... [and] keep abreast of developments in librarianship." The Association recommends that four to six working days per year be devoted to continuing education. Bryant (1995, 3) says, "Ironically, the difficulties which solo librarians and information workers commonly experience in attending formal events may encourage them to become more adept at exploiting a wider range of informal and work-based opportunities." What is the end result of continuing education? Continuing education boosts your professional esteem and demonstrates your professional attitude to yourself and to your manager (St. Clair 1987). By participating in continuing education, you empower yourself, you increase your sense of self-worth, you improve your productivity and the value of your services, and you provide the structure for life-long success.

ONE MORE PAIR OF HANDS—OR ONE LESS: DOWNSIZING AND OUTSOURCING

This section deals with how to grow an additional pair of hands and add hours to the clock (outsourcing) and how to cope with losing some of your staff (downsizing). Some people equate outsourcing with downsizing and are afraid of both, but they are not the same at all. *Downsizing* is reducing the number of people working in the library. Many OPLs become OPLs by being downsized from a larger staff; an OPL also can be downsized by losing clerical support. Of course, the ultimate downsizing is cutting all staff and closing the library. In contrast, *outsourcing* is the contracting out of some services, while keeping the library open. Rather than something to be feared, outsourcing can be a boon to the OPL when handled properly.

Downsizing

Downsizing is now a business reality. As librarians, we know that the *real* way to save money is to have more well-trained information intermediaries and fewer expensive end-users doing their own searching for information. But not all managers understand this. Libraries are not alone in being downsized. Many companies are doing away with lower-paid secretaries and having higher-paid professionals doing word processing and photocopying, which makes about as much sense to me as having librarians empty wastebaskets and sweep the floors. But that's the way it is. Many OPLs are concerned about losing their jobs as a result of outsourcing or downsizing of the library. Whereas the existence of a library used to be a given in many organizations, it is no longer seen as absolutely necessary (except perhaps in academia where the library is necessary for accreditation). Corporations, law firms, and not-for-profit organizations are consolidating, merging, and just plain closing their libraries. For instance, in the past, a medical library with a degreed librarian was required in the U.S. for accreditation; however, today, The U.S. Joint Commission on Accreditation of Hospital Organizations only requires access to the appropriate resources, which unfortunately can be accomplished easily without a library or librarian. Even public libraries are not immune to downsizing. Branches close, hours are cut, and librarians are replaced with clerks. All librarians must prove their worth. The closing of a library is always a possibility. You need not worry too much if you are (1) doing a good job and (2) are prepared.

Reasons for Downsizing

Fifteen percent of the organizations surveyed by Prusak and Matarazzo in 1990 had closed their libraries by 1995, and the number is probably higher now. What makes our profession so vulnerable to downsizing, and is there a way to avoid it? Bryant (1995, 7) says "solo librarians are perpetually vulnerable to 'downsizing,' and ignore ... reports of the dissatisfaction of employers at their peril." In a note of hope, St. Clair (1996c) writes that libraries in corporations, law firms, and so on, might be less vulnerable to downsizing because they (presumably) meet specialized needs. However, considering the findings of my own research, I cannot agree. OPLs are especially vulnerable because they are smaller and often less visible.

Cram (1995, 107) has written the following:

Two issues play a critical role in contributing to the vulnerability of libraries to closure or gradual withdrawal of support: the tendency of librarians to market their libraries and library services as a product class rather than as a unique service delivering specific and quantifiable benefits; the view of the library as a cost centre, a vulnerability exacerbated by the tendency of librarians not to take the needs of the accountants and lawyers who manage our organisation seriously.

Sometimes a new management theory can contribute to downsizing. A hot new code word for downsizing is *disintermediation*, which means doing away with the intermediary (you, the librarian) and going directly to the end-users. The increase in use of the Internet has contributed to the comfort level of management with end-user searching. I am not a fan of end-user searching. Do you want your high-priced engineers (e.g., scientists and salespeople) spending their time looking for information on systems with which they are not familiar, using search logic and databases they do not fully understand? It would be better to have (relatively) low-priced information professionals who are well-versed in both sources and methods of searching doing it for them, and in a better, faster, and less expensive way. Because most organizations lack methods to evaluate and value the library, libraries are often seen only as overhead. Management does not understand how libraries can help obtain information (and organize and disseminate it) and thereby increase productivity or profitability, or both. Another problem leading to library closings or downsizing is competition from other departments in the organization who think they can do the work of the library. In addition, outsourcing some library services could lead to contracting out of *all* services.

An organization's attitude toward information is of vital importance to a library's success. If management does not value information, then find a way to change the attitude; if management does value information, then nurture this attitude. The library must understand the stated (and unstated) mission of the organization and the library's role and relationship to the mission: there must be a connection,and the library must be seen as being *mission-critical*. The library must be perceived as supplying information in whatever form is necessary, not just in books and journals. Often, those who have the authority to close or downsize a library are not library users and have no vested interest in the library. Because it is not valuable to them, they think the library is not valuable to anyone.

Another reason for this vulnerability is that special librarians (and librarians in public libraries and academia) have allowed others to fight their battles. DiMattia (1995) writes: "We're waiting for someone else to do the work, wave the magic wand, and give us ammunition to fight the fight on our personal battlefield. We adopted the same tactics with the image issue, asking our professional associations to wage broad-based campaigns to improve the image of librarians." It didn't work, because it is our issue. We have to fight it on a library-by-library basis. DiMattia goes on to say: "Special librarians continually maintain that they don't have the time nor the expertise to conduct research [on the value of the library to the organization] in addition to fighting the daily battles to stay employed." They should make the time, and they must "be integrated in the organization and so well connected to the corporate political strength that you have a vivid understanding of the decisions being made on high. [This is much easier said than done.] The bottom line is to convince corporate managers that even though information may not be their core business, information is at the core of their business and their competitive advantage in the marketplace."

How to Avoid Downsizing

There is no way to guarantee that your library will not be outsourced or downsized, but here are some ideas on how to prevent it from happening. You should be doing these things anyway; if you aren't, then you should start now.

- Rethink what you are doing. Do you provide information to the chief executive officer? Do you know his or her information

needs? Have you made a presentation to the board recently? Find
new roles for the library to replace ones that are obsolete, little
used, or that can be outsourced. "Are you performing duties simply
because you've always done them?" (Wilson and Mount 1997).
Write a mission statement reflecting the strategic objectives of the
organization and promote the mission statement to the organization. Review your procedures. Are you doing your best?

- Think like a chief financial officer. What are the financial drivers
  of the organization? Short-term? Long-term? Where is the organization positioned? What is its market share? Is the organization
  expanding? Which departments are growing? Which are contracting? Which departments are critical to the mission of the organization? Which are profit centers? Answers to these questions may
  tell where the money is, and where it will be in the future.
  Identify the person in upper management who controls the
  library's money and make sure he or she understands the library
  and its advantages (Bates 1997).

- Collect "meaningful" statistics, and make sure they are presented
  to top management, that is, the decision-makers. Include sales
  closed or contracts won because of information from the library,
  the amount you billed back to other departments (costs avoided),
  the time and money saved. Do not include circulation figures,
  size of the collection, interlibrary loans, and so on. Prepare a
  report showing the unique services you can provide that outsourcing may not be able to (such as timeliness, internal control,
  and confidentiality). Librarians often make the mistake of marketing only to users. You must market to the ultimate decision-
  makers. Give them a list of companies that downsized their
  libraries but later reconsidered. Make the library a profit center,
  even if the dollars are just internal ones. Charge back by projects.
  Establish value-added services that other departments are willing
  to pay for.

- Keep your skills up-to-date (both technical skills and business
  skills). Make sure the library looks up-to-date, modern, neat, and

uncluttered. Look at your publicity. Could you insert any library's name in place of yours, or is your library unique? Is it of high quality? Does it adequately convey all the facets of your services? Participating in organizational task forces allows you to demonstrate competencies to upper management. Show that you are a valuable and contributing member of the team.

- Identify key customers that can be your advocates. Make sure they realize that information expertise and knowledge were required to fill their requests; that is, not just anyone could have done what they asked for. Ask users how the information received from the library contributed to their achieving departmental or organizational goals. Be sure to ask not just regular visitors, but also those who rely on the library and those who are in line (revenue-stream, as opposed to staff or supporting) positions, whether or not they actually use the library themselves.

- Make yourself indispensable. Become a guru. Management expert Tom Peters makes several good suggestions: specialize— know a lot about something particular, such as finding business information or patent searching; advertise—become known by networking and talking to other people; get mentors who can give you the confidence to sell yourself, score the points; and be known for accomplishing something or achieve "brand-dom"— make your name synonymous with expertise [or information]. Finally, says Peters (1998, 37): "Shake them up. It's at least as important to be provocative as it is to be right. I have to shake you up to be memorable. To some extent, I'm saying I don't care if you agree with me or not. What I really want you to do is rethink a handful of things."

- Understand the corporate culture of your organization. Mark Estes (in Quint 1996b, 16) says: "If you, the librarian, don't know your world you're a fool. It's the responsibility of any professional librarian to pay attention to their work environment."

- In the spring of 1995, after a very large law firm, Baker and McKenzie, closed its library and outsourced its services, the American Association of Law Libraries (AALL) formed a Task Force on the Value of Law Libraries in the Information Age. The aim was to prepare materials to assist law librarians in explaining their value to their bosses, their clients, and themselves. Because most AALL members work in small, mostly one-person libraries, they have been especially vulnerable to downsizing. Most other library associations have similar resources available—use them.

- Beat them to the punch. Take information to the desktop—before you are asked to. Develop a virtual library—before you are required to. Benchmark library services—before you have to.

Perhaps the problem is that no one in the decision-making upper echelons knows who you are. To increase your visibility, try some of these ideas:

- Write. If your institution has a magazine or newsletter, write something for it: for example, a regular column or a feature article, or anything. If there is no in-house publication, start a library newsletter. Put in it new acquisitions, features on services, your credentials, your philosophy, and interviews with users.

- Submit an article to a professional journal or newsletter and make sure management gets a copy of it. (Don't forget about submitting articles to local or subject chapter publications. They are always looking for material.)

- Make sure your name and the name of the library are on everything that goes out. This is one of the basic tenets of marketing. It is better if the library name is actually on the printout or copy, rather than on an attachment. That way your patron cannot remove the name and present it as, "Look what I found."

- Get and use business cards. If your company will not provide them, have some made yourself. I have seen them as low as

U.S. $20 per thousand at office supply stores. Give them to all
visitors and attach them to all materials that you send out, even
books (see the caveat above first).

• Consider displaying your professional credentials (diploma and
certificates) on the wall of your office and on your business
cards. Doing so will help establish your professional status in the
minds of your colleagues. If you don't have a library degree, display certificates of completion of library-related workshops and
other education.

• If you are called on to become a profit center and generate revenue, consider expanding existing services to new clients, such as
using subscription management software to manage professional
memberships. Sell existing clients new services based on extensions of existing services.

• Disaggregate some services, enhancing and repackaging the
parts. For instance, move from only circulating journals to advertising that you can locate lost or missing issues or articles, or
document delivery service with a new slant. Having users pay
small amounts for some services does not make the library a cost
center. Charging only for added-value services gives the message
that core services are not valuable. Be sure to include capital, collection, operational, and personnel costs in the "cost" of the
library when calculating return on investment. Include intangible
benefits, but relate them to costs or value. However, I warn you
that many times the conversion of a library from service center to
a profit center can be the kiss of death. It is very difficult to
recover all the costs of a library at a price that the users will pay.

Dealing with Downsizing

What can you do if your efforts at downsizing have failed? Guy St.
Clair (1996c) suggests that you be proactive—offer to downsize what
you can (it makes you look loyal and sacrificing). Be sure you know
how downsizing will affect your customers and make management

aware of the effects. You may need to realign information services, make new partnership and alliances, consolidate units, or shed responsibilities. Regarding outsourcing, St. Clair (1996e) says:

1. "Outsourcing is not a dirty word." Outsource the tedium, the out-of-scope, the I-don't-have-time things that you do.

2. "Management's job is to control and to evaluate." It is the job of management to find ways to economize, and it is your job to make sure cutting library services is not the way.

3. "External consultants are in business." They are not the ogres.

4. "Ethics is still important." Beware the consultant that comes in and says you need to outsource the library—to them!

5. "The one-person librarian is the information expert for the organization, enterprise, institution, or community in which she is employed." If management does not see this, it is probably your fault.

6. "Advocacy is not a passive activity." Lobbying is good, library committees are good, and advocates are good.

7. "The grapevine exists." Use it. Know what is going on before it happens, and don't let yourself be blindsided.

8. "When it's too late, it's too late." Once the decision has been made to outsource an entire library function, it is too late for the OPL to do anything. Don't panic. And don't try to fight back. Just go quietly.

Herb White (1984) describes three stages of dealing with a cutback in resources. The first stage is that the condition is temporary and the problem will disappear. Unfortunately, this is seldom true and it usually gets worse. The second stage is that the organization can continue as it has, doing more with less. This rarely works and is counterproductive.

If we *can* do more, then management says we were not working as hard as we could have been. If we *can* make do with less, then management says we had too much. The last stage is that a change in resources requires a reassessment of goals, objectives, and strategies. We must decide on new priorities and how to reach them with the new level of resources. Let your customers know of the changes and their implications and that the library will continue to help them, although maybe differently. Do not fall victim to the temptation to cut back-office services such as cataloging, filing help, and so on. First, cut something that will affect your user, that is, some highly visible service or resource. Drop a major journal or database subscription. Be sure to tell patrons that you cannot provide the information because management felt the service was no longer necessary. If you have to cut, cut something that will affect the users. Bates (1997, 21) advises:

> If you simply absorb the cuts by buying fewer resources, using the Internet rather than a commercial online service (which often saves money but wastes time), or cutting back on professional development, it sends the message to upper management that the library had fat it could cut. If everyone who uses the library sees the curtailed services or is otherwise directly affected by the reduction in service, they are much more likely to be strong advocates for restoring funding to the library.

Doing so is a bit dramatic and a hardship on those whose questions go unanswered but can be an effective way to make a point. But be prepared for the fact that this will not always work. If cost-cutting has been a way of life in your organization, your customers may have had enough experience to just adapt to the cuts and not protest to upper management.

Concentrate on the essentials, delegate what you can, and use partnerships and alliances. Ask, "Why are *we* doing this task?" Is the library the best place for this task, or could someone do it better?

What would be the consequences of letting someone else do it? Is this task integral (critical or strategic) to the mission of the organization? To the mission of the library? What are the costs associated with doing this task? What would be the cost of outsourcing this task? In other words, go down your list of tasks and ask for each, "Is this trip necessary?" Perhaps you can downsize your space. Do you really need it all? Can you weed some books or journals? Can you share resources with another institution? Can you become more of a "virtual" library? St. Clair points out (1996b, 7) that "The delivery of information is not constrained by space."

If it is decided to outsource all library functions, make sure management realizes the consequences. There will be lower levels of service and quality. The advantage of employees who understand the organization, its products, services, and corporate culture will be lost. The outsourcer's staff will not be able to anticipate information needs of the organization in the future, and undoubtedly there will less customized and personalized service. The employees of the outsourcer do not have a personal investment in the library, so there may be a higher turnover and financial incentive to cut services and provide less comprehensive searches. Remind management of the dangers and economic implications of making decisions without adequate information, of opportunities that may be missed and projects delayed.

Not all closings are the librarian's fault. Some are political, some have ulterior motives, and some are just budgetary. But in some cases it is the librarian's fault. The library and information services were not promoted to the right people, the decision-makers, or did not keep up with what was needed. Professional skills were not updated in terms of computer literacy, technical orientation, or business techniques. Our jargon or services did not keep up with needs. The library continued to concentrate on buying and circulating books and journals and not on information, competitive information, and the Internet.

Four Case Studies in Downsizing

Case Study 1: From six to two in easy stages. An OPL at a large branch of one of the top 10 law firms says that at first there were three librarians (a manager, an assistant librarian, and cataloger) and three clerical people. First one clerical position was eliminated, then the cataloger. Then the library manager left. The OPL became the manager-librarian-cataloger, and he outsourced the filing. He was down to one clerical person, a filer. He said, "I don't know what these extra people did! Yes, sometimes I'm stretched but eventually I catch up and the attorneys are super!"

Case Study 2: They did it right, but got downsized anyway. They did everything right. They publicized the library with a logo, a brochure, well-attended open houses, visits to off-site facilities and department staff meetings, new employee orientations, user surveys, and even a special reception for management. Their statistics demonstrated growing usage across all business areas. So, how did they go from a staff of 11 (five professionals and six support staff members) in 10,000 square feet to a staff of two in 2,500 square feet? The fact is you can do everything recommended by library management books and gurus and still not be able to save your library. A library, like the other units in a company, is subject to all the management tools (or fads) of the moment. Downsizing is a way of life in the corporate world and can hit anywhere. The library is neither exempt nor singled out.

Although automation and more efficient procedures led to substantial savings, management was insistent on complete cost recovery (including space at premium rent charges; the cost of all support services provided, such as accounts payable and mail; and even a percentage of administrative costs above the actual costs of the library). The library instituted cuts even without management pressure. When staff members left they were not replaced. The collections were weeded, and library space needs were reduced. Now there were eight (four librarians and four support staff members) in 5,000 square feet. Then came the corporate mandate to all units to "decentralize." They presented a report to top management documenting negative cost and service implications, but it didn't matter. Decentralization was to happen, regardless of cost, service, or anything else. The corporate library was reduced to three librarians providing reference and research services and document delivery through an outside vendor. They moved into a suite of office cubicles. The business groups made other provisions for meeting their information needs.

Two years later, the pendulum swung back. Cost savings was the key corporate objective. Where they had "decentralized," now they "consolidated." Two major collections that had not been part of the original library were added, but when the dust settled they were down to a staff of four (two librarians and two support staff members). A year later, a major business segment accounting for 40 percent of library use moved to another site. The library dropped one librarian and one very capable support person. They manage to keep up with customer requests for information and documents; however, just about everything else falls behind, and outsourcing is still a threat.

Case Study 3: Being Proactive and Anticipating Downsizing. Dan Trefethen (1996) then of TRA Associates in Seattle, Washington, was faced with losing his assistant, who was just finishing up a records management certificate program at the university. Trefethen developed a win-win situation—or at least one that he could live with—a phased-in layoff. He went to his boss, the financial-administrative manager of the firm. He was a bottom-line guy. Like most bosses, he knew nothing substantial about the library. The thing management hates most is for a librarian to dump a problem on them, especially one that costs money they weren't counting on spending. However, the thing management likes most is for their people to come to them and say, "We have an opportunity here to improve your bottom line and the job situation here." Then they listen.

Trefethen told his boss they could cut his assistant, but he just wanted to do it in an orderly fashion. First: Set a target date. Second: Tell the assistant what he needed to accomplish by that time. Third: Decide what he was going to have to *not* do when he was a true OPL. This was the perfect chance to get rid of non-essential tasks. He worked with the departments to reassign some of them to other units that now had more staff. He even exchanged some clerical tasks for information tasks from the other units or for computer upgrades. You might even pick up some projects because of downsizing in other departments, so you will need additional resources to handle them. You offer to fall on your sword (as the Roman Centurions did), because it is not as bad as the alternative. Trefethen (1996) says, "One advantage: the librarian 'mystique.' If they don't really know how you do what you do, they're not in a good position to micromanage you or to critique your downsizing strategy. We always say that knowledge is power. The corollary is that lack of knowledge is lack of power. Use the knowledge to your advantage."

Case Study 4: A Tale of Two Libraries—What's the Moral? In the first case, management hired a consulting firm to study the library. They found only a small core of users. The librarian declined to be involved in the study. The library was closed. No one was too upset, except the librarian. In case two, the librarian heard rumors of a corporate reorganization and went to his prime users with a questionnaire on library services and satisfaction. He followed up on it, raising users' awareness of the library. The library was not downsized, even though every other department was. The moral? You have to be proactive. Don't wait until they come to you. Assume there is going to be downsizing and cutbacks and have a plan (St. Clair 1994).

Final Thoughts on Downsizing

All is not bleak. Downsizing may not be permanent. One OPL's chief executive officer thought eliminating the library could save lots of bucks. Three months later she was asked to return. "A budget cut isn't necessarily forever"—the point is to survive until they realize how valuable you are and restore funding for the library (Bates 1997, 21).

One OPL has been steadily "upsizing" her library for the past seven years. Over the years she's gone from part-time status, with administrative assistant responsibilities, to full-time status, with archive responsibilities. She did this by giving people services they might not have thought they needed. It paid off. Management always knew a library was "a good thing" or she'd have been laid off a long time ago. Management is finally seeing that having information is paying off, and that's been good for the librarian. Thus, you can see that all businesses and institutions do not downsize, but it is important for you to make yourself as essential as possible to management so the value of your position can be seen.

When closing a library, management usually asks, "What do we do with the books?" Instead, management should ask, "What do we do without the service?" (Prusak 1993). When one company I worked for closed my library, someone asked what were the users going to do? I replied, "Without." It is up to us to make sure that management asks the right question and that our users do not have to "do without." By making ourselves indispensable to the organization, keeping plugged into what's going on, being proactive and prepared, and providing the best service possible, we will be doing all we can to avoid the spectre of the ultimate downsizing.

Outsourcing

Outsourcing is a part of business life. Most major corporations now outsource at least some services. There is little chance of change. The trend to outsource will continue as long as there is pressure to cut costs. However, outsourcing, that is, paying someone else to do a part of your job, can be a big time saver for OPLs. What should you outsource? What should you *not* outsource? You must decide which of your services are mission-critical and which can be done only, or best, by you.

There are two kinds of outsourcing: internal and external. You can either outsource work to another department within the organization or to another organization. Both have pros and cons. It might seem safer to outsource internally. But librarians are sometimes criticized for "collaborating with other departments in our organizations that are involved with information delivery and information transfer [outsourcing stuff] that 'by right' should come to us" (St. Clair 1996d, 1). But there should be no problem with internal outsourcing as long as we make sure there is added value; we are just partnering inside the organization rather than outside of it. OPLs have been partnering with our colleagues in the organizations where we work for a long time, and as St. Clair (1996d, 1) has said, "No one-person librarian would dare to think that, as a professional information services employee, he or she should stand alone. Cooperating, partnering, participating in the achievement of the corporate good, is what one-person librarians do."

What about external outsourcing? Some outsourcers approach senior management directly, saying the library is not cost-effective and information services should be outsourced. Managers, in their ignorance, may believe it. The information customer is caught in the middle of this vendor-librarian "fight." The decision is made, not by the customer, not by the librarian, not by the vendor, but by management. "And by the time management has made the decision, it is probably too late to do much about it"(St. Clair 1996d, 6). In other words, if you haven't already sold management on the value of your information expertise, it may be too late.

The question arises as to when you should outsource. The general rules are you should outsource when it is to your advantage, when you can control it, when it can improve service levels at no extra cost, when a contractor would more easily be able to stay current with technology, and when you need expertise not available in-house. Caldwell (1996) says, "What we outsource is not our organization's core business, but it is that of the vendor, who is in a better position to deliver a quality product." Outsourcing can allow you to increase services without adding head count, something management is always trying to avoid. You may not have time to supervise an employee anyway. Outsourcing can also take care of a temporary overload. We all face times when everyone wants something at the same time; outsourcing can help. Outsourcing is also appropriate when you will be absent from the library for a relatively long period of time (for a vacation, illness, or professional development). By outsourcing you won't have to hire a substitute and run the risk of the organization letting you go and hiring the sub. Finally, outsourcing can be a good way to offer a new service with minimal risk. If it doesn't go over well, you can just drop the outsourcer.

What You Should Outsource

Herb White (1984) suggests you try to contract out only clerical or non-professional tasks, but I disagree. Contract out those tasks you do not do well so that you can concentrate on what you do best. If you are not a cataloger, contract out cataloging to give you more time to do the online searching or database building that you do outstandingly. Dr. David Bender, executive director of SLA, suggests four questions to ask before outsourcing (in Quint 1996b, 8):

- "How would outsourcing this function affect the corporate memory?"

- "How would it affect the integrity of our data?"

- "What is the standing and/or reliability of this contractor?"

- "What are the cost advantages and disadvantages?"

"If outsourcing could satisfy one's needs in some way, then there's no reason not to pursue it." But be careful to only outsource non-strategic work, because you do not want to lose control of those activities essential to the institution's mission. The most common library services outsourced are journal subscriptions, document delivery (books and articles), cataloging, and online searching.

Subscriptions

If you take care of lots of subscriptions, either for the library or for the whole organization, you probably need either an assistant or a subscription service. Using a subscription service does *not* save money but does save time. A subscription service costs more, unless you count savings from centralized billing and elimination of multiple subscriptions. One librarian suggested that the yearly cost for handling subscriptions could be the equivalent of one-half of a person, without benefits, if the collection were big enough. Just make sure that when you are figuring the time and cost it will take to do the subscriptions yourself, you also must include the amount of other services you provide that will have to be cut because you are spending time managing the subscriptions. People always tend to sit up and take notice when something they want might be taken away. The big subscription services handle thousands of journals and are set up to do it far more efficiently that you could. They can place the orders, handle address changes, and take care of claiming lost issues. Some will even add routing slips for you. The may have more clout when handling missing issues, claims, and so on, since they purchase many subscriptions from each publisher. This is all done through one phone number and can simplify your life. Of course, if you have only a few subscriptions, it probably won't be necessary or worthwhile. When negotiating with subscription services, know your collection and the needs of your patrons; establish priorities; compare prices and services; negotiate credits and service charges (almost everything is negotiable, and don't be afraid to tell one vendor another offered you a smaller service charge); be open to smaller, no-name vendors; get everything in writing; remember that your first loyalty is to your library; and evaluate the vendor's attitude as well as technical competence. You also should not be afraid to complain to the vendor or even switch vendors when service is unsatisfactory. One caution is that switching vendors is a time-consuming and frustrating process that itself may degrade service in terms of duplicate or lost issues. It should not be done just to save half of a percentage point in service charges, but only as a last resort.

Document Delivery

Document delivery, both of photocopies and books, is at best a time-consuming and mind-numbing job. Why not pay someone else to locate the items, arrange payment, and ship them to you? If you have access to a good ILL network (such as a local consortium or OCLC) or a large public or university library nearby, you may be able to handle most document delivery yourself. But is it worth your time? Are the copyright fees taken care of? A good document delivery service can handle your needs with just one phone call (or e-mail or fax), leaving time for what you do best (or at least better). It may not be much more expensive than ILL. More and more libraries are charging $10 to $15 per filled request, and document delivery services often charge as little as $15 to $20. Most article delivery services will mail or fax documents directly to your patron, but it may be better to have documents sent to you. In this way, you will know when they come in and you can put your name on them so that your patrons will remember who got the documents for them. In choosing a service, be sure to compare turnaround time (which should be one to two days), price (around $15), quality (clean, straight, and no big black margins), ability to get international documents, and payment of the royalty fees. Remember that the total cost, including royalties, is what is relevant. Communication is also important. Will the vendor keep you informed? If you ask for something "rush," you need to know very quickly if it can be delivered in time. If it cannot, you can go elsewhere or at least tell your customer there will be a delay. Remember that not all services provide the same level of service.

Using a book jobber can save you time, money, and aggravation. Let someone else place the orders and deal with short or lost shipments. Jobbers also may get—and pass on to you—discounts that you could not get on your own. You also have only one point of contact to worry about. I calculated that using a jobber gave me 20 percent more free time each day. Some jobbers also pay the shipping costs as well, additional savings that mount up very quickly; remember it is the total cost that counts, not only the discount. You do not have to prepay the jobber as you would a publisher. Therefore, if a book is not published until six months after you order it, you are not out the money until you receive it. Accounting departments love this. They also like the consolidated monthly bill you can get—you pay only one vendor, once a month. Don't forget to evaluate the service of the vendor and if you aren't happy, try another.

Cataloging

The most often outsourced job is cataloging. If you like cataloging, are good at it, and have the time, then by all means do it. But find someone else to do it if you don't like it, aren't good at it, and don't have the time. That could be OCLC, your book jobber, the state library, or a colleague. Many OPLs outsource cataloging. (I did.) Anderson and Pawl (1979, 274) say: "Don't waste time and money on original cataloging and processing in a one-person library .... Your time will be much better spent serving a user." You can save time and money and not hire a cataloger. A cataloging service can maintain quality and consistency of cataloging better because the service does it all the time and can afford the training to keep up-to-date. Some services can prepare the book for the shelf (pockets, call numbers, and even property stamping). However, you usually need to send items away, which can be expensive and delay availability to customers. Finally, there is the cost of the service. Only you can determine if the positives outweigh the negatives.

Online Searching

You can use outsourcing to add expertise that you don't have. If you have a project that will require a lot of detailed chemical searching, but you aren't a chemist, why not outsource those searches to an expert chemical searcher? The expert will do it better than you could, making your patron happy and, indirectly, making you look good. But most librarians feel, and rightly so, that this is the most professional and most valuable of their services and that this is the one service they should retain in-house. It should be outsourced only to add value or as a last resort.

Sometimes outsourcers (consultants or firms) are asked to bid on projects without the approval (or even knowledge) of the librarian or the current outsourcer. Although it is done, it is not ethical. It also is not a good idea for outsourcers to do this, because if they treat their current information provider this way, can you expect to be treated better? This may be the reason for the real (or perceived) adversarial relationship between librarians and vendors. We constantly demand more from our vendors, just as our customers are asking more of us. However, librarians and vendors must understand each other's business needs. We cannot squeeze their margins so tight that they go out of business. Doing so isn't good for either party. Assuming you like their service, it is in your best interest to keep your vendors in business. If they go out of business, you get *no* service.

Besides vendors, you may find yourself working with information brokers. James Dobbs defined an information broker as "one who collects a fee for acting as an intermediary" (LaForte 1982, 84). Information brokers can serve the same purpose as the vendors mentioned above, giving us more expertise and time. Many librarians are afraid to use information brokers because they challenge some basic library assumptions concerning the role of the library in society: that we might become expendable; that information is being sold when it should be a free right; and that "free" libraries will be abused by brokers and other for-profit institutions and individuals. When used judiciously and only for special projects or services, however, information brokers can be valuable additions to our OPL bag of tricks. Information brokers can do many things: document delivery, subject bibliographies, online searches, translations, data collection, primary and secondary market research, abstracting and indexing, writing and editing, library setup, library evaluation, providing current awareness reports, and locating experts. Eiblum (1995, 22) says, "Working in partnership with librarians, information brokers can provide the *product*, allowing the librarian to focus attention on the *client* .... " That is, after all, what we were hired to do.

In summary, outsourcing is not the be-all and end-all of one-person librarianship. Appel (1996) advises: "Stay in close touch with your users so you know the quality of [work] done and your users know that you have access to additional and different info. Depending on the business you're in you will find one service suits you better than another." You need to constantly re-evaluate outsourcing. What made sense to outsource last year may not make sense today. For example, at one time I outsourced all journal subscriptions. It made sense when I handled all the subscriptions for the entire company (over 350 subscriptions). But later, when I had fewer library subscriptions, it became more trouble than it was worth. Some managers objected to the service charge and having to pay for next year's subscriptions out of this year's funds. At least two vice presidents said to me, "What else do you do down there besides screw up my subscriptions?" (How was I to know when they ordered a certain journal that they already had a subscription. They were now getting two copies and blamed me.) It had become a lose-lose situation. The best I could possibly hope for was that all subscriptions would arrive on time, all the time—not an event having a high probability of occurring. Because I was getting no glory, only grief, for doing the subscriptions, I returned this task to the departments. This example illustrates the importance of continual re-evaluation of outsourcing.

KNOWLEDGE MANAGEMENT

Knowledge management currently is one of the most-often-heard terms in librarianship and management. Is knowledge management just the latest buzzword, a passing fad, or here to stay? What is knowledge management? How does it affect the OPL?

What Is Knowledge?

We all know of the trilogy of data, information, and knowledge. Data are the raw materials—the names, numbers, and simple facts. Information is the organized and rational presentation of data, often with some analysis or selection, or both. Knowledge is, according to Thomas Davenport (Davenport, DeLong, and Beers 1998, 43), one of the knowledge management gurus, "information combined with experience, context, interpretation, and reflection." In other words, knowledge is information ready to be put to use.

What Is Knowledge Management?

Marianne Broadbent (1997, 24–25), educator and consultant, says that knowledge management is "the purposeful management processes which capture often personal and conceptual information that can be used for the organization's benefit. [It] is a form of expertise-centered management focusing on using human expertise for business advantage." The purpose is to deliver value to the business. Nigel Oxbrow and Angela Abell (1997) of TFPL Ltd. in the U.K. say:

> Knowledge management is the art of making creative, effective and efficient use of all the knowledge and information available to an organization—for the benefit of clients. Its implementation requires a review of the organization's values, culture, infrastructure, and management of intellectual assets. Knowledge management is a new focus on information and knowledge, creating a knowledge-valuing environment, where information is shared, managed and used.

The important features of knowledge management can be summarized as follows:

1. Knowledge management is purposeful, not random or accidental.

2. Specific, funded processes are in place to capture organizational knowledge.

3. Human, experiential, tacit information is captured that otherwise would be lost.

4. The information is used, not just collected.

5. The information is used to increase the organization's competitive advantage.

Knowledge management is a very hot topic as I write this book. Whether it will still be hot and called knowledge management when you read this, I don't know; however, the principles of knowledge management always will be important. Some of the factors that make knowledge management important are the globalization of markets and the economy, the presence of increasingly rapid change, customers' demanding more from organizations, a more mobile workforce and the change in employer-worker relationships, and the availability of technology to aid in knowledge management.

Oxbrow and Abell (1997) wrote that the core of the knowledge proposition is to create value. The specific objectives of knowledge management include increasing competitiveness; responding quickly to change; improving decision-making; leveraging intangible assets; and reducing risks, costs, and duplication of effort. The success of a knowledge management project can be measured by an increase in the resources assigned to the project, an increase in the content and usage of knowledge, and the project becoming part of the organization and not dependent on particular individuals. Jay Liebowitz, Professor of Management Science, George Washington University, said that success is relative. Progress, not a quantitative target, is the ultimate goal. Evaluation focuses on cost of missing or under-utilizing a business opportunity or avoiding or minimizing a threat. Another way to make a knowledge management project a success is to link the project to economic performance or industry value such as money saved or earned; indirect benefits, such as cycle time and customer satisfaction; operational improvements, which may be limited to a particular process or function; economic benefit; or competitive advantage.

Measuring the value of knowledge management is a new concept; however, measures are absolutely essential, and the process of measuring itself has value. Everything can be measured, but you may have to be creative. Oxbrow and Abell (1997) suggest two kinds of measures: those that relate to where you want to be and intermediate measures along the way. However, measures are tools and are only worthwhile if they lead to action.

Which Skills Are Required for Effective Knowledge Management?

Judith J. Field (SLA 1997) said that knowledge management requires a creative or innovative information specialist who becomes known as the expert in internal as well as external data sources, the monitor of technical standards, and the person who can make use of his or her ability and experience in training users on information systems. Oxbrow and Abell (SLA 1997) said that you must add to this a knowledge of the business, the ability to communicate and to be a team player, confidence and a willingness to take risks, a mastery of information technology applications and tools, negotiation skills, and an understanding of internal and external information sources. Nicholson (SLA 1997) put it this way. "Knowledge managers must know about information technology, industry or subject knowledge, information management, value-added skills (analysis/synthesis, of information) training and skills transfer, teamwork, communication and interpersonal skills, change management."

What Are the Consequences of Not Having a Knowledge Management System?

Lewis Perelman (SLA 1997, 61–62) wrote, "The essential 'worst practice' is ignorance. And the costliest, most disastrous ignorance commonly is not simple lack of information—it is a dynamic, devious force that shrouds decisions from reality." Unfortunately, dynamic ignorance often is built into overall system-corporate architecture. Mike Bonaventura of Sequent Computer Systems (SLA 1997) said that the usual pattern in an organization is that there is no commonly held mode for knowledge creation and dissemination, no process or systems to support it, and no metrics or systems for evaluating and measuring it. Oxbrow reminded us that a good knowledge management system enables an institution to avoid excess costs, duplication of effort, mistakes and their repetition, wasted time, and missed opportunities. R.M. Taylor (SLA 1997) called this organizational amnesia. Organizations fail to retain knowledge acquired and lessons learned in the past and the people who had the knowledge leave and no retrievable record remains. This results in sub-optimal decision-making, failing to capitalize on potential new initiatives, restriction of the growth and development of the organization, and the over-use of some knowledge resources.

How Does Knowledge Management Require Changing of the Corporate Culture?

Knowledge is a cultural product, created through human interaction. Therefore, Bonaventura (SLA 1997) says that we need to "Create a culture where individuals are encouraged, if not given incentives, to share knowledge. The essence of knowledge management is connection and collection." Both connecting people with information and connecting people with people are important. The organization must encourage sharing and use of information and enable conversion of information into knowledge. Constraints or barriers to this process include the following:

- Time (pressure to get it done quickly, not necessarily collaboratively)

- "Knowledge is power" syndrome (no rewards for sharing, rewards for what you know, not what you accomplish)

- NIH ("not invented here") or a reluctance to consider non-traditional ideas

- Lack of coherent knowledge vision and leadership

If the corporate culture isn't suitable, no knowledge management project can succeed. You don't need to change the entire corporation at once. If you start in one area and are successful there, other departments will want to adopt your approach.

To succeed, make sure all stakeholders buy into and commit to knowledge management. An important tactic is quick wins. Focus on the impact of knowledge management on the business and emphasize quick, visible results to make participants feel good. International cultural differences also impact the implementation of a knowledge management system. Knowledge management in the U.S. is more technology-driven and process-driven. In Asia, knowledge management is more about interaction of people, in teams. Europe is in the middle, being more into the culture of knowledge management, facilitating change rather than forcing it (Young 1998, 21).

Who Is Doing Knowledge Management Now?

At the time this book was written, most formal knowledge management projects were being done in large corporations and consulting firms such as Cooper & Lybrand and Ernst & Young. Also on the forefront were firms in the oil, pharmaceutical, financial, chemical, high technology, manufacturing, and public-governmental sectors. These firms may have the following characteristics: they are global, they do a great deal of research and development, they are regulated, they are highly competitive, and they need fast decisions in rapidly changing markets. However, informal knowledge management programs and initiatives using parts of the process, but not called knowledge management, were being implemented in many smaller organizations.

Few knowledge management projects involve librarians and even fewer have librarians as their leaders. Oxbrow (Oxbrow and Abell 1997) said that knowledge management is more than traditional librarianship and that the instigator of a knowledge management project is unlikely to be the librarian. This may have been true in the past, but there is no reason it should be true now or in the future. Librarians have the skills to lead knowledge management initiatives. All we need are the will and the opportunity.

Broadbent (1997, 30, 32) says:

> Knowledge work emphasizes the use of professional intellect in activities which use individual and external knowledge to produce outputs characterized by information content. If your work can be or is totally routinized, then you are an administrative worker, not a knowledge worker. If you describe what you do as organizing things for others to access, you come close to being an administrative worker rather than a knowledge worker.

Stephen Abram (SLA 1997, 180) of Micromedia Limited in Canada reminds us, "Our core mandate is not to create data, but information about data (metadata)." He adds, "I believe this is a higher-level calling in the knowledge continuum." We already operate at a higher level than knowledge management; we are "key catalysts" in the knowledge continuum. Michael E.D. Koenig (1997), Dean Emeritus, Graduate School of Library and Information Services, Dominican University, Chicago, Illinois, (SLA 1997, 196) put it this way: "If the management of knowledge and intellectual capital is a continuous iterative process then it needs continuous management attention." Librarians need to be a key part of the team that provides that continuous attention.

In a sales presentation, one knowledge management vendor emphasized that the knowledge management process should not become too automatic. It still must involve human input and thinking on such issues as how to categorize knowledge, what each item means, and why it is in the repository. Who better to provide that input than librarians? At the European Business Information Conference in 1998, Ellen Knapp, Vice Chairman and CKO of Coopers & Lybrand, predicted, "As organisations sort out their technology and cultural issues they will then realise the true value of information skills—and information specialists are going to get rich very soon." (Or at least more valued and noticed.)

Can a One-Person Librarian Do Knowledge Management?

Of course you can. In fact you are probably doing some knowledge management already.

- Do you have the skills? If you are a successful OPL, you probably already do. If not, you can learn them.

- Do you have the desire? Are you ready to be an active participant in a knowledge management project? Do you have the commitment and confidence? This is something only you can decide.

• Do you have the time? You'll find the time if you really want to do it.

• Is your organization ready for knowledge management? Make sure you really understand the corporate culture and structure. See below for the decision criteria.

Is Knowledge Management for Everyone?

No, knowledge management is not for everyone. There are some organizations in which a knowledge management project will not work. Coccia (1988, 32) gives an example: an organization "that thrives on control and exists in a constant state of crisis." Broadbent (1998, 34) added:

> Some organizations act as though their major competitors are other parts of their own organization rather [than] external firms or agencies. This is often reinforced by reward systems that focus on individual performance only, despite the fact that the organization might espouse notions of 'empowerment' and 'team based work groups.' Where [this] feudal model is prevalent, justification processes would not accommodate decisions about the needs of the whole organization, rather than that of its specific parts ... [whereas a monarchist or federalist organization with a more extensive infrastructure is more suited to knowledge management.] ... If the cultural soil isn't fertile for a knowledge project, no amount of technology, knowledge content, or good project management practices will make the effort successful.

Should you try anyway? Davenport, DeLong, and Beers (1988, 53) caution us: "Evangelistic knowledge proponents can have some effect, but they will probably be both happier and more successful if they take a different job in a setting that already has a knowledge-friendly culture." In other words, if your organization does not have the proper orientation, approach knowledge management at your own risk. You might want to ask the following questions before starting a knowledge management project:

- Does the corporate culture support knowledge sharing?

- Are people rewarded for sharing?

- Do the knowledge workers have the tools to support sharing?

- Where are the centers of information?

- Are the people who created these centers still at the company?

- Is there a high turnover of knowledge workers?

- Do people trust information from others?

- Are people admired or frowned on for sharing knowledge?

- How do people find experts when they have questions?

In the final analysis, knowledge management is not just another management fad. It is not going to go away. We need to know what it is and how we can contribute to it. Then we need to let others know what we can do and have the confidence to go out and do it.

9

The Future of One-Person Librarianship

This chapter first looks at what people are saying about the future of librarianship in general, then about the specific future of the one-person or one-professional library. Closing the chapter are my own observations and expectations.

Before speculating about the future of librarians, there is a basic question that Raitt (1994, 275) stated well: "Will librarians still be around in 2024, and if so, what are they likely to be doing?" Do teachers, doctors, or lawyers ask this about their profession? Of course not. I don't understand why we librarians continue to question our continued existence. Is it because information is becoming more available or because librarians are insecure? It is probably more the latter (insecurity) than the former (the threat of technology). As discussed earlier in this book, librarians have a historically poor self-image, which leads to more introspective questioning of the future than is probably either necessary or healthy. But, because the question has been asked, this chapter will try to provide some answers.

TECHNOLOGY

We librarians cannot overestimate the impact technology will have on our future. The greatest impact may come from client-server technology providing information at the desktop, with graphics, sound, and video; in full text with copyrights taken care of; from databases of internal documents; and by way of personalized news updates—all available from anywhere in the world to anywhere else. There is the ever-present danger of techno-lust, that new is always better than old, the future is always better than the present. There is a tendency to assume that any and all improvements are worthwhile. In addition, there is always the nerd's cry of "Gotta have it now."

The library must add value along with the technology, not just add the technology, lest it be overwhelmed. Prusak (1995) points out four steps to bringing new value to the organization:

1. Decide whom you want to help and choose them with care; find clients with a clear need for information and who value information, and abandon universal service.

2. Get to know those in the group well and use their vocabulary; people don't know what they don't know and may be reluctant to admit they don't know, especially to junior staff.

3. Figure out what information would add value for them.

4. Learn their concerns and mission-critical projects, and build core services and products to serve them. Read what they read.

In addition, we have another decision to make. How do we deal with technological change? A computer industry analyst (Stear 1997, 80) has said that librarians have two choices:

1. "Manage the change created by the Information Revolution. Move from the role of processor to become a process manager."

2. "Resist change if you believe that your skill as an intermediary searcher is invaluable. Stand your ground if you can be the lowest cost provider of this service. There are still some highly skilled craftsmen who can repair typewriters."

At the American Library Association Midwinter Conference in January 2000, the Library and Information Technology Association discussed the top technology trends for libraries—Y2K. Here are some of their predictions for our future:

1. We will soon be working with the Internet, not against it.

2. We will make progress in finding our role in the world of "ubiquitous electronic information."

3. We will find that a major trend will be convergence—a blurring and even dropping of the line between us (librarians) and them (our users).

4. We will be involved in more partnerships with those outside of the library world.

5. We will see that privacy will continue to be an issue, but a greater issue will be libraries learning to make the best use of our electronic data while still maintaining patron privacy.

6. We will need to educate ourselves about e-books because they are not going to go away.

A decade or so ago some experts confidently predicted a paperless society. What happened to it? Information has been moving to electronic form for years, first to CD-ROM (still widely used), then to dial-up services (which still have a place), and now to the World Wide Web (WWW). I am sure that even more technologies will appear in the future. However, all the various forms of information—including paper—will continue to exist side-by-side with the new. Each improvement adds to, rather than replaces, the old.

Paper will persist for several reasons. Acid-free paper remains the best archival medium, accessible to all without added technology. Even if e-books become inexpensive and user-friendly, some people will still prefer paper (for its disposability, smell, feel, or a myriad of other reasons). (I, for one, will not be impressed with e-books until I can take one into the bathtub without fear of destroying it if I drop it into the water.). At the National Online Meeting in May 1995, Vance Opperman, president of West Publishing, said:

> There is no doubt that some print publications should disappear. Those that are used primarily on a paragraph-by-paragraph basis (ready reference, dictionaries, and statistics), whose probable use is less than 10 percent of the whole over its life (back runs of little used serials, government documents, and conference proceedings), and those for which delays in publication outdate the information (consumer and price guides and financial information) are probably best done electronically—but not everything.

Technology must be seen and designed as just another tool to solve problems, not an end in itself, leading us only to find new ways to use new technology. We must weigh the costs, benefits, and impact on users of any proposed innovation. We should rethink the entire service, not just automate it (and only automate what is improved with automation). Crawford and Gorman (1995) also identify a potential problem with an all-electronic library, the danger of losing perspective. If we only look at pre-selected topics (the ones in our computerized profile, online newspaper, or custom alert), we may not get a well-rounded view of the world. (For example, who would choose Bosnia as a keyword? Very few, but most of us will at least glance at the headlines about it.) The researcher runs the risk of only finding the material available online. If it hasn't been indexed, it becomes invisible. The researcher also may make document retrieval decisions based on what's available online in full-text rather than what will present a well-balanced view of the issues. There is also the danger of "The Young Scholar's Peril." The Young Scholar will define a field so narrowly and search so restrictively that he or she will miss important research. He or she will spend so much time keeping up with new postings in this area that there will be no time to organize, analyze, and synthesize all that constitutes original research.

In 1988, Riggs and Sabine asked library leaders to predict what libraries would be like in 1998. We are just past this date, so let's see what has become of their predictions:

- School librarians will be more involved in teaching. This has come true, as it has become true of public librarians and special librarians.

- More in-house databases will exist. True, but many are not physically in-house, but on the WWW.

- More and more computers will be networked together. True.

- More full-text periodicals will be available electronically. True, but there are probably not as many as they expected.

- More people will access the library from home. This has come true, but even more access information on the WWW rather than their local library. Many customers of special libraries access the services of their organization's library at the desktop, and the number is increasing every day.

- Libraries will be connected by fax machines. This is true, but more and more inter-library communication is done by e-mail these days.

- More multimedia will be available. Boy, is this true!

- Artificial intelligence will be used for searching. This isn't true yet, but many companies are working hard on developing usable search engines using artificial intelligence.

- Basic reference questions will be answered by technology, making reference more of a reader's advisory function. This hasn't happened yet and does not seem to be looming on the horizon.

- Public librarians will serve as advisors, more like special librarians. Increasingly, this is being seen as an appropriate role for public librarians but is not universal yet.

- Document delivery will be done online. This is true in some cases but is not the rule and definitely is not happening as fast as our customers would like.

- More active research will be done by librarians for a fee. More and more public and academic libraries are developing fee-based information services, and more and more special libraries are charging in-house customers for their services.

Riggs and Sabine (1988) also asked what library users would be like in 1998. Their respondents predicted the following:

- The client will expect materials from anywhere in the world available instantly. This is true, especially for users of special libraries. Unfortunately, this ideal service is not available yet.

- More library education will occur in public schools. This varies widely, both in the schools and in other organizations. Librarians still need to make sure that their customers understand which services their library can provide and how to use them most effectively.

- Users will have raised expectations. This is most definitely true, thanks to the WWW.

- Users will be more adept at using technology. Younger and more affluent users are very techno-savvy, but older and less affluent users have not really had the opportunity or access to develop these skills. It remains our job to educate our users.

- Users will be more visually oriented. This is especially true of younger users.

Finally, the question was posed as to what the impact of technology would be. They forecasted the following:

- Productivity will increase. This is partly true. Technology helps us do things faster, but we are also asked to do more things. Overall, it is a draw.

- New job responsibilities and positions will be created for librarians. This is increasingly true, especially in corporate libraries.

- Technology will not result in reduced staff but in the creation of more positions. This is not true for most of us who find downsizing a constant threat.

- Too much emphasis will be placed on technology and not enough on results. Unfortunately, this too has come true.

- Finally, less physical contact with our users will occur. This is increasingly the situation as we deliver more services to remote users by way of the Internet, intranets, and the WWW.

Some people think the future is already here. Clare Hart (2000, 169-170), CEO of the newly created information giant Factiva, said:

> Today's online librarian has shifted from being the sole source of knowledge to really managing the process by which people, user[s], gain and apply that knowledge. The entire information culture has become much less controlling in nature and now resembles a more open-access, free-range environment. It is the librarian, acting in many important capacities, who plays the pivotal role in bringing these impressive knowledge networks to internal and external audiences. The librarian is seen, and respected, as the Knowledge Professional who steers their organizational efforts, exerting a great deal of influence on the creation, development and management of network content and

delivery. It's not just how much you know, but the relevant value of what you know that is the truest measure of information quality. Once again it is the trusted librarian who will protect and define that quality standard, ideally before it ever becomes an issue for end-users.

Although I know we all hope that this will actually be true for all librarians, I don't think this is true—yet.

THE LIBRARY OF THE FUTURE

In 1998, the BUSLIB-L electronic list asked for predictions about the library collection of the future, circa 2002. Some expected it to be nearly all electronic. ("We won't need to store much in paper. Some internal publications will also be stored in digital form.") Many reference materials will be in electronic form, especially business, science, and engineering. Others are not as optimistic about a virtual future. ("It may be 30 years or more before everything will be electronic.") Nearly everyone agrees that print will still be needed, however. ("We are still going to need books and periodicals, only far fewer, we will be 'just in time,' not 'just in case.'" "We will still want to purchase books on current, hot topics but their life will be less than 5 years.") Historical information and physical and artistic collections will most likely still be in traditional forms. Those libraries heavily dependent on such information may not change much.

In regard to customer service, there were many expectations that the user will not have to come to the library at all, relying on Internet, telephone, and e-mail access. Reference books are definitely candidates for replacement by electronic versions. There will be an increasing demand for international materials, and they will be increasingly available as a result of networking and online access.

The physical library may change, with more offices or "privacy spaces" where librarians can consult with clients confidentially. It will be "computer-heavy," existing more as a space for people to meet, space for training people how to search, an exciting—but not necessarily a quiet—place. The library will become more of an archival or records management function, will need significant space for training users, will have less need for clerical workers, and will have a greater need for techno-savvy librarians.

In 1996, Michael Gorman focused on three aspects of the library of the future, that is, the madness—a network of human and electronic resources available in only one form, that is, electronic; the reality—the library as a place with or without walls, influenced by money or the lack of it, requiring us to do more with less; and the dream—a library freely available to all, staffed by skilled professionals, marked by local and national cooperation, intelligently using technologies old and new, with free access to remote resources. In their book, *Future Libraries: Dreams, Madness, and Reality,* in the section on "Deconstructing Dreams of the All-Electronic Future," Crawford and Gorman (1995, 87) questioned the vision of all data-information-knowledge being on line and universally available; everyone being able to make effective use of this data and happy to pay; and copyright problems being solved as "irresponsible, illogical, and unworkable." Libraries as physical entities will not cease to exist, nor will print. The authors also pointed out the dangers of the "Enemies of the Library," which include enemies within, such as the suicidal librarian (those who call themselves information specialists and library managers without library educations), and doomsayers among library school faculty (predicting the death of print and removing the word "library" from the name of the school). "Librarianship will die if librarians and library educators kill it off" (1995, 107). Also on the enemies list are those who deny or minimize the professionalism of reference librarianship; those who encourage users to develop the research skills needed to replace the librarian, that is, assuming that they even want to do so; and the new barbarians who believe that facts are all that are important, not knowledge, organization, or preservation.

In an article in *Library Journal,* Schement (1996, 35) saw the threat coming from another direction: "In the long run, the decline of community threatens librarians most severely. However, the information society is evolving away from the traditional notion of community." The library of the future must first teach *mediacy skills* (a term coined by Toni Carbo, who defined *mediacy skills* as literacy plus knowing where to find information plus knowing what to do with it). Next, the library should be put in every household (by way of television, the Internet, reference resources, and mediacy services). Finally, new communities of the 21st Century should be built, that is, virtual communities. Thus the library turns from a territorial institution to a functional institution. Libraries must act decisively; talk with other libraries, museums, schools, and media; develop alliances because "not only do librarians have a great stake in the information society, but all of us as citizens have a great stake in the success of libraries" (Schement 1996, 36).

Much of what is predicted is based on false assumptions. Libraries never were the primary source for up-to-date information. First there were newspapers and then television for that. In the past, people used to buy more books; however, recent trends show that bookstores are booming and more books are sold than ever before. If information becomes totally electronic, public libraries may or may not be obsolete because people will still need a place to go. In addition, electronic data will not replace the library's role in preservation of information and culture for future generations. Remember also that there is no ultimate library or patron because "different libraries and different library users have different needs and problems" (Crawford and Gorman 1995, 130). Finally, the importance of "and" not "or" is stressed. Adopt the new, but keep the old: print *and* electronic communication, linear *and* hypertext, mediation *and* end-user access, collections *and* access, library as edifice *and* interface.

FUTURE ROLES OF THE LIBRARIAN

The only thing that we can count on in the future is that it won't be the same as the past or the present. The only thing constant in life is change. If we keep doing what we did yesterday, we, as librarians, will be passed over, made obsolete. Guy St. Clair (St. Clair and Berner, 1996) wrote:

> I love librarianship and all it stands for, and I am quick to say to any young person who comes to me for career advice that librarianship is the best of all careers because it can engage you intellectually while you are being of service—truly of service—to others. But I also tell them that it is a career in which everything changes. It always has and it always will, and they must be willing to deal with change throughout their careers. That, in a nutshell, is what's exciting about librarianship.

What Changes Might We See in Our Roles?

As information is seen as a commodity, organizations will want to decrease their information acquisition costs. Librarians can serve as central purchasing clearinghouses, eliminating duplication, negotiating contracts, advising on the best providers, and so on. (Note that I wrote "seen as a commodity," not "becomes a commodity." Non-librarians often do not realize that the interface, ease of use, reliability, and product service of an information product or source are just as important—and in many cases more important—than the information itself. We, of course, have known this all along.)

Another effect of the commoditization of information is that librarians must market their services as products following "the same product development process that commercial vendors do" (Corcoran, Dagar, and Stratigos 2000, 34). Marketing in all its various forms will become increasingly important in the future.

More and more of us will be working outside of libraries. Whether in an organization or on our own, the location of a librarian in a physical library may be unnecessary and, in some cases, undesirable. In the corporate sector, librarians are moving out of the library into the business units, working alongside other professionals to provide the information needed for informed decisions right at the point of the decision.

D. Scott Brandt (in O'Leary 2000, 22) says that, in the future, our new roles may not be "itemized in job descriptions and obtained through training regimens. Instead, 'new roles' must be understood as attitudes, aptitudes, and approaches, as a set of capabilities that can be quickly and effectively applied to whatever new need or opportunity arises. These new roles are harder to define, to acquire, and to apply, yet they are and will be more important to the survival and success of librarians than anything to which a position announcement can be attached." We may even have to unlearn some old roles and rules.

How we react to change says a lot about our future position in society. Ferguson (1996, 10) urges "librarians [to] take off your black arm bands, stop the funeral dirge, cease the endless wringing of hands, stop sounding the death knell of collection development, stop moaning about the end of librarianship as we know it today. We are all going to be busier in the future than in the past." Mickey (2000, 7) says, "Pay attention to the changes, stay flexible, and be proactive about the role [we] play in the information environment." Users will need even more guidance through the "chaos" of the Internet, because it is continually changing. Collection development will take more time because digital materials need more evaluation than do books. The safeguarding of intellectual property will be more complicated and require more technical competence. Ferguson (1996, 89) said, "Our shelves may be digital, but the work of filling them and keeping them filled continues to be complicated and important. Job security for the information professional is assured." Cataloging will still be necessary. It will be a long time before machines can replace indexing done by a trained professional who is familiar with the information needs and information-seeking behavior of the potential users. Ten years ago, Quint (1991, 59) said, "The good librarian defines performance by a service ethic to clients." There will always be a need for good customer service, and we are the experts in customer service. To survive, we librarians will need to carve out a specific niche based on our own unique competencies. More importantly, we will need to demonstrate the value of these competencies to those who employ us.

In 1995, *Working Woman* (1995, 40) magazine predicted that the career of corporate librarian would be one of the 25 hottest careers: "The explosion of on-line research is sure to sustain demand for well-trained information specialists." Already the job descriptions in library want ads are changing. More and more employers are looking for technical skills such as proficiency in computers and networks, Internet, intranet, Web site creation, and even e-commerce. Innovative and entrepreneurial skills also are sought after by library and corporate employers. There has been some concern that the "best and brightest" graduates of library schools are taking jobs outside of the traditional library sector—at startup Internet companies and computer technology firms. While it may be true that some graduates are doing this, I question if they are the " best and brightest." I personally think that it is quite bright to go into traditional library work. And who is to judge that they are the "best?"

The definition of what librarians are is evolving from mere clerical drudges or question-answerers to highly trained, technically competent, service-oriented information advisors. There may be little room in the future for the stereotypical little old lady with a bun and clunky shoes. Merry (1994) said, "Those librarians who continue to focus primarily on acquisition and distribution of information ... will likely be absorbed into other functions ... or be increasingly relegated to the sidelines of an exciting business environment."

Partnering or team-building skills will become even more vital in the future. In the corporate world, one promising partnership is in knowledge management or creating in-house expert networks. Partnering is increasing outside the for-profit arena because librarians are increasingly required to work as part of research or project teams in organizations, participate in clinical rounds in hospitals, and support teams of attorneys working on large involved cases. In the electronic future, the librarian's world will become wider. St. Clair and Berner (1996) focused on "insourcing," which emphasizes the relationship between the information professional and the quite possibly narrowly defined customer base. The librarian is no longer a "support" function, but a critical member of the team. (Another term for insourcing might be partnering or even just good one-person librarianship, because what we try to do is bond with our users and tailor our services to their needs.)

We cannot aim low. Merry (1994) noted that in the organization of today the chief information officer (CIO) usually is an IS/MIS/IT (computer) person. This position should actually be called the CTO, or chief technology officer. The CIO should be a librarian or an information professional. Some librarians have already made it to the top. Librarians are now bank vice presidents (Carol Ginsburg at Bankers Trust, now Deutsche Bank, New York, New York), partners in consulting firms (Trish Foy at PriceWaterhouseCoopers, Stamford, Connecticut), and confidants to chief executive officers (CEOs) (Lisa Guedea Carreno at Highsmith, Fort Atkinson, Wisconsin) (in Buchanan 1999), to name a few. This will be a hard sell, but it is how we *all* should envision our role in the future and labor to make it so.

THE FUTURE FOR SPECIFIC TYPES OF LIBRARIANS

The special librarian is also predicted to survive. Ferguson and Mobley (1984, 177–178) wrote, "We believe there will be librarians operating in the future [and] we firmly believe that the special librarian can make a more successful transition to the future than any other type of practitioner in the profession." These authors feel that the librarian of the future may be more of an intermediary, packager, or interpreter of information than he or she is now.

The Fifth Information Innovator's Institute, held in 2000, focused on the role law librarians would play in law firms in the next five years. The participants found that the added value of being current has diminished—become a given—and the new added value is in linking information from diverse sources to save lawyers' time. This linking system

1) must be a masterable, integrated system; and 2) must contain a built-in, transparent system "to link words, concepts, and ideas from a variety of disciplines" (Shaffer 1996, 5). For example, if an attorney enters the administrative code section dealing with a specific type of drug, the system should automatically generate links to medical journal articles about related research. Another finding of the institute was that we have moved from computer systems designed, implemented, and maintained in-house to ones purchased off the shelf or located on the Internet and accessed from around the world. Because we no longer have to spend time developing the products, we can now focus on content (information) instead of technology. Shaffer (1996, 5) says, "The law librarian of the future is not merely a passive information manager; the law librarian [can be] a key knowledge creator." Finally, while the idea of the physical library may now be "an antiquated idea" in the future, the library will still serve as "a source of organized, authenticated, user oriented information."

Medical librarians are already moving out of the library and into the future. One example is clinical librarianship, where the medical librarian receives special, accelerated medical training and then becomes a part of the patient team. The librarian accompanies physicians on rounds. Equipped with a laptop computer, a wireless modem, an Internet connection, and access to medical databases, the librarian can often provide instant answers to clinical questions. When the answer cannot be found immediately, the librarian returns to the library (or his or her desk or cubicle) and engages in a lengthy search, delivering the answer (not raw data or articles) to the physician within hours.

The small public library is also changing and will continue to do so. More emphasis is on non-print collections (videos, CDs, and DVDs). Access to the Internet is both a boon and a bane. The public library is probably the best institution to offer Internet access to the person who does not own a computer, but cost and content are big problems. Who will provide the technology? Who will train all the librarians on the new hardware, software, and services? Who will make time for librarians to keep up-to-date on all the Web sites that the public will ask about? (Is the average citizen going to understand when he or she sees a librarian surfing the Internet on duty?) I don't see any end to the filtering debate in the near future. Public librarians will continue to be caught between a dedication to access and the public outcry for deletion of "objectionable" information. (I do not envy them at all.) The new services will bring more patrons to the library, creating expansion pressure. Fortunately, networking may help by enabling patrons to access the library from the comfort of their own homes. Libraries are already seeing this phenomenon among students doing research for papers (Leibovich 2000).

What of academic libraries? Gillies (2000) asked, "Will the university library still exist in 20 years?" In what form? As a unit of the university, a unit of a nation-wide university, or as a private entity (franchised out, perhaps to an international publisher)? If the library is franchised, will there be access to information from all publishers? Academic libraries face most of the same issues as do public libraries, namely a changing collection, costs, training, and remote access. Will the library be able to afford all this electronic information? However, as referral centers and de facto archives, there is one big additional challenge. What is going to be done about preserving the knowledge of the present (and past) for future generations of scholars? As more and more information goes online in the form of Web sites, electronic journals, and now electronic books, who will archive it? Who will catalog and index it? And who will make it available to the public?

Gillies (2000) says, "Information provision [could] become a momentary [and monetary] thing, rather than the product of diligent collection over the ages." He concludes a bit more optimistically, saying, "I am sure that many physical libraries will survive as places of scholarly refuge, dedicated to social learning [by this he means students studying together rather than accessing the library remotely and independently] and collecting items that do not easily digitize ...." This is not a bad future, I think.

THE FUTURE OF ONE-PERSON LIBRARIANSHIP

Back in 1986, Guy St. Clair was confident that one-person librarians (OPLs) would continue to exist and their numbers would increase. He predicted that in the future there would be more interaction among OPLs and more literature written about them. This has all come to pass. The Solo Librarians Division of the Special Libraries Association (U.S.) grew in 10 years (1991–2000) from 100 to over 1,000 members and was, in the year 2000, the fourth largest of SLA's 28 divisions. OPL or solo groups have sprouted in Australia, Germany, Israel, the U.K., and who knows how many other countries. Books about OPLs have been written in the U.S. (by Berner, Williamson and Siess), in Germany (by Peeters), and in Australia (by Dartnall). Many articles about OPLs have appeared in the library literature around the world, and some have even been seen in the non-library press (such as the profile of Highsmith's librarian and her CEO—"The smartest little company in the world"—in *Inc.*). These trends will only continue.

Instead of OPLs being downsized out of existence, it is likely that more will be created. Some of these, unfortunately, will be from the downsizing of larger libraries. Many more, however, will come from the realization that information is absolutely necessary for an organization's success and that a trained information professional, that is to say a librarian and not a computer person, is the best one to handle this responsibility. To quote St. Clair (1987, 267), managers "will find that they get more value for their money by employing one highly skilled and effective librarian/information specialist instead of a team— however small—of generalists who are not as skilled" and "there is also recognition in the profession that one-person librarianship just might become a standard for library staffing in the future. [Often] one excellent, efficient, and enthusiastic librarian or information specialist is preferable to two or more who do not provide the same level of service for users." Although there have been drastic changes in the information climate since he wrote those words, the desire for good library service and good information delivery has not changed. Because of the following, the OPL more than ever is able to serve an organization's information needs with little or no assistance:

- Advances in technology, including networking, electronic information available online or on the WWW at little or no cost (in money or time).

- Concentration of librarian resources on mission-critical functions and outsourcing or elimination of non-essential services.

- Increasing capability of users to find answers to non-complex questions, or, for law librarians, attorneys using electronic resources to do their own legal research, thus allowing librarians to focus on business, medical, or international issues.

- Better training and education for librarians, in general, and OPLs, in particular.

- A heightened sense of "professional self-worth and organizational allegiance" by OPLs, accompanied by more attendance at continuing education events and increased interpersonal networking and establishing of professional cooperative relationships.

We will, of course, continue to have challenges. The idea that "everything, for free" is on the Internet is an obstacle we all have to face. We must show our patrons that they have only found the tip of the iceberg and the rest is in "professional databases," which we can help them navigate. Rhea Austin, 1996–1997 Chair of the Solo Librarians Division, said, "A real, live librarian can provide more information than they already have." A second major challenge is downsizing. "We need to show our management how invaluable we are so we will not be downsized right out the door." We have a responsibility to those who follow us—to help newcomers find out how great it is to be an OPL. "If we do our best, we can have a very rewarding future!"

Mary Ellen Bates (1997), a consultant and author in Washington, D.C., believes "that the future of solo librarians is very positive. Solos are in the front line of the battle for the hearts and minds of information consumers—they can run lean and mean operations within their organizations to educate, consult with, and provide in-depth research for the professionals within their organizations." Their roles will be to teach consumers how to shop around and select the most appropriate information resources, train them in the most cost-effective search techniques, and support them when they need more complex research done that goes beyond the capabilities of the end-user's search tools. Sometimes it is difficult to give up some of the online searching—this is the part that many OPLs enjoy the most. But in handing over the basic tools to library patrons, OPLs can build their jobs into that of information consultant and guru instead of information gofer. And remember, patrons will still come back when they find that they're not finding what they want ... and they have a much higher appreciation of the information gathering and analysis skills of librarians as a result.

MY VIEW OF THE FUTURE

I said in *The SOLO Librarian's Sourcebook* (Siess 1997) that librarianship would increasingly depend on technology. This is still true. In fact, technology will probably be even more important than we can imagine. Therefore, we must be sure we become the masters of technology, rather than letting it dominate us. We must ensure we do not let it co-opt our role in the transfer of knowledge (just as the computer people have co-opted the term information.) We need to find a way to get information back where it belongs—in the library. Because it is unlikely that our current or prospective employers will jump to train us in the new technology, it remains our responsibility to find, obtain, and—all too often—pay for this training ourselves.

We must realize that we are the only ones who can make our own future. We are responsible for our destiny. The computer or the Internet will not be able to answer every question, will not replace the human touch, cannot greet the user with a smile, cannot enjoy the thanks of a grateful customer.

To make the future come out the way we want it to, we must:

1. Decide where we are now.

2. Decide what we want our future to be.

3. Figure out what it will take to get us there.

4. Prepare a plan.

5. Implement the plan.

It is clear that to remain part of the information mainstream, we must change our roles and become information and knowledge leaders, facilitators, mediators, and advisors. No longer will it be enough to be passive information providers; we will have to take a proactive role in promoting information services and the importance of our role in the process. Our educational system will have to change so that library schools produce graduates who meet the needs of their future workplaces, whether in a traditional library or not. We must change our image with the public. We must quit demanding respect and begin earning it by our actions.

It is almost certain that in the future there will be more OPLs in corporate and other institutional settings and probably even in public and academic settings. Some may see this as a bad thing, but I see it as an opportunity for those of us who enjoy working alone. To succeed, however, we need to have more contact and interchange among OPLs. Networking is now and will continue to be imperative for survival. Fortunately, networking is getting easier every day. There are multitudes of electronic discussion lists. Organizations serving OPLs are growing and beginning to cooperate. For those in developing countries, networking is even more important. Therefore, it is incumbent on experienced OPLs to establish and maintain mentoring relationships with OPLs elsewhere so that they will no longer feel unprepared and alone. We can also communicate to library students, prospective students, and those new to the profession the joy of working in a one-person library and increase the odds that they will find productive and enjoyable employment.

Note that I use "we" throughout these thoughts. None of us can sit back and wait for the future to happen—for "them" to make changes. We all have to take an active part in making the future happen the way we envision it. We need to have the right education, the right attitude, and the right image. We need to make sure that not only are we are experts, but that we are experts in the right things. We need to have the breadth and depth of knowledge required by our employers, customers, and society; we also need to make sure that they know what we have to offer. We have to convince them that we are the best (maybe the only) ones to help them meet their goals. We must position ourselves to become an indispensable part of their business plan. Then, and only then, will we not have to worry about the future. Then, and only then, will we be paid what we are worth. Then, and only then, will we become full partners in the worldwide information process.

As the Hebrew sage Hillel said, "If I am not for myself, who will be for me? If I am for myself alone, what am I? If not now, when?" We must be for our profession and ourselves. No one is going to do this for us. But we also have to be for our customers, because that is our mission. And there is no tomorrow—the future is now!

Organizations

Some of the most important sources of information, guidance, and help for one-person librarians (OPLs) are organizations, both library and otherwise. Organizations are almost always happy to answer your questions or send you information, whether or not you are a member. (Of course, they will be more helpful to members.) Here are lists of useful organizations in the U.S., Canada, and other countries, along with their addresses, phone numbers, e-mail addresses, if available. They are arranged alphabetically within the following categories:

• Especially for OPLs

• General Library Organizations

• Specialized Library Organizations

• Law Library Organizations

• Medical Library Organizations

• Church and Synagogue Library Organizations

• Other Organizations

• Alternative Careers

ESPECIALLY FOR OPLs

Australia

One Person Australian Libraries (OPAL), a special interest group of the Australian Library and Information Association (ALIA); membership in ALAI is required to join OPAL; see ALIA listing for more information; Web site: http://www.alia.org.au/sigs/opals.

Germany

OPL-Kommission-fur One-Person Librarians, part of the Verein der Diplom-Bibliothekare (VdDB) and Berufsberband Information und Bibliothek (BIB), c/o Regina Peeters, Europaisches Ubersetzer-Kollegium, Kuhstrasse 15-19, 47638 Straelen, Germany; voice: 02834-7158, fax: 02834-7544, e-mail: euk.straelen@t-online.de, Web site: http://homepages.uni-tuebingen.de/juergen.plieninger/vddb-opl/, Electronic list: send e-mail to majordomo@izn.niedersachsen.de, "subscribe opl".

Mexico

Check out http://www.enbiblioteca.com, the Web site of a group of special librarians, mostly OPLs, based in Monterrey, Nuevo Leon. You can also contact Lic. Reymundo Juarez Jimenez at reyjuarez@hotmail.com.

United States

Solo Librarians Division, a division of the SLA; membership in SLA is required to join the Solo Division; see SLA listing for more information; Web site: http://www.sla.org/division/dsol.

GENERAL LIBRARY ORGANIZATIONS

International

Association of Libraries & Information Bureau (ASLIB), Information House, 20-24 Old St., London EC1V 9AP, England, voice: 44-(0)71-253-4488, fax: 44-(0)71-430-0514, Web site: http://www.aslib.co.uk. This is an association of libraries, not librarians, but it has an excellent journal, *Managing Information*. There is a One-Man Band interest group, but it has been inactive in recent years.

International Federation of Library Associations (IFLA), P.O. Box 95312, 2509 CH The Hague, the Netherlands, voice: 31-790-314-0884, fax: 31-70-383-4827, e-mail: ifla@ifla.org, Web site: http://www.ifla. org. Division of Special Libraries, Hans-Christooph Hobohm, Chair, e-mail: hobohm@fh-potsdam.de.

Australasia
Australian Library and Information Association (ALIA), P.O. Box E441, Kingston ACT 2604, Australia, voice: 61-02-6285-1877, fax: 61-02-6282-2249, e-mail: enquiry@alia.org.au, Web site: http://www.alia.org.au. The ALIA holds a Specials, Legal and Medical conference every other year.

Library and Information Association of New Zealand (LIANZA), Level 8, Petercorp House, 86 Lambton Quay, Wellington North, New Zealand, 04-473-5834, Web site: http://www.lianza.org.nz. There is a Special Libraries & Information Services (SLIS) group that is quite active, also a northern (Auckland) branch of SLIS and New Zealand Law Librarians Group (NZLLG).

Canada
Canadian Library Association (CLA), 328 Frank Street, Ottawa, Ontario, Canada K2P 0X8, voice: 1-613-232-9625, fax: 1-613-563-9895, Web site: http://www.cla.ca. The CLA is to Canada as the American Library Association (ALA) is to the U.S., but they do have a special libraries division (Canadian Association of Special Libraries and Information Services [CASLIS]).

United Kingdom
Institute of Information Scientists, 44-45 Museum Street, London WC1A 1LY, England, voice: 44-(0)171-831-8003, fax: 44-(0)171-430-1270, e-mail: iis@dial.pipex.com, Web site: http://www.iis.org.uk. As of Fall 2000, a merger with The Library Association is planned.

The Library Association (LA), 7 Ridgmount Street, London, England WC1E 7AE, voice: 44-(0)71-636-7543, Web site: http://www. la-hq.org.uk. This is the UK's equivalent of the American Library Association (ALA). Of interest to OPLs are the Industrial & Commercial Libraries Group (many are OPLs), Health Libraries Group, Special Libraries Committee, and School Libraries Group.

Library Association of Ireland, 53 Upper Mount Street, Dublin 2, Ireland I-619000, voice: 353-(0)65-21616, fax: 353-(0)65-42461, e-mail: lai@iol.ie, Web site: http://www.iol.ie, Academic & Special Libraries Section.

Scottish Library Association (SLA) and Scottish Library and Information Council (SLIC), Scottish Centre for Library and Information Services, 1 Jon Street, Hamilton, ML3 7EU, Scotland, voice: 44-(0)1698-458888, fax: 44-(0)1698-456899, e-mail: sla@ liberator.amlibs.co.uk or slic@liberator.amli8bs.co.uk, Web site: http://www.slainte.org.uk.

United States

American Library Association (ALA), 50 E. Huron Street, Chicago, Illinois 60611-2795, U.S.A., voice: 1-800-545-2433, Web site: http://www.ala.org. ALA is the major library organization in the USA. It is dominated by public and academic libraries, but within the Public Library Association (PLA) there is the Small & Medium Sized Libraries Division.

American Society for Information Science & Technology (ASIS&T), 8720 Georgia Avenue, Suite 501, Silver Spring, Maryland 20910-3602, U.S.A., voice: 1-301-495-0900, e-mail: asis@cni.org, Web site: http://www.asis.org. Formerly just ASIS, the society has a split personality—half information science (e.g., citation analysis) and half practical management and searching.

National Federation of Abstracting and Information Services (NFAIS), 1518 Walnut Street, Suite 307, Philadelphia, Pennsylvania 19102-3403, U.S.A., voice: 1-215-893-1561, fax: 1-215-893-1564, e-mail: nfais@nfais.org, Web site: http://www.nfais.org.

Special Libraries Association (SLA), 1700 18th St., NW, Washington, D.C. 20009, U.S.A., voice: 1-202-234-4700, Web site: http://www.sla.org. SLA is the major voice of special librarians in the U.S. and Canada and perhaps in the world. Divisions of interest are Solo Librarians and Library Management. There are also major subject divisions such as Science-Technology, Museums-Arts-Humanities, Legal, and so on.

Others Worldwide

Italian Library Association, Assoociazione italiana bilioteche (AIB), c/o Biblioteca nazionale centrale, viale Castro Pretorio 105, I-00185,

Roma, Italy, voice: 39-6-446-3532, fax: 39-6-444-1139, e-mail: aib@aib.it, Web site: http://www.aib.it.

Library and Information Association of South Africa (LIASA), P.O. Box 1598, Pretoria 0001, Republic of South Africa, voice: 27-012-429-3061, fax: 27-012-429-2925, e-mail: ferrenm@alpha.unisa.ac.za, Web site: http://www.imaginet.co.za/liasa. The unification of the South African Institute for Librarianship and Information Science (SAILIS) and the African Library Association of South Africa (ALASA).

SPECIALIZED LIBRARY ORGANIZATIONS

South Africa
Gauteng & Environs Library Consortium (GAELIC), Johannesburg, Web site: sunsite.wits.ac.za/gaelic/gaelic_home_page.htm.

Organisation of South African Law Libraries (OSALL), Web site: http://www.sunsite.wits.ac.za/osall, also has a list and newsletter.

SABINET, Web site: http://www.sabinet.co.za. Although organized for interlibrary loan (ILL) and database access, SABINET also organizes events for information professionals.

Special Libraries & Information Services (SLIS) group, Web site: http://www.specialibraries.org.za/slis, has its own electronic list and newsletter.

Special Libraries Interest Group (SLIG), a Cape Town–based interest group, Web site: http://www.specialibraries.org.za/slig.

LAW LIBRARY ORGANIZATIONS

American Association of Law Librarians (AALL), 53 W. Jackson Boulevard, Suite 940, Chicago, Illinois 60604, U.S.A., voice: 1-312-939-4764, Web site: http://www.aallnet.org.

British-Irish Association of Law Libraries (BIALL), 26 Myton Crescent, Warwick CV34 6QA, U.K., voice/fax: 44-(0)1926-491717, e-mail: susanfrost@compuserve.com, Web site: http://www.biall.org. uk. International Association of Law Libraries, c/o Marie-Louise Bernal, Secretary, P.O. Box 5709, Washington, D.C. 20016-1309, U.S.A., e-mail: mber@loc.gov, Web site: http://www.iall.org.

Lex Mundi: A global association of 143 independent law firms, for the exchange of professional information about local and global practice, 1800 West Loop South, #1880, Houston, Texas 77027-3211, U.S.A., voice: 1-713-626-9393, e-mail: lexmundi@lexmundi.org, Web site: http://www.hg.org/lm.html.

National Federation of Paralegal Associations, P.O. Box 33108, Kansas City, Missouri 64114, U.S.A., voice: 1-816-941-4000, fax: 1-816-914-2725, e-mail: info@paralegals.org, Web site: http://www. paralegals.org/home.html.

New Zealand Law Librarians Group, Web site: http://www. knowledge-basket/co/na/nzllg.

PIUG, Patent Information Users Group, Web site: http://www. piug.org. "An organization of individuals having a professional, scientific or technical interest in patents."

MEDICAL LIBRARY ORGANIZATIONS

Association of Academic Health Sciences Library Directors (AAH-SLD), c/o Joyce Welch, HAM-TMC Library, 1133 M.D. Anderson Boulevard, Houston, Texas 77030, U.S.A., voice: 1-713-790-7060.

Canadian Health Libraries Association, P.O. Box 94038, 3332 Yonge Street, Toronto, Ontario, Canada M4N 3R1, voice: 1-416-485-0377, fax: 1-416-485-6877, e-mail chla@inforamp.net, Web site: http://www.med. mun.ca/chla.

European Association for Health Information and Libraries, Secretariat, Plompetorengracht 11, 3512 CA Utrecht, the Netherlands, voice: 31-3-261-9663, fax: 31-30-231-1830, e-mail: eahil-secr@nic. surfnet.nl, Web site: http://www.eahil.org (U.S. membership available through the Medical Libraries Association [MLA]).

Medical Libraries Association (MLA), 6 N. Michigan Avenue, Suite 300, Chicago, Illinois 60602, U.S.A., voice: 1-312-419-9094, fax: 1-312-419-8950, e-mail: info@mlanet.org, Web site: http://www. mlanet.org.

CHURCH AND SYNAGOGUE LIBRARY ORGANIZATIONS

American Theological Library Association (ATLA), 250 S. Wacker Drive, Suite 11600, Chicago, Illinois 60606-5834, U.S.A., voice: 1-888-665-2852 or 1-312-454-5100, fax: 1-312-454-5505, e-mail: atla@atla.com, Web site: http://www.atla.com.

Association of Christian Librarians, P.O. Box 4, Cedarville, Ohio 45314, U.S.A., voice: 1-937-675-3799, e-mail: info@acl.org, Web site: http://www.acl.org, worldwide organization.

Association of Jewish Libraries, 15 E. 26th Street, Room 1034, New York, New York 10010, U.S.A., voice: 1-212-725-5359, e-mail: ajl@jewishbooks.org, Web site: aleph.lib.ohio-state.edu/www/ajl.html, worldwide organization.

Catholic Library Association, 100 North St., #224, Pittsfield, Massachusetts 01201-5109, U.S.A., voice: 1-413-443-2352, fax: 1-413-442-2352, e-mail: cla@vgernet.net, Web site: http://www.cathla. org.

Church & Synagogue Library Association (CSLA), P.O. Box 19357, Portland, Oregon 97280, U.S.A., voice: 1-800-542-2752 or 1-503-244-6919, fax: 1-503-977-3734, Web site: http://www.worldaccessnet.com/~csla, annual conference, publications, local chapters; CSLA affiliates: Church Library Council (Washington, D.C.), Church & Synagogue Librarians Fellowship (Baltimore, Maryland), Pacific Northwest Association of Church Librarians, Congregational Librarians Association of British Columbia, Church Library Association (Toronto, Ontario), Lutheran Church Library Association, and Catholic Library Association.

OTHER ORGANIZATIONS

American Association of Museums (AAM), 1225 Eye Street, NW, Washington, D.C. 20005, U.S.A., voice: 1-202-289-1818, fax: 1-202-289-6578, Web site: http://www.aam-us.org.

American Association of School Librarians (AASL), 50 Huron Street, Chicago, Illinois 60611, U.S.A., voice: 1-312-944-6780, e-mail: aas@ala.org, Web site: http://www.ala.org/aasl.

American Translators Association, 225 Reinekers Lane, Suite 590, Alexandria, Virginia 22314, U.S.A., voice: 1-703-683-6100, fax: 1-703-683-6122, Web site: http://www.atanet.org.

American Zoo and Aquarium Association Librarians Special Interest Group (AZA/LSIG), 7970-D Old Georgetown Road, Bethesda, Maryland 20814, U.S.A., voice: 1-301-907-7777, Web site: http://www.aza.org.

Art Libraries Society, North America (ARLIS/NA), 329 March Road, Suite 232, P.O. Box 11, Kanata, Ontario, Canada K2K 2E1, voice: 1-800-817-0621, fax: 1-613-599-7027, e-mail: arlisna@lgs. neet, Web site: http://www.arlisna.org.

Art Libraries Society (ARLIS/UK and Ireland), 18 College Road, Bromsgrove, Worcestershire, B60 2NE, England, voice/fax: 44-(01)1527-579298, e-mail: sfrench@arlis.demon.co.uk, Web site: arlis.nal.vam.ac.uk.

Association of Mental Health Librarians (AMHL), Web site: http://www.mhlib.org.

Council on Botanical and Horticultural Libraries, c/o John F. Reed, Treasurer, New York Botanical Gardens, 200th Street and Southern Boulevard, Bronx, New York 10458, U.S.A., voice: 1-718-817-8705, ext. 8729, e-mail: jfreed@nybg.org, Web site: http://www.huntbot. andrew.cmu.edu/CBHL/CBHL.html.

International Association of Music Libraries (IAML), Archives and Documentation Centres, Web site: http://www.cilea.it/music/iaml.

International Association of School Librarianship (IASL), Department. 962, P.O. Box 34069, Seattle, Washington 98124-1069, U.S.A., fax: 1-604-925-0566, e-mail: iasl@rockland.com, Web site: http://www. hi.is/~anne/iasl.html.

Music Library Association, Bonna J. Boettcher, Executive Secretary, Music Library and Sound Recording Archives, William T. Jerome Library, Bowling Green State University, Bowling Green, Ohio 43403-0179, U.S.A., voice: 1-419-372-9929, fax: 1-419-372-7996, e-mail: bboettc@bgnet.bgsu.edu.

National Association of Government Archives & Records Administrators (NAGARA), Bruce Dearstyne, Executive Director,

College of Library & Information Services, University of Maryland, 4105 Hornbake Building, South Wing, College Park, Maryland 20742-4345, U.S.A., voice: 1-301-405-2001, fax: 1-301-314-9145, e-mail: bd58@umail.umd.edu.

Society of Competitive Intelligence Professionals, 1700 Diagonal Road, Suite 600, Alexandria, Virginia 22314, U.S.A., voice: 1-703-739-0696, fax: 1-703-739-2524, e-mail: info@scip.com, Web site: http://www.scip.org. *The* organization for competitive intelligence, chapters throughout the U.S. and in other countries, too.

Society of School Librarians International, Jeanne Schwartz, Executive Director, 19 Savage Street, Charleston, South Carolina 29401, U.S.A., e-mail: sbssteve@aol.com, Web site: http://falcon.jmu.edu/~ramseyil/sslihome.htm.

Theatre Library Association, The Shubert Archive, 149 W. 45th Street, New York, New York 10036, U.S.A., Web site: http://www.brown.edu/Facilities/University_Library/beyond/TLA.

Western Association of Map Libraries (WAML), Web site: http://www.waml.org.

ALTERNATIVE CAREERS

American Library Association (ALA) Discussion Group for Alternative Careers, Independent Librarians Exchange Round Table.

Association of Independent Information Professionals (AIIP), 7044 S. 13th Street, Oak Creek, Wisconsin 53154-1429, U.S.A., voice: 1-414-766-0421, fax: 1-414-768-8001, e-mail: aiipinfo@aiip.org, Web site: http://www.aiip.org. The premiere organization for independent librarians outside of traditional libraries, members must own or rent their own facilities (not for library fee-based services within libraries). Special Libraries Association (SLA) Caucus on Professional Librarians in Alternative Non-Traditional Careers (PLIANT), Consultants Section of Library Management Division.

11

Books and Journals

In addition to the sources listed in the bibliography, which are quoted in this book, I have compiled a list of other resources. I have read most of them and chose them for their relevance to the issues presented earlier in this book. When a relatively old book is included, it is either a classic or the latest I could find on a subject. The addresses for many of the publishers are listed at the end of this chapter. The prices listed were effective in late 2000 and are in U.S. dollars, unless otherwise specified.

The categories are given here. The listings under the categories are alphabetized by author. Books come first, followed by articles. Lists of journals also are included.

- One-Person or Solo Librarianship

- About the Profession

- General Management

- Space Planning

- Business

- Communication

- Marketing and Public Relations

- Financial Matters

- Strategic Planning

- Time Management

- Outsourcing and Downsizing

- Knowledge Management

- Technical Services

- Medical and Hospital Libraries

- Law Libraries

- Small Public Libraries

- Church and Synagogue Libraries

- U.S. Religious Publishers

- Other Kinds of Libraries

- Technology, Internet, and Online Searching

- Education and Alternative Careers

- Non-U.S. Essential References

- Miscellaneous

- Publishers

ONE-PERSON OR SOLO LIBRARIANSHIP

Books

Berk, Robert A. 1989. *Starting, Managing, and Promoting the Small Library.* Armonk, New York, U.S.A.: M.E. Sharpe, $71.

Berner, Andrew, and Guy St. Clair. 1990. *The Best of OPL: Five Years of The One-Person Library.* Washington, D.C., U.S.A.: Special Libraries Association. ISBN: 0-87111-438-0,

$34.50. Especially great if you are new to being an OPL, a history of the profession in very readable form. Contents include general considerations, management strategies, advocacy, marketing, profiles, helpful tips, and bibliography.

_____. 1996. *The Best of OPL, II: Selected Readings from The One-Person Library: A Newsletter for Librarians and Management, 1990–1994.* Washington, D.C., U.S.A.: Special Libraries Association, ISBN 0-87111-438-0, $34.50. The latest summary of OPL, worth a re-read if you are subscriber.

Bolef, Doris. 1988. "The special library." In *The How-To-Do-It Manual for Small Libraries,* edited by Bill Katz. New York, New York, U.S.A.: Neal-Schuman Publishers, pp. 54-61.

Lang, Jovan P., ed. 1992. *Reference Sources for Small and Medium-Size Libraries,* 5th ed. Chicago, Illinois, U.S.A.: American Library Association, $36 members, $40 non-members, ISBN 0-8389-3406-4.

Managing Small Special Libraries: An SLA Information Kit. 1992. Washington, D.C., U.S.A.: Special Libraries Association, $27, ISBN 0-87111-404-6. A classic.

Peeters, Regina, ed. 1997. *Das Robinson Crusoe-Syndrom und was mandagegen tun kann (The Robinson Crusoe Syndrome and What You Can Do About It).* Regensberg, Germany, New York, U.S.A.: Regina Peeters, ISBN 3-924659-28-1. DM 16. 24 detailed descriptions of OPLs in Germany with a strong emphasis on pragmatic approaches to problem solving. In German.

St. Clair, Guy L. 1996. *One-Person Libraries: Checkliste als Orienteirungshilfe fur den Betreib von OPLs.* Berlin, Germany, New York, U.S.A.: Deutsches Bibliotheksinstitut. ISBN 3-87068-490-9. In German.

_____. 1998. *One-Person Libraries: Aufgaben und Management. Handlungshilfe fur den Betrieb von OPLs* (Arbeitshilfen fur Spezialbbliotheken, Band 8). Berlin, Germany, New York, U.S.A.: DBI. ISBN 3-87068-969-2. In German.

_____. 2000. *One-Person Libraries: Checkliste als Orienteirungshilfe fur den Betreib von OPLs.* Tokyo, Japan: National Institute of Informatics. ISBN 4-924600-86-5. In Japanese, translated from the German by Setsuko Kuwabara.

St. Clair, Guy, and Joan Williamson. 1986. *Managing The One-Person Library.* Stoneham, Massachusetts, U.S.A.: Butterworth-Heineman. ISBN: 0-408-01511-X, $30. No OPL should be without this and the next one on this list.

_____. 1992. *Managing the New One-Person Library,* 2nd ed. New York, New York, U.S.A.: Bowker-Saur. ISBN 0-86291-630-5, $35. Profiles, isolation, education and continuing education, advocacy, managing, time management, collection development, finances, technology, and marketing.

Special Reports

SMR Special Reports, New York, New York, U.S.A.: SMR International:

1. Paul, Meg and Sandra Crabtree, *Strategies for Special Libraries*, 1995.

2. St. Clair, Guy, *The One-Person Library in the Organization*, Report 2, 1995.

3. St. Clair, Guy, *One-Person Librarianship: The Authority of the Customer*, Report 3, 1995.

4. St. Clair, Guy, *What The One-Person Library Does*, 1995.

5. St. Clair, Guy, *Finances and Value: How The One-Person Library is Paid For*, 1995.

6. St. Clair, Guy, *Dealing with Downsizing: A Guide for the Information Services Practitioner*, 1996.

Journals

Flying Solo, SOLO Librarians Division, Special Libraries Association, quarterly, free with membership.

National Network, Hospital Libraries Section, Medical Libraries Association, quarterly, included with membership. Anne Tomlin writes a column on One-Person Librarianship in every issue.

The One-Person Library: A Newsletter for Librarians and Management, Information Bridges International, Inc., 477 Harris Road, Cleveland, Ohio, U.S.A. 44143-2537. ISSN 0748-8831, $69–$100. If you subscribe to just one journal, this is the one it should be.

Rural Libraries, semi-annual, $10/year, ISSN 0276-2048, Center for the Study of Rural Librarianship, Clarion, Pennsylvania, U.S.A.

Rural Library Services Newsletter, NORWELD, 251 N. Main St., Bowling Green, Ohio 43402, U.S.A., voice: 1-419-352-2903, e-mail: shill@ohionet.org, $20/year.

ABOUT THE PROFESSION

Books

Continuing Professionalism: Education and IFLA: Past, Present and a Vision for the Future, 1994, London, England: Bowker-Saur, ISBN 3-598-21794-3, $110.

Eberhart, George M. 2000. *The Whole Library Handbook 3: Current Data, Professional Advice, and Curiosa About Libraries and Library Services*, Chicago, Illinois, U.S.A.: American Library Association, ISBN 0-8389-0-7814, $40. At last, SOLO librarians are recognized by the ALA.

Gorman, Michael. 1997. *Our Singular Strengths: Meditations for Librarians*, Chicago, Illinois, U.S.A.: American Library Association, ISBN 0-8389-0724-5, $20. For when you need inspiration.

Mintz, Anne P., ed. 1990. *Information Ethics: Concerns for Librarianship and the Information Industry*. Jefferson, North Carolina, U.S.A.: McFarland, ISBN 0-89950-514-7, $20.

White, Herbert S. 1989. *Librarians and the Awakening from Innocence: A Collection of Papers*. Boston, Massachusetts, U.S.A.: G.K. Hall, ISBN 0-8161-1892-2, $40. The first collection of White's writings, should be read, memorized, and followed by all librarians.

_____. 1995. *At the Crossroads: Librarians on the Information Superhighway*. Englewood, Colorado, U.S.A.: Libraries Unlimited, Inc., ISBN 1-56308-165-2, $60. White's later writings, the introductions to the sections are especially enlightening.

Articles

Corcoran, Mary. 2000. "Changing roles of information professionals: Choices and implications." *Online* 24(2):72-74.

DiMattia, Susan S. 2000. "Going solo: Wise is a force of one." *Library Journal* 125(12):40-41. Cover article, profile of Olga Wise, Compaq, Austin, TX, U.S.

Siess, Judith. 1995. "The MLS is not enough: One SOLO librarian's view." *The One-Person Library* 12(5):4-7.

_____. 1997. "The Future of SOLO Librarianship". *AALL Spectrum* 2(2):10-12. Cover article in journal of the American Association of Law Libraries.

_____. 1999. "Flying solo: Librarian, manage thyself." *American Libraries* 30(2):32-34.

Young, Peter R. 1994. "Changing information access economics: New roles for libraries and librarians." *Information Technology & Libraries* 13(2):103-144.

Journals

American Libraries (ALA) ISSN 0002-9769, American Library Association's official publication, American Library Association, Chicago, Illinois, U.S.A.

ASLIB Proceedings (U.K.), ISSN 0001-253X, scholarly, U.K. orientation.

Canadian Library Journal, ISSN 0008-4352.

Current Awareness Abstracts: A review of information management literature, U.K. orientation, 10/year, ISSN 1350-5238, also available electronically with hard copy subscription, Portland Press Ltd., Commerce Way, Whitehall Industrial Estate, Colchester CO2 8HP, U.K., e-mail: sales@portlandpress.co.uk.

The Informed Librarian: Professional Reading for the Information Professionals. Infosources Publishing (Arlene Eis), 140 Norma Rd., Teaneck, New Jersey 07666. U.S.A., $99/year, monthly. A table of contents, current awareness tool for librarians, a great way to keep up without the expense of subscribing to lots of journals, photocopy service available at a very reasonable cost.

Information Advisor, R. Berkman, editor, FIND/SVP, Inc., 625 Avenue of the Americas, New York, New York 10011 U.S.A., voice: 1-212-645-4500, monthly, $130/year, pp. 1050-1576.

Information Broker, ISSN 0895-9927, Burwell Enterprises, 6/year (formerly *Journal of Fee-Based Information Services*).

Information World Review, Learned Information Europe Ltd., P.O. Box 359, Sittingourne, Kent ME9 8DL, U.K., voice: 44-(0)1795-414964, fax: 44-(0)1795-414555, e-mail: iwr@galleon.co.uk, Web site: http://www.iwr.co.uk, £41 U.K., £51 elsewhere. *Journal of Business and Finance Librarianship,* ISSN 0895-0277, The Haworth Press, Binghamton, New York U.S.A., quarterly, $36 individual, $75 libraries.

Library Journal; ISSN 0024-2594, Cahners, New York, New York U.S.A. This is the one publication you should get to stay abreast of the non-OPL library world, worth the price just for the reviews and columns.

Library Trends, ISSN 0024-2594, more scholarly, but very readable.

Managing Information, 10/year, ISSN 1352-0229, ASLIB's official publication, current issue available free on the ASLIB Web site, http://www.Aslib.co.uk/man-inf, archive of back issues, Portland Press Ltd., Commerce Way, Whitehall Industrial Estate, Colchester CO2 8HP, U.K., e-mail: sales@portlandpress.co.uk.

GENERAL MANAGEMENT

Books

Allen, Kenneth B. 1997. *Enhancing Competitiveness in the Information Age. Strategies and Tactics for Special Librarians and Information Professionals,* Washington, D.C., U.S.A.: Special Libraries Association, ISBN 0-87111-476-3, $29.

Berkman, Robert I. 1995. *Rethinking the Corporate Information Center: A Blueprint for the 21st Century,* New York, New York, U.S.A.: Find/SVP Inc., ISBN 1-56241-214-0, $95.

Boccialetti, Gene. 1995. *It Takes Two: Managing Yourself When Working with Bosses and Other Authority Figures*, San Francisco, California, U.S.A.: Jossey-Bass, ISBN 0-7879008-5, $30.

Brinkman, Rick, and Rick Kirschner. 1994. *Dealing With People You Can't Stand: How to Bring Out the Best in People at Their Worst*, New York, New York, U.S.A.: McGraw-Hill, ISBN 0-07-007838-6, $12.95 (paper). Their "10 Most Unwanted List": the Tank, the Sniper, the Grenade, the Know-it-all, the Yes Person, the Maybe Person, the Nothing Person, the No Person, the Whiner.

Caputo, Janette S. 1991. *Stress and Burnout in Library Service*. Phoenix, Arizona, U.S.A.: Oryx Press, ISBN 0-897746023, $25.

Carson, Paula Phillips, et al. 1995. *The Library Manager's Deskbook: 102 Expert Solutions to 101 Common Dilemmas*. Chicago, Illinois, U.S.A.: American Library Association, ISBN 0-8389-0655-9, $32.

Curzon, Susan C. 1989. *Managing Change: A How-To-Do-It Manual for Planning, Implementing, and Evaluating Change in Libraries*. New York, New York, U.S.A.: Neal-Schuman Publishers, ISBN 1-55570-032-2, $45.

Ellis, Albert. 1988. *How to Stubbornly Refuse to Make Yourself Miserable About Anything—Yes, Anything*, New York, New York, U.S.A.: Carol Publishing Group (600 Madison Ave., New York, New York 10022, U.S.A.), ISBN 0-8184-0456-6, $12, paper.

Gasaway, Laura N., and Sarah K., Winant. 1994. *Libraries and Copyright: A Guide to Copyright Law in the 1990s*. Washington, D.C., U.S.A.: Special Libraries Association, $40 members, $50 nonmembers, ISBN 0-87111-407-0. Written by the SLA expert on copyright, it has all you need to know and more.

Giesecke, Joan, ed. 1992. *Practical Help for New Supervisors*, 2nd ed. Chicago, Illinois, U.S.A.: American Library Association, $18 members, $20 nonmembers, ISBN 0-8389-3408-0, $24.

Hernon, Peter, and Ellen Altman. 1998. A*ssessing Service Quality: Satisfying the Expectations of Library Customers*, Chicago, Illinois, U.S.A.: American Library Association, ISBN 0-8389-3489-7, $40.

The Information Audit: An SLA Information Kit. 1995, Washington, D.C., U.S.A.: Special Libraries Association, $16 members, $21 nonmembers, ISBN 0-87111-452-6, with input from Guy St. Clair, how to find out how your organization uses information.

The Information Services Management Series, Guy St. Clair, London, U.K. Bowker-Saur:

- *Customer Service in the Information Environment*, ISBN
  1-85739-004-0, 1994, $34.95.

- *Entrepreneurial Librarianship: The Key to Effective Information Services Management*, ISBN 1-85739-014-8, 1996, $45.

- *Power and Influence: Enhancing Information Services Within the Organization*, ISBN 0-85739-098-9, 1994, $34.95.

- *Total Quality Management in Information Services*, ISBN 0-85739-039-3, 1996, $45.

- *Human Resources in Information Services Management* (with Meg Paul), ISBN 1-85739-118-7, August 1997.

- *Corporate Memory: Information Management in the Electronic Age*, ISBN 1-85739-158-6, May 1997.

- *Knowledge for Europe: Librarians and Publishers Working Together*, ISBN 3-598-11164-9, 1993, $65.

Kahn, Miriam B. 1997. *Disaster Response and Planning for Libraries*, Chicago, Illinois, U.S.A.: American Library Association, ISBN 0-08389-0716-4, $38.

Know How Guides, London, U.K: ASLIB, various, available from Portland Press Ltd., Commerce Way, Whitehall Industrial Estate, Colchester CO2 8HP, U.K., e-mail sales@portlandpress.co.uk. Over 25 titles on all kinds of subjects. Sample titles include "Promotional Strategies," "Intranets and Push Technology," "Managing Change," "Moving Your Library," and "Legal Information."

Lock, Dennis, ed. 1998. *The Gower Handbook of Management*, 4th ed. Aldershot: Gower, U.K. ISBN 0-566-07938-0. In a review in the *Journal of Documentation* it was called a publication "that takes your breath away" and "*The* management title to sit on your shelves."

Managing Information Reports, London, U.K.: ASLIB, various, available from Portland Press Ltd., Commerce Way, Whitehall Industrial Estate, Colchester CO2 8HP, e-mail: sales@portlandpress.co.uk. Sample titles include "Document Delivery" and "Meeting Managers' Information Needs."

Matarazzo, James M. 1990. *Corporate Library Excellence*. Washington, D.C., U.S.A.: Special Libraries Association, ISBN 0-87111-367-8, $49. Profiles of 13 corporate libraries voted outstanding by the boards of six Special Libraries Association chapters.

Matarazzo, James M., and Miriam A. Drake. 1994. *Information for Management: A Handbook*. Washington, D.C., U.S.A.: Special Libraries Association, $49, ISBN 0-87111-427-5. How to present information to upper management, information needs assessment, organizational dynamics, communication with management, records management, TQM, virtual library, nonprofits, and information technology.

Murphy, Marcy. 1988. *The Managerial Competencies of Twelve Corporate Librarians.* Washington, D.C., U.S.A.: Special Libraries Association. (SLA Research Series No. 2), ISBN 0-8711-332-5, $9.

Porter, Cathy A., ed. 1997. *Special Libraries: A Guide for Management,* 3rd ed. Washington, D.C., U.S.A.: Special Libraries Association, ISBN 0-87111-466-6, $32. Newest version of Elin Christensen's classic.

Porter, Michael E. 1985. *Competitive Advantage: Creating and Sustaining Superior Performance.* New York, New York, U.S.A.: Free Press/Simon & Schuster, ISBN 0-02-925090-0, $37.50. One of the best introductions to how business works.

Weingand, Darlene E., 1997. *Customer Service Excellence: A Concise Guide for Librarians,* Chicago, Illinois, U.S.A.: American Library Association, ISBN 0-83890689-3, $30.

Willis, Mark. 1999. *Dealing with Difficult People in the Library.* Chicago, Illinois, U.S.A.: American Library Association, ISBN 0838907601, $28.

Woodsworth, Anne, and James F. Williams II. 1993. *Managing the Economics of Owning, Leasing and Contracting Out Information Services,* Aldershot, Hampshire, U.K.: Ashgate Publishing, IASBN 1-85743018-7, $68.

Articles

Barter, Richard F., Jr. 1994. "In search of excellence in libraries: The management writings of Tom Peters and their implications for library and information services." *Library Management* 15(8):4–15.

Bauwens, Michel. 1994. "The BP nutrition virtual library: A case study." In *Information for Management: A Handbook,* Washington, D.C., U.S.A.: Special Libraries Association, pp. 159–165.

"How Do You Manage?" Continuing column in *Library Journal.* Although most of the examples are from public libraries with multiple professionals, the solo can learn a lot from the suggestions made by practitioners. (This column was the inspiration for OPL's "What Would You Do?" feature.)

Kearns, Kevin P. 1997. "Managing upward: Working effectively with supervisors and others in the hierarchy." *Information Outlook* 1(10):23–27.

Parris, Lou B. 1994. "Know your company and its business." In *Information for Management: A Handbook,* edited by James M. Matarazzo and Miriam A. Drake, Washington, D.C., U.S.A.: Special Libraries Association.

St. Clair, Guy. 1995. "Looking at that volatile 'vendor/senior management/information practitioner' relationship." *InfoManage* 2(12):6–7.

_____. 1996. "'Adding value'—What's it mean?" (Column: The Practical Information Manager), *InfoManage* 3(3):6–8.

Journals

Information Today, Information Today, Inc., 11/year, ISSN 8755-6286, $47.95 U.S., $59.95 Canada and Mexico, $65 rest of world, news about the library and information world, book reviews.

Information World Review, Information Today, Inc., 11/year, ISSN 0950-9879, $62.95 U.S., $72.95 Canada and Mexico, European information industry reports.

Journal of Library Administration, ISSN 0193-0826, quarterly, Binghamton, New York, U.S.A.: The Haworth Press, $40 individual, $105 libraries.

Library Management, ISSN 0143-5124.

Library Management Quarterly, ISSN 0271-3306, Washington, D.C., U.S.A.: Special Libraries Association, SLA Library Management Division, free with membership.

Supervisory Management, American Management Association, monthly, ISSN 0039-5919. Very helpful tips for supervising—and for dealing with your supervisor.

SPACE PLANNING

Books and Articles

Dahlgren, Anders C. 1990. *Planning the Small Library Facility*, 2nd ed., Chicago, Illinois, U.S.A.: American Library Association (Small Library Publications No. 23), ISBN 0-8389-0681-8, $15.

Dancik, Deborah, and Emelie J. Schroeder, eds. 1995. *Building Blocks for Library Space: Functional Guidelines*. Chicago, Illinois, U.S.A.: American Library Association. Out of print.

Fraley, Ruth A., and Carol Lee Anderson. 1990. *Library Space Planning: A How-to-Do-It Manual for Assessing, Allocating and Reorganizing Collections, Resources and Facilities*, 2nd ed. New York, New York, U.S.A.: Neal-Schuman Publishers, ISBN 1-55570040-3 (paper), $45.

Habich, Elizabeth Chamberlain. 1998. *Moving Library Collections*, Westport, Connecticut, U.S.A.: Greenwood Publishing, ISBN 0-31329330-9, $79.50.

McDonald, A. 1994. *Moving Your Library*. London, U.K: ASLIB, ISBN 0-85142-328-0.

Mount, Ellis, ed. 1988. *Creative Planning of Special Library Facilities*, Binghamton, New York, U.S.A.: The Haworth Press, ISBN 0-86656697-X, $40.

Pellizzi, Tom, 1998. Two-Part Series on "Space Planning." *The One-Person Library* 15(3):6-8 and15(4):5-6.

Tucker, Dennis C. 1999. *Library Relocations and Collection Shifts*. Medford, New Jersey, U.S.A.: Information Today, ISBN 1-57387069-2, $35.

Wells, Marianna, and Rosemary Young. 1997. *Moving and Reorganizing a Library.* Aldershot, Hampshire, U.K.: Ashgate Publishing, ISBN 0-56607701-9, $74.95.

BUSINESS

Books

Bates, Mary Ellen. 1999. *Super Searchers Do Business: The Online Secrets of Top Business Researchers.* Medford, New Jersey, U.S.A.: CyberAge Books, an imprint of Information Today, Inc. ISBN 0-910965-33-1 (paper), $24.95. Simply the best book on business searching I have ever seen.

Berinstein, Paula. 1998. *Finding Statistics Online: How to Locate the Elusive Numbers You Need.* Medford, New Jersey, U.S.A.: Information Today, Inc. ISBN 0-910965-25-0, $29.95.

Berkman, Robert I. 1994. *Find It Fast: How to Uncover Expert Information on Any Subject,* 3rd ed. New York, New York, U.S.A.: Harper Collins, ISBN 0-06-0964863, $12. Elias, Stephen. 1996. *Patent, Copyright and Trademark: A Desk Reference to Intellectual Property Law.* Berkeley, California, U.S.A.: Nolo Press, ISBN 0-87337-236-0, $25.

Fuld, Leonard J. 1994. *Competitor Intelligence: How to Get It, How to Use It,* 2nd ed. New York, New York, U.S.A.: John Wiley, ISBN 0-471-585-09-2 $25.

Harris, Sherwood. 1991. New York *Public Library Book of How and Where to Look It Up.* New York, New York, U.S.A.: McMillan, ISBN 0-13-614728-3, $30.

Hillstrom, Kevin, and Laurie Collier Hillstron.1998. *Encyclopedia of Small Business.* Detroit, Michigan, U.S.A.: Gale Group, 2 vols., ISBN 0-7876-1864-0, $395.

How to Find Information About Companies, 14th ed. 1998. Washington, D.C., U.S.A.: Washington Researchers, voice 1-202-333-3499, 3 vols., ISBN 1-56365086-X, $395 per volume. Contains sources, techniques, and case studies.

Lavin, Michael R. 2001. *Business Information, How to Find It, How to Use It,* 3rd ed. Phoenix, Arizona, U.S.A.: Oryx Press, ISBN 8-89774-643-0, $48.50.

McGonagle, John J., Jr., and Carolyn M. Vella, 1990. *Outsmarting the Competition.* Naperville, Illinois, U.S.A.: Sourcebooks. Out of print.

Pagell, Ruth, and Michael Halperin. 2000. *International Business Information: How to Find It, How to Use It,* 2nd ed. Phoenix, Arizona, U.S.A.: Oryx Press, ISBN 1-88899883-0, $65.

Reynard, Keith W., ed. 1999. *The ASLIB Directory of Information Sources in the United Kingdom,* 10th ed. London, U.K: ASLIB, ISBN 0-85142-409-0, $550. Also available with CD-ROM at extra cost.

Journals

Blue Book of Canadian Business, ISSN 0381-7245, Web site: http://www.bluebook.ca. Included are 2,700 Canadian firms with annual revenue of $10 million or more and/or assets of $10 million.

Business Information Alert: Sources, Strategies, and Signposts for Information Professionals, ISSN 1042-0746, Chicago, Illinois, U.S.A.: Alert Publications, 10/year, $152, $99 for public and academic libraries.

Competia (competitive intelligence), Web site: http://www.competia.com.

Forthcoming International Scientific and Technical Conferences, quarterly, ISSN 0046-4686, Portland Press Ltd., Commerce Way, Whitehall Industrial Estate, Colchester CO2 8HP, U.K., e-mail: sales@portlandpress.co.uk.

Scott's Canadian Sourcebook 2000, Southam Information Product Group. Economic statistics on business, industry, and trade in Canada; summary of federal and provincial labor legislation and a full listing of Canadian trade unions and labor organizations; lists of libraries, magazines, newsletters, associations, education, and books.

COMMUNICATION

Books

Axtell, Roger E. 1992. *Do's and Taboos of Public Speaking,* New York, New York, U.S.A.: John Wiley, ISBN 0-47153670-9, $16.95.

Beckwith, Harry. 1997. *Selling the Invisible: A Field Guide to Modern Marketing,* New York, New York, U.S.A.: Warner Books, ISBN 0-446-52094-2, $20. The "invisible" is service. Must reading for all customer-driven librarians.

Brinkman, Rick, and Rick Kirschner. 1994. *Dealing With People You Can't Stand: How to Bring Out the Best in People at their Worst,* New York, New York, U.S.A.: McGraw-Hill, ISBN 0-07-007838-6, $13.

Articles

Bridges, Peggy Bass, and Suzette Morgan. 2000. "Creatively marketing the corporate library." *Marketing Library Services* 14(2):1–3.

Paul, Meg. 1999. "On the necessity of being political." *The One-Person Library* 15(9):3–4.

_____. 1998. "Dealing with your manager." *The One-Person Library* 15(7):6–7.

Siess, Judith. 1998. "How to write an annual report." *The One-Person Library* 15(8):3–4.

_____. 1999. "Confronting international clients' styles and needs." *The One-Person Library* 16(7):7.

_____. 1999. "Dealing with your boss." *The One-Person Library* 16(7):1–4.

St. Clair, Guy. 1993. "To memo or not to memo." *The One-Person Library* 10(1):6.

_____. 1995. "How well do you know your boss?" *The One-Person Library* 11(12):3.

_____. 1997. "How 'elevator management' can work for the OPL." *The One-Person Library* 13(10):5–6.

_____. 1997. "The OPL as information spokesperson." *The One-Person Library* 14(3):6.

_____. 1997. "Take a look at how you look." *The One-Person Library* 14(6):6.

White, Herbert S. 1987. "How to cope with an incompetent supervisor." In *Librarians and the Awakening from Innocence: A Collection of Papers*, Boston, Massachusetts, U.S.A.: G.K. Hall, 1989, pp. 213–221 (originally published in *Canadian Library Journal* 44:381–384, December 1987).

Journals

Harvard Management Communication Letter: A Newsletter from Harvard Business School Publishing, ISSN 1524-5519, $79/year, monthly, Web site: http://www.hbsp.harvard.edu, e-mail: HMCL@hbsp.harvard.edu.

DOING BUSINESS WORLDWIDE

Books and Journals

Axtell, Roger E. 1990. *Do's and Taboos of Hosting International Visitors*, New York, New York, U.S.A.: John Wiley, ISBN 0-471-51570-1, $18.

_____. 1997. *Gestures: The Do's and Taboos of Body Language Around the World*, New York, New York, U.S.A.: John Wiley, ISBN 0-471-8342-3, $16.

_____. 1993. *Do's and Taboos Around the World: A Guide to International Behavior*, 3rd ed. New York, New York, U.S.A.: John Wiley, ISBN 0-47159528-4, $16.

_____. 1994. *The Do's and Taboos of International Trade: A Small Business Primer*, rev. ed. New York, New York, U.S.A.: John Wiley, ISBN 0-47100760-9, $19.

_____. 1995. *Do's and Taboos of Using English Around the World*, New York, New York, U.S.A.: John Wiley, ISBN 0-047130841-2, $15.

Axtell, Roger E., and John P. Healy 1994. *Do's and Taboos of Preparing for Your Trip Abroad*, New York, New York, U.S.A.: John Wiley, ISBN 0-47102567-4, $13.

Axtell, Roger E., et al. 1997. *Do's and Taboos Around the World for Women in Business*, New York, New York, U.S.A.: John Wiley, ISBN 0-471-14364-2, $18.

Braganti, Nancy L., and Elizabeth Devine. 1984. *The Travelers' Guide to European Customs and Manners: How to Converse, Dine, Tip, Drive, Bargain, Dress, Make Friends, and Conduct Business while in Europe*, New York, New York, U.S.A.: Meadowbrook/Simon and Schuster, ISBN 0-671-54493-4.

_____. 1986. *The Travelers' Guide to Asia Customs and Manners: How to Converse, Dine, Tip, Drive, Bargain, Dress, Make Friends, and Conduct Business while in Asia*, New York, New York, U.S.A.: St. Martin's Press, ISBN 0-312-811610-3, $17.

_____. 1989. *The Travelers' Guide to Latin American Customs and Manners: How to Converse, Dine, Tip, Drive, Bargain, Dress, Make Friends, and Conduct Business while in Latin America*, New York, New York, U.S.A.: St. Martin's Press, ISBN 0-31202303-0, $17.

Culturgrams, David M. Kennedy Center for International Studies, Brigham Young University, Provo, Utah, U.S.A., voice: 1-801-378-6528, Web site: http://fhss.byu.edu/kenncent/publications. Available for over 100 countries, these cover greetings, visiting etiquette, food, language, religion, lifestyle, climate, holidays, economy, and traveler precautions in only four pages.

Devine, Elizabeth, and Nancy L. Braganti. 1991. *The Travelers' Guide to Middle Eastern and North African Customs and Manners: How to Converse, Dine, Tip, Drive, Bargain, Dress, Make Friends, and Conduct Business while in Middle East and North Africa*, New York, New York, U.S.A.: St. Martin's Press, ISBN 0-312-05523-4, $14.

Doing Business In (various countries) ... from Ernst and Young, New York, New York, U.S.A.; voice: 1-800-726-7330, $162/set or $3 each. E & Y also has a CD-ROM version called EY Passport, but you may have to be an E & Y client to get it.

Dun & Bradstreet's Guide to Doing Business Around the World, ISBN 0-13531-4844, 1997, $26.

Hinkleman, Edward G., ed. *Country Business Guide Series*, World Trade Press, includes China, Japan, Korea, the Philippines, Hong Kong, Mexico, Singapore, $25.

Kurtz, Patricia L. 1994. *The Global Speaker: An English Speaker's Guide to Making Presentations Around the World*, New York, New York, U.S.A.: Amacom/American Management Association, ISBN 0-8144-7878-6, $17.

Morrison, Terri, Wayne A. Conaway, and George A. Borden. 1994. *Kiss, Bow, or Shake Hands: How to Do Business in Sixty Countries*, Holbrook, Massachusetts, U.S.A.: Bob Adams, ISBN 1-55850-444-3, $20.

Simons, George. 1989. *Working Together: How to Become More Effective in a Multicultural Organization*, Los Altos, California, U.S.A.: Crisp Publications, ISBN 0-0961931-85-8, $13.

MARKETING AND PUBLIC RELATIONS

Books

Dean, Sharon. 1990. *Winning Marketing Techniques: An Introduction to Marketing for Information Professionals* (self-study). Washington, D.C., U.S.A.: Special Libraries Association, ISBN 0-87111-390-2, $60 members, $75 nonmembers.

Hart, Keith. 1998. *Putting Marketing Ideas into Action.* London, U.K.: Library Association Publishing ISBN 1-85604182-4, $30.

Jain, Abhinadan K., et al. 1999. *Marketing Information Products and Services: A Primer for Librarians and Information Professionals.* New Delhi, India: IDRC/Tata McGraw-Hill, ISBN 0-88936-817-1, $25.

Karp, Rashelle S., ed. 1995. *Part-Time Public Relations with Full-Time Results.* Chicago, Illinois, U.S.A.: American Library Association, LAMA PR Section, ISBN 0-83890661-2, $18.

Kotler, Philip, and Alan Andreasen. 1996. *Strategic Marketing for Nonprofit Organizations*, 5th ed. Englewood Cliffs, New Jersey, U.S.A.: Prentice Hall, ISBN 0-13232547-0, $90.

LEXIS-NEXIS. 1996. *Marketing Tips for Information Professionals: A Practical Workbook*, ISBN 0-926578-15-4, $7.95.

Phillips, Michael, and Salli Rasberry. 1997. *Marketing Without Advertising*, 2nd ed. Berkeley, California, U.S.A.: Nolo Press, ISBN 0-87337608-0, $25.

Walters, Suzanne. 1992. *Marketing: A How-To-Do-It Manual for Librarians*, New York, New York, U.S.A.: Neal-Schuman Publishers, ISBN 1-44470095-0, $45.

Weingand, Darlene E. 1998. *Future-Driven Marketing*, Chicago, Illinois, U.S.A.: American Library Association, ISBN 0-8389-0735-0, $25.

Wolfe, Lisa A. 1997. *Library Public Relations, Promotions, and Communications: A How-To-Do-It Manual for Librarians*, New York, New York, U.S.A.: Neal-Schuman Publishers, ISBN 1-5570-266-X, $45. Highly recommended by Kathy Miller, editor of *Marketing Library Services.*

Articles

Bauwens, Michel 1996. "Marketing the cybrary." *Marketing Library Services* 10(4):1–3.

_____. "The Cybrarian's Guide to Cyber-Marketing," Web site: http://www.iocom.be/pilot/cybermarketing.

Bertelli, Frances. 2000. "How do you spell public relations?" *AALL Spectrum* 4(7):34.

Carpenter, Beth. "Your attention, please! Marketing today's libraries." *Computers in Libraries* 18(8):62–66, September 1998. Carpenter is electronic resources librarian, Outagamie Waupaca Library System, Appleton, Wisconsin.

Muir, Robert F. 1993. "Marketing your library or information service to business." *Online* 17:41–46.

Powers, Janet E. 1995. "Marketing in the special library environment." *Library Trends* 43:478.

Journals

MLS: Marketing Library Services, ISSN 0896-3908, Medford, New Jersey, U.S.A.: Information Today, 8/year.

FINANCIAL MATTERS

Books

Crismond, Linda, ed. 1994. *Against All Odds: Case Studies on Library Financial Management*. Fort Atkinson, Wisconsin, U.S.A.: Highsmith Press, ISBN 0-917846-28-1, $19.

Daubert, Madeline J. 1993. *Financial Management for Small and Medium-Sized Libraries*. Chicago, Illinois, U.S.A.: American Library Association, $34.20 members, $38 nonmembers, ISBN 0-8389-0618-4, $38.

_____. 1995. *Money Talk: Accounting Fundamentals for Special Libraries. An SLA Self-Study Program*. Washington, D.C., U.S.A.: Special Libraries Association, ISBN 0-87111-445-3, $85.

_____. 1996. *Control of Administrative and Financial Operations in Special Libraries*, Washington, D.C., U.S.A.: Special Libraries Association, ISBN 9087111-457-7, $70 members, $85 nonmembers.

_____. 1997. *Analyzing Library Costs for Decision-Making and Cost Recovery. An SLA Self-Study Program*. Washington, D.C., U.S.A.: Special Libraries Association, ISBN 0-87111-464-X, $85.

Davenport, Elisabeth. 1997. *Costing and Pricing in the Digital Age: A Practical Guide for Information Services*, New York, New York, U.S.A.: Neal-Schuman Publishers, ISBN 1-55570311-9.

Koenig, Michael, E.D. 1980. *Budgeting Techniques for Libraries and Information Centers*. Washington, D.C., U.S.A.: Special Libraries Association Professional Development Series 1. Out of print.

Martin, Murray S., ed. 1983. *Financial Planning for Libraries*. New York, New York, U.S.A.: Haworth Press, ISBN: 0-86656-118-8, $40.

Smith, G. Stevenson. 1999. *Accounting for Librarians and Other Not-for-Profit Managers,* 2nd ed. Chicago, Illinois, U.S.A.: American Library Association. ISBN: 0-8389-0758-X, $82. Very detailed instructions for fund accounting and financial analysis, with exercises.

Warner, Alice Sizer. 1992. *Owning Your Numbers: An Introduction to Budgeting for Special Libraries,* (self-study), ISBN 0-87111-387-2, Washington, D.C., U.S.A.: Special Libraries Association, $60 members, $75 nonmembers.

_____. 1998. *Budgeting. A How-To-Do-It Manual for Librarians,* New York, New York, U.S.A.: Neal-Schuman Publishers, ISBN 1-55570288-0, $50.

Articles

Caprusso, Stefano. 1998. "Negotiating the deal and price from an end-user point of view." *Information Outlook* 2(3):25–28.

Kinder, Robin. 1988. "Agreeing to disagree: The relationship between librarians and brokers." *The Reference Librarian* (22):1–3.

McQueen, Judy, and N. Bernard Basch. 1991. "Negotiations with subscription agents." *American Libraries* 22:644–647.

Pack, Thomas. 2000. "The Changing Role of the Information Vendor." *Online* 24(2):36–40.

Snyder, Herbert and Elizabeth Davenport. 1997. "What does it really cost? Allocating indirect costs." *Bottom Line* 10(4):158–164.

Spiegelman, Barbara M. 1997. "Beach budget bingo." *Library Management Quarterly* 20(4):8–9.

"Where did all the $ Go?" *Library Benchmarking Newsletter* 4(4):1, 3–4, Jul/Aug 1997.

White, Gary W., and Gregory A. Crawford. 1997. "Cost/benefits analyses of library services." *MLS Marketing Library Services* 11(5):4–5.

Journals

Bottom Line: A Financial Magazine for Librarians, New York, New York, U.S.A.: Neal-Schuman Publishers, quarterly, ISSN 0888-045X.

STRATEGIC PLANNING

Books

Bremer, Suzanne. 1994. *Long Range Planning: A How-To-Do-It Manual for Public Libraries.* New York, New York, U.S.A.: Neal-Schuman Publishers, ISBN 1-55570-0162-0, $45.

Danner, Richard A. 1996. *Strategic Planning: A Law Library Management Tool for the 90's and Beyond,* 2nd ed. Dobbs Ferry, New York, U.S.A.: Glanville Publishers, ISBN 0-87802110-8, $55.

Giesecke, Joan, ed. 1998. *Scenario Planning for Libraries,* Chicago, Illinois, U.S.A.: American Library Association, ISBN 0-8389-3482-X, $30.

Jacob, M.E.L. 1990. *Strategic Planning: A How-To-Do-It Manual for Libraries.* New York, New York, U.S.A.: Neal-Schuman Publishers, ISBN 1-55570074-8, $45.

Articles

Balas, Janet L. 1999. *Online* treasures: "Online help for library strategic planners." *Computers in Libraries* 19(1):40–42.

Brewerton, Antony. 1999. "First, find some visionaries." *Library Association Record* 101(6):354–356.

Bridgland, Angela, and Helen M. Hayes. 1995. "Strategic planning for libraries." *Australian Library Review* 12:1–57. Special issue.

Callaghan, Anne. 1998. "Strategic planning in a tertiary library." *Pathways to Knowledge, ALIA 5th Biennial Conference Proceedings,* Sydney: Australian Library & Information Association, pp. 125–130.

Corrall, Sheila M. 1994. "Strategic planning for library and information services." *Managing Information* 1(11/12):41.

_____. 1995. "Strategy: Who needs it?" *Library Manager* (3):9.

Dyson, Cathy. 1998. "A strategic plan for Information at Zurich Reinsurance." *Management Information* 5(9)30–32.

Feinman, Valerie Jackson. 1999. "Five steps toward planning today for tomorrow's needs." *Computers in Libraries* 19(1):18–21.

Gooijer, J.D. 1995. "Strategic planning: taking a scenario analysis approach." *Australian Library Review* 12(1):11–14.

Henderson, C. 1996. "Effective strategic planning." *Bulletin of the Special Libraries Association.* Florida and Caribbean Chapter Review Issue, pp. 59–60.

Hobrock, Brice G. 1991. "Creating your library's future through effective strategic planning." *Journal of Library Administration* 14(3):37–57.

Hoffman, U. 1995. "Developing a strategic planning framework for information technologies for libraries." *OCLC Systems and Services* 11(4):22–32.

Hopwood, Susan H. 1999. "Long-range planning and funding for innovation." *Computers in Libraries* 19(1):22–27.

Kennedy, Mary Lee. 1996. "Positioning strategic information: Partnering for the Information Age." *Special Libraries* 87(2):120-131.

Line, Maurice B. 1995. "Editorial: Is strategic planning outmoded?" *Alexandria* 7(3):135–137.

Lombard, Carol. 1999. "Principles to include in formulating an information policy for a resource center." *The One-Person Library* 15(11):2–5.

Lyon, J. 1995. "The best laid plans." *Library Manager* (7):6–9.

Mackenzie, C. 1997. "From forward plan to business plan: strategic planning in public libraries." *Australasian Public Libraries and Information Services* 10(4):191–200.

Morgan, Eric Lease. 1999. "Libraries of the future: Springboards for strategic planning." *Computers in Libraries* 19(1):32–33.

Penniman, W. David. 1999. "Strategic planning to avoid bottlenecks in the age of the Internet." *Computers in Libraries* 19(1):50–52.

Raber, D. 1995. "A conflict of cultures: planning versus tradition in public libraries." *Reference Quarterly (RQ)*: 35(1):50–62.

St. Clair, Guy. 1996. "Thinking about: Link strategic planning to OPL management." *The One-Person Library* 13(2):1–3.

Siess, Judith. 1999. "Thinking about planning: What to plan and how to get started." *The One-Person Library* 16(4):1–4.

Wilt, C., and C.C. Wilt. 1995. "Library networking issues and strategic issue analysis." *Resource Sharing & Information Networks* 10 (1/2):33–48.

Zimmerman, Michael C. 1997. "Your library's strategic plan: Plan the writing before you write the plan." *Information Outlook* 1(12):40–41.

TIME MANAGEMENT

Books

Allen Kathleen R. 1995. *Time and Information Management that Really Works!* Lincolnwood, Illinois, U.S.A.: NTC Business Books, ISBN 0-8442-2998-9, $13.95.

Bly, Robert W. 1999. *101 Ways to Make Every Second Count: Time Management Tips and Techniques for More Success with Less Stress.* Franklin Lakes, New Jersey, U.S.A.: The Career Press, ISBN 1-56414-406-2, $14.99.

Cochran, J. Wesley. 1992. *Time Management Handbook for Librarians.* New York, New York, U.S.A.: Greenwood Press, ISBN 0-313-27842-3, $48.

Davis, Martha, Elizabeth Robbins Eshelman, and Matthew McKay. 2000. *The Relaxation and Stress Reduction Workbook*, 5th ed. New York, New York, U.S.A.: New Harbinger Publications, ISBN 1-57224214-0, $20. Especially Chapter 16, "Goal Setting and Time Management;" and Chapter 18, "Job Stress Management."

Hemphill, Barbara 1998. *Taming the Office Tiger: The Complete Guide to Getting Organized at Work*, 2nd ed. Washington, D.C., U.S.A.: Kiplinger Books, ISBN 0-93872158-5, $15.

Koch, Richard. 1998. *The 80/20 Principle: The Secret of Achieving More With Less*, New York, New York, U.S.A.: Doubleday, ISBN 0-385-49174-3, $15.

Mackenzie, Alec. 1997. *The Time Trap*, 3rd ed. New York, New York, U.S.A.: Amacom. ISBN 0-81447926-X, $18.

Mayer, Jeffrey J. 1999. *Time Management for Dummies*, 2nd ed. Foster City, California, U.S.A.: IDG Books, ISBN 0-7645-5145-0, $19.99.

McConkey, Dale. 1994. *No-Nonsense Delegation*, New York, New York, U.S.A.: AMACOM, Out of print.

Articles

Berner, Andrew. 1997. "Overcoming procrastination: A practical approach." *Information Outlook* 1(12):23–26.

Pawlak, Jim. 1999. "To avoid self-destruction, know when to say 'no.'" *The [Cleveland, Ohio] Plain Dealer,* page 3-H, 10 October.

Saunders, Rebecca M. 2000. "Asserting yourself: How to say 'no' and mean it." *Harvard Management Communication Letter* 3(7):9–11.

Urgo, Marisa. 1996. "A new formula for the OPL: Substitution + Simplicity + Time over money = Successful time management." *The One-Person Library* 13(7):6–8.

OUTSOURCING AND DOWNSIZING

Books

Hirson, Arnold, and Barbara Winters. 1996. *Outsourcing Library Technical Services: A How-To-Do-It Manual for Librarians.* New York, New York, U.S.A.: Neal-Schuman

Publishers, ISBN 1-55570-221-X, $45, accompanying disk of ready to import RFP specifications, ISBN 1-55570-272-4, $20.

Kascus, Marie A., and Dawn Hale, eds. 1995. *Outsourcing Cataloging, Authority Work, and Physical Processing: A Checklist of Considerations.* Chicago, Illinois, U.S.A.: American Library Association, ISBN 0-8389-3449-8, $13.50 members, $15 nonmembers.

Khosrowpour, Mehdil. 1995. *Managing Information Technology Investments with Outsourcing.* Hershey, Pennsylvania, U.S.A.: Idea Group Publishing, ISBN 1-878289-20-9, $59.95.

Portugal, Frank. 1997. *Exploring Outsourcing: Case Studies of Corporate Libraries,* Washington, D.C., U.S.A.: Special Libraries Association, ISBN 0-08711-468-2. Out of print.

Articles

Anonymous. 1993. "The incredible shrinking staff: Supervisors deal with downsizing." *Library Personnel News* 7(6):3–4. From ALA/LAMA sessions at annual conference.

Bates, Mary Ellen. 1997. "Outsourcing, co-sourcing, and core competencies: What's an information professional to do?" *Information Outlook* 1(12):35–37.

Davidson, Ann C. 1996. "Obedience to the unenforceable: The ethics of outsourcing." *Searcher* 4(4):28–30.

Field, Judith J. 1995. "Downsizing, reengineering, outsourcing and closing: Words to lose sleep over." *Library Management Quarterly* 18(4):4.

Khan, Marta. 1987. "Successful downsizing strategies." *Canadian Library Journal* 44:393–399.

St. Clair, Guy, and Andrew Berner. 1996. "Insourcing: The evolution of information delivery (new management trends for OPLs)." *The One-Person Library* 13(4):1–4.

KNOWLEDGE MANAGEMENT

Books

Burden, Paul. 2000. *Knowledge Management: The Bibliography* (ASIS&T Monograph Series), Medford, New Jersey, U.S.A.: Information Today, Inc. ISBN 1-57387-101-X. Based on the bibliography originally created by Morgen MacIntosh and T. Kanti Srikantaiah and published in *Knowledge Management for the Information Professional.*

Choo, Chun Wei. 1998. *Information Management for the Intelligent Organization: The Art of Scanning the Environment,* 2nd ed. Medford, New Jersey, U.S.A.: Information Today, Inc. ISBN 1-57387-057-9.

Cortada, James, and John Woods. 2000. *The Knowledge Management Yearbook 2000–2001,* Woburn, Massachusetts, U.S.A.: Butterworth-Heinemann, ISBN 0-7506-7258-7, $89.95, voice: 1-800-366-2654, fax: 1-800-446-6529, Articles on current state of knowledge management, lists of literature, online resources, organizations, periodicals, and vocabulary. An excellent new reference work.

Enhancing Competitiveness in the Information Age: Strategies and Tactics for Special Librarians and Information Professionals. 1997. Washington, D.C., U.S.A.: Special Libraries Association, ISBN 0-87111-476-3, $29.

Knowledge Management: A New Competitive Asset. Washington, D.C., U.S.A.: Special Libraries Association, 1977, 1997 SLA State of the Art Institute. ISBN 0-87111-480-1, $40. Chapters include the following:

- Judith J. Field, "Information + Technology + You equals knowledge management."

- Alison G. Tucker, "From information to knowledge: A new competitive asset."

- Nigel Oxbrow and Angela Abell, "Putting knowledge to work: What skills and competencies are required?"

- Patricia S. Foy, "Lessons from the field—Part I."

- Jay Liebowitz, "A look towards valuating knowledge."

- Lewis J. Perelman, "DYNAMIC ignorance."

- Dr. J. Michael Pemberton, "Chief knowledge officer: The climax to your career?"

- Soumitra Dutta, "Strategies for implementing knowledge-based systems."

- Mike Bonaventura, "The benefits of a knowledge culture."

- Stephen Abram, "Post Information Age positioning for special librarians: Is knowledge management the answer?"

- Michael E.D. Koenig, "Intellectual capital and how to leverage it."

Prusak, Laurence. 1997. *Knowledge in Organizations.* Newton, Massachusetts, U.S.A.: Butterworth-Heinemann, 1997.

O'Dell, Carla, and C. Jackson Grayson, Jr. 1998. *If We Only Knew What We Knew,* The Free Press. ISBN 0-68484474-5, $30.

Tiwana, Amrit. 2000. *The Knowledge Management Toolkit,* Englewood Cliffs, New Jersey, U.S.A.: Prentice Hall, ISBN 0-13012853-8, $45 for book and CD-ROM. Very practical.

Articles

Abram, Stephen. 1997. "Post information age positioning for special librarians: Is knowledge management the answer?" *Information Outlook* 1(6):18–25.

Bonaventura, Mike. 1997. "The benefits of a knowledge culture". *ASLIB Proceedings* 49(4):82–89.

Bridgland, Angela. 1998. "The linking of knowledge and skills to hanging work practices." *Education for Library and Information Services: Australia (ELIS:A)* 15(1):11–27.

Broadbent, Marianne. 1997. "The emerging phenomenon of knowledge management." *Australian Library Journal* 46(1), February 1997.

_____. 1998. "The phenomenon of knowledge management: What does it mean to the information profession?" *Information Outlook* 2(5):23–36.

Chase, Rory L. 1998. "Knowledge navigators." *Information Outlook* 2(9):17–24.

Coccia, Cynthia. 1998. "Avoiding a 'toxic' organization." *Nursing Management* 29(5):32–33. This very important article tells when knowledge management will not work.

Corcoran, Mary, and Rebecca Jones. 1997. "Chief knowledge officers? Perceptions, pitfalls, and potential." *Information Outlook* 1(6):30–36.

Davenport, Tom. 1996. "Some principles of knowledge management." Web site: http://www.strategy-business.com/strategy/96105/ page1.html.

Davenport, Thomas H., David W. De Long, and Michael C. Beers. 1998. "Successful knowledge management projects." *Sloan Management Review* 39(2):43–57. They studied 31 knowledge management projects in 24 companies.

Davenport, Thomas H., S.J. Jarvenpaa, and Michael C. Beers. 1996. "Improving knowledge work processes." *Sloan Management Review* 37(4):53–65.

Davenport, Thomas H., and Laurence Prusak. 1993. "Blow up the corporate library." *International Journal of Information Management* 13(6):405–412.

Delio, Michelle. 2000. "Grass roots are greener." *Knowledge Management* 3(2):47–50.

Doyle, Diane, and Adline du Toit. 1998. "Knowledge management in a law firm." *ASLIB Proceedings* 50(1):3–8.

Eddison, Betty. 1997. "Our profession is changing: Whether we like it or not." *Online* (1):72–81.

Gray, J.A. Muir. 1998. "Where's the chief knowledge officer? To manage the most precious resource of all." *British Medical Journal (BMJ)* 317:832–840.

Head, Alison J. 1997. "Managing computers and work: Are companies informated yet?" *Information Outlook* 1(9):24–30.

Helfer, Joe. 1998. "Order out of chaos: A practitioner's guide to knowledge management." *Searcher* 6(7):44–51.

Klobas, Jane. 1997. "Knowledge partners: Information professionals in the new information environment." *Australian Special Libraries* 30(4):103–116.

Macintosh, A. 1998. "Organisational knowledge management, position paper on knowledge asset management," Web site: http://www.aiai.ed.ac.uk/~alm/kam.htm.

Marshall, Lucy. 1997. "Facilitating knowledge management and knowledge sharing: New opportunities for information professionals." *Online* 21(5):92–98.

Nicolson, Marion. 1998. "The remaking of librarians in the knowledge era: skills to meet future requirements." *Education for Library and Information Services: Australia (ELIS:A)* 15(1):33–35.

Oxbrow, Nigel, and Angela Abell. 1997. "The realities of implementing knowledge management." *Business & Finance Bulletin* (Business and Finance Division, Special Libraries Association) 106:43–47.

_____. 1997. "Knowledge management: Competitive advantage for the 21st Century." *Records Management Bulletin* 83:5–10, 12.

_____ . 1998. "The role of information management in knowledge management, stimulating creativity and innovation through information," Continuing education course, Pittsburgh, Pennsylvania, U.S.A.: American Society for Information Science, 25 October 1998.

Pemberton, Michael J. 1997. "Chief knowledge officer: The climax to your career." *Records Management Quarterly* 31(2):66–69.

Platt, Nina. 1997. "Knowledge management: Can it exist in a law office?" LLRX—Law Library Resource Exchange, 1 December, Web site: http://www.llrx.com.

Shand, Dawne. 1999. "Return on knowledge." *Knowledge Management* 2(4):32–39.

Skyrme, David J. 1997. "From information to knowledge management: Are you prepared?" *Online Information 97*: Proceedings of the 21st International Online Information Meeting Held in London, 9–11 December 1997, edited by David I. Raite, Oxford: Learned Information, pp. 109–118.

St. Clair, Guy. 1998. "Knowledge management for OPLs?—Why not?" *The One-Person Library*, 14(9):1–2.

Taylor, R.M. 1996. Knowledge management. Web site: http://ourworld.compuserve. com/homepages/roberttaylor/km.htm.

Journals

The Information Advisor, Knowledge Management Quarterly Supplement, ISSN 1050-1576, FIND/SVP Inc., 625 Avenue of the Americas, New York, NY 10011, U.S.A., voice: 1-212-645-4500.

Knowledge Management: The Magazine for Knowledge Professionals. ISSN 1463-1822, Learned Information Europe Ltd., Woodside, Hinksey Hill, Oxford OX1 5BE, U.K., voice: 44-(01)865-388-8000, Web site: http://www.knowledgemanagement. co.uk, £40 per year U.K. £50 elsewhere.

Knowtes, ISSN 1093-8583, Burton Knowledge Services, $50, 4/year, voice: 1-315-488-0800, e-mail, burton@future.dreamscape .com, Web site: http://www.dream-scape.com/burton/kmmeet.htm. "A discussion of knowledge management with a holistic approach to the issues."

TECHNICAL SERVICES

Books

Hoffman, Herbert. 1986. *Small Library Cataloging*, 2nd ed. Metuchen, New Jersey, U.S.A.: Scarecrow. ISBN: 0-8108-1910-4; $25. For those with no formal cataloging training, simplified, with examples.

Mitchell, Eleanor, and Sheila Walters. 1995. *Document Delivery Services: Issues and Answers.* Medford, New Jersey, U.S.A.: Information Today, ISBN 1-57387-003-X, $42.50.

Northeast Document Conservation Center. 2000. *Handbook for Digital Projects: A Management Tool for Preservation and Access.* Andover, Pennsylvania, U.S.A.: Northeast Document Conservation Center, $38, Web site: http://www.nedcc.org.

Olson, Nancy B. 1998. *Cataloging of Audiovisual Materials and Other Special Materials: A Manual Based on AACR2*, 4th ed. Minneapolis, Minnesota, U.S.A.: Minnesota Scholarly Press, ISBN 0-93347453-9, $75.

Palmer, Joseph. 1992. *Cataloging and the Small Special Library.* Washington, D.C., U.S.A.: Special Libraries Association, ISBN 0-87111-370-8, $22.50 members, $28 nonmembers.

Swan, James. 1996. *Automating Small Libraries.* Ft. Atkinson, Wisconsin, U.S.A.: Highsmith Press, ISBN 0-917846-78-8, $19.

Journals

Against the Grain, ISSN 1043-2094, Katina Strauch, Citadel Station, Charleston, South Carolina 29409, U.S.A., voice: 1-803-723-3536. About libraries, publishers, jobbers, subscription services, 5/year, $30 U.S., $40 foreign.

ASLIB Book Guide: An international guide to English language scientific and technical books, monthly, ISSN 001-2521, Portland Press Ltd., Commerce Way, Whitehall Industrial Estate, Colchester CO2 8HP, U.K., e-mail: sales@portlandpress.co.uk.

Internet Reference Services Quarterly, ISSN 1087-5301, Binghamton, New York, U.S.A.: The Haworth Press, $36 individual, $48 libraries.

Journal of Interlibrary Loan, Document Delivery and Information Supply, ISSN 1072-303X, Binghamton, New York, U.S.A.: The Haworth Press, quarterly, $36 individual, $60 libraries.

Kirkus Reviews, ISSN 0042-6598, 200 Park Avenue, New York, New York 10003, U.S.A., fax: 1-212-979-1352, 24/year. Adult and children's pre-publication book reviews.

MEDICAL AND HOSPITAL LIBRARIES

Books

American Medical Association Manual of Style, 9th ed. 1998. Chicago, Illinois, U.S.A.: American Medical Association, ISBN 0-68340206-4, $40.

Berow, Robert. 2000. *Merck Manual of Medical Information.* New York, New York, U.S.A.: Pocket Books, ISBN 0-88737729-7, $28.95.

Darling, Louise, ed. 1993. *Handbook of Medical Library Practice* (reissue). Lanham, Maryland, U.S.A.: Scarecrow Press, ISBN 0-91217612-1, $70. Three volumes: technical services, public services, health sciences librarianship and administration.

Delafosse, Veronica. 1995. *Resources for Health Sciences: A Guide for Australia.* Adelaide, South Australia, Australia: AUSLIB Press (P.O. Box 622, Blackwood South Australia 5051, Australia), AU$30 plus AU$5 for shipping. Bibliographic data for 1,022 books, 454 journals, and 78 other references.

Detwiler, Susan, 2000. *Super Searchers on Health & Medicine: The Online Secrets of Top Health & Medical Researchers.* Medford, New Jersey, U.S.A.: Information Today, Inc., ISBN 0-910965-44-7, $24.95.

Detwiler, Susan, ed. 2001. *Detwiler's Directory of Health & Medical Resources,* 2001-2002 ed. Medford, New Jersey, U.S.A.: Information Today, Inc., ISBN 1-57387-119-2, $195.

Dorland, W. Newman, ed. 2000. *Dorland's Illustrated Medical Dictionary,* 29th ed. Philadelphia, Pennsylvania, U.S.A.: W.B. Saunders, ISBN 0-72166254-4, $50.

Friedman, Howard S., ed. 1998. *Encyclopedia of Mental Health.* New York, New York, U.S.A.: Academic Press, 3 vol., ISBN 0-12-226675-7, $550.

Geissler, Elaine. 1998. *Pocket Guide to Cultural Assessment,* 2nd ed. Philadelphia, Pennsylvania, U.S.A.: Mosby, ISBN 0-81513633-1, $25.

Guidelines for Design and Construction of Hospital and Health Care Facilities. 1996. Washington, D.C., U.S.A.: American Institute of Architects Press, ISBN 1-55835151-5, $60.

Hague, H. 1997. *Core Collection of Medical Books and Journals 1996/7.* Manchester, U.K.: Haigh and Hochland Ltd. (Precinct Centre, Oxford Road, Manchester M13 9QA, U.K., voice: 44-(0)161-2734156, fax: 44-(0)161-2734340). A core collection list with a more European focus.

Hamilton, Betty, and Barbara Guidos. 1987. *The Medical Word Finder: A Reverse Medical Dictionary,* New York, New York, U.S.A.: Neal-Schuman Publishers, ISBN 1-55570-01-X, $45. Translates layperson's language into medical terminology.

Haubrich, W.S. 1984. *Medical Meanings: A Glossary of Word Origins.* San Diego, California, U.S.A.: Harcourt Brace Jovanovich, ISBN 0-94312656-8, $30.

Holst, Ruth, and Sharon A. Phillips. 2000. *The Medical Library Association Guide to Managing Health Care Libraries,* New York, New York, U.S.A.: Neal-Schuman Publishers, ISBN 1-55570-397-6, $75.

Huth, Edward J. 1999. *Writing and Publishing in Medicine,* 3rd ed. Philadelphia, Pennsylvania, U.S.A.: Williams & Wilkins, ISBN 0-68340447-4, $35.

Jablonski, S., editor. 1998. *Dictionary of Medical Acronyms and Abbreviations,* 3rd ed. Philadelphia, Pennsylvania, U.S.A.: Hanley & Belfus. ISBN 1-56053264-5, $20.

Joint Commission on Accreditation of Healthcare Organizations. 1995. *An Introduction to the Management of Information Standards for Healthcare Organizations,* Oak Brook Terrace, Illinois, U.S.A.: JCAHO, ISBN 0-86688-429-7, $50. Section 9, The Management of Knowledge-Based Information.

Longe, E. and K. Thomas. 1998. *Consumer Health Resource Centers: A Guide to Successful Planning and Implementation.* Chicago, Illinois, U.S.A.: American Hospital Association Press, ISBN 1-55648231-0, $26.

Magalini, Sergio I. 1997. *Dictionary of Medical Syndromes,* 4th ed. Philadelphia, Pennsylvania, U.S.A.: Lippincott-Raven Press, ISBN 0-39758418-0, $99.

McCall, K., ed. 1999. *Marketing the Consumer Health Information Service.* Chicago, Illinois, U.S.A.: Medical Library Association, DocKit 12.

McCullough, Laurence B. 1998. *Surgical Ethics,* New York, New York, U.S.A.: Oxford University Press, ISBN 0-19510347-5, $55.

Miller, B.F., and C.B. Keane. 1997. *Encyclopedia and Dictionary of Medicine, Nursing, and Allied Health*, 6th ed. Philadelphia, Pennsylvania, U.S.A.: W.B. Saunders.

Moore, Dorothy L., ed. 1997. *Guide for the Development and Management of Nursing Libraries and Information Resources*. New York, New York, U.S.A.: National League for Nursing Press, ISBN 0-88737-729-7, $28.95.

Morton, Leslie, and Shane Godbolt, eds. 1992. *Information Sources in the Medical Sciences*, 4th ed. New York, New York, U.S.A.: Bowker-Saur, ISBN 0-86291-596-1, $100.

Mould, Richard F. 1996. *Mould's Medical Anecdotes: Omnibus ed.* London, U.K.: Institute of Physics, ISBN 0-75030390-5, $35.

Netter, Frank H. 1998. *Atlas of Human Anatomy*. East Hanover, New Jersey, U.S.A.: Novartis Medical Education, ISBN 0-9141688-0, $90.

Rees, A.M., editor. 2000. *Consumer Health Information Source Book*, 6th ed. Phoenix, Arizona, U.S.A.: Oryx Press, ISBN 1-57356123-4, $70.

Roper, Fred, and J.A. Boorkman. 1994. *Introduction to Reference Sources in the Health Sciences*, 3rd ed. Metuchen, New Jersey, U.S.A.: Medical Library Association and Scarecrow Press, ISBN 0-81082889-8, $37.

Rinzler, Carol A. 1999. *A Dictionary of Medical Folklore*. Lincolnwood, Illinois, U.S.A.: Wordsworth Editions Ltd./Contemporary Books NTC, ISBN 1-85326434-0, $10.95.

Schanz, Stephen J. 1999. *Using the Internet for Health Information: Legal Issues*. Chicago, Illinois, U.S.A.: American Medical Association, ISBN 0-89970977-X. $35.

Segen, J.C. 1995. *Current Med Talk: A Dictionary of Medical Terms, Slang and Jargon*. Stamford, Connecticut, U.S.A.: Appleton & Lange, ISBN 0-83851464-2, $45.

Spector, Rachel. 1999. *Cultural Diversity in Health and Illness*, 5th ed. Englewood Cliffs, New Jersey, U.S.A.: Prentice Hall, ISBN 0-83851536-3, $36.95.

Spilker, B. 1995. *Medical Dictionary in Six Languages*. Baltimore, Maryland, U.S.A.: Raven Press/Lippincott Williams & Wilkins. Sections in English, French, German, Japanese, Italian and Spanish.

Stedman, Thomas. 2000. *Stedman's Medical Dictionary*, 27th ed. Baltimore, Maryland, U.S.A.: Williams & Wilkins, ISBN 0-68340007-X, $50.

Troidl, Hans, et al. 1998. *Surgical Research: Basic Principles and Clinical Practice*, 3rd ed. New York, New York, U.S.A.: Springer, ISBN 0-38794693-3, $98.

Wayne-Doppke, Jennifer, ed. 1998. *Medical Internet Toolkit*. Santa Barbara, California, U.S.A.: COR Healthcare Resources, ISBN 0-9645369-6-4.

Wood, M. Sandra, ed. 1994. *Current Practice in Health Sciences Librarianship, vol. 1: Reference and Information Services in Health Sciences Libraries*. Chicago, Illinois,

U.S.A.: Medical Library Association, ISBN 0-8108-2765-4, 41.50. Future volumes include: educational services, information access and delivery, collection development, acquisitions, bibliographic management, health sciences environment and librarianship, administration and management.

_____. 2000. *Health Care Resources on the Internet: A Guide for Librarians and Health Care Consumers*. Binghamton, New York, U.S.A.: The Haworth Information Press. ISBN 0-7890-0911-0, $25.

Articles

Albrecht, Stephen, and Kay Wellik. 1997. "Surviving reengineering: Coping in today's health care environment." *Medical Reference Services Quarterly* 16(4):75–81.

Antes, E. Jean. 1982. "A librarian for the small hospital." *Nursing Times* 78(40):1683–1685, 6–12. Circuit-rider librarian.

Bigby, Michael. 1998. "Evidence-based medicine in a nutshell: Guide to finding and using the best evidence in caring for patients." *Archives of Dermatology* 134(12):1609–1618.

Blansit, B. Douglas, and Elizabeth Connor. 1999. "Making sense of the electronic resource marketplace: trends in health-related electronic resources." *Bulletin of the Medical Library Association* 87(3):243–250.

Calabretta, Nancy. 1996. "The hospital library as provider of consumer health information." *Medical Reference Services Quarterly* 15(3):13–22.

Cheng, Grace Y.T, and Louisa M.C. Lam. 1996. "Information-seeking behavior of health professionals in Hong Kong: A survey of thirty-seven hospitals." *Bulletin of the Medical Library Association* 84(1):32–40.

Collins, Barbara W., and Ann B. Sasser. 1998. "Medical self-managing—the hospital librarian's role." *Medical Reference Services Quarterly* 17(3):59–70.

Feuer, Sylvia. 1977. "The circuit rider librarian." *Bulletin of the Medical Library Association* 65(3):349–353.

Glitz, Beryl, et al. 1998. "Hospital library service and the changes in national standards." *Bulletin of the Medical Library Association* 86(1):77–87.

Grey-Lloyd, Joanna. 2000. "Branching out with the net." *Library Technology* 5(1):17, 20. Service to remote customers.

Grosman, Jane, and Betsy Larson. 1996. "Team building with information system departments: A hospital librarian's experience in coexisting, collaborating, and cooperating." *Bulletin of the Medical Library Association* 84(2):196–199.

Greer, Marsha C. 1998. "The medical librarian as chief information officer." *Bulletin of the Medical Library Association* 86(1):88–94.

Herin, Nancy J. 1991. "The liability of the hospital librarian: Why you need a professional medical librarian." *Hospital Topics* 69(3):26–29.

Hill, D.R., and H.N. Stickell. 1999. "Brandon/Hill selected list of books and journals for the small medical library." *Bulletin of the Medical Library Association* 873(2):145–169, published every other April.

_____. 1998. "Brandon/Hill selected list of books and journals in allied health." *Bulletin of the Medical Library Association* 86(4):447–463.

_____. 2000. "Brandon/Hill selected list of print nursing books and journals." *Nursing Outlook* 48(1):10–22.

Hollander, S. 1996. "Consumer health information partnerships: the health science library and multitype library systems." *Bulletin of the Medical Library Association* 84(2):247–252.

Holtum, Edwin A. 1999. "Librarians, clinicians, evidence-based medicine, and the division of labor." *Bulletin of the Medical Library Association* 87(4):404–407.

International Committee of Medical Journal Editors. 1997. "Uniform requirements for manuscripts submitted to biomedical journals, 5th ed." *Journal of the American Medical Association* 277(11):927–934.

Isaacs, David, and Dominic Fitzgerald. 1999. "Seven alternatives to evidence based medicine." *British Medical Journal (BMJ)* pp. 1618, 18 December, Web site: bmj.com/cgi/content/full/319/7225/1618. Humorous.

Jacobson, Susan. 1994. "Reorganization: premises, processes, and pitfalls." *Bulletin of the Medical Library Association* 82(4):369–374.

Kronenfeld, Michael R., and Fernande Hebert. 1997. "Electronic 'library without walls' in a hospital library." *Bulletin of the Medical Library Association* 85(2):198–201.

Larson, Eric B. 1999. "Evidence-based medicine: is translating evidence into practice a solution to the cost-quality challenges facing medicine?" *The Joint Commission Journal on Quality Improvement* 25(9):480–485.

Larson, Wendy. 1997. "Space: The final frontier: maximizing space in the hospital library." *National Network* 22(2):8.

LaBeause, Jan, et al. 1999. "GaIN (Georgia Interactive Network for Medical Information) study of health professionals; search requests and continuing education needs." *Medical Reference Services Quarterly* 18(2):81–89.

McKnight, Michelynn. 1997. "Get out of your library and learn what your customers need." *National Network* 22(2):11.

Milks, Deborah, and Susan Siefert. 1997. "Contracting educational and library services." *Journal of Healthcare Resource Management* 15(3):22–24. Outsourcing of a medical library in Columbus, Ohio, U.S.A.

Moran, Bronte. 1996. "The role of the medical departmental library." *Bulletin of the Medical Library Association* 84(1):25–31.

Murray, S., and D. Giustini. 1999. "The Web and electronic information (EI) in Canadian Consumer Health libraries: Perceptions of twenty public, hospital and special librarians." *Bibliotheca Medica Canadiana* 20(3):128–131.

Ohles, Janet. 1996. "The Internet: A valuable resource for the hospital librarian." *Bulletin of the Medical Library Association* 84(1):110–111.

Orchanian, A., J. Bayne, and P. Catton. 1999. "Restructuring the hospital-based library." *Bibliotheca Medica Canadiana* 20(4):169–172.

Palmer, Raymond A. 1991. "The hospital library is crucial to quality healthcare." *Hospital Topics* 69(3):20–25.

Perkins, Eva. 2000. "Healthcare resources on the Internet: A primer." *Searcher* 8(10):53–57.

Raeder, Aggi. 1996. "Finding medical information (Column: The Internet Express)". *Searcher* 4(4):40–43.

Stanley, Eileen. 2000. "Competencies for hospital librarians." *National Network* 24(2):12–13,20. The SLA competencies with hospital specific examples. A very important read.

Straus, S.E. 1992. "Evidence-based medicine as a tool." *Hospital Medicine* 59(10):762–765.

Suttles, Cheryl. 1998. "Bare necessities for information sources in small rural hospitals." *National Network* 22(4):10.

Todd Smith, Bernie. 1992. "Strategic planning: the hospital library perspective." *Bibliotheca Medica Canadiana* 13(3):146–153.

Urquhart, Christine, and John Hepworth. 1995. "The value of information supplied to clinicians by health libraries: devising an outcomes-based assessment of the contribution of libraries to clinical decision-making." *Health Libraries Review* 12(3):201–213.

Walker, Mary E. 1994. "Maslow's hierarchy and the sad case of the hospital librarian." *Bulletin of the Medical Library Association* 82(3):320–322

Journals

Bulletin of the Medical Library Association. ISSN 0025-7338.

CINAHL (Cumulative Index to Nursing and Allied Health Literature). Adventist Medical Center, bimonthly.

Health Care on the Internet, ISSN 1089-4187, Binghamton, New York, U.S.A.: The Haworth Press, quarterly, $38 individual, $85 libraries.

Health Industry QuickSource, ISSN 1077-9469, QuickSource Press, voice: 1-415-851-2556, fax: 1-415-851-9347 (descriptions and contact information for periodicals, CD-ROM, online databases, updated annually, 1,000 pp.), $225 ($180 public libraries and nonprofit organizations).

Interactive Healthcare Report, $129 for libraries, with prepayment, add $20 for non-U.S., voice: 1-888-354-6600 (U.S. only), 1-573-449-1200, e-mail: graphiced@graphiced.com.

Medical Reference Services Quarterly, ISSN 0276-3869, Binghamton, New York, U.S.A.: The Haworth Press, $32 individual, $105 libraries.

National Network, Hospital Libraries Section, Medical Library Association, quarterly.

LAW LIBRARIES

Books

Blackman, Josh. *The Legal Researcher's Internet Directory*, self-published, voice: 1-718-399-6136, $49.95.

Canadian Guide to Uniform Legal Citation, 4th ed. 1998. Scarborough, Ontario, Canada: Carswell, ISBN 0-45923799-3, $39.

Cohen, Morris L. 1989. *How to Find the Law*, 9th ed. St. Paul, Minnesota, U.S.A.: West Information, ISBN 0-31453318-4, $42.10.

Dukelow, Daphne A., and Betsy Nuse. 1995. *Dictionary of Law*, 2nd ed. Scarborough, Ontario, Canada: Carswell, ISBN 0-45955289-9, $55.

Garson, Marjorie, et al. 1988. *Reflections on Law Librarianship: A Collection of Interviews*. Littleton, Colorado, U.S.A.: FB Rothman, ISBN 0-83770128-7, $35.

The Law Society's Directory of Solicitors and Barristers. 2000. Marston Book Services, Abingdon, Oxford, U.K.: Law Society Publishing. "The only official directory of solicitors in England and Wales."

Moys, Elizabeth M., ed. 1987. *Manual of Law Librarianship: The Use and Organization of Legal Literature*, 2nd ed. Buffalo, New York, U.S.A.: GK Hall for the British and Irish Association of Law Librarians, ISBN 0-81611854-X, $65.

Panella, Deborah S. 1991. B*asics of Law Librarianship (Haworth Series in Special Librarianship, vol. 2)*. Binghamton, New York, U.S.A.: The Haworth Press, ISBN 0-86656-989-8, $40.

Price, Miles Oscar, et al. 1979. *Effective Legal Research*, 4th ed. Boston, Massachusetts, U.S.A.: Little Brown, ISBN 0-31671832-7, $35.

Prince, Mary Miles. 1997. *Bieber's Dictionary of Legal Citations: Reference Guide for Attorneys*. Buffalo, New York, U.S.A.: William S. Hein, ISBN 1-57588285-X, $39.50.

Snyder, Esther M. 2000. *Israel: A Legal Research Guide (Legal Research Guides vol. 37)*. Buffalo, New York, U.S.A.: William S. Hein ISBN 1-57588528-X, $47.

Svengalis, Kendall F. 2000. *Legal information Buyer's Guide and Reference Manual*. Barrington, Rhode Island, U.S.A.: Rhode Island Lawpress, ISBN 0-96510323-4, $99.

Voges, Mickie A. 1988. *Building Your Law Library: A Step-by-Step Guide*. Chicago, Illinois, U.S.A.: American Bar Association, ISBN 0-89707-361-4, $30. Videotape also available.

Wren, C., and J. Wren. 1999. *Legal Research Manual: A Game Plan for Legal Research and Analysis,* 3rd ed. Littleton, Colorado, U.S.A.: Legal Education Publishers, ISBN 0-91695122-7, $12.95.

Articles

Abraham, Sharon. 1998. "Librarians training lawyers." *Law Library Journal* 90(1)71–75.

Bennett, D.S. 1997. "Effectively managing the human side of change." *Law Library Journal* 89(3):355-348.

Butler, Yvonne. 1998. "Six months in a leaky boat: Issues for Australian and NZ law librarians." *The Law Librarian* 29(4):229–233.

Chanen, Jill Schahner. 1998. "Kissing law books goodbye. Many small firms are retooling their libraries via new technologies". *ABA [American Bar Association] Journal,* 84:76.

Curci-Gonzalez, Lucy. 2000. "All I really need to know about law library marketing I learned watching commercials during the Super Bowl." *AALL Spectrum* 4(6):16.

Elliott, Franki. 1998. "Legal research products on the Web." *Searcher* 6(6):64–70.

Estes Mark. 1998. "Case sensitive: Law librarians adapt to net expectations." *Library Journal* 123(12):44–46.

Griffith, C. 1997. "Law librarians embrace change." *Information Today* 14(6):18–19.

Jurek, Ken. 1999. "Law libraries no longer bound solely to books." *Crain's Cleveland Business,* 1 March:19.

Leiter, Richard. 1997. "Your role as librarian." *Legal Assistant Today* 14(3):80–81.

Lewis, Sheri. 1997. "Leadership skills for the law library manager." AALL Institute. (Baltimore). *AALL Spectrum* 2(1).

O'Toole, Susan, Charles Knuth, and Kellee Selden-Althouse. 1995. "Automated alternatives are alluring." *National Law Journal* (October 2):B9–10.

Quint, Barbara. 1996c. "The best defense is a good offense: Interview with AALL's Mark Estes." *Searcher* 4(7):12–17.

Reinke, Janet. 1999. "The informed law librarian." *Legal Information Alert* 18(3):1–5, 14. Provides a good list of resources.

Shaffer, Roberta. 1996. "The future of the law library and law librarian." *LEXIS-NEXIS Information Professional Update* (3):37.

_____. 2000. "The information innovator's institute: Divine dis-intervention." *Law Librarians in the New Millennium* 2(2):4–5, Eagan, Minnesota, U.S.A.: The West Group.

Siebers, Susan P. 1997. "Law librarians—Positioning for our future impact on the legal community: Change is inevitable, and as our parent institutions redefine their goals and objectives, so must we." *AALL Spectrum* 1(8):5.

Sih, Julie. 1995. "Are we mice, or are we marketers?" *Trends in Law Library Management and Technology* 7(4):1–4.

Westwood, Karen. 1994. "Prison law librarianship: A lesson in service for all librarians." *American Libraries* 25:152–154.

Journals

Copyright & New Media Law Newsletter, 16 pp., 3/year with two free electronic supplements, Handshake Publications, Web site: http:///www.copyrightlaw.com.

Current Publications in Legal and Related Fields, ISSN 0011-3859.

Cyberspace Lawyer, Glasser Legal Works, 150 Clove Rd., Little Falls, New Jersey 07424, U.S.A., voice: 1-800-308-1700 or 1-973-890-0008, fax: 1-973-890-0042, e-mail: legalwks@aol.com, Web site: http://www. legalwks.com, 11/year, $300. "The best source of information on legal and business developments affecting online commerce." Covers intellectual property, contract law, business arrangements, government regulation, liability, criminal law.

"Digital Technology Law Journal," from the Asia Pacific Intellectual Property Law Institute at Murdoch University, Western Australia, quarterly, Web site: http://www.law.murdoch.edu/au/dtlj /index.html.

Law Library Journal, ISSN 0023-9283.

Law Office Computing, ISSN 1055-128X, Costa Mesa, California, U.S.A.: James Publishing Group, voice: 1-800-394-2626, bimonthly, Web site: http://www. lawofficecomputing.com. Covers new computer applications from a lawyer's viewpoint.

Law Technology Product News, ISSN 0738-0186, New York Law Publishing Company, Web site: http://www.ltpn.com.

Leader's Legal Tech Newsletter, New York Law Publishing, voice, 1-800-888-8300, monthly, Web site: http://www.ljextra.com.

Legal Information Alert, ISSN 0883-1297, Chicago, Illinois, U.S.A.: Alert Publications, 16-20 pp., 10/ year, $169, e-mail: alertpub@compuserve.com.

Legal Information Management Reports, Library Specialists, Inc., Marietta, Georgia, U.S.A., voice: 1-770-578-6200, fax: 1-770-578-6263, quarterly.

Legal Looseleafs in Print, ISSN 0275-4088.

Legal Newsletters in Print, ISSN 8755-416X.

legal.online, Legal Communications Ltd., Philadelphia, Pennsylvania, voice: 1-800-722-7670, e-mail: lawline@ix.netcom .com, monthly, $149/year. "First newsletter dedicated to guiding lawyers through the maze of legal resources and information on the Internet."

Legal Reference Services Quarterly, Binghamton, New York, U.S.A.: The Haworth Press, $40 individual, $115 libraries.

LegaNet, $99 per year (U.S.$110 per year non-U.S.A.), contact Legamed, Inc., 8364 Six Forks Rd., Suite 104, Raleigh, North Carolina 27615, U.S.A., Web site: http://www.legamed.com. "Designed to quickly and concisely summarize important legal, legislative and regulatory developments affecting the use of the Internet by physicians, nurses, lawyers, and those disseminating health information electronically." The company also publishes Telemed Law and Carelaw.

Patent, Trademark & Copyright Journal, ISSN 0148-7965, Bureau of National Affairs, 12311 25th St., NW, Washington, D.C. 20037, U.S.A., voice: 1-202-452-4200, weekly, $1,366/year.

PLL Perspectives (Private Law Libraries special interest section, American Association of Law Libraries), included in membership.

Research Advisor: Information Solutions for Today's Legal Professionals, Alert Publications, Inc., 6/year, $49 U.S., $59 Canada and Mexico, $20 elsewhere.

State, Court and County Law Libraries Newsletter (special interest section, American Association of Law Libraries), included in membership.

Trends in Law Library Management and Technology, Fred B. Rothman & Co., bimonthly, voice: 1-800-457-1986. "Thought-provoking articles."

World Intellectual Property Report, ISSN 0952-7613, Bureau of National Affairs, 1231 25th St., NW, Washington, D.C. 20038, U.S.A., voice: 1-202-452-7549, e-mail: marketing@bnai.com, $950/year in U.S.A. and Canada, £560 rest of world, mail alerting available at no additional cost, 2nd and subsequent subscriptions half price. "Monthly news and analysis on IP law, regulation and policy from around the world."

SMALL PUBLIC LIBRARIES

Books

Campbell, William D. 1987. *A Bookkeeping System for Small Public Libraries.* Clarion, Pennsylvania, U.S.A.: Center for the Study of Rural Librarianship, $7.95.

_____. 1987. *A Budgeting Manual for Small Public Libraries.* Clarion, Pennsylvania, U.S.A.: Center for the Study of Rural Librarianship, $6.95. Very detailed.

Dahlgren, Anders C. 1996. *Planning the Small Library Facility*, 2nd ed., Small Libraries Publication 23, Chicago, Illinois, U.S.A.: American Library Association, ISBN 0-8389-0681-8, $15.

Fox, Beth Wheeler. 1990. *Behind the Scenes at the Dynamic Library: Simplifying Essentials. Technical Services in the Small Library.* Chicago, Illinois, U.S.A.: American Library Association, ISBN 0-8389-0531-5, $15.

Gervasi, Anne, and Betty Kay Seibt. 1988. *Handbook for Small, Rural, and Emerging Public Libraries.* Phoenix, Arizona, U.S.A.: Oryx, ISBN 0-89774-303-2, $31.50. Excellent, very detailed.

Henri, James, and Roy Sanders, eds. 1987. *Libraries Alone: Proceedings of the Rural and Isolated Librarians Conference.* Wagga Wagga, New South Wales, Australia: Libraries Alone. ISBN 0-7316-1766-2. One hundred seventy participants from all over Australia and New Zealand; keynote from Bernard Vavrek.

Katz, Bill, ed. 1988. *The How-To-Do-It Manual for Small Libraries.* New York, New York, U.S.A.: Neal-Schuman Publishers. ISBN 1-55570-016-0, $50.

Koenig, Michael E.D. 1980. *Budgeting Techniques for Libraries and Information Centers. Special Libraries Association Professional Development Series 1.* Washington, D.C., U.S.A.: Special Libraries Association.

Larson, Jeannette, and Herman L. Totten. 1998. *Model Policies for Small and Medium Public Libraries.* New York, New York, U.S.A.: Neal-Schuman Publishers, ISBN 1-55570-343-7, paper, $50.

Vavrek, Bernard. 1993. *Assessing the Role of the Rural Public Library.* Clarion, Pennsylvania, U.S.A.: Clarion University of Pennsylvania.

Weingand, Darlene E. 2000. *Administration of the Small Public Library*, 4th ed. Chicago, Illinois, U.S.A.: American Library Association, ISBN 0-8389-0794-6.

Wynar, Bohdan S., ed. 2000. *Recommended Reference Books for Small and Medium Sized Libraries and Media Centers*, Englewood, Colorado, U.S.A.: Libraries Unlimited, ISBN 1-56308838-X, $60.

LAMA Small Libraries Publications Series, Chicago, Illinois, U.S.A.: American Library Association, $4.50 members, $5 nonmembers. Publications on trustees, budgeting, PR, administration, cooperation, buildings, reference, AV, collection development, automation, personnel, and volunteer management.

Neal-Schuman (various). *How-To-Do-It Manuals for Librarians.* New York, Neal-Schuman Publishers. Subjects covered include trustees, boards, managing time.

Articles

Hardsog, Ellen L. 1992. "The small town library: discovering relevancy." *The Reference Librarian* (38):31–39.

Hennen, Thomas J., Jr. 1986. "Attacking the myths of small libraries." *American Libraries* 17:803.

Kadanoff, Diane G. 1986. "Small libraries—No small job!" *Library Journal* 111:71–73.

Kenneally, Adele. 1998. "Mobile services: Australian style." *Bookmobile and Outreach Services* 2(1):26–38.

Kramer, Pamela K., 1989. "Salute to the 'super SOLOs'—School librarians who do it all." *Illinois Libraries* 71:282-283. By a non-SOLO.

Pitts, Roberta L. 1994. "A generalist in the age of specialists: A profile of The One-Person Library director." *Library Trends* 43(1):121–135.

Pungitore, Verna, compiler. 1990. "Life in small public libraries of Indiana." *Indiana Libraries* 9(1):23–37. Essays by four small public librarians.

Stipek, Kathleen. 1988. "The public library." In *The How-To-Do-It Manual for Small Libraries*, edited by Bill Katz. New York, New York, U.S.A.: Neal-Schuman Publishers, pp. 3–13.

White, Herbert S. 1994. "Small public libraries—Challenges, opportunities, and irrelevancies." *Library Journal* 119(7):53–54.

Journals

Emergency Librarian, ISSN 0315-8888, Rockland Press, P.O. Box C34069, Dept. 284, Seattle, Washington 98124-1069, U.S.A., voice: 1-604-825-0266, fax: 1-604-925-0566, 284-810 W. Broadway, Vancouver, British Columbia, Canada V5Z 4C9, 5/year, $49 billed, $44 prepaid. Library services for children and young adults.

CHURCH AND SYNAGOGUE LIBRARIES

Books

Caughman, Ginger. 1990. *Church Library Promotion: A Handbook of How-To's*, Jefferson, North Carolina, U.S.A.: McFarland, ISBN 0-899502-881, $35.

Church and Synagogue Library Association Guide Series, Church and Synagogue Library Association, P.O Box 19357, Portland, Oregon 97219, U.S.A. How to set up a library, cataloging, policy manuals, reference, and so on.

Dotts, Maryann. 1988. *You Can Have a Church Library: Start, Enhance and Expand Your Religious Learning Center, A Step-by-Step Guide for Church Leaders*, rev. ed. Nashville, Tennessee, U.S.A.: Abingdon, ISBN 0-68704604-1, $6.

Harvey, John, ed. 1980. *Church and Synagogue Libraries*. Metuchen, New Jersey, U.S.A.: Scarecrow. ISBN: 0-8108-1304-1, $25.

McMichael, Betty. 1998. *The Church Librarian's Handbook: A Complete Guide for the Library and Resource Center in Christian Education*, 3rd ed. Grand Rapids, Michigan, U.S.A.: Baker Book House. ISBN: 0-8010-5772-8, $18.

Rodda, Dorothy. 1992. *Church and Synagogue Library Resources*, 5th ed. Portland, Oregon, U.S.A.: Church and Synagogue Library Association, ISBN 0-915324334, $7.10.

Saul, Arthur K. 1980. *121 Ways Toward a More Effective Church Library*, Victor Books (location unknown), ISBN 0-88207-171-8.

Tucker, Dennis C. 2000. *Research Techniques for Scholars and Students in Religion and Theology*. Medford, New Jersey, U.S.A.: Information Today, Inc. ISBN 1-57387-089-7.

Walls, Francine. 1980. *The Church Library Workbook*, Winona, Indiana, U.S.A.: Light and Life Communications, ISBN 0-89367048-0, $3.

Reference

Achtemeier, Paul J., ed. 1996. *HarperCollins Bible Dictionary*. New York, New York, U.S.A.: Harper Collins, ISBN 0-06060037-2, $45.

McGee, J. Vernon. 1984. *Thru the Bible*. 5 vols. Nashville, Tennessee, U.S.A.: Thomas Nelson, ISBN 0-78520041-X, $125.

Meeks, Wayne A., ed. 1997. *HarperCollins Study Bible*. New York, New York, U.S.A.: Harper Collins, ISBN 0-06065527-5, $27.

The New Interpreter's Bible. 2000. 12 vols. Nashville, Tennessee, U.S.A.: Abingdon, ISBN 0-68723547-1, $770.

Pritchard, James B., ed. 1997. *HarperCollins Atlas of the Bible*. New York, New York, U.S.A.: Harper Collins, ISBN 0-06251499-7, $25. Reprint.

Journals

Christian Bookseller and Librarian, ISSN 0749-2510.

Christian History, ISSN 0891-9666, Carol Stream, Illinois, U.S.A.: Christianity Today.

The Christian Librarian, ISSN 0412-3131.

Christian Media Journal (formerly Church Media Library Journal), Nashville, Tennessee, U.S.A.: The Sunday School Board of the Southern Baptist Convention.

Christian Periodical Index, ISSN 0069-3871.

Creation Care (formerly Green Cross), Wynnewood, Pennsylvania, U.S.A.: Evangelical Environmental Network.

Horizons, Louisville Kentucky, U.S.A.: Presbyterian Women, Presbyterian Church, U.S.

Journal of Religious and Theological Information, Binghamton, New York, U.S.A.: The Haworth Press, biannual, $24 individual, $48 libraries.

Presbyterians Today, ISSN 1083-2181, Louisville, Kentucky, U.S.A.: Presbyterian Church, U.S.

Provident Book Finder, Scottsdale, Pennsylvania, U.S.A.: Provident Bookstores.

Publishers Weekly Religion Bookline, ISSN 0000-1694, P.O. Box 6457, Torrance, California 90504-0457, U.S.A., voice: 1-800-278-2991 or 1-310-978-6916, fax: 1-310-978-6901, 2/month, $79 U.S., higher rest of world.

OTHER KINDS OF LIBRARIES

Books

AALL Standing Committee on Law Library Service to Institution Residents and American Correctional Association. 1991. *Correctional Facility Law Libraries: An A to Z Resource Guide*. Chicago, Illinois, U.S.A.: American Association of Law Libraries, ISBN 0-929310-55-1, $16.

Bierbaum, Esther Green. 2000. *Museum Librarianship: A Guide to the Provision and Management of Information Services*, 2nd ed. Jefferson, North Carolina, U.S.A.: McFarland, ISBN 0-7864086-7, $40.

Collins, Marcia. 1977. *Libraries for Small Museums,* 3rd ed. Museum Brief 7, Columbia Missouri, U.S.A.: Museum of Anthropology, University of Missouri, ISBN 0-91313490-2, $2.50.

Dobzhansky, Theodoi. 1981. *Library Service: A Guide for Librarians and Jail Administrators*. Chicago, Illinois, U.S.A.: American Library Association, ISBN 0-8389-3258-4, $19.

Rubin, Rhea J., and Daniel S. Suvak. 1995. *Libraries Inside: A Practical Guide for Prison Libraries*. Jefferson, North Carolina, U.S.A.: McFarland, ISBN 0-93533711-1, $41.50.

Rudin, Claire. 1990. *The School Librarian's Sourcebook.* New York, New York, U.S.A.: R.R. Bowker, ISBN 0-8352-2711-1, $38.

Sager, Donald J. 2000. *Small Libraries: Organization and Operation*, 3rd ed. Fort Atkinson, Wisconsin, U.S.A.: Highsmith Press, ISBN 1-5795-5-87, $19. Includes chapters on public, school, church and synagogue, law, business, medical, museum, and other libraries.

Werner, Oliver James. 1990. *Werner's Manual for Prison Law Libraries*, 2nd ed. Littleton Colorado, U.S.A.: F.B. Rothman for the American Association of Law Libraries, ISBN 0-83770136-8, $22.50.

Articles

Bierbaum Esther G. 1996. "Museum libraries: The more things change." *Special Libraries* 87(2):74–78.

Carns, Brenda. 1989. "Locked up libraries." *Colorado Libraries* 15(3):17–18.

Skapura, Robert. 1988. "The school library." In *The How-To-Do-It Manual for Small Libraries*, edited by Bill Katz. New York, New York, U.S.A.: Neal-Schuman Publishers, pp. 14–26.

Journals

American Archivist, ISSN 0360-9081.

Information Processing and Management, ISSN 03-6-4573.

International Journal of Information Management, ISSN 0268-4012.

Journal of Management Information, ISSN 0742-1222.

Records Management Journal, 3/year, ISSN 0956-5698, Portland Press Ltd., Commerce Way, Whitehall Industrial Estate, Colchester CO2 8HP, U.K., e-mail: sales@portlandpress.co.uk. Also available electronically with hard copy subscription.

Records Management Quarterly, ISSN 1050-2343.

TECHNOLOGY, INTERNET, AND ONLINE SEARCHING

Books

Banks, Michael A. 2000. *The Modem Reference: The Complete Guide to PC Communications,* 4th ed. Medford, New Jersey, U.S.A.: CyberAge Books. ISBN 0-910965-36-6, $29.95. Also includes chapters on faxing, "The Internet Defined," browsers, data conversion, troubleshooting, and lists of equipment manufacturers and vendors.

Basch, Reva. 1994. *Secrets of the Super Searchers: The Accumulated Wisdom of 23 of the World's Top Online Searchers.* Medford, New Jersey, U.S.A.: CyberAge Books, ISBN 0-910965-12-9, $39.95. A combination of tips and tricks and confirmation that you have been doing it right, check the Super Searchers website (http://www.infoto-day.com/supersearchers) for other excellent books in this series.

Benson, Allen C. 1995. *The Complete Internet Companion for Librarians.* New York, New York, U.S.A.: Neal-Schuman Publishers, $49.95, ISBN 1-55570-178-7, $50. Many lists of useful places to find information on the Internet.

Carroll, John A. 1994. *The Canadian Internet Handbook.* Toronto, Ontario, Canada: Prentice Hall, Canada, $16.95, ISBN 0-13-304-395-9, $13.

Ensor, Pat, ed. various. *Key Guide to Electronic Resources Series.* Medford, New Jersey, U.S.A.: Information Today, Inc., *Art and Art History,* 1996 (ISBN 1-57387-020-X), *Engineering,* 1995 (ISBN 1-57837-008-0), *Health Sciences,* 1995 (ISBN 1-57387-001-3), and *Agriculture* (ISBN 1-57837-000-5), $39.50 each.

Glossbrenner, Alfred, and Emily Glossbrenner. 1994. *Internet Slick Tricks.* New York, New York, U.S.A.: Random House, ISBN 0-679-75611-6, $16.

Graef, Jean. 1996. *Leveraging Know-How: The Internet's Role in the Corporate Knowledgebase.* The Montague Institute, 18 Main St., P.O. Box 8, Montague, Massachusetts 01351-0008, U.S.A., voice: 1-413-367-0245, e-mail: jgraef@mon-tague.com, Web site: http://www.montague.com, $30.

Head, Alison J. 1999. *Design Wise: A Guide for Evaluating the Interior Design of Information Resources.* Medford, New Jersey, U.S.A.: CyberAge Books, ISBN 0-910965-39-0 (hardcover), ISBN 0-910965-31-5 (paper), $29.95 (paper). Divided into two sections: "Interface Design Basics" and "Interface Design Analyses" (including CD-ROMS, web sites, and online databases).

Hogarth, Michael, MD, and David Hutchinson, RN. *An Internet Guide for the Health Professional,* 2nd ed. Houston, Texas, U.S.A.: Majors Scientific Books, ISBN 0-96514120-9, $30.

Ladner, Sharyn J., and Hope N. Tillman. 1993. *The Internet and Special Librarians; Use, Training and the Future.* Washington, D.C., U.S.A.: Special Libraries

Association, $26.50 members, $33 nonmembers, ISBN 0-87111-413-5. Result of a survey.

Li, Xia and Nancy B. Crane. 1996. *Electronic Styles: A Handbook for Citing Electronic References*. Medford, New Jersey, U.S.A.: Information Today, Inc. ISBN 1-57387-027-7. Covers both APA Embellished Style and MLA Embellished Style.

Metz, Ray E., and Gail Junion-Metz. 1995. *Using the World Wide Web and Creating Home Pages: A How-To-Do-It Manual for Librarians*. New York, New York, U.S.A.: Neal-Schuman Publishers, ISBN 1-55570-241-4, $55.

Morris, A., and H. Dyer. 1998. *Human Aspects of Library Automation*, 2nd ed. Aldershot, Hampshire, England: Gower, ISBN 0-56607504-0, $100.

Newby, Gregory B. 1993. *Directory of Directories on the Internet: A Guide to Information Sources*. Westport, Connecticut, U.S.A.: Mecklermedia, ISBN 0-88736-786-2, $55.

Paul, Nora and Margot Williams. 1999. *Great Scouts! CyberGuides for Subject Searching on the Web*. Medford, New Jersey, U.S.A.: CyberAge Books. ISBN 0-910965-27-7, $24.95. Includes Life and Times (education, food, health and medicine, politics, religion, travel), Business and Professional Resources (management, governement, law, news, reference), Arts and Entertainment (architecture, crafts, literature, libraries, sports), and Science and Technology (computer, environment).

Poulter, Alan, Debra Hiom, and Gwyneth Tseng. 2000. *The Library and Information Professional's Guide to the Internet*, 3rd ed. London, U.K.: Library Association Publishing, 2000, ISBN 1-85604-376-2, $40. Written by and for librarians, very comprehensive, U.K. and the rest of the world, Includes discussion lists, electronic journals and newsletters, general reference, software, networking guides, training materials, information servers and gateways, subject listings and indexing services, online public access catalogs.

Still, Julie M. 2001. *Creating Web-Accessible Databases: Case Studies for Libraries, Museums, and Other Nonprofits*. Medford, New Jersey, U.S.A.: Information Today, Inc. ISBN 1-57387-104-4.

Tillman, Hope, ed. 1995. *Internet Tools of the Profession: A Guide for Special Librarians*. Washington, D.C., U.S.A.: Special Libraries Association, ISBN 0-87111-4677-4, $30 members, $37.50 nonmembers.

The Virtual Library: An SLA Information Kit, 1994, Washington, D.C., U.S.A.: Special Libraries Association, $15 members, $20 nonmembers, ISBN 0-87111-428-3, $20. A compilation of articles on how to go virtual.

Articles

Balas, Janet L. 1999. "The 'don'ts' of Web page design." *Computers in Libraries* 19(8):46–48.

Cronin, Blaise, et al. 1994. "The Internet and competitive intelligence: A survey of current practice." *International Journal of Information Management* 14(3):204–222.

Glinert, Susan. 1999. "Top of the ranks." *Home Office Computing* 17(11):105–106.

Guenther, Kim. 1999. "Publicity through better web site design." *Computers in Libraries* 19(8):62–67.

Jacso, Peter. 2000. "Be savvy! Sometimes the free resources are better." *Computers in Libraries* 20(5):58–59.

Nicholls, Paul. 1996. "Why did you think they called it the World Wide Web?" *Searcher* 4(5):20–27. Good list of international Web sites.

Journals

Computers in Libraries, Medford, New Jersey, U.S.A.: Information Today, Inc., ISSN 1041-7915, 10/year, $87.95 U.S., $97.95 Canada and Mexico, $105.95 rest of world. Includes Internet Librarian and CD-ROM Librarian, Libraries of the Future, and Current Cites.

EContent (formerly Database), 6/year, Online, Inc., $49.50, http://www.onlineinc.com/database.

The Electronic Library, Learned Information Ltd., 0264-0473, 6/year, $120.

Information Highways: Canada's Magazine for Consumers of Strategic Electronic Information. 162 Joicey Blvd., Toronto, Ontario, Canada M5M 2V2, voice: 1-416-488-7372, fax: 1-416-488-7078. CA$68/year in Canada.

Information Technology Newsletter, ISSN 1057-7939, Idea Group Publishing, 4811 Jonestown Road, Suite 230, Harrisburg, Pennsylvania 17109-1751, U.S.A., voice 1-717-541-9150, fax: 1-717-541-9159, e-mail: 75364.3150@compuserve.com, semi-annually, free.

Link-Up: The Newsmagazine for Users of Online Services, CD-ROM, and the Internet, 0739-988X, Medford, New Jersey, U.S.A.: Information Today, Inc., 6/year, $28.95 U.S., $35 Canada and Mexico.

Online, ISSN 0146-5422, Online, Inc., $49.50, 6/year, Web site: http://www.onlineinc.com onlinemag.

Online and CD Notes, 10/year, ISSN 0144-025X, also available electronically with hard copy subscription, Portland Press Ltd., Commerce Way, Whitehall Industrial Estate, Colchester CO2 8HP, U.K., e-mail: sales@portlandpress.co.uk.

Online Currents: Covering the Australian and international online and optical information industry, ISSN 0816-956X, Enterprise Information Management Pty Ltd., P.O.

Box 215, Lindfield, New South Wales 2070 Australia, voice: 61-2-9880-9000, fax: 61-2-9880-9001, e-mail: olc@pnc.com.au, Web site: http://www.sofcom.com.au/olc, 10/year, print or electronic only: A$165 (Australia), A$185 (overseas); print plus electronic: A$200 (Australia), A$220 (overseas). A very good summary of online/Internet happenings in Australia and elsewhere. Also covers conferences, hardware, and books.

Searcher: The Magazine for Database Professionals. Medford, New Jersey, U.S.A.: Information Today, Inc., ISSN 1070-4795, 10/year, $55.95 U.S., $67 Canada and Mexico, $78 rest of world. Invaluable for what's new in online and for Barbara Quint's unique point of view.

EDUCATION AND ALTERNATIVE CAREERS

Books

Allen, Lawrence A. 1974. *Continuing Education Needs of Special Librarians.* New York, New York, U.S.A.: Special Libraries Association, (SLA State-of-the-Art Review 3).

Burwell, Helen P. 2001. *The Burwell World Directory of Information Brokers.* Dallas, Texas, U.S.A.: Burwell Enterprises, ISBN 0-93851919-0, $59.50.

Coffman, Steve, and Pat Weidensohler. 1993. *The FISCAL Directory of Fee-Based Research and Document Supply Services,* 4th ed. Los Angeles, California, U.S.A.: County of Los Angeles Public Library, ISBN 0-8389-2161-2, ISSN 1067-7674, $75.

The EIRENE Directory (European Information Researchers' Network), £55, London, U.K.: First Contact, Ltd., voice: 44-(0)71-490-5519, fax: 44-(0)71-490-4610.

Everett, John H., and Elizabeth Powell Crowe. 1994. *Information for Sale: How to Start and Operate Your Own Data Research Service,* 2nd ed. New York, New York, U.S.A.: Windcrest/McGraw-Hill. ISBN: 0-070199507, $17.

Garoogian, Rhoda. 1985. *Careers in Other Fields for Librarians.* Chicago, Illinois, U.S.A.: American Library Association, ISBN 0-8389-0431-9, $15.

Griffiths, Jose-Marie, and Donald W. King. 1986. *New Directions in Library and Information Science Education.* White Plains, New York, U.S.A.: Knowledge Industry Press for American Society for Information Science, ISBN 0-31325779-5, $75.

Horton, Forest Woody, Jr. 1994. *Extending the Librarian's Domain: A Survey of Emerging Occupational Opportunities for Librarians and Information Professionals.* Washington, D.C., U.S.A.: Special Libraries Association (Occasional Papers Series 4). ISBN: 0-87111-419-4, $38.

Mount, Ellis, ed. 1993. *Opening New Doors: Alternative Careers for Librarians.* Washington, D.C., U.S.A.: Special Libraries Association. ISBN: 0-87111-408-9; $39, profiles of 12 entrepreneurs and 16 workers in nontraditional positions.

_____. 1997. *Expanding Technologies—Expanding Careers: Librarianship in Transition.* Washington, D.C., U.S.A.: Special Libraries Association, ISBN 0-87111-465-8, $45. A newer version of the above; includes a chapter by Judith Siess.

Plumez, Jacqueline H., and Karla Dougherty. 1986. *Divorcing a Corporation: How to Know When—and If—a Job Change is Right for You.* New York, New York, U.S.A.: Villard Books, ISBN 0-394-54457-9, $17. I did not look at this, but from the title it sounds fascinating.

Rochester, Maxine, ed. *Education for Librarianship Series.* London, U.K.: Mansell, Published as of 2000: Australia, New Zealand and the Pacific Islands, Scandinavia, U.S., U.K., c. $100 each.

Rugge, Sue, and Alfred Glossbrenner. 1997. *The Information Broker's Handbook.* New York, New York, U.S.A.: McGraw-Hill. ISBN: 0-07057871-0, $35.

Sellen, Betty-Carol. 1997. *What Else Can You Do With a Library Degree?* New York, New York, U.S.A.: Neal-Schuman Publishers, ISBN 1-55570264-3, $33.

Sellen, Betty-Carol, and Dimity S. Berkner. 1984. *New Options for Librarians: Finding a Job in a Related Field.* New York, New York, U.S.A.: Neal-Schuman Publishers, ISBN: 0-918212-73-1, $40.

Warner, Alice Sizer. 1987. *Mind Your Own Business: A Guide for the Information Entrepreneur.* New York, New York, U.S.A.: Neal-Schuman Publishers, ISBN 1-555-70014-4, $30.

Articles

Brees, Mina Akins. 1973. "The challenge for library schools: A student's view." *Special Libraries* 64(10):433–438.

Eismark, Henrik. 1995. "The business of entrepreneurship in Europe: Would-be information brokers click here." *Searcher* 3(10):18–22.

Hill, Linda. 1993. "Education for library and information management careers in corporate environments." *Library Trends* 42(2):225–368.

Piggott, Sylvia. 1996. "Charting the course to the 21st Century: Managing your career and your profession." *LMD Quarterly* 19(1) 4–6. Summary of findings from workshops held October to November at Eastern Canada, Baltimore, and Washington SLA chapters.

Williams, W.W. 1994. "Library journal career survey part 3: Alternative careers: You can take your MLS out of the library." *Library Journal* 119(19):43–46.

Williamson, Joan. 1988. "One person libraries and information units: Their education and training needs." *Library Management* 9(5):1–72.

Willner, Richard A. 1993. "Education for library and information management careers in business and financial services." *Library Trends* 42(2):232–248.

Wooley, Marcus. 1988. "The One-Person Library: Professional Development and Professional Management." *Library Management* 9(1). One British OPL's first year, written for his certification.

NON-U.S. ESSENTIAL REFERENCES

U.K.

ASLIB Directory of Information Sources in the U.K., 10th ed. 1999, London, U.K.: ASLIB, Web site: http://www.aslib.co.uk/pubs/ index.html, ISBN 0-85142409-0.

The Civil Service Yearbook (annual). London, U.K.: The Stationery Office, ISBN 0-11430158-1, £40.

Councils, Committees and Boards, Including Government Agencies and Authorities, 10th ed. 1999. Beckenham, Kent, U.K.: CBD Research. ISBN 0-900246-84-7, ISSN 0070-1211.

Dale, Peter. 1998. *Guide to Libraries and Information Units in Government Departments and Other Organisations.* London, U.K.: British Library. ISBN 0-7123-0845-8, £37.

_____. 2000. *Guide to Libraries and Information Sources in Medicine and Healthcare*, 3rd ed. London, U.K.: British Library. ISBN 0-7123-0856-3, £40.

Directory of British Associations and Associations in Ireland. 2000. CBD Research, Web site: http://www.glen.co.uk/cbd, ISBN 0-90024686-3, £175.

Henderson, S.P.A., and A.J.W. Henderson, eds. 2000. *Directory of Hospitals and NHS Trust*s. London, U.K.: Informa Healthcare, ISBN 1-85978569-7, £99.

Henderson C.A.P., ed. 1999. *Benn's Media: U.K, Europe, World.* Tonbridge, Kent, U.K.: Miller Freeman U.K. Ltd., ISBN 1-89148289-0, £142.50.

Municipal Yearbook (annual). Newman Books, Hemming Group, Web site, http://www.h-info.co.uk, 2 vols., ISBN 0-790796993-X, £144.

Philips Great World Atlas, 4th ed. 1994. London, U.K.: George Philip.

Turner, Barry, ed. 2001. *Statesman's Yearbook.* London, U.K.: Palgrave, ISBN 0-33377566-X, £60.

Whitaker's Almanack. 2001. London, U.K.: The Stationery Office, Web site: http://www.whitakers-almanack.co.uk. ISBN 0-11-702261-6, £40. (also Scottish Almanack, London Almanack, Obituary Almanack, and Olympic Almanack).

Whitehall Companion 2000. London, U.K.: Stationery Office, ISBN 0-11702263-2, £165.

Who's Who (U.K.). 2000. London, U.K.: A&C Black, ISBN 0-7136-5158-X.

MISCELLANEOUS

Books

Amende, Coral. 1999. *Random House Famous Name Finder*. New York, New York, U.S.A.: Random House, ISBN 1-37570602-X, $14. "Concise biographies of over 10,000 legendary people, indexed four ways."

Cibbarelli, Pamela, ed. 2000. *Directory of Library Automation Software, Systems, and Services*. Medford, New Jersey, U.S.A.: Information Today, Inc., ISBN 1-57387088-9, $89.

Soukhanov, Anne H., ed. 1999. *Encarta World English Dictionary*. New York, New York, U.S.A.: St. Martin's, 1999, ISBN 0-312-22222-X, $50. Entries for all variations of English—U.K., Australia, U.S., and so on—not comprehensive, but highly recommended.

Journals

Keesing's Record of World Events, ISSN 0950-6128, Keesing's Worldwide LLC, P.O. Box 5590, Washington, D.C. 20010-1190, U.S.A., voice: 1-800-332-3535 or 1-301-718-8770, fax: 1-301-718-8494, U.K. and Europe 44-(01)1223-508050, e-mail: info@keesings.com. A monthly digest of world news, also available on the Internet.

PUBLISHERS

To find addresses of publishers not found here, try http://www.mediafinder.com.

Alert Publications, Inc., 401 W. Fullerton Parkway, Suite 1403E, Chicago, Illinois 60614-2805, U.S.A., voice: 1-773-525-7594, fax: 1-773-525-7015, e-mail: info@alertpub.com, Web site: http://www.alertpub.com.

American Library Association, 50 E. Huron St., Chicago, Illinois 60611, U.S.A., voice: 1-800-545-2433, Web site: http://www.ala.org; in Canada: order through CLA, voice: 1-613-232-9625, ext. 310. Primarily for public libraries, but some publications are of interest to all.

Books on Tape, Inc., P.O. Box 7900, Newport Beach, California 92658, U.S.A., voice: 1-800-541-5525 or 1-714-825-0021, fax: 1-714-825-0756, Web site: http://www.booksontape.com, unabridged audiobooks.

R.R. Bowker, 121 Chanlon Rd., New Providence, New Jersey 07974, U.S.A., voice: 1-888-269-5372, e-mail: info@bowker.com, Web site: http://www.bowker.com. A wide range of reference books, especially in the library/book area.

Center for the Study of Rural Librarianship, The Small Library Development Center, Clarion University of Pennsylvania, Clarion, PA 16214, U.S.A., $2 each. A mix of scholarly and very useful publications, including bibliographies on subjects such as rural library service, public relations, administration, technical service, and so on.

Gale Group, 27500 Drake Rd., Farmington Hills, Michigan 48331, U.S.A., voice: 1-248-699-3253, fax: 1-248-699-8064, e-mail: galeord@galegroup.com, Web site: http://www.galegroup.com. Mostly reference books.

The Haworth Press, Inc., 10 Alice St., Binghamton, New York 13904-1580, U.S.A., voice: 1-800-342-9678 or 1-607-722-5857, fax: 1-800-895-0582 or 1-607-722-6362, e-mail: get info@haworthpressinc.com, Web site: http://www.haworthpressinc.com. Books and serials on reference and technical services.

HW Wilson Co., 950 University Ave., Bronx, New York 10452, U.S.A., voice: 1-800-367-6770 or 1-718-588-8400, fax: 1-718-5900, Web site: http://www.hwwilson.com.

Information Today, Inc., 143 Old Marlton Pike, Medford, New Jersey 08055, U.S.A., voice: 1-800-300-9868 or 1-609-654-6266, fax: 1-609-654-4309, e-mail: custserv @infotoday.com, Web site: http://www.infotoday.com. Books, directories, journals, and conferences for librarians, information professionals, and knowledge workers.

Libraries Unlimited, P.O. Box 6633, Englewood, Colorado 80155-6633, U.S.A., voice: 1-800-237-6124 or 1-303-770-1220, fax: 1-303-220-8843, e-mail: lu-books@lu.com, Web site: http://www. lu.com. Library textbooks and reference works, much for educators and school librarians.

Marquis Who's Who, 121 Chanlon Rd., New Providence, New Jersey 07974, U.S.A., voice: 1-800-521-8110 or 1-908-464-6800, fax: 1-908-665-6688, e-mail: info.marquiswhoswho@renp.com, Web site: http://www.marquiswhoswho.com. Biographical reference books.

Neal-Schuman Publishers, Inc., 100 Varick St., New York, New York 10013, U.S.A., voice: 1-212-925-8650, fax: 1-800-584-2414, e-mail: info@neal-schuman.com, Web site: http://www.neal-schuman.com. Mostly library and information science books.

Online, Inc., 213 Danbury Rd., Wilton, Connecticut 06897-4007, U.S.A., voice: 1-800-248-8466 or 1-203-761-1466, fax: 1-203-761-1444, e-mail: info@onlineinc.com, Web site: http://www.onlineinc .com. Publishers of eContent and database magazines.

O'Reilly and Associates, Inc., 103 Morris St., Suite A, Sebastopol, California 95472, U.S.A., voice: 1-800-998-9938 or 1-707-829-0515, Web site: http://www.oreilly.com. Internet and computer books.

Public Library Association, a division of the American Library Association, 50 E. Huron St., Chicago, Illinois 60611, U.S.A., voice: 1-800-545-2433, Web site: http://www.ala.org.

SMR International (Guy St. Clair), 527 Third Ave., New York, New York 10116, U.S.A., voice: 1-212-683-6285, fax: 1-212-683-2987, e-mail: guystclair@cs.com. Publications especially for Solos and library managers.

Special Libraries Association, 1700 18th St., NW, Washington, D.C. 20009-2508, U.S.A., voice: 1-202-234-4700, fax 1-202-265-9317, Web site: http://www.sla.org.

12

Vendors and Suppliers

All libraries need to purchase supplies or services. The dilemma is how to get the best product at the best price. How do you solve this problem? Talk to vendors at library conferences. Spend as much time as you can at the exhibits. If possible, do so a time when fewer people are at the exhibits so that you will have more time to talk with the vendors. I usually try to make one pass through the exhibits to see what is there, and then return to talk to the vendors who interest me the most. Leave your business card and ask them to send their literature to your office. You can also talk to *selected* vendors in your office. You shouldn't say yes to every vendor who calls you on the phone or sends you literature, but you should talk to any that sell services you need now or are likely to need in the future. Set aside an hour or so and listen to what they have to say. Use salespeople as you would a resource: ask questions, ask for samples of their work, and ask for references. I always ask for a free sample of their services, a demo search, a month of free service, and so on. The worst they can do is say no; when they say yes, you get a real chance to evaluate their service. (In fact, I will not buy a service *without* a free sample of the work up front.) It is very important that you don't create an adversarial relationship. Be open and honest and, if possible, share information with them. Remember that the vendors cannot succeed without customers. It is to their advantage to make us happy. If they don't, tell them and tell others. To be fair, if they do a good job, tell them and others as well. The customer is, or should be, always right. Sometimes you will have to remind the vendor of this. If the vendor doesn't get it, if they won't work the way you want to work, then change vendors! You always have alternatives.

You should always ask other librarians for their opinions of a potential vendor. Listservs on the Internet are excellent places to do this. I have seen many questions and discussions on LIBREF-L, BUSLIB-L, SOLOLIB-L, and MEDLIB regarding vendors, with many varied but always useful responses. There is even a listserv dedicated to discussions of document delivery issues, which has many discussions on quality of service.

Most of the vendors in this chapter were recommended by at least one OPL. A few were chosen by reputation or because they often appear at SLA conference exhibits. Not all vendors are represented, but this chapter should give you a place to start looking. If there is a vendor that you recommend that is not listed, please let me know. Also, if you have had a bad experience with a listed vendor, let me know so I can consider removing the name from future editions of this book.

This chapter is organized as follows:

- Guides to products and services.

- Print resources: booksellers and bookstores, used books, subscription services, competitive intelligence and market research, document delivery, patents, and standards.

- Electronic resources: library automation; and online, CD-ROM, and other electronic media.

- Other: suppliers, library consultants, copyright authorities, translation services, and library movers.

For information about services available on the Internet, see Chapter 12. Most vendors can serve customers anywhere in the world, so I have arranged them by the country in which they are located. Don't forget to check out suppliers outside of your own area.

With all the consolidation and merging and buying-out going on in the information arena today, all these addresses are subject to change or deletion. The information here was accurate as of Fall 2000.

GUIDES TO PRODUCTS AND SERVICES

The Librarian's Yellow Pages, P.O. Box 79, Larchmont, New York 10538, U.S.A., voice: 1-800-235-9723, Web site: http://www. librariansyellowpages.com. Includes 800 numbers, fax numbers, e-mail, and World Wide Web home pages.

Library Journal Sourcebook: The Reference for Library Products and Services, supplement to the December issue of *Library Journal*, Cahners Publishing, 249 West 17th Street, New York, New York 10011, U.S.A., voice: 1-212-463-6819, fax: 1-212-463-6734. Directory of products, services, suppliers, and a showcase of products.

PRINTED RESOURCES

Booksellers and Bookstores

Australia and New Zealand
Lexis Legal/Butterworths, voice: 1-800-772-7772 (Australia only), Web site: lexislegal.com. Has news as well as books.

Canada
Renouf Books, 1-5369 Canotek Rd., Ottawa, Ontario, K1J 9J3, and other stores in Toronto and Quebec City, voice: 1-613-745-2665, fax: 1-613-745-7660, Web site: http://www.renoufbooks.com; U.S. office: 812 Proctor Ave., Ogdensburg, New York 13669-2205, U.S.A., voice: 1-888-551-7420 (all of North America), fax: 1-888-568-8546 (U.S. only). Governmental, international, current affairs, business, and legal publications.

France
Librairie Erasmus, 28 rue Basfroi, 75011 Paris, voice: 33-1-43-480320, fax: 33-1-43-481424, e-mail: erasmus@erasmus.fr, Web site: http://www.erasmusbooks.nl.

Italy
Viella Libreria Editrice, via delle Alpi 32, I-00198, Roma, voice: 06-841-7758, fax: 06-853-5396, Web site: http://viella@flashnet.it.

The Netherlands
Erasmus Boekhandel, P.O. Box 19140, 1000 GC Amsterdam, voice: 31-20-627-6952, fax: 31-20-620-6799, e-mail: erasmus@erasmusbooks.nl.

Burgersdijk & Niermans, Templum Salamonis, Niewsteeg 1, 2311 RW Leiden, voice: 31-71-5121067 or 31-71-5126381, fax: 31-71-5130461, e-mail: burgersdijk@b-n.nl, Web site: http://www.b-n.nl. For specialized academic books, out-of-print books, and so on.

Nijhoff, P.O. Box 1853, 2700 CZ Zoetermeer, voice: 31-079-368-4400, fax: 31-079-61-5698, e-mail: info@nijhoff.nl, Web site: http://www.nijhoff.nl.

South Africa
Butterworths Publishers, 8 Walter Place, P.O. Box 4, Mayville 4001, voice: 27-031-268-3111, fax: 27-031-268-3100, Web site: http://www.butterworths.co.za.

Juta and Jutastat, P.O. Box 14373, Kenwyn 7790, voice: 27-21-797-5101, fax: 27-21-797-0121, e-mail: books@juta.co.za, Web site: http://www.juta.co.za or http://www.jutastat.com. Legal, tax, and accounting; also University of Cape Town Press; stores all over the country.

Kalahari Net, Web site: http://www.kalahari.net. South Africa's answer to Amazon.com. Online bookshop with frequent specials and sales on business titles.

Red Pepper Books, P.O. Box 22764, Helderkruin 1733, voice: 27-011-768-1145, fax: 27-011-768-1110, Web site: http://www.redpepperbooks.co.za. South African book supplier to libraries, companies, and training organizations.

United Kingdom
Blackwell's, Beaver House, Hythe Bridge St., Oxford OX1 2ET, 44-(0)1865-792792, fax: 44-(0)1865-791438, e-mail: lbdus@blackwell. co.uk, Web site: http://www.blackwell.com. Home page is in Italian, French, Spanish, German, and English.

Books Etc. Professional, 54 London Wall, London EC2M 5RA, voice: 44-(0)20-7628-9708, e-mail: sales@lw.books-etc.co.uk.

Dawson Book Division, Crane Close, Wellingborough NN8 1QG, voice: 44-(0)1933-274444, fax: 44-(0)1933-225993, e-mail: bksales @dawson.co.uk, Web site: http://www.dawson.co.uk.

Heffers Online Bookshop, 20 Trinity St., Cambridge CB2 1TY, voice: 44-(0)1223-568568, fax: 44-(0)1223-568591, e-mail: hefferws@ heffers.co.uk, Web site: http://www.heffers.co.uk.

Peters Bookselling Services, 120 Bromsgrove St., Birmingham B5 6RJ, voice: 44-(0)121-666-6648, fax: 44-(0)121-666-7033. Library supply and general books.

The Stationery Office (U.K.), formerly Her Majesty's Stationery Office, 51 Nine Elms Lane, London SW8 5DR, voice: 44-(0)20-7873-8812, Web site: http://www.ukstate.com (very slow). Publishes in areas of health and pharmaceutical, social issues, nautical, information technology and management, reference and statistics, business and professional, international banking and finance, museums and heritage, environment, and travel and tourism.

W.H. Smith Online, 6 Isis Business Centre, Pony Road, Oxford OX4 2RD, voice: 44-(0)1865-771772, fax: 44-(0)1865-771-766, e-mail: suuport@whsmithonline.co.uk, Web site: http://www.bookshop.co.uk. About 1.4 million U.K. and U.S. books at savings of up to half from one of the most ubiquitous book chains in the U.K. You can even register for "Jenny, your personal librarian" who will let you know whenever new books in your area of interest are published.

United States

Amazon.com, 2250 First Ave., South, Seattle, Washington 98134, voice: 1-206-622-0761, fax: 1-206-622-2405, Web site: http://www. amazon.com. Amazon has over one million titles listed, and many OPLs use it as a bookstore or at least to look up prices, ISBN numbers, and so on.

Amazon.com.uk, same features as the U.S. version, but with a large selection of U.K. and European books.

Baker & Taylor Books, 2709 Water Ridge Pkwy, Charlotte, North Carolina 28217, voice: 1-704-357-3500 or 1-800-775-1800, fax:

1-704-329-8989, e-mail: BTinfo@btol.com, Web site: http://www. btol.com. Books, audiovisual, software, electronic ordering, cataloging, and processing.

Barnes and Noble, voice: 1-800-843-2665 or 1-201-272-3651, Web site: http://www.bn.com. Similar to amazon.com. Check both for the lower price.

Barton Business Services, 45 New Amwell Rd., Hillsborough, New Jersey 08844-1268, voice: 1-800-244-5707 or 1-908-281-1411, fax: 1-800-244-5698, e-mail: bbsbooks@aol.com, Web site: http://www. bartonbooks.com (a really neat website; you can even search for books by ISBN). Any book in print can be supplied from anywhere in the world to anywhere in the world. Shipping is included in the U.S. This is my own personal jobber, and I have had wonderful service from them.

Bernan/UNIPUB, 4611-F Assembly Dr., Lanham, Maryland 20706, voice: 1-800-274-4888 or 1-301-459-7666, fax: 1-800-865-3450 or 1-301-459-0056, e-mail: query@bernan.com, Web site: http://www.bernan.com, exclusive U.S. distributor for the U.S. government, United Nations, and other agencies (including National Educational, Scientific and Cultural Organization [UNESCO], Food and Agriculture Organization [FAO], International Atomic Energy Association [IAEA], Her Majesty's Stationery Office [HMSO], European Commission [EC]).

Book Clearing House, 46 Purdy St., Harrison, New York 10528, voice: 1-800-431-1579 or 1-914-835-0015, fax: 1-914-835-039, e-mail: bchouse@book-clearing-house.com, Web site: http://www.book-clearing-house.com. Small, with very personalized service.

The Book House, Inc., 208 W. Chicago St., Jonesville, Michigan 49250, voice: 1-800-248-1146 or 1-517-849-2117, fax: 1-800-858-9716, e-mail: bkorders@thebookhouse.com, Web site: http://www. thebookhouse.com. Any book in print, CD-ROMs, and software.

Christian Book Distributors, P.O. Box 7000, Peabody Massachusetts 01961-7000, voice: 1-978-977-5060, fax: 1-978-977-5010, Web site: http://www.christianbook.com.

Corporate Book Resources, 305 Main Street, Sutton, West Virginia 26601, voice: 1-800-222-7787, fax: 1-800-932-0033, e-mail: e-mail@cbrbk.com, Web site: http://www.cbrbk.com. Any book in print, shipping included. A founding sponsor of the Solo Librarians Division.

Emery-Pratt Company, 1966 W. Main St., Owosso, Michigan 48867-1372, voice: 1-800-248-3887 or 1-517-723-5291, fax: 1-800-523-8379 or 1-517-723-4677, e-mail: mail@emery-pratt.com, Web site: http://www.emery-pratt.com. For all libraries, including medical libraries.

Fatbrain.com, 1-888-328-2724, e-mail: contact-us@fatbrain.com. Online only for technical, business, and scientific books.

Ingram Library Services Inc., One Ingram Blvd., La Vergne, Tennessee 37086-1986, voice: 1-800-937-5300, fax: 1-615-793-3810, Web site: http://www.ingramlibrary.com. Books, audiovisual, and multimedia.

The Lawbook Exchange, Ltd., 965 Jefferson Ave., Union, New Jersey 07083-8605, voice: 1-800-422-6686 or 1-908-686-1998, fax: 1-908-686-3098, Web site: http://www.lawbookexchange.com. Current and antiquarian law and legal history of the U.S. and U.K.

Libros Sin Fronteras (Books Without Borders), P.O. Box 2085, Olympia, Washington 98507-2085, voice: 1-800-464-2767 or 1-206-357-4332, fax: 1-206-357-4332, e-mail: info@ librossinfronteras.com, Web site: http://www.librossinfronteras.com. Distributor of Spanish-language books, compact discs, and audiovisual; specializes in schools and public libraries.

Majors Scientific Books, 1401 Lakeway Dr., Lewisville, Texas, voice: 1-800-633-1851 or 1-214-247-2929, fax: 1-214-888-4800, e-mail: dallas@majors.com; or the Science and Technology Division, 9464 Kirby Dr., Houston, Texas USA, voice: 1-713-662-3984, fax: 1-713-662-9627, e-mail: houston@majors.com, Web site: http://www.majors.com. Distributor of health, science, and scientific books and media.

Matthews Medical & Scientific Books, Inc., 11559 Rock Island Ct., Maryland Heights, Missouri 63043, voice: 1-800-633-2665 or 1-314-432-1400, fax: 1-800-421-8816 or 1-314-432-7044, e-mail: ask@mattmccoy.com, Web site: http://www.mattmccoy.com. Health sciences, medical nursing, dental, and bioscience books, and electronic media.

Midwest Library Service, 11443 St. Charles Rock Rd., Bridgeton, Missouri 63044-2789, voice: 1-800-325-8833 or 1-314-739-3100, fax: 1-800-952-1009 or 1-314-739-1326, e-mail: mail@midwestls.com, Web site: http://www.midwestls.co. Small titles, technical processing.

Orderpoint, Minneapolis, Minnesota, voice: 1-800-999-9174 or 1-612-920-4171, fax: 1-612-730-6911, e-mail: info@orderpoint.com, Web site: http://www.orderpoint.

Planet JSD Bookstore, 839-L Quince Orchard Blvd., Gaithersburg, Maryland 20878-1614, voice: 1-800-573-5010 or 1-301-977-4424, fax: 1-301-977-4507, Web site: http://www.PlanetJSD.com. Scientific, technical, and professional books and document delivery.

Powell's Technical Bookstore, 33 NW Park Ave., Portland, Oregon 87209, voice: 1-800-225-6911 or 1-503-228-3906, fax: 1-503-228-0505, e-mail: help@powells.com, Web site: http://www.powells.com.

Research Books, Inc./Scholium International, 38 Academy Street, P.O. Box 1507, Madison, Connecticut 06443, voice: 1-800-445-3359 or 1-203-245-3279, fax: 1-203-245-1830, e-mail: order@researchbooks .com, Web site: http://www.researchbook.com. Will handle small orders.

Rittenhouse Book Distributors, 511 Feheley Drive, King of Prussia, Pennsylvania 19406, voice: 1-800-345-6425 or 1-610-277-1414, fax: 1-800-223-7488, Web site: http://www.rittenhouse.com. Specializes in health science, print, and electronic media.

Schoenhof's Foreign Books, Inc., 76A Mt. Auburn St., Cambridge, Massachusetts 02138, voice: 1-617-547-8855, fax: 1-617-547-8551, e-mail: info@schoenhofs.com, Web site: http://www.schoenhofs.com. Importer of foreign-language books.

Tatnuck Bookseller, Marketplace and Restaurant, 335 Chandler, Worcester, Massachusetts 01602, voice: 1-800-642-6657 or 1-508-756-7644, fax: 1-708-756-9425, Web site: http://www.tatnuck.com.

Total Information, Inc., 844 Dewey Avenue, Rochester, New York 14613, voice: 1-800-786-4636 or 1-716-254-0621, fax: 1-716-254-0153, e-mail: orders@totalinformation.com, Web site: http://www. totalinformation.com.

YBP Library Service (Yankee Book Peddler), 999 Maple St., Contoocook, New Hampshire 03229, voice: 1-800-258-3774 or 1-608-746-3102, fax: 1-608-746-5628, Web site: http://www.ybp.com. A part of Baker & Taylor serving academic and special libraries, books and audio only.

To find addresses and websites of firms specializing in law and legal materials, check out the Web site: http://www.everlaw.com/legal_publishers.htm.

Used Books

Abracadabra Booksearch International, Web site: http://www.abrabks.com.

Advanced Book Exchange, Web site: http://www.abebooks.com.

Amazon.com. If the book you want is out of print, you can just click to get a list of used book suppliers with prices and online ordering. I tried it. It works.

Best Book Buys (comparison shopping), Web site: http://www.bestbookbuys.com.

BookFinder, Web site: http://www.bookfinder.com.

Bookshop (U.S.), Web site: http://www.bookshop.co.uk.

UHR Books (medical and nursing books), Web site: http://www.uhrbooks.com.

Subscription Services

In a survey on subscription services on the SOLOLIB-L listserv in late 2000, Faxon/RoweCom/Dawson was the overwhelming first choice, with EBSCO second, and Basch Subscriptions third.

Australia
Blackwell's Periodicals (Australia and New Zealand), Locked Bag 538, French's Forest, New South Wales 2086, voice: 61-2-9986-7080, fax: 61-2-9986-7090.

DA Information Service Pty Ltd., 648 Whitehorse Rd., Mitcham, Victoria 3132, voice: 61-3-9210-7788, e-mail: service@dadirect. com.au.

Globe Subscription Agency Pty Ltd., P.O. Box 41, Double Bay, New South Wales 1360, voice: 61-2-9389-9988.

Hinton Information Services, HIS Australia Pty Ltd., Locked Bag 7, Eastwood, New South Wales 2122, voice: 61-2-9876-2299, e-mail: hinton@ihs.co.au.

Tait Information Service Pty Ltd., P.O. Box 5005, Alphington, Victoria 3108, voice: 61-3-9497-3233.

University Co-op Bookstore, P.O. Box 54, Broadway, New South Wales 2007, voice: 61-2-9212-3373.

Canada
RoweCom Canada, P.O. Box 2382, London, Ontario N6A 5A7, voice: 1-800-263-2966 or 1-519-472-1003, fax: 1-519-472-1072, Web site: http://www.rowecom.ca.

Denmark
Munksgaard Direct, P.O. Box 173, DK-1005, Copenhagen K, voice: 45-77-333377, e-mail: direct@munksgaarddirect.ck.

Germany
Buchhandlung Biazza, Corneliusstrassee 6, D-80469 Munich, voice: 49-89-23-500523, e-mail: buch.biazza@t-online.de.

Ex Libris, Ferdinand-Dirichs-Weg 28, 60529, Frankfurt am Main, voice: 49-69-356099, e-mail: exlibris@t-online.de.

Otto Harrassowitz Buchhandlung, 65174 Wiesbaden, voice: 49-611-530560, e-mail: sedrvice@harrassowitz.de.

Israel
Teldan Information System, Subscription Department, P.O. Box 18094, Tel Aviv 61180, Israel

The Netherlands
Swets & Zeitlinger BV, P.O. Box 800, 2160 SAZZ Lisse, voice: 31-252-435-111.

United Kingdom

Blackwell's Periodicals Division, Oxford Service Center (U.K.), P.O. Box 40, Hythe Bridge Street, Oxford, England OX1 2EU, voice: 44-(0)1865-792792, fax: 44-(0)1865-791438, e-mail: persales@ blackwell.co.uk, Web site: http://www.blackwell.co.uk.

Swets Blackwell, 32 Blacklands Way, Abingdon Business Park, Abingdon OX14 1SX, Web site: http://www.swetsblakwell.com. Clear favorite.

Tomlinson's, South Lodge, Gravesend Road, Wrotham, Kent TN15 7JJ, voice: 44-(0)1732-824000, fax: 44-(0)1732-8223829.

United States

American Overseas Book Company, 550 Walnut St., Norwood, New Jersey 06480, e-mail: books@aobc.com, Web site: http://www.aobc. com.

American Scientific Publications, Inc., 507c Main St., Fort Lee, New Jersey 07024, voice: 1-201-944-0414.

Basch Subscriptions, Inc., 88 Main St., Concord, New Hampshire 03301, voice: 1-800-226-5310 or 1-603-250-5109, fax: 1-603-226-9443, e-mail: subs@basch.com, Web site: http://www.basch.com. The owner, "Buzzy" Basch, was instrumental in the creation of the Solo Librarians Division of the Special Libraries Association; his company provides personalized service.

Blackwell's Periodicals Division, New Jersey Service Center (North America), P.O. Box 1257, Blackwood, New Jersey 08012, voice: 1-800-458-3706, fax: 1-609-232-5397, Web site: http://www. blackwells.com.

CSS Agency Inc., 85 Chestnut Ridge Road, Montvale, New Jersey 07645, voice: 1-201-930-8608.

EBSCO Subscription Services. P.O. Box 1943, Birmingham, Alabama 35201-1943, voice: 1-205-991-6600, fax: 1-205-995-1518, Web site: http://www.ebsco.com. Servers (and service) around the world; service change may be higher than others, but service is excellent.

E.V.A. Subscription Services, Suite 339, 290 Turnpike Rd., Westborough, Massachusetts 01581, voice: 1-508-843-9826.

Fennell Subscription Services, 1002 W. Michigan Ave., Jackson, Michigan 49202.

Harrassowitz Library Services, 820 University Blvd., South, Suite 4B, Mobile, Alabama 36609, voice: 1-800-348-6886, fax: 1-334-342-5732.

National Organization Services, Inc., 4515 Fleur Drive, #301, Des Moines, Iowa 50321.

RoweCom, Inc., 1005 West Pines Rd., Oregon, Illinois 61061-9570, voice: 1-888-837-7287 or 1-815-732-21123, fax: 1-617-497-6825, Web site: http://www.rowe.com. Now operates Faxon, ISA, and Dawson.

Scholarly Publications, Inc., 14601 Bellaire Blvd, #60, Houston, Texas 77083, voice: 1-281-504-4460, fax: 1-281-504-4642.

Swets Subscription Service, 440 Creamery Way, Suite A, Exton, Pennsylvania 19341, voice: 1-610-524-5355, fax: 1-610-624-5366. Specializing in foreign subscriptions, current awareness, and document delivery services.

Wolper Sales Agency, Inc., 6 Centre Square, Suite 202, Easton, Pennsylvania 18042.

WT Cox Subscriptions, Inc., 411 Marcia Dr., Goldsboro, North Carolina 27530, voice: 1-800-553-8088, fax: 1-919-734-3332, e-mail: info@wtcox.com, Web site: http://www.wtcox.com.

Competitive Intelligence and Market Research

Find/SVP, Inc., 625 Avenue of the Americas, New York, New York 10011-2002 U.S.A., voice: 1-800-346-3787 or 1-212-645-4500, fax: 1-212-807-2676, Web site: http://www.findsvp.com. Also has a subscription custom research service.

The Freedonia Group, Inc., 767 Beta Drive, Highland Heights, Ohio 44143, U.S.A., voice: 1-440-684-9600, fax: 1-440-648-0484, e-mail: info@freedoniagroup.com, Web site: http://www.freedoniagroup.com. Market reports.

MIRC/Frost & Sullivan, 2525 Charleston Road, Mountain View, California 94043, U.S.A., voice; 1-650-961-9000, fax: 1-650-961-5042, e-mail: straskos@frost.com, Web site: http://www.frost.com. Also has offices in the U.K., Germany, and France.

Technical Insights, Inc. (John Wiley & Sons), 605 Third Ave., New York, New York 10158, U.S.A., voice: 1-212850-8600, Web site: http://www.wiley.com/technical_insights. Technical intelligence for executives, via print, Internet, disk, and fax.

Teltech/Sopheon, 2850 Metro Dr., Bloomington, Minnesota 55425, U.S.A., voice: 1-952-851-7500, fax: 1-952-851-7744, e-mail: info_us@sopheon.com, Web site: http://www.teltech.com or http://www.sopheon.com; in the U.K.: Sopheon U.K. Ltd., Stirling House, Stirling Road, Surrey Research Park, Guildford, Surrey, GU2 7RF, U.K., voice: 44-(0)1483, 88-3000, fax: 44-(0)1483-88-3050, e-mail: info_uk@sopheon.com. Other offices in the Netherlands. Technical and business intelligence, consulting, location of technical experts and vendors, document delivery. (I recommend you use this company for location of technical experts and vendors only. **Use with caution because the company has been known to approach management to outsource libraries.**)

Document Delivery

For a list of document delivery services with their main offices outside the U.S., go to http://www.docdel.com/Document_Delivery_Outside_US.html. The list is not exhaustive, concentrating on major governmental, university-based, and a few commercial services, but it gives you a place to start.

Canada
Canada Institute for Scientific and Technical Information (CISTI), voice: 1-613-998-8544, fax: 1-613-952-9112, e-mail: info.cisti@nrc.ca, Web site: http://www.cisti.nrc.ca. Also provides services for health libraries.

The Netherlands
Netherlands Institute for Scientific Information Services, P.O. Box 95110, 1090 HC, Amsterdam, voice: 31-20-462-8600, fax: 31-20-665-8013, also a branch in The Hague, voice: 31-70-314-0251,

e-mail: info@niwi.knaw.nl, Web site: http://www.niwi.knaw.nl. Add "/us" at end of URL to get the information in English.

United Kingdom
British Library, Boston Spa, Wetherby, West Yorkshire LS23 7BQ, voice: 44-(0)937-546060, fax: 44-(0)937-546333, Web site: http://www.bl.uk. Extensive coverage of the world's literature.

Databeuro, The Rufus Centre, Steppingley Road, Flitwick, Bedford MK45 1AH, voice: 44-(0)1525-752689, fax: 44-(0)1525-526 90, e-mail: books@databeuro.com, Web site: http://www.databeuro.com. "Official representatives for OECD publications and data" and IMF publications.

United States
Advanced Information Consultants/Infotrieve, P.O. Box 87127, Canton, Michigan 48187-0127, voice: 1-800-929-3789 or 1-734-459-9090, fax: 1-734-459-8990, e-mail: info@advinfo.com, Web site: http://www.advinfo.com.

Chemical Abstracts Service, 2540 Olentangy River Rd., P.O. Box 3012, Columbus, Ohio 43210, voice: 1-800-753-4227 or 1-614-447-3670, fax: 1-614-447-3750, (also free phone numbers from all over the world, see http://www.cas.org/support/custserv.html), e-mail: help@cas.org, Web site: http://www.cas.org. Outstanding collection of chemical literature.

FOI Services, Inc., 11 Firstfield Rd., Gaithersburg, Maryland 20878-1704, voice: 1-301-975-9400, fax: 1-301-975-0702, e-mail: infofoi @foiservices.com, Web site: http://www.foiservices.com. Specializing in Food and Drug Administration (FDA) information, document retrieval, reference books, and online databases, publisher of DIO-GENES: FDA Regulatory Information Online.

Information Express, 3221 Porter Dr., Palo Alto, California 94304, voice: 1-650-812-3588, fax: 1-650-812-3573, e-mail: service@ ieonline.com, Web site: http://www.ieonline.com.

Linda Hall Library, 5109 Cherry St., Kansas City, Missouri 64110-2498, voice: 1-800-662-1545 or 1-816-363-4600, e-mail: requests@ lindahall.org, Web site: http://www.lindahall.org. Extensive technical collection; took over the Engineering Societies Library collection.

The Medical Library Center of New York (MLCNY), 5 E. 102nd St., 7th Floor, New York, New York 10029-5288, voice: 1-212-427-1630, fax: 1-212-876-6697, e-mail: mlcny@metgate.metro.org.

The Public Register's Annual Report Service (PRARS), 440 Route 198, Woodstock Valley, Connecticut 06282, voice: 1-800-426-6825 or 1-860-974-2223, fax: 1-860-974-2229, Web site: http://www. prars.com.

The Research Investment, 20600 Chagrin Blvd., Suite 650, Cleveland, Ohio 44122-5334, voice: 1-216-752-0300, fax: 1-216-752-0330, e-mail: orders@researchinvest.com. This is my personal document supplier.

TDI Library Services, 11340 W. Olympic Blvd., #355, Los Angeles, California 90064-1639, voice: 1-310-268-0601, fax: 1-310-268-0701, e-mail: tdi@tdico.com, Web site: http://www.tdico.com.

Patents

Airmail Patent Service, P.O. Box 1732, Rockville, Maryland 20849, U.S.A., voice: 1-301-424-7692, fax: 1-301-424-8211. U.S. and foreign patents and trademarks.

FaxPat, 5350 Shawnee Road, #110, Alexandria, Virginia 22312, U.S.A., voice: 1-800-866-1323, e-mail: service@faxpat.com, Web site: http://www.faxpat.com; 1790.com, http://111.1790.com (for older U.S. patents); European Office: 235 Southwark Bridge Rd., Pocock House, London, SE1 6LY, England, voice: 44-(0)20-7450-5105, e-mail: uk@micropat.com.

Great Lakes Patent and Trademark Office, part of the Detroit, Michigan Public Library (U.S.A.), voice: 1-800-547-0619. Good for old U.S. and foreign patents; inexpensive (U.S.$5).

MicroPatent/IHS, 250 Dodge Ave., East Haven, Connecticut 06512, U.S.A, voice: 1-800-648-6787 or 1-203-466-5054, e-mail: info@micropat.com, Web site: http://www.micropat.com.

Standards

American National Standards Institute (ANSI), 1819 L St., NW, 6th Floor, Washington, D.C. 20036, U.S.A., voice: 1-202-293-8020, fax: 1-202-293-9287, New York Office: 11 E. 42nd St., 13th Floor, New York, New York 10036 U.S.A., voice: 1-212-642-4900, fax: 1-212-398-0023, e-mail: ansionline@ansi.org, Web site: http://www.ansi.org. All American National Standards Institute-(ANSI) approved standards; must be prepaid.

American Society for Testing and Materials (ASTM), 100 Barr Harbor Dr., West Conshohocken, Pennsylvania 19428-2959, U.S.A., voice: 1-610-832-9585, fax: 1-610-832-9555, Web site: http://www. astm.org. Prepay or additional cost for shipping.

Canadian Standards Association (CSA), 178 Rexdale Blvd., Rexdale, Ontario, Canada M9W 1R3, voice: 1-416-747-4000.

Document Center, 111 Industrial Road, Unit 9, Belmont, California 94002, U.S.A., voice: 1-650-591-7600, fax: 1-650-591-7617, e-mail: info@doccenter.com, Web site: http://www.document-center.com. Can supply all standards; strong supporter of the Solo Division; woman-owned business.

Global Engineering Documents, 15 Inverness Way, East, Englewood, Colorado 80112-5704, U.S.A., voice: 1-303-397-7956, fax: 1-303-397-2740, e-mail: global@ihs.com, Web site: http://www. global.his.com. Can supply almost any document but somewhat expensive; many offices in other countries; see the website for details.

National Center for Standards and Certification Information (NIST), Building 411, Room MS 2150, Gaithersburg, Maryland 20899-2150, U.S.A., voice: 1-301-975-4040, fax: 1-301-926-1559, e-mail: ncsci@nist.gov, Web site: http://ts.nist.gove/ts/htdocs/210/217/bro.htm. Joanne Overman can help with standards information, no standards supplied, e-mail: joanne.overman@nist.gov.

National Technical Information Service (NTIS), 5295 Port Royal Rd., Springfield, Virginia 22161, U.S.A., voice: 1-800-553-6847 or 1-703-605-6000, fax: 1-703-605-6900, e-mail: info@ntis.gov, Web site: http://www.ntis.gov. Deposit account or credit card; can order online; relatively slow but rush service is available at extra cost. Government publications of all types.

Underwriters' Laboratories, Inc. (UL), 333 Pfingsten Rd., Northbrook, Illinois 60062, U.S.A., voice: 1-847-272-8800, fax: 1-847-509-6220, e-mail: northbrook@ul.com, Web site: http://www.ul.co. Must prepay.

ELECTRONIC RESOURCES

Library Automation

Canada

Best-Seller Inc., 3300 Cote-Vertu, Suite 203, Ville Saint-Laurent, Quebec, Ontario H4R 2B8, voice: 1-514-337-3000, fax: 1-514-337-9690, e-mail: info@bestseller.com, Web site: http://www.bestseller.com.

Eloquent Systems Inc., 25-1501 Lonsdale Ave., North, Vancouver, British Columbia V7M 2J2, voice: 1-800-663-8172 or 1-604-980-8358, fax: 1-800-660-9537 or 1-604-980-9537, e-mail: info@eloquent-systems.com, Web site: http://www.eloquent-systems.com.

ILS International Library Systems/SydneyPlus, 1135-13560 Maycrest Way, Richmond, British Columbia V6V 2J7, voice: 1-604-278-6717, fax: 1-604-278-9161, e-mail: sales@sydneyplus .com, Web site: http://www.ils.ca.

Jaywil Software Development, Inc., P.O. Box 25005, Guelph, Ontario N1G 4T4, voice: 1-800-815-8370 or 1-519-837-8370, fax: 1-519-837-8656, email: info@resourcemate.com, website: http:// www.resourcemate.com, producers of ResourceMate©, a full-featured but low-cost online catalog.

Special Libraries Cataloguing, 4493 Lindholm Rd., Victoria, British Columbia V9C 3Y1, voice: 1-250-474-3361, fax: 1-250-474-3362, e-mail: mac@slc.bc.ca, Web site: http://www.slc.bc.ca.

United Kingdom

Alice Executive Library Management Software, Softlink, 26 Hanborough House, Hanborough Business Park, Long Hanborough, Oxfordshire OX8 8LH, voice: 44-(0)1993-883401, fax: 44-(0)1993-883799, e-mail: alice@softlink.co.uk, Web site: http://www.softlink. co.uk. For special libraries and schools.

ILS International Library Systems/SydneyPlus, voice: 44-(0)115-955-5936, fax: 44-(0)115-955-5937, e-mail: sales@sydneyplus.co.uk, Web site: http://www.ils.ca.

Information Management & Engineering (IME), 140-142 St. John St., London EC1V 4JT, voice: 44-(0)171-253-1177, fax: 44-(0)171-608-3599.

United States

Brodart Automation, 500 Arch St., Williamsport, Pennsylvania 17705, voice: 1-800-233-8467, ext. 6581, fax: 1-570-327-9237, e-mail: salesmkt@brodart.com, Web site: http://www.brodart.com.

CASPR Library Systems, Inc., 100 Park Center Plaza, #100, San Jose, California 95113, voice: 1-800-852-2777 or 1-408-522-9800, fax: 1-408-522-9806, e-mail: sales@caspr.com, Web site: http://www.caspr.com.

DRA, 1276 N. Warson Rd., St. Louis, Missouri 63132, voice: 1-800-325-0888 or 1-314-432-1100, fax: 1-314-993-8927, e-mail: sales@dra.com, Web site: http://www.dra.com. Client-server library automation and network design.

Epixtech (formerly Ameritech Library Services), 400 W. 5050 North, Provo, Utah 84604. voice: 1-800-288-8020 or 1-801-223-5200, fax: 1-801-223-5202, Web site: http://epixtech.com.

Follett Company, 2233 West. St., River Grove, Illinois 60171-1895, voice: 1-800-621-4345 or 1-708-583-2000, fax: 1-708-452-9347, e-mail: marketing@fsc.follett.com, Web site: http://www.follett.com. Especially for schools.

Gateway Software Corp., P.O. Box 367, Fromberg, Montana 59029-0367, voice: 1-800-735-3637 or 1-406-668-7661, fax: 1-406-668-7665, e-mail: gateway@gscweb.com, Web site: http://www.gscweb.com.

Inmagic, Inc., 800 W. Cummings Park, Woburn, Massachusetts 01801, voice: 1-800-229-8398 or 1-781-938-4442, fax: 1-781-938-6393. Strong supporter of the Solo Division, "most popular" library automation among U.S. special libraries.

Library Associates, 8845 W. Olympic, #100, Beverly Hills, California 90211, voice: 1-800-987-6794 or 1-310-289-1067, fax: 1-310-289-9635, e-mail: info@libraryassociates.com, Web site:

http://www.libraryassociates.com. Cataloging, foreign languages, retrospective conversion.

The Library Corp., Research Park, Inwood, West Virginia 25428-2733, voice: 1-800-325-7759, fax: 1-304-229-0295, e-mail: info@tlcdelivers.com, Web site: http://www.tlcdelivers.com.

Marcive, Inc., P.O. Box 47508, San Antonio, Texas 78265-7508, voice: 1-800-531-7678 or 1-210-646-6161, fax: 1-210-646-0167, e-mail: info@marcive.com, Web site: http://www.marcive.com.

On Point, Inc./TLC Total Library Computerization, 2606 36th St., NW, Washington, D.C. 20007-1419, voice: 1-202-338-8914, fax: 1-202-337-7107, e-mail: tlc@onpointinc.com, Web site: http://www.onpointinc.com.

Professional Software, 21 Forrest Ave., Glen Ridge, New Jersey 07028, voice: 1-201-748-7658, fax: 1-748-680-9536. Low prices cataloging, serials, and holdings.

Right On Programs, 775 New York Ave., Suite 210, Huntington, New York 11743, voice: 1-516-424-7777, fax: 1-516-424-7207, e-mail: customerservice@rightonprograms.com, Web site: http://www.rightonprograms.com. Inexpensive circulation, online catalog, periodical manager, inventory, and so on.

VTLS, Inc., 1701 Kraft Dr., Blacksburg, Virginia 24060, voice: 1-540-557-1200, Web site: http://www.vtls.com.

Winnebago Software Co./Sagebrush Corporation, 12219 Nicollet Ave., South, Burnsville Minnesota 65337, voice: 1-800-533-5430 or 1-507-724-5411, fax: 1-507-724-2301, e-mail: info@sagebrush.com, Web site: http://www.sagebrush.com. Circulation, catalog, acquisitions, card programs, retrospective conversion services.

Online, CD-ROM, and Other Electronic Media

Australasia

Australian Public Affairs—Full Text, RMIT Publishing, P.O. Box 12058, A'Beckett St., Melbourne, Victoria 8006, Australia, voice: 61-03-9925-8100, fax: 61-03-9925-8299, e-mail: info@informit.com.au, Web site: http://www.informit.com.au/apaft. Indexes over 200 Australian journals; scanned images of complete articles.

Elsevier Science Australia and New Zealand, Tower 2, 475 Victoria Ave., Chatswood, New South Wales 2067, Australia, voice: 61-02-9422-2006, fax: 61-02-9422-2915, e-mail: sally.stone@reed-elsevier.com.au. Represents ScienceDirect, Adonis, and BioMedNet.

NuMedia Pacific Pty Ltd, P.O. Box 525, Sandy Bay, Tasmania 7006, Australia, voice: 61-03-6223-4568, fax: 61-3-6224-0814, e-mail: tasinlaw@niumedia.com.au, Web site: http://www.niumedia.com.au. Laws of Tasmanian and Papua New Guinea.

Canada
iSCAN Intelligent Scanning Inc., 2255 St. Laurent Blvd., Suite 304, Ottawa, Ontario K1G 4K3, voice: 1-800-668-SCAN or 1-613-526-7226, fax: 1-613-526-1496. Backfile conversion to CD-ROM or microform.

Statistics Canada, Tunney's Pasture, Ottawa, Ontario K1A 0T6, voice: 1-800-263-1136, fax: 1-613-951-0581, Web site: http://www. statcan.ca. Print and electronic socioeconomic data.

The Netherlands
Adonis B.V., Postbus 993, 1000 AZ Amsterdam, the Netherlands, voice: 31-(0)-20-485-3870, fax: 31-(0)-20-485-3871, e-mail: info@adonis.nl, Web site: http://www.adonis.nl, full-text. U.S.: 1-800-944-6415 or 1-508-877-6400, fax: 1-508-877-6464; e-mail: infousa@adonis.nl. Includes pharmaceutical literature, over 900 journals.

United Kingdom
Chadwyck-Healey Inc., The Quorum, Barnwell Road, Cambridge CB5 8SW, voice: 44-(0)1223-215512, fax: 44-(0)1223-215513, e-mail: mktg@chadwyck.com, Web site: http://www.chadwyck.co.uk. U.S. office: 1101 King St., Suite 380, Alexandria, Virginia 22314, U.S.A., voice: 1-800-752-0515 or 1-703-683-4890, fax: 1-703-683-7589. Reference products on CD-ROM, microform, and print.

Context Ltd., Grand Union House, 20 Kentish Town Road, London NW1 9NR, voice: 44-(0)20-7267-8989, 44-(0)20-7267-1133, e-mail: enquiries@context.co.uk, Web site: http://www.context.co.uk. JUSTIS, CD-ROM, and EU documents.

Health Communication Network (HCN), Omega Park, Alton, Hampshire GU34 2PG, voice: 44-(0)1420-82005, fax: 44-(0)1420-89889, e-mail: info@hcn.org.uk, Web site: http://www.hcn.org. Publishes various health-related databases, including the British Nursing Index.

Instant Library Ltd., The Charnwood Wing, Gas Research & Technology Centre, Ashby Road, Loughborough, Leicestershire LE11 3GS, voice: 44-(0)1509-268292, fax: 44-(0)1509-232748, e-mail: enquiries@instant-library.com, Web site: http://www.instant-library.com. Scanning, document managing, and cataloging.

Turpion Electronic Journals, Turpin Distribution Services Ltd., Blackhorse Road, Letchworth, Hertfordshire SG6 1HN, voice: 44-(0)1462-672555, fax: 44-(0)1462-480947, e-mail: turpin@rsc.org, Web site: http://www.turpion.org. For Russian language scientific journals, 5 years full-text electronic archive available at no extra cost. A joint venture of the Royal Society of Chemistry, Russian Academy of Sciences, and London Mathematical Society.

United States
Bowker Electronic Publishing, 121 Chanlon Rd., New Providence, New Jersey 07974, voice: 1-888-269-5372, e-mail: info@bowker.com, Web site: http://www.bowker.com. *Books in Print, Ulrich's International Periodicals Directory, Directory of Corporate Affiliations*, and Marquis' *Who's Who*.

CINAHL Information Systems, 1509 Wilson Terrace, Glendale, California 91206, voice: 1-818-409-8005 ext. 5341, fax: 1-818-546-5679, e-mail: support@cinahl.com, Web site: http://www.cinahl.com. Nursing and allied health literature, print, CD-ROM, and online.

Factiva, a Dow Jones & Reuters Company, with offices all over the world, e-mail: solutions@factiva.com, Web site: http://www. factiva.com, voice: 1-800-369-8474 (North America), 1-609-627-2256 (Latin America except Brazil), 1-817-304-9810 (Brazil), 44-(0)207-542-3344 (Europe, Middle East, and Africa), 61-(0)2-9373-1781 (Asia-Pacific), 81-3-3432-4287 (Japan).

Federal Information & News Dispatch, Inc. (FIND, Inc.), 236 Massachusetts Ave., NE, #602, Washington, D.C. 20002, voice:

1-202-544-4800, fax: 1-202-544-4825. Government and business information portal, also translators, Federal Register database on DIALOG.

Information Handling Services, 15 Inverness Way East, Englewood, Colorado 80112, voice: 1-800-525-7052 or 1-303-790-0600. Standards are their specialty, also Technical Indexes.

Ingenta, 44 Brattle St., 4th Floor, Cambridge, Massachusetts 02138-0222, voice: 1-617-395-4040, fax: 1-617-395-4099, e-mail: inquiries @ingenta.com, Web site: http://www.ingenta.com. Free access to full text of nearly one million articles from 2,700 research publications, plus MEDLINE with links to full-text articles; document delivery merged with UnCover in 2000.

Kiplinger Business Forecasts, 1729 H Street, NW, Washington, D.C. 20006, voice: 1-202-887-6462, fax: 1-202-778-8976, e-mail: askkip @kiplinger.com, Web site: http://www.kiplingerforecasts.com.

LEXIS-NEXIS (Reed-Elsevier), P.O. Box 933, Dayton, Ohio 45401, voice: 1-937-865-6800, Web site: http://www.lexis-nexis.com. One of the two big legal electronic publishers, plus excellent news and business coverage, includes Congressional Information Service, Martindale-Hubbell, Shephard's, Matthew Bender, and MICHIE.

Moody's Investors Service (Dun & Bradstreet), 99 Church St., New York, New York 10007, voice: 1-212-553-1658, fax: 1-212-553-0882, e-mail: clientservices@moodys.com, Web site: http://www.moodys. com. Business and financial information in print, online, or CD-ROM; offices all over the world.

Online Computer Library Center (OCLC), Inc., 6565 Frantz Rd., Dublin, Ohio 43017, voice: 1-800-848-5878 or 1-614-764-6000, fax: 1-614-764-6096, e-mail: oclc@oclc.org, Web site: http://www.oclc. org. The world's largest cataloging and interlibrary loan database; includes WLN.

Ovid Technologies, 333 Seventh Ave., 4th Floor, New York, New York 10001, voice: 1-212-563-3006, fax: 1-212-563-3784, e-mail: sales and ovid.com, Web site: http://www.ovid.com. Also has offices in Sydney and London. One of the major providers of medical and health sciences information; can be expensive.

SilverPlatter Information, Inc., 100 River Ridge Dr., Norwood, Massachusetts 02062-5043, voice: 1-800-343-0064 or 1-617-769-2599, fax: 1-617-769-8763, e-mail: support@silverplatter.com, Web site: http://www.silverplatter.com. Offices worldwide. Medical, academic, and professional databases on CD-ROM or Internet, host of the SOLOLIB-L electronic list and supporter of the Solo Librarians Division.

Thomson & Thomson, 500 Victory Rd., North Quincy, Massachusetts 02171-1545, voice: 1-800-692-8833 or 1-617-479-1600, fax: 1-617-786-8273, Web site: http://www.thomson-thomson.com. Trademark and copyright research services, online and CD-ROM.

West Group (Thomson Corp.), P.O. Box 64833, St. Paul, Minnesota 55164-0833, voice: 1-800-344-5008 or 1-800-937-8529, e-mail: customer.service@westgroup.com, Web site: http://www.westgroup. com. The other major legal information provider, includes WESTLAW, Clark Boardman, and Callaghan.

Wiley Interscience, 605 Third Ave., New York, New York 10158, voice: 1-800-825-7550 or 1-212-850-6645, fax: 1-212-850-6021, e-mail: uscs-wis@wiley.com. U.K.: 1 Oldlands Way, Bognor Regis, West Sussex PO22 9SA, U.K., voice: 44-(0)1243-843345, fax: 1-44(0)-1243-843232, e-mail: cs-wis@wiley.co.uk (rest of world), Web site: http://www.inter-science.wiley.com. Industrial chemistry.

OTHER

Suppliers

ALA Graphics (American Library Association), 50 E. Huron St., Chicago, Illinois 60611, U.S.A., voice: 1-800-545-2433 or 1-312-280-3252, fax: 1-312-280-2422, Web site: http://www.ala.org. Posters, bookmarks, t-shirts, and so on (includes National Library Week and "READ" series), primarily for public libraries, but some applications for other types as well.

Brodart Co., 1609 Memorial Ave., Williamsport, Pennsylvania 17705, U.S.A., voice: 1-800-233-8959 or 1-717-326-2461, fax: 1-800-283-6087, e-mail: salesmkt@brodart.com, Web site: http://www.brodart.

com. All kinds of supplies, furniture, audiovisual, and computer equipment.

Demco, Inc., 4810 Forest Run Rd., P.O. Box 7488, Madison, Wisconsin 53707-7488, U.S.A., voice: 1-800-356-1200 or 1-608-241-1201, fax: 1-800-245-1329 or 1-608-241-1999, e-mail: custserv@ demco.com, Web site: http://www.demco.com. Library supplies and equipment.

Gaylord Bros., P.O. Box 4901, Syracuse, New York 13090-4001, U.S.A., voice: 1-800-448-6160 or 1-315-457-5070, ext. 287, fax: 1-800-272-3412 or 1-315-453-5040, e-mail: sher@galord.com, Web site: http://www.gaylord.com. Full line of supplies, equipment, furniture, and automation products.

Highsmith Inc., W5527 Highway 106, P.O. Box 800, Fort Atkinson, Wisconsin 53538, U.S.A., voice: 1-800-558-2110 or 1-414-563-9571, fax: 1-800-835-2329, e-mail: service@highsmith.com, Web site: http://www.highsmith.com. Full line of furniture, supplies, and equipment; has a children's division, Upstart.

The Library Store, Inc., 112 E. South St., P.O. Box 964, Tremont, Illinois 61568, U.S.A., voice: 1-800-548-7204, fax: 1-800-320-7706, e-mail: libstore@thelibrarystore.com, Web site: http://www. thelibrarystore.com. Supplies and furniture; also carries church supplies.

Russ Bassett Co., 8189 Byron Rd., Whittier, California 90606, U.S.A., voice: 1-800-350-2445 or 1-562-945-2445, fax: 1-562-698-8972, e-mail:marketingE@russbassett.com, Web site: http://www.russbassett. com. Audio, video, and microform storage systems.

Spacesaver Corporation, 1450 Janesville Ave., Fort Atkinson, Wisconsin 53538, U.S.A., voice: 1-800-492-3434 or 1-562-563-6362, fax: 1-562-563-2702. Compact shelving; Canada: 871 Victoria North, Kitchener, Ontario N2B 3S4 Canada, voice: 1-800-544-3679 or 1-519-741-3684, fax: 1-519-741-3605.

Vernon Library Supplies, Inc., 2851 Cole Court, Norcross, Georgia 30071, U.S.A., voice: 1-770-877-1128, fax: 1-770-446-0165, e-mail: vernon@vernlib.com, Web site: http://www.vernlib.com. Full line of supplies and furniture.

The Worden Co., 199 E. 17th St., Holland, Michigan 49423, U.S.A., voice: 1-800-748-0561, e-mail: info@wordencompany.com, Web site: http://www.wordencompany.com. Furniture and shelving.

Library Consultants

Germany
Thomas Rode, independent information professionals, Meunzstrasse 10, D53332, Bornheim, Germany, voice: 49-2227-924003, e-mail: rode@info.su.edunet.de.

United Kingdom
TFPL, Ltd., 17-18 Britton St., London EC1M 5TL, voice: 44-(0)207-251-5522, fax: 44-(0)207-251-8318, e-mail: central@tfpl. com, Web site: http://www.tfpl.com. Employment, consulting, and knowledge management seminars.

Sylvia James Consultancy, Daymer Birchen Lane, Haywards Heath, West Sussex RM16 1RY, voice and fax: 44-1444-452871, e-mail: 5385418@mcimail.com.

United States
Aaron Cohen Associates Ltd., 159 Teatown Rd., Croton-on-Hudson, New York 10520, voice: 1-914-271-8170, fax: 1-914-271-2434, e-mail: aca@acohen.com, Web site: http://www.acohen.com. Consulting as well as architectural and interior design.

C Berger Group, Inc., 327 E. Gundersen Dr., Carol Stream, Illinois 60188, voice: 1-800-382-4222 or 1-630-653-1115, fax: 1-630-653-1691, e-mail: carol@cberger.com, Web site: http://www.cberger.com. Temporary help in Illinois area, outsourcing, records management, planning, needs assessment, cataloging, and indexing.

Chris Olson & Associates, 857 Twin Harbor Dr., Arnold, Maryland 21012-1027, voice: 1-410-647-6708, fax: 1-410-647-0415, e-mail: chris@chrisolson.com, Web site: http://www.chrisolson.com. Graphics for libraries, consultation on library promotion, and *Marketing Treasures* newsletter available free online.

Library Specialists, Inc., 1000 Johnson Ferry Rd., Suite B-215, Marietta, Georgia 30068, voice: 1-800-578-6200, e-mail:

info@libraryspecialists.com, Web site: http://www.libraryspecialists. com. Cataloging of small libraries (mostly in the Southeast U.S.), staffing, and automation.

The Research Investment, 20600 Chagrin Blvd., Suite 650, Cleveland, Ohio 44122-5334, voice: 1-216-752-0300, fax: 1-216-752-0330, e-mail: orders@researchinvest.com. I have used this service for years.

Teltech/Sopheon, 2850 Metro Dr., Bloomington, Minnesota 55425, voice: 1-952-851-7500, fax: 1-952-851-7744, e-mail: info_us@ sopheon.com, Web sites: http://www.teltech.com or http://www. sopheon.com. (I recommend you use this company for location of technical experts and vendors only; **the company has been known to approach management to outsource libraries.**)

TFPL Inc., 345 Park Avenue South, 10th Floor, New York, New York 10010, voice: 1-212-213-5990, fax: 1-212-213-6887, e-mail: tfpl.inc@tfpl.com, Web site: http://www.tfpl.com. U.K., U.S., and European business information.

Miscellaneous

Copyright Authorities

For countries not listed here, see Web site: http://www.cla.co.uk /http://www.rro.htm.

Australia: Copyright Agency Limited (CAL), Level 19, 157 Liverpool St., Sydney, New South Wales 2000, voice: 61-2-9394-7600, fax: 61-2-9394-7601, e-mail: info@http://www.copyright.com.au, Web site: http://www.copyright.com.au.

Canada: CanCOPY, Canadian Copyright Licensing Agency, 1 Yonge St., #1900, Toronto, Ontario M5E 1E5, voice:1-800-893-5777 or 1-416-868-1620, fax: 1-416-868-1621, e-mail: rarthur@cancopy. com, Web site: http://www.cancopy.com.

U.K.: The Copyright Licensing Agency (CLA), 90 Tottenham Court Road, London W1P 0LP, voice: 44-(0)20-7631-5555, fax: 44-(0)20-7631-5500, e-mail: cla@cla.co.uk, Web site: http://www. cla.co.uk.

U.S.: Copyright Clearance Center (CCC), 222 Rosewood Dr., Danvers, Massachusetts 01923, voice: 1-978-750-8400, fax: 1-978-750-4470, e-mail: info@copyright.com, Web site: http://www.copyright.com.

Translation Companies

For a list of foreign language translation services available free on the Internet, see Chapter 13.

Kenneth Kronenberg, 217 Washington St., Brookline, Massachusetts 02445-6831, U.S.A., voice: 1-617-734-8418, fax: 1-603-452-8269 or 1-617-232-6865, e-mail: kkrone@tiac.net, Web site: http://www.itac. net/users/kkrone. Specializes in medical and legal translation from German to English.

Ralph McElroy Translation Company, 910 West Ave., Austin, Texas 78701, U.S.A., voice: 1-800-531-9977 or 1-512-472-6753, fax: 1-512-472-4591 or 1-512-479-6703, technical translations, e-mail: carolyn@mcelroytranslation.com, Web site: http://www. mcelroytranslation.com.

Nelles Translations, Inc., 11 N. Michigan Ave., Suite 1000, Chicago, Illinois 60603, U.S.A., voice: 1-312-236-2788.

Schreiber Translations Inc., 51 Monroe St., #101, Rockville, Maryland 20850, U.S.A., voice: 1-301-424-7737, fax: 1-301-424-2361, e-mail: translation@schreibernet.com, Web site: http://www.schreibernet.com.

Library Movers

Canada

Boyd Library Moving Services, P.O. Box 9040, 767 Belfast Rd., Ottawa, Ontario K1G 3T8, voice: 1-613-244-4444, Web site: http:// www.boyd.ca/library.htm. Now "teamed up" with Hallett Library Movers.

United States

Hallett Movers, 7535 W. 59th St., Summit, Illinois 60501, voice: 1-800-645-6683 or 1-708-458-8600, fax: 1-708-458-7116, e-mail: sales @hallettmovers.com, Web site: http://www.hallettmovers.com. Best known; can move stacks without removing books; over 35 years experience moving libraries.

National Library Relocations, 70 Bridge Road, Central Islip, New York 11722, voice: 1-800-486-6837 or 1-631-232-2233, fax: 1-631-232-2236, e-mail: scott@nlrbookmovers.com, Web site: http://www.nlrbook movers.com.

Discussion Lists and World Wide Web Sites

ELECTRONIC DISCUSSION LISTS

To join these lists, in almost all cases (exceptions are noted), you can send an e-mail message to the address listed after the name of the list. Leave the subject line blank, and put the following in the message field: Subscribe <name of list> first name last name. For example, subscribe SOLOLIB-L Judith Siess. You will receive an e-mail message from the list with further instructions. Note: e-mail addresses are not case-sensitive, but Web sites definitely are.

The section headings are as follows:

• Other One-Person Librarian (OPL) Lists

• General Library Lists

• Church and Synagogue Libraries

• Museum, Art, and Zoo Libraries

• Law and Government Libraries

• Medical Libraries

• Science and Technology Libraries

313

If you are only going to join one list, it should be this one, from the Solo Librarians Division of the Special Libraries Association (U.S.): SOLOLIB-L, which includes discussions of OPL issues and quick answers to your questions; archives can be found by contacting listserv@silverplatter.com.

Other OPL Lists

ALIAOPAL, listserv@alia.org.au. Official list of One-Person Australian Librarians (OPAL), a special-interest group of the Australian Library and Information Association (ALIA).

Kommission fur One-Person Librarians, majordomo@izn. niedersachsen.de. In German.

SOLO, listproc@listproc.la-hq.org.uk. From The Library Association (U.K.), archives at http://www.la-hq.org.uk/lists/solo.

WORKPLACE, listproc@listproc.la-hq.org.uk. From The Library Association (U.K.), archives at http://www.la-hq.org.uk/cgi-bin/hm_ search?workplace.

General Library Lists

ACQLIBS, mailserv@qut.edu.au. Australian acquisitions librarians.

AIB-CUR, listserv@icineca. Italian Librarians.

ALIANATSPEC, listproc@alianet.alia.org.au. Special library issues in Australia, from the Australian Library and Information Association.

APLA LIST, mailserve@ac.dal.ca. Atlantic Provinces Library Association, Canada.

ASIALIB, majordomo@info.anu.edu.au. Asian librarianship in Australia.

ASIS-L, listserv@asis.org. Discusses information science issues, conferences, and so on.

AW4LIB-L, listproc@scu.edu.au. Australian Web Librarians List.

BACKMED, listserv@sun.readmore.com. Back Issues and Duplicate Exchange Service.

BIBLIO-PROGRESISTAS, biblio-progresistas-subscribe@egroups. com. From the Mexican Circle of Progressive ozlib-announce, autoshare@Tony-Berry.emu.id.au, happenings in Australian libraries, services, databases, conferences, and government regulations.

BUSLIB-L, listserv@listserv.boisestate.edu. Supposedly for business librarians, but deals with all kinds of library issues and reference questions.

CYBRARIAN, majordomo@massey.ac.nz. New Zealand Librarians Accessing Resources on the Internet.

DIGLIB, listserv@infoserv.nlc-bna.ca. Digital library issue.

EURSLA-L, listserv@psuvm.psu.edu. International Information Exchange Caucus, European Chapter, International Relations Committee.

FIDEL, listserv@listserv.redris.es. Information resources in Spain and Latin America; in Spanish.

FIRSTSEARCH, listserv@listserv.boisestate.edu. Discussion of the Online Computer Library Center (OCLC), FirstSearch.

IFLA-L, listerv@infoserv.nlc-bnc.ca. Covers all kinds of international issues, conferences, and so on; official list of the International Federation of Library Associations.

ILL-L, listserv@uvmvm.uvm.edu.

INETBIB, maiser@zb.ub.uni-dortmund.de. Internet usage in German or German-speaking libraries.

INFO CAREER TRENDS, imailsrv@lisjobs.com. Personal professional development.

IWETEL, listserv@listserv.redris.es. Library events in Spain (mostly); in Spanish.

LIB-L, maiser@zb.ub.uni-dortmund.de. German and German-speaking libraries.

LIBPER-L, listserv@ksuvm.ksu.edu, Library personnel and organizational development.

LIBREF-L, listerv@listserv.kent.edu. Reference questions and issues.

LIBSUP-L, listproc@washington.edu. Library support staff.

LIS-FORUM, listserv@ncsi-iisc-ernet.in. From India.

LITA-L, listserv@uicvm.uic.edu. Library and Information Technology Associations.

MELANET-L, listproc@cornell.edu. Middle East Librarians Association.

NEWLIB-L, listproc@usc.edu. Originally designed for library students and new librarians, this list also discusses general library education and professional issues.

OZBIZ, listproc@gu.edu.au. Australian business librarians.

PACS-L, listservg@listserv.uhupvm1.uh.edu. Public access catalog issues.

PUBLIB-NET, listserv@nysernet.org. Internet use in public libraries.

PUBYAC, listserv@nysernet.org. Library services to children and young adults in public libraries.

REFEX, listserv@listserv.arizona.edu. Exchange of reference materials.

REFLIBS, reflibs-request@newcastle.edu.au. Australian reference librarians.

RESOURCE, to join visit http://www.mailbase.ac.uk/lists/resourcenews. U.K. Council for Museums, Archives and Libraries.

STUMPERS-L, mailserv@cfr.cuis.edu. Here is the place to post your "impossible" reference questions.

SYSLIBS, syslibs-request@library.adelaide.edu.au. Australian systems librarians.

TECH, listserv@ukcc.uky.edu. Technical services in special libraries.

WAIN, listproc@info.curtin.edu.au. Library and information profession in Western Australia.

WEB4LIB, listserv@library.berkeley.edu. Library web issues.

Church and Synagogue Libraries

ATLANTIS, listserv@harvarda.harvard.edu. Church and synagogue libraries.

HASAFRAN, listserv@lists.acs.ohio-state.edu. Association of Jewish Libraries.

Museum, Art, and Zoo Libraries

ARCLIB-L, listserv@irlearn.ucd.ie. Irish and U.K. architectural librarians.

ARLISANZ, majordomo@info.anu.edu.au. Arts Libraries Society of Australia and New Zealand.

ARLIS-L, listserv@ukcc.uky.edu. Art Libraries Association of North America.

MLA-L, listserv@iubvm.ucs.indiana.edu. Music Library Association.

Law and Government Libraries

ANZ-LAW-LIBRARIANS, ANZ-LAW-LIBRARIANS@uow.edu. Academic law librarians in Australia and New Zealand.

FLIN-L, listproc@nla.gov.au. Australian Federal Libraries Information network.

GOVDOC-L, listserv@psuvm.psu.edu. Government documents.

INT-LAW, listserv@listhost.ciesin.org. International Law.

JURIST, listserv@law.pitt.edu. Reviews of forthcoming scholarly and trade law books, for faculty, from Law Professors' Network.

LAW-LIB, listserv@ucdavis.edu.

LAWLIBREF-L, listproc@lawlib.wuacc.edu.

LEGALREC-L, listserv@netcom.com, American Association of Law Libraries, Private Law Libraries Special Interest Group, and Records Management Group.

LIBKNOW-L, majordomo@teleport.com. Knowledge management for librarians.

NET-LAWYERS, listserv@peach.ease.lsoft.com.

NEWLAWLIB-L, contact Stephanie Davidson, sdavidso@iupui. edu. Archives at http://php.iupui.edu/~sdavidso/docs/archives.html.

PLL-OPLL-L, listproc@aall.wuacc.edu. From the American Association of Law Libraries (AALL), Private Law Libraries (PLL) Section, focuses on OPLs in private law firms.

PRIVATELAWLIB-L, listproc@aall.wuacc.edu. Private law libraries.

SLALAW, listserv@listserv.uh.edu. Special Libraries Association (U.S.) Legal Division.

TECHNOLAWYER, nsquillante@netsquire.dom.

Medical Libraries

BIB-MED, listserv@listserv.rediris.es. Medical libraries; in Spanish.

CANMEDLIB, listserv@morgan.ucs.mun.ca. Canadian Health Sciences Libraries.

DENTALIB, listproc@usc.edu. Dental Librarians List.

LIS-MEDICAL, mailbase@mailbase.ac.uk. U.K. Health Sciences Libraries.

MEDIBIB-L, medbib-l-request@uni-muenster.de. German medical libraries discussion; in German.

MEDLIB-L, listserv@ubvm.cc.buffalo.edu. Medical issues and reference questions; archives at http://listserv.ubvm.cc.buffalo.edu/archives/medlib-l.html.

MLA-EBHC, majordomo@mlahq. Evidence-based health care.

Science and Technology Libraries

CHINF-L, listserv@iubvm.ucs.indiana.edu. Chemical information sources.

LIS-SCITECH, mailbase@mailbase.ac.uk. U.K. Science and Technology Libraries.

WORLD WIDE WEB SITES

These sites were active and the URLs were checked as of late Fall 2000. Things may have changed by the time you read this, but this list will give you an idea of what is available out there. Remember, URLs are case sensitive—be sure to type them in exactly as printed here.

The section headings are as follows:

• Just for OPLs

• General Reference

• News

• Business Resources

• Strategic Planning Resources

• Directories

• Law Resources

• Government Resources

• Intellectual Property Resources

• Library and Information Science Resources

• Knowledge Management Resources

• Technical Services

• Medical and Health Resources

• Science and Technology Resources

• Internet, World Wide Web, and Computer Technology Resources

Just for OPLs

International
The One-Person Library: A Newsletter for Librarians and Management, from Information Bridges International, Inc., http://www.ibi-opl.com.

The Solo Librarians Division, Special Libraries Association, http://www.sla.org/divisions/dsol.

Australia
One-Person Australian Librarians (OPAL), http://www.alia.org.au/sigs/opals.

Germany
Kommission fur One-Person Librarians, VdDB, http://homepages.uni-tuebingen.de/juergen.plienger/vddb-opl.

United Kingdom
The Library Association, SOLO archives at http://www.la-hq.org.uk/lists/solo/, WORKPLACE archives at http://www.la-hq.org.uk/cgi-bin/hm_search?workplace.

General Reference

Bartleby.com—"Great Books Online," http://www.bartleby.com. Searchable reference books, including the *Columbia Encyclopedia, World Factbook, American Heritage Dictionary, Roget's Thesaurus, The King's English, The Elements of Style, Bartlett's Familiar Quotations, The Bible* (KJV), *Cambridge History of English and American Literature, The Oxford Shakespeare, Gray's Anatomy, Fannie Farmer's Cook Book, Emily Post's Etiquette, Robert's Rules of Order*, and Inaugural Addresses of the Presidents of the United States. There are also works of fiction, nonfiction, and verse. A truly amazing site!

The Best Information on the Net (BIOTN), http://vweb.sau.edu/bestinfo. Links to just about *anything* you could want to find, from the librarians at O'Keefe Library, St. Ambrose University, Davenport, Iowa, especially good on general news and news on specialized topics.

Blue Mountain, http://www.bluemountain.com. For worldwide and regional holiday and celebration dates; some are very obscure. For more like this, try http://www.rubicon.com/passport/holidays/ holidays/htm (sorted by day of the month), or The Worldwide Holiday and Festival Site, http://www.holidayfestival.com (search by month, religion, or country).

For a list of foreign language translation services available free on the Internet, see http://www.translate-free.com. Also try http://www. freetranslation.com for a "quick and dirty" instant translation.

How Far is It?, http://www.indo.com/distance. Very fast and can even give you driving directions.

Information Please Almanac, http://www.infoplease.com. The print version plus online-only features.

Instructions to Authors, http://www.mco.edu/lib/instr/libinsta.html. From the Medical College of Ohio. Over 3,000 journals, including links to journal home pages.

The Internet Movie Database, http://us.imdb.com.

Kasamba, http://www.kasamba.com. Find an expert and ask a quick question, or hire the expert; an interesting concept.

Merriam-Webster Online, http://www.m-w.com. Dictionary and thesaurus.

OneLook Dictionaries, http://www.onelook.com. Access to nearly 500 works.

Online English Grammar Helper, http://www.edunet.com/english/ grammar/index.html

Quickforms, http://www.quickforms.com. Sample forms.

Time Zone Converter, http://www.timezoneconverter.com.

The Universal Currency Converter, http://www.xe.net/ucc, 180 currencies, updated once a minute.

Xrefer, http://www.xrefer.com. Fact search engine "powered by encyclopedias, dictionaries, books of quotations and other [trusted] reference works," delivers authoritative answers rather than links.

yourdictionary.com, http://www.yourdictionary.com. Quick lookups in *Merriam-Webster's Collegiate Dictionary and Thesaurus*, with good and lengthy definitions. Also language dictionaries; multi-lingual dictionaries; translations; and specialty dictionaries, such as law, business, and finance.

International
CIA World Factbook, http://www.odci.gov/. Lots of information on countries of the world.

Asia-Pacific
Asia-Pacific Information, http://asiabiz.com.

Australia, http://www.nla.gov.au/oz/gov.

National Library of New Zealand, http://www.natlib.govt.nz/ flash.html.

New Zealand and Pacific Islanders, http://tepuna.natlib.govt.nz/ web_directory.

United States
Ask ERIC, http://www.askeric.org/Eric. General social science and humanities index.

Peterson's Education Center, http://www.petersons.com.

U.S. Public Broadcasting Service, http://www.pbs.com

U.S. Zip Code server. http://www.cedar.buffalo.edu/adserv.html. Input a name and address and get the zip code.

Rest of the Americas
Latin American Network, http://lanic.utexas.edu. From the University of Texas.

Mexico and Central America, http://www.mexonline.com/grupoam 1.htm

Micromedia Limited (Canada's Information People), http://www. mmltd.com.

Peruvian Web site, http://www.rcp.net.pe. Introduction in English or Spanish, and articles in Spanish.

United Kingdom
American-English/English-American Translation Guide, http:// www.scit.wlv.ac.uk/~jphb/american.html.

The Best of British: An American's Guide to Speaking British, http://www.effingpot.com/index.html.

The British Council Education Information Service, http://www. brit-coun.de/oldsite/index.htm. Information on study and education in the U.K., mostly in German.

Get Mapping, http://www.getmapping.com. Aerial views by postal code of which you can buy a copy.

Great Britain: A Complete Touring Guide, http://www.great-britain. co.uk. A to Z listings, travel information, regional information, accommodations (including country house hotels), history, culture, sports, and people; searchable.

History of the U.K., Primary Documents, http://library.byu.edu/~rdh/eurodocs/uk.html. From Brigham Young University (U.S.). Maps, royal proclamations, newspapers, treaties, Word War I documents, Winston Churchill's speeches, explanation of the British legal system. Also on BYU's site is similar coverage for Andorra, Austria-Hungary, Belgium, Denmark, Finland, Germany, Greece, Iceland, Ireland, Italy, Liechtenstein, Luxembourg, Netherlands, Norway, Portugal, San Marino, Spain, Sweden, Switzerland, Vatican City, and "Europe as a Supernational Region."

Know U.K., http://www.knowuk.co.uk. "Online answers about the people, places and institutions of the United Kingdom." from Chadwyck-Healey Ltd.

Lifestyle U.K., http://www.lifestyle.co.uk. Search for information on living, the environment, communities, education, health, travel, jobs, real estate, news, shopping, entertainment, sports, computing, and women's sites.

Maps, http://www.lonelyplanet.com.

Office for National Statistics, http://www.statistics.gov.uk. Includes the census, education, StatBase, and statistical publications; searchable.

Oxford University Press Reading Room, http://www.oup.co.uk. Reading room; sample chapters from new books from the Press (as PDF files), free. All academic subject areas covered.

U.K. Index, http://www.ukindex.co.uk.

U.K. Plus, http:www.ukplus.co.uk.

U.K. Politics, http://www.ukpol.co.uk. Searchable database and links to elections and politics in the U.K.. Includes biographies of the members of Parliament, local election results, officers, and issues.

U.K. Theatre Web, http://www.uktw.co.uk. A "comprehensive" guide to the performing arts in the U.K.

The U.K. Travel Guide, http://www.uktravel.com. Links to cities, castles, the Royal Family, picture, travel, lodging, and so on; searchable. You can even send a postcard of London to a friend via the Internet.

The U.K. Travel Guide, http://www.uktravel.com. Links to cities, castles, the Royal Family, pictures, travel, and lodging; searchable.

Rest of Europe

Belgium, http://www.cais.net/U.S.

Northern Ireland, http://www.nics.gov.uk.

Spain, http://www.docuweb.ca/sispain.

Statistics Netherlands, http://www.cbs.nl.

Statistics Norway, http://www-open.ssb.no/www-open.

Statistics Sweden, http://www.scb.se.

Statistisches Bundesamt (Germany), http://statistik-bund.de.

Switzerland, http://swissinfo.ch/main/oben_r.htm.

News

Aileena World Wide Media Index, http://www.aileena.ch/aileena.htm. Links to many, many newspapers and radio and television stations.

The Boston Globe, http://www.globe.com.

British Broadcasting Corporation, http://www.bbc.co.uk. Some transcripts, news reviews and analysis, and more.

CNN News Interactive, http://www.cnn.com. Today's news.

Der Spiegel (in German), http://www.spiegel.de.

The Electronic Newsstand, http://www.enews.com. *Business Week*, *The Economist*, and *Scientist*.

The Financial Times, http://www.ft.com. Free searching of all main U.K. newspapers in their archives.

JournalismNet, http://www.journalismnet.com. Links to newspapers in the U.S., Canada, the U.K., and France. Also how to find news, search help, and journalism schools.

London Daily Telegraph, http://www.telegraph.co.uk.

The London Times, http://www.the-times.co.uk.

The New York Times, http://www.nytimes.com.

Newsdesk, http://www.newsdesk.com. Press releases, free.

Newswire Canada, http://www.newswire.ca. Press releases.

Online newspapers, http://www.onlinenewspapers.com. Over 4,100 newspapers.

Philadelphia Inquirer and *Daily News*, http://www.phillynews.com.

San Jose Mercury News, http://www.sjmercury.com.

Business Resources

Canada
Consumer Price Index, http://www.statcan.ca/english/Subjecs/Cpi/cpi-en.htm

Insurance Canada, http://www.insurance-canada.ca. Directory and searchable news from 1994 forward.

Germany
Statistics, http://www.statistik-bund.de/basis/be_ueber.htm or http://www.germany-inf.olg/newcontent/index_gic.html.

International
Business Information on the Net, http://www.rba.co.uk/sources/index.htm.

Business Researcher's Interests, http://www.pitt.edu/~malhotra/interest.html From Yogesh Malhotra at University of Pittsburgh, Katz Graduate School of Business, Pittsburgh, Pennsylvania.

Corporate Information metasite, http://www.corporateinformation. com. Over 350,000 international company profiles (20,000 on their site) and research reports. You can search by industry or country. Also available in French or Spanish for companies in which either is the dominant language.

Exchange Rates, http://www.x-rates.com. Tables only, both current and historical (up to 120 days), importable to Excel, multi-lingual.

Financial Times U.K. Company Briefing, http://www.globalarchive. ft.com/cb/cb_search.htm, Quoted company briefs and financials, free with registration; much of the content of the *Dow Jones World Reporter* is available.

Find/SVP, http://www.findsvp.com. Market research.

FreePint, http://www. Freepint.co.uk. Free bimonthly newsletter, plus great online tips and discussion list; U.K.-oriented but covers world. One of the best business pages around; it can be addictive.

Gale full-text, http://www.findarticles.com. Free access to "some" business and premium magazines from the past one to two years. Not all journals are there, but if they are, they are full-text and free.

Gartner Group and Dataquest, http://www.gartner.com or http://www. dataquest.com. Market research and information.

Government Statistics Agencies of the World, http://www.scb.se/scbeng/ishtm/andrakallorasiaeng.htm.

Hoover's Online, http://www.hoovers.com. Company profiles, stock quotes, Securities and Exchange Commission documents, directory of 10,000 companies, Initial Public Offering documents, links to corporate Web sites; some services are available free, the rest are by subscription ($9.95/month).

International Business Resources on the Web, http://ciber.bus. msu.edu/busres.htm. Extensive gateway from Michigan State University's Center for International Business Education and Research; also has some feature articles, international conference announcements, and executive summaries of the *Journal of International Marketing.*

International Monetary Fund, http://dsbb.inf.org/gddsindex.htm. General data dissemination system, individual countries and general information, standards and codes, publications, and fund rates.

International salary calculator, http://www.homefair.com/homefair/cmr/salcalc.html.

Layperson's Guide to Online Market Research, http://www.vivamus.com.

Open Market's Commercial Sites Index, http://www.directory.net.

Prices and earnings around the globe, http://www.ubsw.com/e/index/about/research/pcc/publications.html. From the Union Bank of Switzerland.

United Kingdom
Companies House Direct, http://www.direct.companies-house .gov.uk. U.K.'s equivalent of the U.S. Securities and Exchange Commission. Much of the information is free, some documents are downloadable for a small fee.

Company Finder (U.K.), http://www.hoovers.co.uk.

ICC, http://193.133.118.15/iccweb/icchome.htm. Online credit and business information, every Companies House document, every British shareholder and director; not free.

U.K. Businesspark, http://www.ukbusiness park.co.uk. Business news, mostly mergers and acquisitions.

U.K. Company Researcher, http://www.ukcompanyresearcher.com. Links to company information and actual corporation websites.

United States
Addresses for U.S. public companies, http://www.quicken.com/investments.

ASI's Market Research Center, http://www.asiresearch.com.

Big Yellow, http://www.bigyellow.com. Web access to the Yellow Pages throughout the U.S.

EDGAR, http://www.sec.gov/edaux/searches.htm. U.S. Securities and Exchange Commission (electronic copies of most filings).

NAICS (North American Industry Classification System), the successor to the SIC system, http://www.census.gov/epcd/www/naics. html.

Thomas Register, http://www.thomasregister.com. Free.

Rest of the World

Australia on Display, http://www.austrade.gov.au/AOD/index.asp. Easy-to-use gateway to Australian companies.

Japan Corporate Information Bank, http://www.dir.co.jp. Information on Japanese corporations.

Japan External Trade Organization (JETRO), http://www.jetro.go.jp.

Strategic Planning Resources

Global Electronic Nonprofit Information Express, http://www.support-center.org/sf/spgenie.html. Planning retreats, mission statements.

The Management Center, http://www.tmcenter.org. Nonprofits.

National Center for Nonprofit Boards, http://www.ncnb.org.

New Mexico State University Library Strategic Plan Working Documents, http://lib.nmsu.edu/aboutlib/plan/index.html.

Special Libraries Association (U.S.) Strategic References on Strategic Planning, http://www.sla.org/membership/irc/libstrat.html.

Strategies, http://strategis.ic.gc.ca. From the Canadian government, English and French, includes a quiz "offering to help confirm the need for strategic planning."

Directories

International

Directory of Electronic Journals, Newsletters, and Academic Discussion Lists, http://arl.cni.org/scomm/edir.

Kapitol International Telephone Directory, http://www.infobel.be/infobel/infobelworld.html, Business directories.

Kompass, http://www.kompass.com. Links to 1.5 million company listings, many not found elsewhere.

Universities Worldwide, http://geohttp://www.uibk.ac.at/univ/. 89 countries, over 3,000 institutions.

Whois, http://www.networksolutions.com/cgi-bin/whois/whois. Search of the main domain name registry.

WhoWhere?, http://www.whowhere.lycos.com/. Searchable database of e-mail, phone, and postal addresses.

World Wide Web Virtual Library, http://vlib.org/Overview.html. Hierarchical subject index, worldwide.

United Kingdom
InfoSpace U.K., http://www.infospace.com/intldb/intl-uk.html.

PhoneNet U.K. Online Phone Directory, http://www.bt.co.uk/phonenetuk. Searchable, U.K. only.

U.K. Phonebook.com, http://www.ukphonebook.com/servlet/home.

YELL: Yellow Pages U.K., http://www.yell.co.uk. Directory and search service, U.K. only.

United States
GTE SuperPages, http://yp.gte.net. Yellow Pages.

Telephone area codes and country codes, http://www.xmission.com/~americom/aclookup.html.

U.S. Zip Code server, http://www.cedar.buffalo.edu/adserv.html. Input a name and address, and get the zip code.

Law Resources

International
Digital Technology Law Journal, http://wwwlaw.murdoch.edu/au/dtlj/index.html. From the Asia Pacific Intellectual Property Law Institute at Murdoch University, Western Australia; quarterly.

Directory of Law Sites on the Web, http://www.dm.net.lb/tmalouli/links/legsites.htm. Articles, international sites (France, Lebanon, and the U.S.), law schools and libraries, forms and contracts, associations, and attorneys and firms.

Eur-Lex European Union Law, http://www.europa.eu.int/eurlex/en/index.html. *The Official Journal*, treaties, legislation, and case law.

International Law Overview, http://www.llrx.com/resources4.htm. Newsletter-type directory.

List of legal Web sites from David Zyngier of Sandoz Partners, Australia, contact David at sandoz@labyrinth.net.au.

Canada

Alberta Courts, http://www.albertacourts.ab.ca/webpage.jdb/jdb.com.

Best Guide to Canadian Legal Research, http://legalresearch.org. From Catherine Best.

British Columbia Courts: http://www.courts.gov.bc.ca.

Canadian statutes and regulations, http://canada.justice.gc.ca/Loireg/index_en.html.

Federal Court of Canada judgments, http://www.fja.gc.ca/en/cf.

Guide to Canadian Legal Research, http://www.llrx.com/features/ca.htm. From Ted Tjaden, Law Library, University of Toronto; check out his website at http://www.fis.utoronto.ca.

Ontario Courts: http://www.ontariocoutsw.on.ca.

Supreme Court of Canada judgments, http://www.lexum.umontreal.ca/csc-scc/en/inex.html.

University of Calgary Law Library, http://www.ucalgary.ca/library/law.

And many subscription services such as Quicklaw (http://www.quicklaw.com), eCarswell (http://www.carswell.com), LEXIS-NEXIS (http://www.lexis-nexis-canada.com), CCH iWorks (http://www.ca.cch.com), and Canada Law Book (http://www.canadalawbook.ca).

United Kingdom

British and Irish Legal Information Institute, http://www.bailii.org. "Comprehensive access to freely available British and Irish public legal information."

Hemscott Legal, http://www.hemscottlegal.com. Links to U.K., European, Australaisan, and U.S. sites.

Legal Resource Pages from the U.K., Delia Venables, http://www.pavilion.co.uk/legal and Nick Holmes http://www. infolaw.co.uk.

Web Journal of Current Legal Issues, http://webjcli.ncl.ac.uk. From the University of Newcastle (U.K.) and Blackstone Press.

United States
AALLNET, American Association of Law Libraries, http://www. aallnet.org.

Bytes in Brief, http://www.senseient.com. Free monthly digest of Internet law and technology through e-mail.

CLE Advisor, http://www.oceanalaw.com. Costs about U.S. $50 per year, but has a searchable database of U.S. and Canadian continuing legal education programs.

Cornell University's Legal Information Institute, http://www.law. cornell.edu/index.html.

Electronic Licensing Issues, http://www.arl.org/scomm/licensing.

EXACTA, http://www.excata.com.au. A great free Australian legal news service.

FindLaw, http://www.FindLaw.com. Named "best legal website over-all" by one online publication.

Internet Skills and Strategies for the Legal Researcher, http://www. virtualchase.com/legalresearcher. Designed by Genie Tyburski of Ballard Spahr Andrews & Ingersoll, Philadelphia, Pennsylvania, U.S., to accompany her six-hour classes on finding, using, and evaluated legal Web sites.

Law Guru, http://www.lawguru.com. Access to over 435 legal search engine forms and legal databases, also state legal research sections, questions and answers searchable database, search court opinions in 21 states from one interface at the same time.

Law Journals and Firm Articles, http://www.Loundy.com/Law_articles.html.

Law News Network, from American Lawyer Media (including Counsel Connect and Law Journal EXTRA) http://www.lawnewsnetwork.com and a catalog of books, newsletters, and journals at http://www.lawcatalog.com.

Law Runner, http://www.lawrunner.com. Legal research tool.

Legal Resources, http://www.paralegals.org/LegalResources/home.html. National Federation of Paralegal Associations.

Lex Mundi, http://www.hg.org. A comprehensive law and government Web site for the legal profession.

LLRX (Law Library Resource Exchange), http://www.llrx.com. Mentioned on everyone's good legal Web site list.

Martindale-Hubbell Lawyer Locator, http://lawyers.martindale.com/marhub.

Public Library Collection Guidelines for a Legal Research Collection, http://www.allnet.org/sis/lisp/collect.htm.

Seamless Website, Law and Legal Resources, http://seamless.com.

Virtual Chase Legal Research on the Internet, http://www.virtualchase.com. Research guides, online teaching tools from Ballard Spahr Andrews & Ingersoll, Philadelphia, Pennsylvania.

Washburn University College of Law http://www.washlaw.edu.

West's Legal Dictionary, http://www.westpub.com.

Zimmerman's Research Guide, http://www.llrx/com/guide.

Government Resources

International
CORDIS, http://www.cordis.lu. Information on European Union-supported research and development activities.

Electronic Embassy, http://www.embassy.org.

Embassy Page, http://www.globescope.com.

Eudralex, http://dg3.eudra.org. European pharmaceutical legislation.

European Union/Commission: http://europa.eu.int/index.htm.

Intelligence Services, http://www.kimsoft.com/kim-spy.htm#1g. By country.

International Court of Justice, http://www.icj-cij.org.

KIOSK: Journal of Geo-Politics, http://fowlerlibrary.com/Kiosk. Online news sources in world politics.

United National Development Programme, http://www.undp.org, United Nations documents, conferences, and directories.

WWW Virtual Library of International Affairs Resources, http://www.etown.edu/vl.

Canada

Canada's Parliament, http://www.parl.gc.ca. Full-text bills, committee reports, and debates.

Canadian Who's Who, http://www.utpress/utoronto.ca/cww/cw2w3.cgi. The 1997 edition was the latest as of Fall 2000.

Federal and provincial government links, http://www.sympatico.ca/Contents/Government. From Lycos, Canada.

United Kingdom

BOPCAS: British Official Publications Current Awareness Service, http://www.bopcas.com. Database of British official publications, searchable.

Commonwealth information, http://www.fco.gov.uk.

The Home Office (U.K.), http://www.homeoffice.gov.uk. List of acts, press releases, statistics, and office directories.

National Statistics, http://www.statstics.gov.uk. "The official U.K. statistics site." Census, social surveys, births, marriages and deaths, publications, and StatBase online encyclopedia of official statistics.

Office of the Prime Minister (U.K.), http://www.number-10.gov.uk. News items, information center, tour, list of prime ministers, biography of the current prime minister. Note: the prime minister's office now has its first librarian (Michael Lee, as of Fall 2000).

Open.gov.uk, http://www.open.gov.uk/. Links and information for many U.K. government departments.

Public Record Office, http://www.pro.gov.uk. Online catalog of over eight million document references.

U.K. Politics, http://www.ukpol.co.uk. Searchable database and links to elections and politics in the U.K.. Includes biographies of the members of Parliament, local election results, officers, and issues.

ukstate, http://www.ukstate.com/portal.asp. "Opening up official information" from the Stationery Office (official publisher of U.K. information, formerly HMSO), links to 10 Downing Street, U.K. Parliament, Houses of Lords and Commons, Scottish Parliament, National Assembly for Wales, and Northern Ireland Assembly.

United States

Census information, http://www.census.gov:80.

CIA World Factbook, http://www.odci.gov. Lots of information on countries of the world.

General gateway, http://firstgov.gov or http://www.fedworld.gov.

NAICS, http://www.census.gov/epcd/www/naics.html. Guide to the North American Industry Classification System, the successor to the SIC system.

Occupational Safety and Health Administration (OSHA), http://www.osha.gov.

Statistical Abstract of the U.S., http://www.census.gov:80/stat_ abstract.

U.S. Congress, http://thomas.loc.gov/home/thomas2.html. Full text of Bills, and so on.

U.S. Supreme Court, http://supct.law.cornell.edu/supct/index.html. From Cornell Legal Information Institute. Opinions, complete from 1990 to the present and over 600 older ones; also the Court calendar; easy to use, very current.

Intellectual Property Resources

Copyright and Copyleft: The Educational Cyberplayground's Copyright Links, http://www.edu-cyberpg.com/Internet/copyrightleft.html.

DNI-Copyright Discussion Group, http://www.cni.org/Hforums/cni-copyright.

FindLaw Intellectual Property Center, http://www.findlaw.com/01topics/23intellectprop/index.html.

The Intellectual Property Center, http://www.ipcenter.com.

Intellectual Property, Copyright, and Fair Use Resources, http://www.albany.edu/~ls973/copy.html.

Intellectual Property Rights Helpdesk, http://www.ipr-helpdesk.org/t_en/home.asp.

International Trademark Association (includes discussion group), http://www.inta.org.

Links to patent and other intellectual property information resources, British Library Science, Technology and Business Patents Information Service, http://www.bl.uk/servicews/stb/etalmenu.html. A very long and good list of gateways, databases, subjects-based databases, classification schemes, patent agents, national and international legislation, and so on.

U.S. Patent and Trademark Office, http://www.uspto.gov.

Library and Information Science Resources

International and General
BUBL Information Service, http://bubl.ac.uk. Gateway for library and information science professional, mostly U.K.

Cyberlibrarian's Rest Stop: Web-Savvy: Keeping Current with Web-based Resources, http://www.thelearningsite.net/cyberlibrarian/elibraries/cybecurr.html. Links to newsletters, search tools, news services, and current awareness.

Documents in Information Science (DoIS), http://dois.mimas.ac.uk/DoIS/. Jointly managed by a European volunteer team. Indexes over a 1,000 articles and papers, all downloadable from the site.

EARL, http://www.earl.org.uk/. Includes "Ask a librarian" service.

Hypertext Library Lingo: A Glossary of Library Technology, http://www.wcsu.edu/library/odlis.html. From Joan Reitz, Western Connecticut State University.

IFLA Internet and Library Software Archive, http://ifla.org/II/software.htm.

Instructions to Authors, http://www.mco.edu/lib/instr/libinsta.html. Compiled by the librarians, Medical College of Ohio. For over 3,000 journals.

The Internet Public Library, http://www.ipl.org. Links and reference service, U.S.

Librarians' Index to the Internet, http://lii.org/. Prepared by Carole Leita. Very complete list of links, also has an electronic list to join.

Libraries-Online, http://www.libraries-online.com. Gateway, world-wide.

Library-oriented lists and electronic serials, http://www.wrlc.org/ liblists.

Libweb, http://sunsite.berkeley.edu/Libweb/. List of over 3,000 library-based Web sites worldwide.

Lib-web-cats, http://staffweb.library.vanderbilt.edu/Breeding/libwebcats. html. Directory of library Web pages, online catalogs, and profiles.

Multilingual Glossary for Art Librarians. http://www.ifla.org/ VII/s30/pub/mg1.htm. Published by the International Federation of Library Associations (IFLA) Section of Art Libraries, in English with indexes in Dutch, French, German, Italian, Spanish, and Swedish.

Online Citation Styles, http://www.bedfordstmartins.com/online/ citex.html. Compilation of citation guidelines to a range of electronic and other journals.

Researcha, http://www.researcha.com. "The community for information professionals." Free, recruitment, discussions, interviews, news and features, database of free market reports, and help with research questions or finding a researcher.

The Researching Librarian, http://www2.msstate.edu/~kerjsmit/ trl/index.html. Web resources helpful for librarians doing research.

Resource Directory Network, http://www.rdn.ac.uk/. Network of information gateways, including health, medicine, engineering, computing, social sciences, business, and law.

Salary Information, http://www.salary.com, http://www.jobsmart. org/tools/salary/sal-prof.htm, and http://www.scip.com.

Zoo library sites, http://www.mindspring.com/~zoonet/www_virtual_ lib/zoos.html, http://www.aza.org and http://www.sandiegozoo.org.

Canada
Canadian Library Gateway, http://www.nlc-bnc-.ca/gatepasse/index _e.htm. "... Connecting Canada's libraries."

United Kingdom
BAILER WWW Server (British Association for Information and Library Education and Research), http://www.staff.livjm.ac.uk/ busjofar/bailer/. Directory of U.K. library schools and some in the rest of the world.

British Library, http://portico.bl.uk. More than the online catalog, operating hours, contents of special collection, exhibitions, and services; searchable.

Bookseller Links, http://http://www.thebookseller.com. Publications, directories, analysis of the U.K. book business, jobs, who owns whom, and debates and dialogs on e-commerce.

Library and Information Statistics Unit (U.K.), http://www.lboro.ac. uk/departments/dis/lisu/lisuhp.html. Statistical information on U.K. libraries.

Library World, http://www.libraryworld.co.uk. "A directory designed by library professionals *for* library professionals." Lots of good links to all aspects of librarianship, with an electronic bulletin board and reference desk; updated weekly.

Paul Pedley's Homepage, http://www.paulpedley.com or http:// website.lineone.net/~p.d.p. Lots and lots links to library, economics, market research and other websites. Paul is at *The Economist* and is active in the Library Association's Industrial and Commercial Libraries Group.

Knowledge Management Resources

American Productivity and Quality Center, http://www.apqc.org.

@BRINT: The Premier Network for Business, Technology and Knowledge Management, http://www.brint.com.

Harvard Business Review, http://www.hbsp.harvard.edu/frames/ groups/bhr/indexx.html. Articles on knowledge management, almost monthly.

Intelligent Enterprise, http://www.iemagazine.com.

Intranet/Knowledge Management Resource Center, http://www. uni-hohenheim.de/~miepple/ikcenter.html.

KM World, http://www.kmworld.com.

Knowledge-at-Work, http://www.knowledge-at-work.com/. Practical matters from Knowledge Management Associates, Inc.

Knowledge Management and Innovation Conferences and Workshops, http://www.dreamscape.com/dream2000/discover/discover.htm. Sponsored by Burton Knowledge Services.

Knowledge Management Forum, http://revolution.3-cities.com/~ bonewman/. Hosted by Bo Newman.

Knowledge Management Magazine, Knowledge Transfer International, http://www.ktic.com/topic6/km.htm.

Knowledge Management Server, http://www.bus.utexas. edu/kmam/. Knowledge management glossary, resources, and case studies.

Knowledge Resources from Knowledge Inc., http://www. knowledgeinc.com.

NetAcademy at Knowledge Media, http://www.knowledgemedia.org.

Robert Buckman, http://www.knowledge-nurture.com. Go to the Buckman Room.

Technical Services

BackServ, http://www.blackwells.com/services/library/info_services/backserv. From Blackwells, for journal trading.

Bibiofind, http://www.bibliofind.com. Out of print books.

Bookseller Links (U.K.), http://www.thebookseller.com. Publications, directories, analysis of the U.K. book business, jobs, who owns whom, and debates and dialogs on e-commerce.

Bookwire, *Library Journal, School Library Journal, Publishers Weekly*, http://www.bookwire.com.

CARL Uncover http://www.carl.org/carl.html. Tables of contents and document delivery.

Cataloguer's Toolbox, *http://www.mun.ca/library/cat/index.html*. A wonderful Web site with almost everything you could need for cataloging, USMARC, CANMARC, UKMARC, MAB from Germany, and UNIMARC, bibliographic utilities (including Australian Bibliographic Network, A-G Canada, Online Computer Library Center, Research Libraries Information network, and WLN), conferences and meetings, connections to the British Library, National Library of Australia, National Library of Canada, National Library of New Zealand, and the Virtual Canadian Union Catalogue Project.

EBSCO Online, http://www.ebsco.com/online/OnlineTitles.asp. Look up journal titles.

Harvard Library, http://preserve.harvard.edu/resources/disaster/index.html. Disaster preparedness information.

Jake, http://jake.med.yale.edu/. For decoding cryptic journal citations.

JustBooks U.K., http://www.JustBooks.co.uk/. "The largest Internet marketplace in Europe for second-hand and antiquarian books." Over 1.1 million titles and over 250 book dealers.

PubList.com, http://www.publist.com. "Sort of like an online *Ulrich's.*"

Technical Processing Tools Online, http://tpot.ucsd.edu/. Web resources for acquisitions, cataloging, and serials.

The WWW Virtual Library: Publishers, http://www.comlab.ox.ac. uk/archive/publishers.html. Alphabetical list of worldwide publishers with e-mail addresses or websites, and some links.

Medical and Health Resources

General and International

Alternative Medicine, http://www.herbmed.org.

Clinical Medicine NetPrints, http://intl-clinmed.netprints.org.

Drug Index, http://www.rxlist.com.

Drug InfoNet, http://www.druginfonet.com/phrminfo.htm.

Emedicine, http://www.emedicine.com. Good for emergency medicine and pediatrics, definitions, references to images, and so on.

EurekAlert, http://www.eurekalert.org. From the American Association for the Advancement of Science (AAAS), Stanford, global gateway to science, medicine, and technology.

Gray's Anatomy of the Human Body, http://www.bartelby.com/107.

Lists of (mostly medical) full-text books, journals, and clinical guidelines on the Internet, http://www.ladydavidson.com.au/ejournal.htm and http://www.ladydavidson.com.au/etexts. From Toni Kennedy, Lady Davidson Private Hospital, Australia.

Martindale's Health Science Guide, www-sci.lib.uci.edu/HSG/HS Guide.html. Includes multimedia.

MedicineNet, http://www.medicinenet.com. Sort of a newsletter.

Merck Manual, http://merck.com/pubs/mmanual. Free. For the Home Edition, see http://www.merck.com/pubs/mmanual_home/ contents.htm.

MICROMEDEX, http://www.micromedex.com. Information on drugs, decision support, toxicology, and emergency medicine; expensive.

Pharmacy/Pharmacology: http://www.mcp.edu/si/sl/sl_rec.shtml.

PharmInfoNet, http://pharminfo.com/drugdb/db_mnu.html.

Australia

Alzheimer's research: http://werple.mira.net.au/~dhs/ad.html.

Australian Department of Health, http://www.australianprescriber.com.

Australian Medical E-Journals, http://www.oze-mail.com.au/~nldh/ejournal.htm.

Australian Medical E-Texts, http://www.oze-mail.com.au/~nldh/etexts.htm.

United Kingdom

DISCERN, http://www.discern.org.uk. Validated appraisal tool for consumer health information.

Medic8.com, http://www.medic8.com/index.htm. U.K. Medical Information Portal for Healthcare Professionals. Medical resources by clinical specialty, journals, clinical tools, free newsletter, links to other sites, medical discussion forum, latest medical new, medical supply store (books, software, and supplies), site of the month, drug warning and alerts, and searchable peer-reviewed medical sites.

NHS Direct, http://www.nhsdirect.nhs.uk. Patient-oriented portal to the National Health Service.

The Lancet, http://www.thelancet.com.

OMNI: Organising Medical Networked Information, http://www.omni.ac.uk. Gateway to unbiased, high-quality, Internet-based resources for the U.K., nearly 5,000 records.

The Wellcome Trust for the History and Understanding of Medicine, http://www.wellcome.ac.uk.

United States

Acronyms and Initialisms for Health Information Resources, http://www.geocities.com/~mlshams/acronym/acr.htm.

Adam, http://www.adam.com. An interesting new medical site. It looks consumer-oriented but has lots for professionals, including news stories.

American College of Cardiology, http://www.acc.org.

Centers for Disease Control and Prevention, http://www.cdc.gov.

Cut to the Chase, http://www.cuttothechase.com. "Practical information for healthcare management," accreditation, reimbursement, disease management, human resource, information technology, career development, networking, and links to other sites; free.

Dxplain, http://www.lcs.mgh.harvard.edu. Decision support tool.

Emergency Room information, http://herbst7.his.ucsf.edu.

Food and Drug Association, http://www.fda.gov.

Hardin Meta Directory of Internet Health Sources: http://www.arcade.uiowa.edu/hardin-www/md.html.

Harvard University Biopages: http://mcb.harvard.edu/BioLinks. html. A good starting point.

HealthFinder, http://www.healthfinder.com.

HealthWeb, http://healthweb.org. Specific, evaluated information resources for health professionals and consumers.

Hot Topics, http://www.texmed.org/liy/hot_topic_bibliography.asp. From the Texas Medical Association. Bimonthly bibliography on current issues of interest.

HSL Selected Internet Sites, http://ublib.buffalo.edu/libraries/units/hsl/ref/subject.html. From the University of Buffalo Health Sciences Library. Everything from AIDS to Women's Health.

Journal of the American Medical Association, http://www.ama-assn.org.

MD Consult, http://www.mdconsult.com. Formerly only for MDs, full-text medical texts and journals, continuing medical education modules.

Medical/Health Sciences Libraries on the Web, http://www.lib.uiowa.edu/hardin-www/hslibs.html.

MEDLINE Drug Information, http://www.nlm.nih.gov/medlineplus/druginformation.html

MedTech, http://st3.yahoo.com/medtech. Various textbooks.

Medline tutorial, http://www.library.health.ufl.edu/pubmed/pubmed2/. Pubmed tutorial.

The New England Journal of Medicine, http://www.nejm.org. For print subscribers only.

The New Scientist, http://www.newscientist.com.

Pharmacy Info, http://pharminfo.com.

Physicians Assistant site, http://www.halcyon.com.

Primary Care Handbook, http://www.med.ufl.edu/medinfo/baseline

Public Health Information Resources, http://www.mc.vanderbilt. edu/biolib/ph/resources.html. From Vanderbilt University Medical Center.

Evidence-Based Medicine Sites

Bandolier Homepage, http://www.jr2.ox.ac.uk/Bandolier/index. html.

Centre for Evidence-Based Medicine, http://cebm.jr2.ox.ac.uk. From the U.K. National Health Service. Journals, and so on.

EBHC Resources on the Internet, http://mlanet.org/education/tele con/resource.html. From the Medical Library Association. Includes master lists of Web resources, tutorials/how-to sites, search filters, practice guidelines/systematic reviews, organizations, and journals; international coverage.

EBM Bibliography, http://www.ebmny.org/ebmbib.html.

EBM Filters, http://www.urmc.rochester.edu/Miner/Educ/Exper tsearch.html.

Texas Medical Association Library, http://www.texmed.org/lis/gth/ clinical_trials.asp. Links. Hot topics bibliography at http://www. texmed.org/liy/hts/hotbib12.asp.

TRIP, http://www.tripdatabase.com. Searchable collection of over 3,000 links to specific references or documents on evidence-based medicine.

U.S. Medical Libraries Association Resources

Making a Difference: Communications Toolkit, http://www.mlanet. org/publications/tool_kit.

344 The OPL Sourcebook

MLA Benchmarking Initiative, http://mlanet.org/members/benchmark/plan/html.

MLA Librarians Survival Kit, http://www.mlanet.org/resources/survive/survive1.html.

Medical Libraries

Cushing/Whitney Medical Library, Yale-New Haven Medical Center, http://info.med.yale.edu/library.

Galter Health Sciences Library, Northwestern University, http://www.galter.nwu.edu.

Health Sciences Library, SUNY Buffalo, http://ublib.buffalo.edu/libraries/units/hsl.

UNC Literature Exchange, University of North Carolina, Chapel Hill, North Carolina, http://www.uncle.unc.edu.

Weill Medical College, Cornell University, Ithaca, New York, http://lib2.med.cornell.edu/Library/Home.html

Medical Trivia

Absolute Trivia, Totally Trivia Search Engine: http://www.absolutetrivia.com.

Acronym dictionary: http://www.ucc.ie/info/net/acronyms/acro.html.

MedNexus Medical Trivia: http://www.mednexus.com/private/trivia.html.

Science and Technology Resources

Academic Press Dictionary of Science and Technology, http://www.harcourt.com/dictionary. Searchable and free, entirely new work written just for online, and over 130,000 terms defined.

Australian Virtual Engineering Library, http://avel.edu.au. From the Institution of Engineers and seven universities. Gateway for engineers and information technology professionals.

Beilstein Abstracts, http://www.chemweb.com/databases/beilstein. Once you join ChemWeb, unrestricted access to 600,000 titles, authors, and abstracts dating from 1980; free.

BioMed Central, http://www.bomedcentral.com. "Peer-reviewed research across all areas of biology and medicine."

Chemical Abstracts Service, http://www.cas.org.

Gateway to engineering sites, http://www.eevl.ac.uk.

Linda Hall Library, http://www.lhl.lib.mo.us. Very large private science library in Kansas City, Missouri, new home of the Engineering Societies Library collection.

NASA (U.S. government aerospace agency), http://www.gsfc. nasa.gov.

Patent Information Users Group, http://www.piug.org/. Organization for patent search professionals, with a discussion list, newsletter, links to producers and vendors, hosts workshops in the U.S., over 300 members and over 800 on the discussion list.

TechSavvy, http://www.techsavvy.com. Directory of companies, parts and other industry data.

Internet, World Wide Web, and Computer Technology Resources

Hotlinks, http://www.hotlinks.com. You can keep your bookmarks here and can access them from any computer.

Hypertext Library Lingo, http://www.wcsu.edu/library/odlis.html.

Information Infrastructure Task Force, http://iitf.doc.gov.

Internetbookinfo.com, http://www.internetbookinfo.com/. Links to publishing and book selling resources, mostly U.S.

Internet Research Newsletter (U.K.), http://www.hw.ac.uk/lib WWW/irn/irn.htm.

Jargon File Resources, http://www.tuxedo.org/~esr/jargon/. List of jargon used by computer hackers and links to information on hacking.

List of Internet Service Providers, http://www.thelist.com.

LISZT, http://www.liszt.com/. Directory of e-mail discussion groups (listservs). Covers over 50,000 lists from nearly 2,000 sites. (I entered "librarian or librarians" and got 86 lists.)

MacCentral, http://www.maccentral.com. Up-to-date Macintosh information.

McAffee.com Anti Virus Center, http://www.mcaffee.com/centers/anit-virus/. Information and help on viruses.

Media U.K. Internet Directory, http://www.mediauk.com/directory. Contact addresses, e-mail and links, local and national, broadcast and print, U.K. only.

Multilingual Glossary for Art Librarians, http://www.ifla.org/VII/s30/pub/mg1.htm. Published by the International Federation of Library Associations (IFLA) Section of Art Libraries, in English with indexes in Dutch, French, German, Italian, Spanish, and Swedish.

The Newbies Site, http://www.weblearner.co.uk/newbies/index.html. From Web Learner. From basics to advanced, with links and some simple programs.

Newslinx, http://www.newslinx.com. Web, Internet news.

Newspage, http://www.newspage.com. New Web sites, search engines, and so on.

Online Citation Styles, http://www.bedfordstmartins.com/online/citex.html.

Research Buzz, http://www.researchbuzz.com/news/. An extension of Internet Research News. Daily update and searchable archive.

The Scout Report, http://scout.cs.wisc.edu/. To subscribe send e-mail to listserv@cs.wisc.edu, message is "subscribe SRBUSECON."

Search Engine Watch, http://searchenginewatch.com/. How search engines work and ratings and news.

Telecoms Virtual Library, http://www.analysys.com/vlib/. By Analysys Ltd. Other information technology sources.

Ultimate Mac site, http://www.flashpaper.com/umac.

Virtual Computer Library, http://www.utexas.edu/computer/vcl/. Listing of computer resources.

Virus information: http://www.cert.org or http://www.cai.com/virus info/ or http://www.symantec.com/avcenter.

Web-Savvy: Keeping Current with Web-based Resources, http://www.angelfir.com/in/virtuallibrarian/cybercurr.html.

Web Search Strategy, http://Home.sprintmail.com/~debflanagan/main.html. Tutorial for financial research.

Web site ratings from Point Communications, http://www.pointcom.com.

The WWW Acronym and Abbreviation Server, http://www.ucc.ie/info/net/acronyms. Searchable.

Ziff-Davis, http://www.zdnet.com. Excellent source for personal computer-related information.

Internet Search Engines

Alta Vista, http://altavista.digital.com. Allows you to search either Web sites or Usenet newsgroups—and you can look at the news items even if you don't subscribe to the newsgroup; favored by many but not my favorite.

DejaNews, http://dejanews2.dejanews.com. Search Usenet news-groups.

Annotated Bibliography

This is my list of sources quoted with comments on particular books or articles of interest. In order for you to find or order these sources, I have sometimes included ISBN numbers.

Alencar, Maria Cleofas F. 1996. Personal communication, Professor of Library Science, Pontificia Universidade, Catolica de Campenas, Sao Paolo, Brazil.

Allen, Sydney K., and Heather S. Miller. 2000. "Libraries on the book buying merry-go-round: Internet book seller vs. library book vendor." *Against the Grain* 12(2):1, 1618, 1620, 1622.

Alsop, Stewart. 1995. "If you think information is free, you must have stolen this column from someone" (Column: Distributed Thinking). *InfoWorld* 17(49):126.

Anderson, M. Elaine, and Patricia T. Pawl. 1979. "When you are the staff: Tips for managing a small library/media/learning center." *Wisconsin Library Bulletin* 75:271–274.

Appel, L. 1996. Personal communication.

Austin, Rhea. 1996. Personal communication, 1996–1997 Chair of the Solo Librarians Division.

Baker, Brian L. 1995. "Librarians online might get entangled in the Web." *National Law Journal* 2:B13–14.

Bates, Mary Ellen. 1997. "Avoiding the ax: How to keep from being downsized or outsourced." *Information Outlook* 1(10):18–21.

Bauwens, Michel. 1993. "The emergence of the 'cybrarian': A new organizational model for corporate libraries." *Business Information Review* 9(4):65–67.

Beckwith, Harry. 1997. *Selling the Invisible: A Field Guide to Modern Marketing*, New York, New York, U.S.A.: Warner Books, ISBN 0-46-52094-2.

Bender, David R. 1994. "A study of the continuing education needs of SLA members and education activities at SLA conferences." Washington, D.C., U.S.A.: Special Libraries Association Board Memorandum.

Bierbaum, Esther G. 1986. "Professional education doesn't stop with your MLS." *The One-Person Library* 2(12):2.

Bluhdorn, Frances. 1996. "OPALs." *Specialities* (ALIA [Australian Library and Information Association] Special Libraries Section, NSW Group) (18):6–8.

Bott, Ed. 1996. "Internet Lies." *PC Computing*, October. (Quoted in *Library Journal* 122(20):39.)

Brandt, D. Scott. 1996. "Evaluating information on the Internet." *Computers in Libraries* 16(5):44–46.

Brinkman, Rick, and Rick Kirschner. 1994. *Dealing With People You Can't Stand: How to Bring Out the Best in People at their Worst.* New York, New York, U.S.A.: McGraw-Hill, ISBN 0-07-007838-6.

Broadbent, Marianne. 1997. "The emerging phenomenon of knowledge management." *Australia Library Journal* 46(1):6–24.

_____. 1998. "The phenomenon of knowledge management: What does it mean to the information professional?" *Information Outlook* 2(5):23–36.

Bryant, Sue Lacey. 1995. *Personal Professional Development and the Solo Librarian* (Library Training Guides). London, U.K.: Library Association Publishing, ISBN 1-85604-141-7

_____. 1999. "Interesting times for solos in the UK." *The One-Person Library* 16(7):4–5.

Buchanan, Leigh. 1999. "The smartest little company in the world." *Inc.* 21(1):42–54, Cover story on the Highsmith Company and its librarian's close working relationship with the President.

Caldwell, Bruce. 1996. "The new outsourcing partnership." *Information Week* (585):50.

Coccia, Cynthia. 1988. 'Avoiding a 'toxic' organization." *Nursing Management* 29(5):32–33.

Corcoran, Mary, Lynn Dagar, and Anthea Stratigos. 2000. "The changing roles of information professionals: Excerpts from an Outsell, Inc. Study." *Online* 24(2):28–34.

Corrall, Sheila M. 1995. "Strategic management of information resources: Planning for a better future." *The Law Librarian* 26(3):399–403.

Cram, Jennifer. 1995. "Moving from cost centre to profitable investment: Managing the perception of a library's worth." *Australasian Public Libraries and Information Services* 8(3):107–113.

Crawford, Walt. 2000. "Principled libraries: Finding stability in changing times." *Online* 24(2):48–53.

Crawford, Walt, and Michael Gorman. 1995. *Future Libraries: Dreams, Madness, and Reality.* Chicago, Illinois, U.S.A.: American Library Association Editions. ISBN 0-8389-0647-8.

Cronin, Blaise, and Joan Williamson. 1988. "One person libraries and information units: Their education and training needs." *Library Management* 9(5):1–72.

Davenport, Thomas H., David W. DeLong, and Michael C. Beers. 1998. "Successful knowledge management projects." *Sloan Management Review* 39(2):43–57. Studies of 31 knowledge management projects in 24 companies.

DiMattia, Susan. 1995. "When the 'dumb' increases, increase the smarts, sci-tech news." *Corporate Library Update* 4(15):4.

Drake, David. 1990. "When your boss isn't a librarian." *American Libraries*, February 1990:152–153. From an academic librarian but relevant to all.

Duranceau, Ellen Finnie. 1997. "Beyond print: Revisioning serials acquisitions for the digital age." Web site: http://web.mit.edu/waynej/ www/duranceau.htm, accessed 11 September 2000.

Eiblum, Paula. 1995. "The coming of age of document delivery." *Bulletin of the American Society for Information Science* 21(3):21–22.

Eide-Jensen, Inger. 1977. "The one-man library." *Scandinavian Public Library Quarterly* 10(1):15–17.

Ferguson, Elizabeth, and Emily R. Mobley. 1984. *Special Libraries at Work*. Hamden, Connecticut, U.S.A.: Library Professional Publications, ISBN 0-208-01939-1.

Ferguson, Tony. 1996. "The 'L' word." *Against the Grain* 8(2):80, 89.

Fletcher, Lloyd Alan. 1996. "The new economics of online." *Searcher* 4(5):30–44.

Flynn, Louise. 2000. Personal communication.

Garman, Nancy. 1996. "Be a savvy online consumer." *Online User*, July–August:5.

Gervino, Joan. 1995. "Establishing fees for service." *Marketing Treasures* 8(3):4–6.

Gilder, George. 1996. "Feasting on the giant peach." *Forbes ASAP*, August 26:85–96.

Gillies, Malcolm. 2000. "Cybraries will gather no dust." *The Australian*, Web site: http://news.com.au, accessed 2 August 2000.

Gorman, Michael, 1995. "The corruption of cataloging." *Library Journal* (120):34.

———. 1996. "Dreams, madness and reality: The complicated world of human recorded communication." *Against the Grain* 8(1):1,16–18.

Griffiths, Jose-Marie. 1996. Presentation at Betty Burrows Memorial Seminar, Cleveland Ohio, U.S.A., 19 April.

Griffiths, Jose-Marie, and Donald W. King. 1993. *Special Libraries: Increasing the Information Edge*. Washington, D.C., U.S.A.: Special Libraries Association, ISBN 0-87111-414-3.

Hadden, R. Lee. 1991. *An Appeal to Heavenly Library Patrons*. Reston, Virginia, U.S.A.: U.S. Geological Society Library.

Hammerly, Hernan D. 1999. "The success and education of professional librarians: A study of correlations between occupational success and some educational factors as perceived by a group of Argentine librarians." Ph.D. Dissertation, Ann Arbor, Michigan, U.S.A.: The University of Michigan.

Hart, Clare. 2000. "There's a new librarian in town ..." [guest editorial]. *The Electronic Library* 18(3):169–170. President and CEO, Factiva.

Kanter, Rosabeth Moss, 1997. *Rosabeth Moss Kanter on the Frontiers of Management.* Cambridge, Massachusetts, U.S.A.: Harvard Business School Press, ISBN 0-87584-802-8.

Kearns, Kevin. 1997. "Managing upward." *Information Outlook* 1(10):23–28.

Kennedy, Toni. 2000. Personal communication.

Kristensen, Kurt. 1985. "The Norwegian library service: The advantages and disadvantages of small units." *Scandinavian Public Library Quarterly* 18(3):71–73.

Kurtz, Patricia L. 1994. *The Global Speaker: An English Speaker's Guide to Making Presentations Around the World.* New York, New York, U.S.A.: Amacom/American Management Association, ISBN 0-8144-7878-6.

Ladner, Sharyn. 1996. Personal communication, 27 January.

LaForte, Susan R. 1982. "Information brokers: Friend and/or foe?" *Public Library Quarterly* 3:83–91.

Leibovich, Lori. 2000. "Choosing quick hits over the card catalog." *The New York Times* 10 August, Web site: www.nytimes.com/library /tech/00/08/circuits/articls/10thin.html, accessed 10 August 2000.

Library Association. *The Code of Ethics.* London, U.K.: The Library Association.

Line, Maurice B. 1995. "Is strategic planning outmoded?" *Alexandria* 77(3):135–139.

LITA (Library and Information Technology Association, of the American Library Association). 2000. "Top Technology Trends." Web site: www.lita.org/committee/toptech/mw2000.htm, accessed 15 May 2000.

Martin, Mary C. 2000. "Managing your library's computer nerds." *Computers in Libraries* 19(2):8,10.

Matarazzo, James M., and Miriam A. Drake. 1994. *Information for Management: A Handbook.* Washington, D.C., U.S.A.: Special Libraries Association, ISBN 0-87111-427-5.

Merry, Susan A. 1994. "How to talk to senior management." In *Information for Management: A Handbook*, edited by James M. Matarazzo and Miriam A. Drake. Washington, D.C., U.S.A.: Special Libraries Association.

Metcalfe, Bob. 1995. "Predicting the Internet's catastrophic collapse and ghost sites galore in 1996." *InfoWorld* 17(49):61.

Mickey, Bill. 2000. "Thrive or survive." *Online* 24(2):6–7.

Morgan, Eric Lease. 1999. "Libraries of the future: Springboards for strategic planning." *Computers in Libraries* 19(1):32–33.

Morgenstern, Evelin. 1999. "From 'Excuse me please, I am only...' To on everyone's lips: One-person librarians and one-person libraries in Germany." *The One-Person Library* 15(11):6–8.

———. 2000. Personal communication, July and August.

O'Donnell, William S. 1976. "The vulnerable corporate special library/information center: Minimizing the risks." *Special Libraries* 67:179–187.

O'Leary, Mick. 1987. "The information broker: A modern profile." *Online* 11:24–30. Eleven interviews.

———. 2000. "New roles come of age." *Online* 24(2):20–25.

Oxbrow, Nigel, and Angela Abell. 1997. *Putting Knowledge to Work: What Skills and Competencies are Required?* Washington, D.C., U.S.A.: Special Libraries Association.

Paris, Marion, and Herbert S. White. 1986. "Mixed signals and painful choices: The education of special librarians." *Special Libraries* 77(4):207–212.

Paul, Meg, and Sandra Crabtree. 1995. *Strategies for special libraries. SMR Special Report 1.* New York, New York, U.S.A.: SMR International.

Penniman, W. David. 1999. "Strategic planning to avoid bottlenecks in the Age of the Internet." *Computer in Libraries* 19(1):50–53.

Peters, Tom. 1998. Interview. In Cyr, Diane. "The guru game." *Attache* (U.S. Airways Magazine), September:34–37.

Pitts, Roberta L. 1994. "A generalist in the age of specialists: A profile of the one-person library director." *Library Trends* 43(1):121–135.

Prusak, Laurence (Larry). 1993. "Blow up the corporate library." *International Journal of Information Management* 13:405–412.

———. 1994. "Corporate Libraries: A Soft Analysis, a Warning, and Some Generic Advice." In *Information for Management: A Handbook,* ed. by James M. Matarazzo and Miriam A. Drake. Washington, D.C., U.S.A.: Special Libraries Association.

Prusak, Laurence, and James M. Matarazzo. 1990. "Tactics for corporate library success." *Library Journal* 115(15):45–46. A survey of 164 larger U.S. companies.

———. 1995. "The value of corporate libraries: The 1995 survey." *SpeciaList,* November:9,15.

Quint, Barbara. 1991. "Connect time." *Wilson Library Bulletin,* November:59.

———. 1995. "Competition." *Searcher* 3(10):1.

————. 1996a. "Disintermediation." *Searcher* 4(1):4,6.

————. 1996b. "Professional associations react to the challenge." *Searcher* 4(5):8–18.

Raitt, D. 1994. "The future of libraries in the face of the Internet." *Electronic Library* 12(5):275–276.

Ravitch, Diane. Quoted in Leibovich, Lori. 2000. "Choosing quick hits over the card catalog." *The New York Times* 10 August, Web site: www.nytimes.com/library/tech/00/08/circuits/articls/10thin.html, accessed 10 August 2000. Ravitch is a historian of education, New York University.

Riggs, Donald E., and Gordon A. Sabine. 1988. *Libraries in the '90s: What the Leaders Expect*. Phoenix, Arizona, U.S.A.: Oryx Press, ISBN 0-897-74532-9.

Rothstein, Samuel. 1985. "Why people really hate library schools." *Library Journal* 110(1):41–48.

St. Clair, Guy. 1976. "The one-person library: An essay on essentials." *Special Libraries* 67(3):233–238.

————. 1987. "The one-person library: An essay on essentials re-visited." *Special Libraries* 78(4):263–270.

————. 1989. "Interpersonal networking: It is who you know." *Special Libraries* 80(2):107–112.

————. 1993. "To memo or not to memo?" *The One-Person Library* 10(1):6.

————. 1994. "A tale of two corporate libraries." *InfoManage* 1(3):6–7.

————. 1995a. "When you downsize: Focus, connect and network." *InfoManage* 2(6):8.

————. 1995b. "Trish Foy: Matching corporate information services to corporate information needs." *InfoManage* 2(11):1–5.

————. 1995c. *Finances and Value: How the One-Person Library is Paid For. SMR Special Report 5*. New York, New York, U.S.A.: SMR International.

————. 1995d. "How well do you know your boss?" *The One-Person Library* 11(12):3.

————. 1996a. "The OPL profile: Joan Williamson." *The One-Person Library* 12(9);1–5.

————. 1996b. "Real estate management: When it's part of your job." *InfoManage* 3(2):6–7.

————. 1996c. *Dealing with Downsizing: A Guide for the Information Services Practitioner. SMR Special Report 6*. New York, New York, U.S.A.: SMR International.

————. 1996d. "To partner or not to partner?" *The One-Person Library* 13(1):1–3.

_____. 1996e. "Not waiting for it to happen—Outsourcing." *The One-Person Library* 12(2):6-8.

_____. 1997. *25 Years of One-Person Librarianship: Identity, Trends, and Effects.* New York, New York, U.S.A.: SMR International.

St. Clair, Guy, and Andrew Berner 1996. "Insourcing: The evolution of information delivery." *The One-Person Library* 13(4):1.

St. Clair, Guy, and Joan Williamson. 1992. *Managing the New One-Person Library.* New York, New York, U.S.A.: Bowker-Saur, ISBN 0-86291-630-5.

Saunders, Rebecca M. 2000. "Asserting yourself: How to say 'no' and mean it." *Harvard Communication Letter* 3(7):9–11.

Schement, Jorge Reina. 1996. "A 21st Century strategy for librarians." *Library Journal* 121(8):34–36.

Schneiderman, R.A. 1996. "Why Librarians should rule the Net." *e-node* 1(4).

Shaffer, Roberta. 1996. "The future of the law library and law librarian." *LEXIS-NEXIS Information Professional Update* (3):37.

Shuter, J. 1984. *The Information Worker in Isolation.* Bradford, England: MCB University Press.

Siess, Judith A. (1997). *The SOLO Librarian's Sourcebook.* Medford, New Jersey, U.S.A.: Information Today, Inc.

SLA (Special Libraries Association). 1997. *Knowledge Management: A New Competitive Asset* (1997 SLA State-of-the-Art Institute). Washington, D.C., U.S.A.: Special Libraries Association, ISBN 0-87111-480-1.

_____. 1992. *Presidential Study Commission on Professional Recruitment, Ethics and Professional Standards.* Washington, D.C., U.S.A.: Special Libraries Association.

Smock, Raymond W. 1995. "What promise does the Internet hold for scholars?" *The Chronicle of Higher Education*, September 22: B1–2.

Spiller, David, Claire Creaser, and Alison Murphy. 1998. *Libraries in the Workplace. Library and Information Statistics Unit* (Occasional Paper 20, Department of Information and Library Studies). Loughborough, U.K.: Loughborough University, ISBN 1-901786-13-7.

Stathis, Andrew L. 1995. "Technology offers incentive to downsize law libraries." *The National Law Journal* 18(5):B9, B11. President of architectural design firm specializing in law offices, not a librarian.

Stear, Edward B. 1997. "Outsourcing: Competitive threat or technology trend?" *Online* January/February 80. Gartner Group Sr. Research Analyst.

Svoboda, Olga. 1991. "The special library as a competitive intelligence center." *Electronic Library* 9(4/5):239–244.

Tees, Miriam. 1986. "Graduate education for special librarians: What special libraries are looking for in graduates." *Special Libraries* 77(4):190–197.

Tennant, Roy. 1999. "Letter to the editor." *Library Journal* 124(17):8.

Tenopir, Carol. 2000. "I never learned about that in library school." *Online* 24(2):42–46.

Tillman, Hope. 1995. Personal communication.

Tomlin, Anne. 2000. "The OPL column." *National Network* 24(2):10. Librarian, Auburn Memorial Hospital, Auburn, New York.

Trefethen, Dan. 1996. Personal communication.

Vavrek, Bernard. 1987. "Libraries alone: The American experience." In *Libraries Alone: Proceedings of the Rural and Isolated Librarians Conference*, edited by James Henri and Roy Sanders. Wagga Wagga, New South Wales, Australia: Libraries Alone, pp. 5–13.

Walsh, Virginia. 1998. "ALIA explores the value of libraries." *InCite* 19(4):6–7, 20–21. Executive director, Australian Library and Information Association (ALIA).

Weingand, Darlene E. 1994. "Competence and the new paradigm: Continuing education of the reference staff." *The Reference Librarian* (43):173–182.

White, Herbert S. 1984. *Managing the Special Library: Strategies for Success Within the Larger Organization*. White Plains, New York, U.S.A.: G.K. Hall, ISBN 0-86729-088-9.

———. 1988. "Basic competencies and the pursuit of equal opportunity." *Library Journal* 113(12):56–57.

———. 1995. *At the Crossroads: Libraries on the Information Superhighway*. Englewood, Colorado, U.S.A.: Libraries Unlimited, ISBN: 1-56308-165-2. A collection of his writings from 1980 to 1994.

———. 1997. "Planning and evaluation." *Library Journal* 122(9):38–39.

White, Herbert S., and Sarah L. Mort. 1995. "The accredited library education program as preparation for professional library work." In *At the Crossroads: Libraries on the Information Superhighway*, Edited by Herbert S. White, Englewood, Colorado, U.S.A.: Libraries Unlimited, ISBN: 1-56308-165-2, pp. 211–236.

Williamson, Joan. 1984. "How to be an OMB." *Information and Library Manager* 4(2).

Wilson, Marsha, and Ellis Mount. 1997. "Survival of the fittest." *Sci-Tech News* November:19–23.

Working Woman. 1995. July:40.

Young, Ron. 1998. "Cutting the key to the future." (Interview.) *Information World Review* (144):21.

Zamparelli, Roberto. 1999. "Copyright and global libraries: Going with the flow of technology." First Monday (peer-reviewed Internet journal), Web site: www.first-monday.dk/issues/issue2_11/zamparelli/, accessed 11 September 2000.

About the Author

Judith Siess is a recognized expert in one-person librarianship and interpersonal networking. She received her M.S. in Library and Information Science from the University of Illinois at Urbana-Champaign in 1982 and has worked in various industries—industrial process automation, aerospace, biotechnology, and agricultural economics. She founded the Agricultural Economics Reference Organization in 1980, was the first chair of the Solo Librarians' Division of the Special Libraries Association, and was a member of the first People-to-People Citizen Ambassador delegation on Information Management and Special Librarianship to the Republic of South Africa.

Siess is the author of a previous book, *The SOLO Librarian's Sourcebook* (Information Today, Inc., 1997) and is the editor and publisher of *The One-Person Library: A Newsletter for Librarians and Management.*

Index

A

AAHSLD. *See* Association of Academic Health Sciences Library Directors

AALL. *See* American Association of Law Librarians

AAM. *See* American Association of Museums

AASL. *See* American Association of School Librarians

Abram, Stephen, 202

absences, managing, 84–85

academic libraries and librarians, 5–6, 220

accounting programs, 99

activities, typical, 19–23

advantages of OPLs, 12–13, 16

advertising. See marketing; public relations

AIIP. *See* Association of Independent Information Professionals

ALA. *See* American Library Association

Alencar, Maria Cleofas F., 51

ALIA. *See* Australian Library and Information Association

alternative careers, 235, 280–282

American Association of Law Librarians, 231

American Association of Museums, 233

American Association of School Librarians, 233

American Library Association, 230, 235

American Society for Information Science and Technology, 230

American Theological Library Association, 233

American Translators Association, 234

American Zoo and Aquarium Association/Librarians Special Interest Group, 8, 234

AMHL. *See* Association of Mental Health Librarians

annual reports, 115–116

answering machine messages, 81–82

anticipating customer needs, 64–65

Antonir, Anat, 45

Arbeitsgemeinschaft der Spezialbibliotheken, 3

archives and records administrators, 234–235

archiving and preservation, 153, 161–162

Argentina, 47–48

Art Libraries Society, 234

ASLIB. *See* Association of Libraries and Information Bureau

AspB. See Arbeitsgemeinschaft der Spezialbibliotheken

Association of Academic Health Sciences Library Directors, 232

Association of Christian Librarians, 233

Association of Independent Information Professionals, 235

Association of Jewish Libraries, 233

Association of Libraries and Information Bureau, 1, 3, 28, 228

Association of Mental Health Librarians, 234

associations, 228–235. *See also* networking; specific organizations

ATLA. *See* American Theological Library Association

audits, information, 65

Austin, Rhea, 222

Australasian One-Person Library, The, 38
Australia, 36–38
Australian Library and Information
    Association, 3, 36, 229
authorship issues. *See* intellectual prop-
    erty issues
automation, library, 301–303
AZA/LSIG. *See* American Zoo and
    Aquarium Association/Librarians
    Special Interest Group

B

Bates, Mary Ellen, 223
BdDB. *See* Verein der Diplom-
    Bibliothekare
Beckwith, Harry, 134
Bendeich, Therese, 3, 37
Berkman, Bob, 142
Berner, Andrew, 67
Best of OPL, The, 3
BIALL. *See* British-Irish Association of
    Law Libraries
Bluhdorn, Frances, 37
Bonaventura, Mike, 199
book jobbers. *See* booksellers
book sales, 104, 132
bookkeeping, 98–100
books and journals
    alternative careers, 280–282
    business, 247–248
    church and synagogue libraries,
        274–275
    communication, 248–249
    downsizing, 256–257
    education, 280–282
    financial matters, 252–253
    international business, 249–250
    Internet, 277–280
    knowledge management, 257–261
    law libraries, 268–271
    management, 242–246
    marketing, 251–252
    medical and hospital libraries,
        262–268
    miscellaneous libraries, 275–276

non-U.S. essential references, 282
    one-person librarianship, 238–241
    online searching, 277–280
    outsourcing, 256–257
    public libraries, small, 272–273
    public relations, 251–252
    publishers, 283–284
    space planning, 246–247
    strategic planning, 254–255
    technical services, 261–262
    technology, 277–280
    time management, 255–256
Books in Print, 158
booksellers, 157–158, 193, 287–293
Brant, Sue Lacey, 32
Brazil, 51
British-Irish Association of Law
    Libraries, 231
Brittin, Margaret, 4, 28
Broadbent, Marianne, 196
brochures, 128
Bryant, Sue Lacey, 26
budget issues, 43, 57, 95–98, 100–102
    See also downsizing
bulletin boards, 131–132
bulletin boards, electronic. *See* elec-
    tronic discussion lists
business cards, 181–182
business research, 142–143, 247–248,
    325–328

C

Canada, 49–50
Canadian Health Libraries Association,
    232
Canadian Library Association, 229
careers, alternative, 235, 280–282
case studies in downsizing, 186–188
catalogs and cataloging, 63–64, 193–194
Catholic Library Association, 233
CD-ROMs, 153–154
    See also electronic information
characteristics of OPLs, 11–12, 18–19,
    23–24
charge backs, 99–100

chief information officers, 218
chronology of the OPL movement, 2–5
Church and Synagogue Library
    Association, 233
church libraries, 8–9, 233, 274–275, 317
CI. *See* competitive intelligence
CLA. *See* Canadian Library Association
closings. *See* downsizing
colleague communication, 109
collection development and organiza-
    tion, 63–64, 152–156, 212–214
committees, library, 60
communication
    annual reports, 115–116
    books and journals, 248–249
    colleague, 109
    cultural considerations, 112, 117
    customer, 63, 108–110
    difficult persons and, 112–114
    improving, 111–114
    information technology specialists,
        120–123
    management communication,
        107–108
    oral, 112, 116–117
    saying no, 76–78
    with supervisors, 118–119
    telephone, 114
    writing, 114
company librarians, 40–41
competition, 65, 130
competitive intelligence, 10–11, 235,
    296–297
computers. *See* technology
conferences, 85–86, 174
consortia, 155
consultants, library, 309–310
continuing education, 32, 34–36, 137,
    173–175
    See also education
copyright issues, 50, 155–157, 310–311,
    334–335
corporate culture, 56, 200–201
costs, information, 103–105, 154–155,
    182
Council on Botanical and Horticultural

Libraries, 234
Covey, Stephen, 64–65
Crabtree, Chris, 4, 28
cultural considerations in communica-
    tion, 112, 117
customer service
    assisting clients, 63
    avoiding jargon, 63
    collection organization, 63–64
    communication with, 108–110
    communication with clients, 63
    competition, 65
    difficult customers, 112–114
    future needs for, 216–217
    information presentation, 64
    prioritizing services, 61
    proactive, 64–65
    public relations, 134
    summary reports, 62–63
cutbacks. *See* budget issues; downsizing
cyberlibraries. *See* virtual libraries

D

Dale, Georgina, 37
Dartnall, Jean, 4
data conversion, 162
database programs, 99
databases, commercial, 140–141
    See also vendors and suppliers
Davenport. Thomas, 196
DBI. *See* Deutsches Bibliotheksinstitut
decision making, 72–73
definitions
    knowledge, 196
    knowledge management, 196–197
    one-person librarian, 1–2
delegating responsibility, 73–74
Deutsches Bibliotheksinstitut, 3, 5,
    28–29, 35
Dickson, Leslie, 111
difficult persons, 62, 112–114
direction of the organization, 57
directories, Web, 328–329
Directory of State Prison Librarians, 6

disadvantages of OPLs, 13–14, 16–18,
46–47
discount buying, 104
Discussion Group for Alternative
Careers, 235
discussion lists, electronic. *See* electronic discussion lists
disintermediation, 177
Dobbs, James, 195
document delivery, 78, 192–193,
297–299
documentation of value, 111
downsizing, 29, 60
avoiding, 178–182
books and journals, 256–257
case studies, 186–188
evaluating services, 183–185
prioritizing, 184–185
proactive, 187–188
reasons for, 176–178
vulnerability of OPLs, 176–177
See also budget issues
dress, 111
duplication, unauthorized. *See* intellectual property issues

E

education
books and journals, 280–282
distance learning, 171
improvements, 168–169, 172–173
internships, 171–172
preparation for OPL duties, 170
school selection, 168
shortcomings, 165–167
South Africa, 39, 42
special library courses, 172
theory vs. practice, 167
undergraduate degrees, 171
ways to contribute to, 172–173
See also continuing education
efficiency, 72–73
electronic discussion lists
church and synagogue libraries, 317
general library, 314–316

law and government libraries,
317–318
Library Association establishment, 4
managing, 80–81
medical libraries, 318
museum, art, and zoo libraries, 317
OPL, 313–314
science and technology libraries,
318–319
South Africa, 44
United Kingdom, 26
usefulness, 141–142
See also e-mail
electronic information
archiving, 161–162
authorship, 155–156
costs, 154–155
data conversion, 162
disadvantages, 207–208
journals, 156–157
library automation resources,
301–303
licensing agreements, 154–155
life expectancy, 162
media vendors and suppliers,
303–307
print vs., 141–146, 152–156,
163–164, 207–208
search time, 64
e-mail, 80–81, 141
See also electronic discussion lists
employee orientation, 130
end-of-the-month activities, 22–23
end-user searching, 146–150
estimates of OPL numbers, 12
European Association for Health
Information and Libraries, 232
evaluating reference sources, 145–146,
150–151
evaluating services, 90–91, 102–104,
179
Evaluating Websites, 4
evidence-based medicine, 343
exhibits, conference, 86
expense tracking, 98–99

F

failure, 94
fees for service, 103–105, 182
Field, Judith J., 198
Field, Mark, 26
Fifth Information Innovator's Institute, 218
filing, 79–80
financial matters
    bookkeeping, 98–100
    books and journals, 252–253
    budget cuts, 100–102
    budgeting, 95–98
    charge backs, 99–100
    evaluating services, 102–104, 179
    expense tracking, 98–99
    information costs, 103–104
    money-saving, 104–105
Flynn, Louise, 41
"Four Hard Truths," 56
Future Libraries: Dreams, Madness, and Reality, 213
future of OPLs, 205–214, 221–225

G

Gauteng and Environs Library Consortium (GAELIC), 231
general reference Web sites, 320–324
Germany, 28–36
Gervino, Joan, 104
Gilder, George, 159–160
goals, 91
Gorman, Michael, 213
government archives and records administrators, 234–235
government libraries, 317–318
government resources Web sites, 332–334

H

Hadden, R. Lee, 101
Hart, Clare, 211
health resources Web sites, 340–344
history of OPL movement, 2–5
hospital libraries, 7, 262–268

I

IALL. *See* International Association of Law Libraries
IAML. *See* International Association of Music Libraries
IASL. *See* International Association of School Librarianship
image and professionalism, 134–137
Independent Librarians Exchange Round Table, 235
Industrial and Commercial Libraries Group, 28
infopreneurs, 10
information audits, 65
Information Bridges International, Inc., 4
information brokers, 10, 195
information costs, 103–105, 154–155, 182
Information Innovator's Institute, 218
information needs, 109–110
information presentation, 64
information technology. *See* technology
Initiative for Continuing Education in Libraries, Museums, and Archives, 35–36
Institute of Information Scientistis, 229
intellectual property issues, 50, 155–157, 310–311, 334–335
interlibrary loans, 21–22, 99, 154–155, 157
International Association of Law Libraries, 231
International Association of Music Libraries, 234
International Association of School Librarianship, 234
International Federation of Library Associations, 228–229
international issues books and journals, 249–250
international OPLs
    Australia, 36–44
    Brazil, 51
    Canada, 49–50
    Germany, 28–36

International OPLs (cont.)
  Israel, 45
  Latin America, 46–49
  organizations, 228–231
  overview, 25–26
  profiles, 51–53
  Sweden, 50–51
  United Kingdom, 26–28
International Special Libraries Day,
  133
Internet
  advantages and disadvantages,
    144–147
  Backbone Network Service, 161
  books and journals about, 277–280
  business research, 142–143
  end-user searching, 146–150
  evaluating sources, 145–146,
    150–151
  law librarians' use, 143–144
  librarian as searcher, 148
  predicted collapse, 159
  purchasing via, 157–158
  as reference source, 144
  resources, 345–347
  search engines, 140, 347
  searches, 140, 146–147
  See also Web sites
internships, 171–172
interruptions, 75–76
intrapreneurs, 10
ISLIC. See Israeli Society of Libraries
  and Information Centers
isolation, professional, 13–14, 30, 33
Israel, 45
Israeli Society of Libraries and
  Information Centers, 45
Italian Library Association, 230–231

J

jail libraries, 6–7
jargon, avoiding, 59, 63
jobbers, book. See booksellers
journals, electronic, 156–157

K

Kearns, Kevin, 119
Knapp, Ellen, 202
knowledge management
  books and journals, 257–261
  corporate culture and, 200–201
  current players, 201–202
  defined, 196–197
  features, 197
  importance of, 199
  measuring value, 198
  organizational orientation for,
    203–204
  role of librarians, 201–203
  skills, 198–199
  Web sites, 338
Koenig, Michael E.D., 202
Kommission-fur One-Person Libraries,
  228

L

LA. See Library Association
Ladner, Sharyn, 160
law libraries and librarians
  books and journals, 268–271
  electronic discussion lists, 317–318
  functions, 5–6
  future of, 218–219
  Internet and, 143–144
  organizations, 231–232
  reliance on electronic information,
    163
  value of, 181
law resources Web sites, 329–332
Lex Mundi, 232
LEXIS, 163
LIANZA. See Library and Information
  Association of New Zealand
Library and Information Association of
  New Zealand, 229
Library and Information Association of
  South Africa, 231
library and information science
  resources Web sites, 335–337

Library and Information Technology Association, 207
Library Association, 4, 26–28, 174–175, 229
Library Association of Ireland, 229–230
library automation, 301–303
library committees, 60
library movers, 311–312
library schools. *See* education
library types, 5–10
licensing agreements, electronic information, 155
Liebowitz, Jay, 198
location of libraries, 29
logos, 127, 129
Louw, Anna, 40

M

management
    books and journals, 242–246
    communication with, 107–108
    expectations, 110
Managing the One-Person Library, 2
map librarians, 235
market research, 10–11, 296–297
marketing, 30–31, 108, 181, 215, 251–252
    See also public relations
maternity leave, 50
media choice, 152–156
medical libraries and librarians
    books and journals, 262–268
    electronic discussion lists, 318
    future of, 219
    organizations, 232
    Web sites, 343–344
Medical Libraries Association, 7, 232
medical resources, 340–344
meetings, 78–79, 124–125
mental health librarians, 234
mentors, 61
Metcalf, Bob, 159
mission statements, 55–56, 92–93
MLA. *See* Medical Libraries Association
money-saving, 104–105

Morgenstern, Evelin, 3, 28–29
Most Delicate Monster, A: The One-Professional Special Library, 4
museum libraries, 8
music librarians, 234
Music Library Association, 234
myths, 68–69

N

NAGARA. *See* National Association of Government Archives and Records Administrators
National Association of Government Archives and Records Administrators, 234–235
National Federation of Abstracting and Information Services, 230
National Federation of Paralegal Associations, 232
National Library Week, 132–133
National Science Foundation, 161
networking, 27–28, 30, 44, 123–125, 224–225
    See also associations
New Zealand Law Librarians Group, 232
news Web sites, 324–325
newsletters, 60, 128–130
NFAIS. *See* National Federation of Abstracting and Information Services
numbers of OPLs, 12

O

OCLC, 21, 139
One-Man Bands, 1, 3, 28
One-Person Australian Librarians, 3–4, 36–38, 228
One-Person Library: A Newsletter for Librarians and Management, The, 2, 4, 33
One-Person Library Support Group, 49–50
online booksellers, 157–158
Online Computer Library Center (OCLC), 21, 139

online searching. *See* searching, online
OPAL. *See* One-Person Australian
    Librarians
open houses, 20–21, 132
Opperman, Vance, 208
oral communication, 112
oral presentations, 116–117
Organisation of South African Law
    Libraries, 41, 231
organizational issues
    annual reports, 60
    behavioral rules, 58
    boss-librarian relationship, 117–119
    budgets, 57
    communication with management,
        58–59
    corporate culture, 56, 200–201
    customer service, 61–66
    direction of the organization, 57
    gaining knowledge of, 58
    justification of OPL existence, 60
    knowledge management, 196–204
    library importance, 177–178
    mentors, 61
    politics, 61
    prima donnas, 62
    professional status of OPLs, 57
    supervisors, 57, 59–60
organizations. *See* associations
orientation, new employee, 130
OSALL. *See* Organisation of South
    African Law Libraries
outsourcing
    books and journals, 256–257
    cataloging, 193–194
    consequences, 185
    document delivery services, 192–193
    information brokers, 195
    internal vs. external, 189–190
    issues, 183
online searching, 194–195
    re-evaluating, 195–196
    subscriptions, 191–192
    time management and, 73–74, 78
    when to outsource, 190–191
Owens, Gill, 39

P

Patent Information Users Group, 232
patents services, 299
patron saints of libraries, 133
Paul, Meg, 36, 38
Peeters, Regina, 32
Perelman, Lewis, 199
perfectionism, 73
Peters, Tom, 180
physical characteristics of libraries,
    212–213
Pillar, Claire, 37
PIUG, 232
planning, strategic
    books and journals, 254–255
    cornerstones, 92–94
    how to, 90–91
    overview, 89–90
    reasons for, 88–89
    Web sites, 328
politics, organizational, 61
predictions, 207, 209–214
preparation for OPLs, 15
presentation of information, 64
presentations, oral, 116–117
preservation and archiving, 153,
    161–162
prima donnas, 62
print vs. electronic information,
    141–146, 152–156, 163–164,
    207–208
prioritizing, 76, 86–88
prison libraries, 6–7
proactivity, 64–65
procrastination, 74–76
professional isolation, 13–14, 30, 33
professional status, 57, 111, 134–137
promotion, library. See marketing; pub-
    lic relations
public libraries, 9, 219–220, 272–273
public relations
    advertising your services, 129–130
    book sales, 132
    books and journals, 251–252
    brochures, 128
    bulletin boards, 131–332

public relations (cont.)
    cybrarians, 131
    excuses for not engaging in, 125–126
    follow-up, 130
    importance of service, 134
    local politics and, 128
    newsletters, 128–130
    open houses, 132
    vendor materials, 132
publishers, 283–284
purchasing, 97, 157–158

Q

Quint, Barbara, 23, 140

R

reading, 80
Rees-Jones, Lyndsay, 26
reference source, Internet as, 144
reports
    annual, 60, 115–116
    conference, 86
    monthly, 22–23
    summary, 62–63
Rhine, Martha Rose (Marty), 2
Riley, Lis, 4
Robinson Crusoe Syndrome and What
    You Can Do About It, The, 3, 32
roles, library and librarians'
    future, 214–225
    German OPLs, 29
    OPL vs. information technology spe-
        cialists, 120–123
    technology and, 147–151
routines, 76

S

SABINET, 231
salaries, 39–40
SALIS. See South Africa Institute for
    Librarianship and Information
    Science
saying no, 76–78

school libraries and librarians, 9–10,
    233–235
Schwarzwalder, Bob, 108
science and technology libraries, 318–319
science and technology resources,
    344–345
Scottish library associations, 230
Scully, Mike, 142
Searcher, 23
searching, online
    books and journals, 277–280
    difficulties, 146–147
    librarian as searcher, 148
    librarians' role, 148–150
search engines, 140
services, 194–195
service fees, 104–105, 182
Shubert Archive, The, 235
Silson, Toni, 3, 37
SLA. See Special Libraries Association
SLIG. See Special Libraries Interest
    Group
SLIL. See Special Librarians in London
SLIM. See Special Librarians in the
    Midlands
SLIS. See Special Libraries and
    Information Services
Society of Competitive Intelligence
    Professionals, 235
Society of School Librarians
    International, 235
software, 98–99
Solo Librarians Caucus, 2–3
Solo Librarians Division, Special
    Libraries Association, 221, 228
SOLO Librarians Division of SLA, 12
SOLO Librarian's Sourcebook, The, 4,
    141, 223
South Africa, 38–44, 51–53
South Africa Institute for Librarianship
    and Information Science, 39, 41
South African Library Association, 40
space planning information, 246–247
Special Librarians in Cambridge, 4
Special Librarians in London, 4, 28
Special Librarians in the Midlands, 4, 28

special libraries
  defined, 5
  future of, 218
  statistics, 169
Special Libraries and Information
  Services, 231
Special Libraries Association, 22–23,
  133, 221, 228, 230
Special Libraries Interest Group, 231
special reports, 240
Sports Marketing Surveys, 4
spreadsheets, 98–99
St. Clair, Guy, 1–3, 12, 29, 32, 36, 221
St. Jerome, 133
St. Lawrence, 133
stage fright, 116–117
standards services, 300–301
statistics, 116, 179
Stelle, Marion, 37
strategic planning
  books and journals, 254–255
  cornerstones, 92–94
  how to, 90–91
  overview, 89–90
  reasons for, 88–89
  Web sites, 328
subscription services, 191–192, 293–296
summary reports, 62–63
supervisors, 57, 59–60, 62
  boss-librarian relationship, 117–119
suppliers. See vendors and suppliers
Sweden, 50–51
synagogue libraries and librarians, 8–9,
  233, 274–275, 317

T

Taylor, R.M., 199
teaching search techniques, 148–150
team-building skills, 217–218
technical services
  books and journals, 261–262
  Web sites, 339–340
technology
  adding value with, 206
  books and journals, 277–280

  CD-ROMs, 153–154
  current librarian uses, 141–144
  evolution, 139–141
  future impact, 205–212
  librarians' roles and, 147–151
  policy, 151
  preservation issues, 153
  specialists, 120–123
  staying current, 43–44
  support, 43
telephone calls, 81–82, 114
terminology, 59–61, 166
testimonials, 111
Theater Library Association, The
  Shubert Archive, 235
threats to libraries, 213–214
Tillman, Hope, 1451
time management
  80/20 principle, 72–73
  absences, 84–85
  books and journals, 255–256
  conferences, 85–86
  decision making, 72–73
  delegating, 73–74
  difficulties, 13–15, 42–43
  effectiveness, 68
  efficiency, 72–73
  e-mail, 80–81
  evaluating services, 90–91
  filing, 79–80
  goals, 91
  hints, 82–83
  interruptions, 75–76
  meetings, 78–79
  myths about time, 68–69
  outsourcing, 73–74, 78
  perfectionism, 73
  planning, 88–94
  prioritizing, 76, 86–88
  procrastination, 74–76
  reading, 80
  routines, 76
  saying no, 76–78
  telephone calls, 81–82
time studies, 70–72
  wasting time, 69–70

Tomlin, Anne, 101
translation companies, 311
Trefethen, Dan, 187
turnover rate, 50–51

U

Ulrich's International Periodicals Directory, 158
unauthorized duplication. *See* intellectual property issues
United Kingdom, 26–28
upsizing, 188–189
used book sellers, 293

V

vendors and suppliers, 192–195
    book, 157–158
    booksellers and bookstores, 287–293
    cataloging, 193–194
    competitive intelligence, 296–297
    copyright authorities, 310–311
    document delivery, 192–193, 297–299
    electronic resources, 301–303
    guides, 287
    library consultants, 309–310
    library graphics, supplies, furniture, 307–309
    library movers, 311–312
    market research, 296–297
    online, CD-ROM, and other electronic media, 303–307
    online searching, 194–916
    patents services, 299
    public relations and, 132
    standards services, 300–301
    subscription services, 293–296
    translation companies, 311
    used book sellers, 293
Verein der Diplom-Bibliothekare, 3
virtual libraries, 64, 131, 162–164
visibility, 181–182
vision statements, 92–93
Voice-Pro, 111

W

WAML. *See* Western Association of Map Libraries
Washington, Bert, 4
wasting time, 69–70
Web sites
    business resources, 325–328
    computer technology resources, 345–347
    copyright issues, 334–335
    directories, 328–329
    general reference, 320–324
    government resources, 332–334
    Internet resources, 345–347
    knowledge management, 338
    law resources, 329–332
    library and information science resources, 335–337
    medical and health resources, 340–344
    news, 324–325
    OPLs, 320
    science and technology resources, 344–345
    strategic planning, 328
    technical services, 339–340
    World Wide Web resources, 345–347
    See also Internet
week in the life, 19–23
Western Association of Map Libraries, 235
WESTLAW, 163
White, Herb, 24, 101, 107–108
Witowski, Steve, 4
Workplace '99 Initiative, 4
Workplace Libraries discussion list, 4
World Wide Web. *See* Internet
writing, 114, 181

Z

zoo librarians, 8, 234

More Great Books
from Information Today, Inc.

Creating Web-Accessible Databases: Case Studies for Libraries, Museums, and Other Non-Profits

By Julie Still

Libraries, museums, and other not-for-profit institutions are increasingly looking for (and finding) ways to offer patrons and the public Web access to their collections. This book explores the unique challenges non-profit archival institutions face in leveraging the Internet, and presents one dozen case studies showcasing a variety of successful projects and approaches.

2001/200 pp/hardbound • ISBN 1-57387-104-4 • $39.50

The Evolving Virtual Library II
Practical and Philosophical Perspectives

Edited by Laverna M. Saunders

This new edition of *The Evolving Virtual Library* documents how libraries of all types are changing with the integration of the Internet and the Web, electronic resources, and computer networks. It provides a summary of trends over the last 5 years, new developments in networking, case studies of creating digital content delivery systems for remote users, applications in K-12 and public libraries, and a vision of things to come. The contributing experts are highly regarded in their specialties. The information is timely and presents a snapshot of what libraries are dealing with in the new millennium.

1999/194 pp/hardbound • ISBN 1-57387-070-6 • $39.50

Design Wise
A Guide for Evaluating the Interface Design of Information Resources

By Alison Head

"*Design Wise* takes us beyond what's cool and what's hot and shows us what works and what doesn't."
> —*Elizabeth Osder,*
> *The New York Times on the Web.*

Knowing how to size up user-centered interface design is becoming as important for people who choose and use information resources as for those who design them. This book introduces readers to the basics of interface design and explains why a design evaluation should be tied to the use and purchase of information resources.

1999/224 pp/softbound • ISBN 0-910965-31-5 • $29.95
1999/224 pp/hardbound • ISBN 0-910965-39-0 • $39.95

The Extreme Searcher's Guide to Web Search Engines, Second Edition

A Handbook for the Serious Searcher

By Randolph Hock

In this completely revised and expanded version of his award-winning book, the "Extreme Searcher," Randolph (Ran) Hock, digs even deeper, covering all the most popular Web search tools, plus a half-dozen of the newest and most exciting search engines to come down the pike. This is a practical, user-friendly guide supported by a regularly updated Web site.

CyberAge Books/2001/softbound • ISBN 0-910965-47-1 • $24.95

Super Searchers in the News

The Online Secrets of Journalists & News Researchers

By Paula J. Hane
Edited by Reva Basch

Here, for the first time, 10 news researchers reveal their strategies for using the Internet and online services to get the scoop, check the facts, and nail the story. If you want to become a more effective online searcher and do fast, accurate research on a wide range of moving-target topics, don't miss *Super Searchers in the News*. As a bonus, a dedicated Web page links you to the most important Net-based information sources—Super Searcher tested and approved!

2000/256 pp/softbound • ISBN 0-910965-45-5 • $24.95

Super Searchers on Wall Street

Top Investment Professionals
Share Their Online Research Secrets

By Amelia Kassel
Edited by Reva Basch

Through her probing interviews, Amelia Kassel reveals the online secrets of 10 leading financial industry research experts. The Wall Street Super Searchers direct you to important sites and sources, illuminate the trends that are revolutionizing financial research, and help you use online research as part of a powerful investment strategy. As a reader bonus, a directory of top sites and sources is hyperlinked and periodically updated on the Web.

2000/256 pp/softbound • ISBN 0-910965-42-0 • $24.95

For a complete catalog, contact:

Information Today, Inc.

143 Old Marlton Pike, Medford, NJ 08055 • 609/654-6266
email: custserv@infotoday.com • Web site: www.infotoday.com

NOTES

NOTES

NOTES

NOTES